BRITAIN'S SPIDERS

A field guide

Lawrence Bee, Geoff Oxford and Helen Smith

WILD Guides

PRINCETON

Published by Princeton University Press,
41 William Street, Princeton, New Jersey 08540
In the United Kingdom: Princeton University Press, 6 Oxford Street,
Woodstock, Oxfordshire OX20 1TR
nathist.press.princeton.edu

British Library Cataloging-in-Publication Data is available

Library of Congress Control Number 2017931729
ISBN 978-0-691-16529-5

Production and design by **WILD**Guides Ltd., Old Basing, Hampshire UK.
Printed in China

10 9 8 7 6 5 4 3

PRECEDING PAGE *Frosted orb webs are incredible, beautiful and awe-inspiring, and particularly so when the biology of their spider 'architects' is appreciated a little more.*

Contents

THE TYPES OF SPIDER

Pictorial list of families showing the number of genera (dark brown box) and max/min adult body lengths of species within each family. Images are shown at approximately life-size; for families of very small spiders, life-sized images are shown in circles. For the Linyphiidae, sizes are just for the species covered in this book (see *page 10*). For an alphabetical index of genera see *page 480*.

PAGE NUMBERS

Bold Species account
Light Family guide

ATYPIDAE *p. 98*
Purseweb spiders *p. 58*

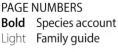

SCYTODIDAE *p. 100*
Spitting spiders *p. 55*

PHOLCIDAE *p. 101*
Cellar spiders *p. 58*

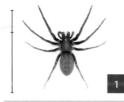

SEGESTRIIDAE *p. 104*
Tubeweb spiders *p. 56*

DYSDERIDAE *p. 106*
Woodlouse spiders *p. 55*

OONOPIDAE *p. 109*
Goblin spiders *p. 54*

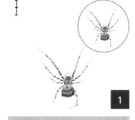

MIMETIDAE *p. 110*
Pirate spiders *p. 61*

ERESIDAE *p. 114*
Velvet spiders *p. 72*

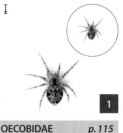

OECOBIIDAE *p. 115*
Discweb spiders *p. 57*

ULOBORIDAE *p. 116, p. 63*
Cribellate orbweb spiders

NESTICIDAE *p. 119, p. 62*
Comb-footed cellar spiders

THERIDIIDAE *p. 120*
Comb-footed spiders *p. 60*

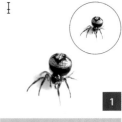

THERIDIOSOMATIDAE
Ray's spiders *p. 163, p. 61*

MYSMENIDAE *p. 164*
Dwarf cobweb spiders *p. 56*

p. 66

TETRAGNATHIDAE *p. 165*
Long-jawed orbweb spiders

ARANEIDAE *p. 177*
Orbweb spiders *p. 63*

LYCOSIDAE *p. 206*
Wolf spiders *p. 71*

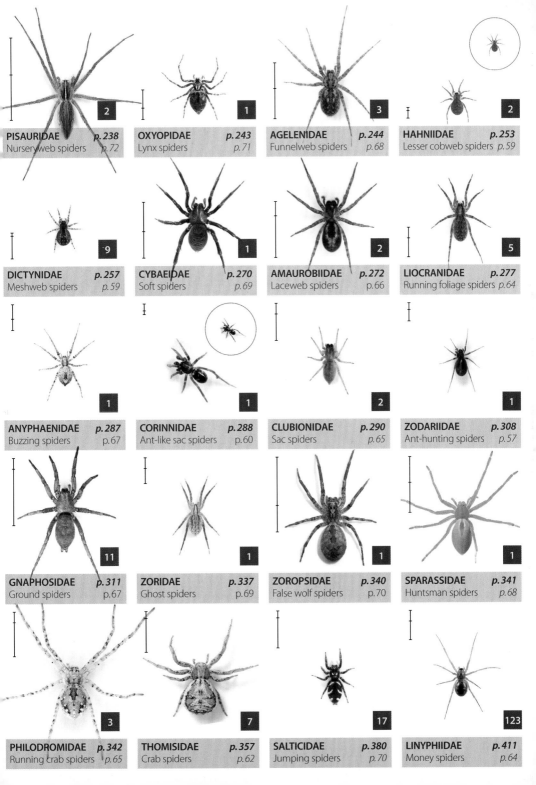

PISAURIDAE *p. 238*
Nurseryweb spiders *p. 72*

OXYOPIDAE *p. 243*
Lynx spiders *p. 71*

AGELENIDAE *p. 244*
Funnelweb spiders *p. 68*

HAHNIIDAE *p. 253*
Lesser cobweb spiders *p. 59*

DICTYNIDAE *p. 257*
Meshweb spiders *p. 59*

CYBAEIDAE *p. 270*
Soft spiders *p. 69*

AMAUROBIIDAE *p. 272*
Laceweb spiders *p. 66*

LIOCRANIDAE *p. 277*
Running foliage spiders *p. 64*

ANYPHAENIDAE *p. 287*
Buzzing spiders *p. 67*

CORINNIDAE *p. 288*
Ant-like sac spiders *p. 60*

CLUBIONIDAE *p. 290*
Sac spiders *p. 65*

ZODARIIDAE *p. 308*
Ant-hunting spiders *p. 57*

GNAPHOSIDAE *p. 311*
Ground spiders *p. 67*

ZORIDAE *p. 337*
Ghost spiders *p. 69*

ZOROPSIDAE *p. 340*
False wolf spiders *p. 70*

SPARASSIDAE *p. 341*
Huntsman spiders *p. 68*

PHILODROMIDAE *p. 342*
Running crab spiders *p. 65*

THOMISIDAE *p. 357*
Crab spiders *p. 62*

SALTICIDAE *p. 380*
Jumping spiders *p. 70*

LINYPHIIDAE *p. 411*
Money spiders *p. 64*

Foreword

From the first time a jumping spider turned to 'look at me' I was bewitched by spiders. Eight, lustrous, obsidian lenses seemed to reflect my own curiosity in their depths. I was looking at an animal that surprised me at such a fundamental level I could never look at one in the same way ever again.

Spiders up until that point hadn't really figured in my life much, other than as the source of the occasional display of squealing hysteria from a genuinely arachnophobic mother.

They had been merely inconvenient things with eight legs to be smuggled out of the house surreptitiously by my Dad before she noticed. They (or their side-effects of cobwebs) may have been a point of shame to my house-proud mother, but that was pretty much it.

Frightening to think how close I came to growing up like the majority of the populace. If it hadn't been for that almost personable brief gaze from a 6 mm specimen of the Zebra Spider *Salticus scenicus,* I might have continued in ignorance.

As it happens, spiders amaze me; they continually blow my mind – not only in their bedizened beauty, but by their ecological ingenuity.

If I ever want to rediscover a sense of adventure, to have my socks well and truly knocked off, or simply to enter a world that is as alien as any my imagination might conceive, then I go and seek out a spider.

With this book in hand I suggest you have a go at doing the same – lower your horizons and get down on your hands and knees and you will soon understand what I've been talking about.

With spiders, contrary to their reputation, there is nothing to fear other than a life of ignorance and with it all the wonderful pleasures that you'll miss out on if you don't. Let them introduce themselves as one of the most diverse, varied, successful groups of animals on earth, and arguably the most misunderstood.

As far as British invertebrates go, this book represents the 'final frontier' of the field naturalist – at last a guide to these amazing creatures (the only photographic guide since the now out-of-print *Country Life Guide to Spiders* by Dick Jones). This book will hopefully mean there will be another generation of enthusiastic naturalists that will be transfixed and entranced by the gaze of a little jumping spider.

Nick Baker

Devon, June 2016

The orbweb of a Wasp Spider *Argiope bruennichi* (Araneidae) showing the zigzag stabilimentum (*page 79*).

The density of spiders is only fully appreciated when myriad webs are revealed on a frosty day.

Introduction

Spiders are one of a very few groups of invertebrates that seem comprehensively to divide people into the fearful and the fascinated. A major purpose of this book is to swing the pendulum towards the 'fascinated'. Spiders certainly need, and deserve, more friends and admirers.

Spiders are found almost everywhere: in gardens, urban spaces and waste ground, from the tops of mountains to the seashore; and, of course, they share our homes. You do not have to go to special places to find and observe them, they are all around you; indeed, it is difficult to ignore them. They will be encountered while gardening, turn up unexpectedly in the bath, or parachute onto your clothes on a sunny day. On any cool, moist morning, or after a night's frost, spiders' intricate webs are displayed in all their architectural glory on buildings and vegetation. It is always striking just how many webs are revealed on these occasions, but also bear in mind that many other spider species will be present that do not spin webs at all. The density of spiders varies widely according to habitat but has been estimated to reach up to 800 in each square metre of an uncut meadow. All spiders are predators and therefore have an impact on prey populations. This can be beneficial to humans by, for instance, controlling the build-up of pests in arable fields. Spiders, in turn, provide food for a wide range of animals including other spiders, birds, mammals, amphibians and reptiles. They therefore play a vital role in most terrestrial ecosystems and deserve a much greater level of understanding and appreciation than they receive at present.

Britain's spider fauna is impoverished compared with that of northern continental Europe – a result of past glaciations and our island status. Even so, there are currently approximately 670 species, which can be split into two broad groups, rather like the more familiar micro- and macro-moths. The 'micros' consist mostly of the money spiders (members of the family Linyphiidae) whereas the 'macros' are all the rest, although there is a certain degree of overlap between them.

This book describes exactly what spiders are, examines their structure, introduces aspects of their intriguing lives and explores the vital roles they play in nature. This leads on to their classification. The recognition of differences between spider families, with their characteristic appearances, life histories, hunting techniques and preferred habitats, is a major step towards identification. Finally, for each **family**, fully illustrated species accounts are provided, enabling names to be put to many distinctive species of British spiders in the field. These accounts, and the following text, also provide information on the distribution and conservation status of Britain's spiders, and how they are recorded.

There is a view amongst some naturalists that good photographs can replace collected specimens as a basis for species identification. Although this is frequently the case for some invertebrate groups, such as macro-moths and butterflies, only a minority of British spiders can be identified with <u>absolute certainty</u> from whole-body photographs. In some cases, macrophotographs of the **genitalia** may be sufficient but often the angle of view is wrong or hairs obscure vital features. It remains the case that the conclusive identification of most spiders is only achieved by examining the genital structures of preserved specimens under a microscope. Although such details are beyond the scope of this book, by using a combination of physical, behavioural, egg-sac and web characteristics, many species or species groups can be recognized in the field.

The identification of spiders in the field often involves the examination of key features that are small and require the animal to be temporarily restrained and examined with a ×10 hand lens (see *page 48)* (or by using binoculars the wrong way round). As a consequence, the majority of the money spiders, which are only a few millimetres long, usually unpatterned and with few diagnostic features visible under ×10 magnification, are not considered in

detail here. However, an annotated *List of British spiders*, covering all species recorded, is provided (*pages 427–462*). Spider webs and, in some cases, egg-sacs can provide clues to the identity of their builders, and so a *Guide to egg-sacs* (*pages 84–95*) and a *Guide to webs* (*pages 73–83*) are therefore included. There is also a *Guide to spider families* (including money spiders) based on externally visible characters of the spiders themselves (*pages 54–72*).

The 'macro' spiders and a minority of money spiders which are larger and patterned, or have unique features or specific habitat characteristics, form the subjects of the 395 separate species accounts which make up the bulk of this book. These accounts provide descriptions and photographs of salient features to look for, details of the habitats in which the species is found, the time of year when adults are likely to be present, and the type of web (if any). Also included are distribution maps showing the density of records and thus, very approximately, the likelihood of encountering the species in any particular area of the country. These maps are based on the roughly one million records held on the British Arachnological Society's Spider Recording Scheme (SRS) database as of mid-2015 (*page 422*). Like many invertebrates, spiders respond to changes in the environment. The SRS data allow the distributions of species to be mapped over time and changes identified; significant shifts in range are discussed in the relevant species accounts. In many cases, closely related species are indistinguishable in the field. For these, the commonest representative(s) within each group is/are illustrated in

A female large house spider *Tegenaria saeva* (Agelenidae) in a familiar setting – a kitchen floor.

the *Species accounts* (*pages 97–420*), and lists given of the similar species that require detailed microscopic examination to tell them apart. The section on *Further reading* (*page 464*) provides information on how to do this.

The books that are currently available on British spiders, such as Michael Roberts' three-volume *The Spiders of Great Britain and Ireland* (1985, 1987) and his *Collins Field Guide to the Spiders of Britain and Northern Europe* (1995), are essential aids to the identification of preserved spiders viewed under a microscope. However, these works are not really designed to be used in the field with a hand lens. Dick Jones' *The Country Life Guide to Spiders of Britain and Northern Europe* (1983), the first comprehensive photographic guide to macro-spiders, is now long out-of-print. The Field Studies Council's (FSC) excellent fold-out chart on *House and Garden Spiders* by Lawrence Bee and Richard Lewington (2002) covers just 40 commonly encountered species. This **WILD**Guide provides a bridge between the FSC chart and the more technical works of Roberts. It aims to encourage many more people to appreciate and enjoy the spiders around them, and to become more involved with their identification and study. There is much still to learn about the biology of even very common species.

Like other organisms, British spiders are in a constant state of flux: new species become established, others extend or contract their ranges, and **taxonomic** understanding evolves. It is intended that the book will be updated and revised to reflect future changes in status and new records and it would be extremely useful to obtain feedback from readers who may have suggestions for improving the book's accuracy or ease of use, or who can supply better images – please contact the authors at wildguide@ britishspiders.org.uk.

Naming spiders

Unlike macro-moths and butterflies, the vast majority of spider species do not have well-established common names. Where common names are established, such as for the Garden Spider *Araneus diadematus* and the Labyrinth Spider *Agelena labyrinthica*, these are used, together with the scientific name (always shown in italics). Where individual species have a unique common name, each name starts with a capital letter (*e. g.* Mouse Spider *Scotophaeus blackwalli*). In a few cases the same common name may be used for two or more closely related species. Here, lower-case letters are used to refer to both the individual species and the collective use of the common name. For instance, there are five species of bright green orbweb spiders in the genus *Araniella* which are similar in appearance. These are collectively and individually known as cucumber spiders; however, one species is referred to specifically as the Common Cucumber Spider *Araniella cucurbitina* and in this case the capital letter convention is used. Common names for families are always in lower-case. We anticipate that more common names will be added as and when the book is revised.

The scientific name is the 'gold standard' and is recognized across the world. The names of spider families always start with a capital letter and end in "idae" (*e. g.* Agelenidae), and a member of that **family** is referred to by the same name without an initial capital letter or the "ae" at the end (in this case, an agelenid). Other conventions that are worth noting are that the name of the genus (the first of the scientific names of a species, which is always shown with an initial capital) is abbreviated in instances where more than one species in that genus is listed (*e. g. Enoplognatha ovata* and *E. latimana*), and that where more than one species is involved this is abbreviated to **spp.** (*e. g. Enoplognatha* spp.).

Distinguishing spiders from other arthropods

Phylum	ARTHROPODA			
Class	ARACHNIDA Spiders and their relatives			INSECTA Insects
Order	**Araneae** TRUE SPIDERS There are about 109 families of spiders in the world, comprising some 45,000 species. In Britain, there are 37 families and approximately 670 species.	**Opiliones** HARVESTMEN This is the group of arachnids most likely to be mistaken for spiders (see table on *page 13*).	**Pseudoscorpionida** PSEUDOSCORPIONS Tiny arachnids that resemble miniature scorpions.	can be distinguished from spiders in several ways (see table *below*).

The **phylum** Arthropoda (arthropods) comprises invertebrates with a hard external skeleton, segmented body and jointed limbs. As well as arachnids, the arthropods also include crustaceans (*e. g.* woodlice, crabs, shrimps), myriapods (*e. g.* millipedes, centipedes) and hexapods (*e. g.* insects, springtails). Spiders belong to the **order** Araneae within the arthropod **class** Arachnida. Other arachnid orders in Britain include harvestmen (27 species), pseudoscorpions (27 species), scorpions (one benign introduced species confined to south coast harbour walls), and over 2,000 species of mites and ticks.

Arachnids can be distinguished from insects by a number of obvious features as shown in the table below.

Representatives of other arachnid orders: a tick *Ixodes ricinus* (TOP) and a mite *Trombidium holosericeum* (BOTTOM).

Feature	**Arachnids**	**Insects**
Body parts	2 (**cephalothorax** and **abdomen**), although the distinction is not obvious in all arachnids	3 (head, thorax and abdomen)
Legs	4 pairs of legs	3 pairs of legs
Eyes	**Simple eyes**	Compound eyes (each comprising a large array of simple photoreception elements)
Wings	Never have wings	Often have wings
Antennae	No **antennae**, but do have **pedipalps**	1 pair of **antennae**
Metamorphosis	Emerge from the egg with all the adult body parts (apart from reproductive organs)	Undergo some sort of metamorphosis: egg → larva → pupa → adult *or* egg → nymph → adult

Pseudoscorpions really do look like miniatures of their better known namesakes but are <u>much</u> smaller (a few millimetres long) and without a stinging tail.

Pseudoscorpions are so distinctive that they are difficult to confuse with spiders and harvestmen. Spiders can be distinguished from harvestmen by the following features:

Knotty Shining Claw
Lamprochernes nodosus × 20

Feature	Spiders	Harvestmen
Body parts	Two clear parts (**cephalothorax** and **abdomen**) separated by a narrow 'waist' (**pedicel**)	One part; **cephalothorax** and **abdomen** fused together into a single structure
Legs	Variable length and thickness	In many species extremely long and thin
Eyes	6 or 8, often at the edges of the **head area**	2 central eyes, usually on a raised 'turret'
Silk	All produce silk	No silk produced

The Daddy long-legs confusion

The confusion generated by using common names is well-illustrated by the term 'Daddy long-legs'. This name is frequently applied to the spider *Pholcus phalangioides*, to harvestmen generally and to species of cranefly (Tipulidae), which are insects.

A spider (*Pholcus phalangioides*)
2 body parts; 8 legs
6–8 simple eyes; pedipalps

A harvestman
(*Phalangium opilio*)
1 body part; 8 legs
2 simple eyes; pedipalps

A cranefly
(*Tipula paludosa*)
3 body parts; 6 legs
2 compound eyes;
wings; antennae

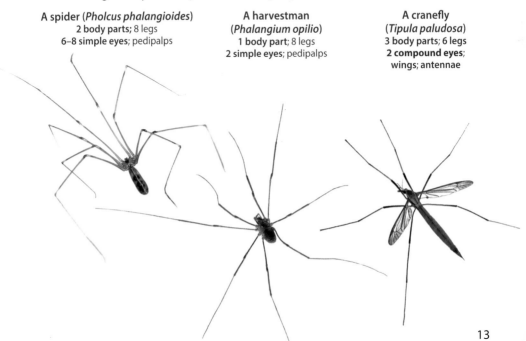

13

Spider anatomy – naming the parts

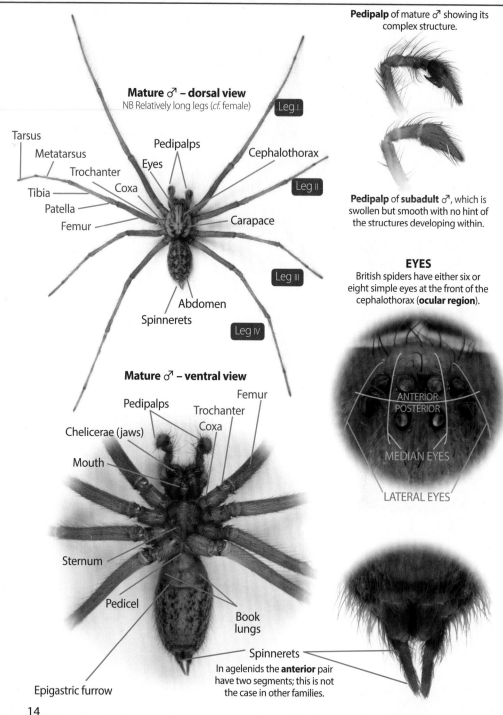

Pedipalp of mature ♂ showing its complex structure.

Mature ♂ – dorsal view
NB Relatively long legs (*cf.* female)

Leg I

Tarsus
Metatarsus
Trochanter
Tibia
Patella
Femur
Coxa
Eyes
Pedipalps
Cephalothorax

Leg II

Carapace

Leg III

Abdomen
Spinnerets

Leg IV

Pedipalp of **subadult** ♂, which is swollen but smooth with no hint of the structures developing within.

EYES
British spiders have either six or eight simple eyes at the front of the cephalothorax (**ocular region**).

ANTERIOR
POSTERIOR
MEDIAN EYES
LATERAL EYES

Mature ♂ – ventral view

Chelicerae (jaws)
Mouth
Pedipalps
Trochanter
Coxa
Femur
Sternum
Pedicel
Book lungs
Epigastric furrow
Spinnerets

In agelenids the **anterior** pair have two segments; this is not the case in other families.

Large house spider *Tegenaria gigantea*

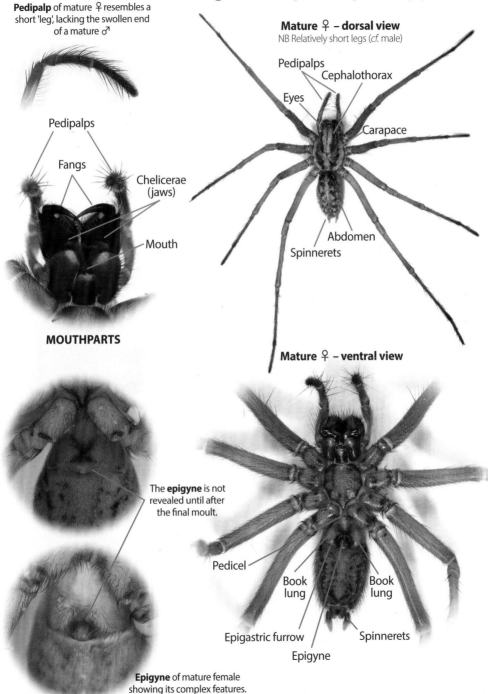

Pedipalp of mature ♀ resembles a short 'leg', lacking the swollen end of a mature ♂

Mature ♀ – dorsal view
NB Relatively short legs (*cf.* male)

Pedipalps
Cephalothorax
Eyes
Carapace
Abdomen
Spinnerets

Pedipalps
Fangs
Chelicerae (jaws)
Mouth

MOUTHPARTS

Mature ♀ – ventral view

The **epigyne** is not revealed until after the final moult.

Pedicel
Book lung
Book lung
Epigastric furrow
Spinnerets
Epigyne

Epigyne of mature female showing its complex features.

Glossary

Photographs showing the locations of terms in **bold brown text** can be found on *pages 14–21* and *page 23*.

abdomen
(adjective: abdominal)
the **posterior** of the two major divisions of the body of a spider

antennae
the 'feelers' on the front of the head of an insect; not present in spiders

anterior
near the front or head end (opposite of **posterior**)

annulation(s)
ring(s) of pigmentation around leg segments

apex/apical
(plural: apices)
tip/towards the tip. In the context of leg segments, farthest from the body

axis
a central line of symmetry

ballooning
the aeronautical activity of spiders, achieved when long strands of silk produced by the **spinnerets** are caught by air currents, enabling the spider to travel through the air (see also **rappelling**)

book lung
an air-filled cavity through which a spider breathes, containing thin vascular sheets arranged like book pages and opening on the underside of the **abdomen**

branchial operculum
(plural: branchial opercula)
a hardened, hairless plate overlying the **book lung**

calamistrum
a comb-like row of small curved spines on **metatarsus** IV of some **cribellate** spiders

carapace
the exoskeletal shield covering the upper surface of the **cephalothorax**

cardiac mark
a tapering, midline mark, starting at the front of the **abdomen** and overlying the heart

cephalothorax
the **anterior** of the two major divisions of the body of a spider, comprising a fused head and **thorax**

chelicerae
(singular: chelicera)
the jaws, each comprising a large basal portion and a **fang**

chitin
(adj.: chitinous)
the tough, protective, semi-transparent substance that forms a spider's **cuticle** – or **exoskeleton**

class
a major **taxonomic** rank of organisms, above an **order** and below a **phylum** or division

book lung, covered by the branchial operculum (the Purseweb Spider *Atypus affinis* (shown above – account on *page 98*) is the only species with two pairs of such structures)

FEATURES USED IN SPECIES DESCRIPTIONS

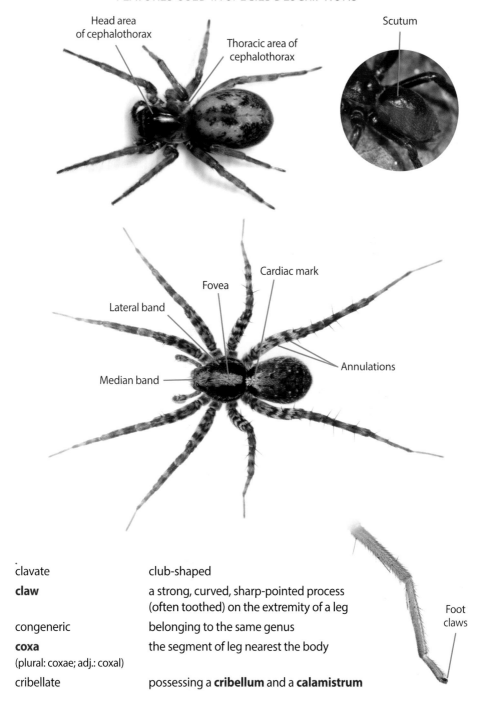

Head area
of cephalothorax

Thoracic area of
cephalothorax

Scutum

Cardiac mark

Fovea

Lateral band

Annulations

Median band

Foot
claws

clavate	club-shaped
claw	a strong, curved, sharp-pointed process (often toothed) on the extremity of a leg
congeneric	belonging to the same genus
coxa (plural: coxae; adj.: coxal)	the segment of leg nearest the body
cribellate	possessing a **cribellum** and a **calamistrum**

17

cribellum	a sieve-like spinning organ in the form of a broad, flat plate, just in front of the **spinnerets** in some (cribellate) spiders
cursorial	adapted to, or specialized for, running
cuticle	the hard, protective layer that forms the outer surface ('skin') of an invertebrate
dentate	a pattern with toothed indentations, like a Holly leaf
dimorphism	a difference in size, body form or colour within a species, characterizing two distinct groups. Examples come from differences between the sexes (sexual dimorphism) and where there are two different (usually genetically-determined) forms within one sex (see also **polymorphism**)
dorsal	on the upper surface, or back (opposite of **ventral**)
duct	an enclosed tube or channel, usually for conveying liquids within the body
ecdysis	moulting, the periodic act of casting off the old **cuticle**
endemic	a species native or restricted to one particular geographical area (*e.g.* Great Britain)
epigastric furrow	a fold and groove separating the region of the **book lungs** and **epigyne** from the rear portion on the underside of the **abdomen**
epigastric region	the general area on the underside of the abdomen where the **epigastric furrow** is located
epigyne	the complex, hardened external structure associated with the reproductive openings of adult females of most spider species
exoskeleton	the hard external supportive covering of all arthropods
exuvia (plural: exuviae)	the part of the **cuticle** cast at **ecdysis** or moult
family	a major **taxonomic** rank of organisms, below an **order** and above **genus**
fang	the claw-like terminal segment of the **chelicera**; the duct from the poison gland opens near its tip
femur (plural: femora; adjective: femoral)	the third segment of the leg or **pedipalp** counting from the body
folium	any broad, leaf-shaped pattern on the **dorsal** surface of the abdomen
fovea	a short, median groove on the **thoracic area** of the **carapace**
genitalia	the copulatory organs: in spiders the external genitalia are the male **pedipalp** and the female **epigyne**

genus	a major **taxonomic** category of organisms that ranks above **species** and below **family**
gossamer	a light film of silk threads which may sometimes be spread over considerable areas; also used to describe silken threads floating in the air
gravid	distended with or full of eggs
guanine	the nitrogen-containing excretory product of spiders, which can also be deposited as a white background within the abdomen against which pigments are displayed
head area	the **anterior** part of the **cephalothorax**
instar	any stage in the development between moults (applies to all arthropods, including spiders)
lenticular	shaped like a lentil, or a biconvex lens
median	in the middle or midline
metatarsus (plural: metatarsi; adj.: metatarsal)	the sixth segment of the leg, counting from the body
morphology	the form and structure of an animal
ocular region	the part of the carapace where the eyes are located
order	a major **taxonomic** rank of organisms, below a **class** and above a **family**
palp (abbrev.)	**pedipalp**
parasitoid	an insect whose larvae live as parasites and which eventually kill their hosts
patella (plural: patellae; adj.: patellar)	the fourth segment of the leg or **pedipalp**, counting from the body
pedicel	the narrow stalk connecting the **cephalothorax** and **abdomen**
pedipalp	jointed appendages on the **cephalothorax**, resembling short legs and originating behind the **chelicerae** but in front of the legs. Greatly modified in adult male spiders for sperm transfer
penultimate instar	the **instar** immediately before the moult to sexual maturity; spiders are described as **subadult** during this instar
phenology	the study of the impact of seasonal and interannual variations in climate on the occurrence, growth and development of an organism

pheromone (adjective: pheromonal)	a chemical, secreted by an animal in minute amounts, which produces a behavioural response in another animal, frequently the opposite sex of the same species, and sometimes over considerable distances
phylum	a principal **taxonomic** category that ranks below a kingdom but above a **class**
polymorphism	size, body form or colour differences within a species that characterize two or more discrete groups (see also **dimorphism**)
posterior	nearer the rear end (opposite of **anterior**)
process (plural: processes)	a projection from the main structure
rappelling	short-distance aerial movements using silk lines (see also **ballooning**)
recurved	curved backwards
reticulated	having a pattern of interlacing lines like a net
scutum	a hard, frequently shiny, plate on the **abdomen** of some spiders
sexual dimorphism	differences between (usually mature) males and females of a species in coloration or **morphology**

Recurved eye row(s)

silk glands	glands inside the **abdomen** of a spider from which silk issues via the **spinnerets**
simple eye	an eye containing a single lens, as found in spiders (by comparison, the compound eyes of insects comprise many units, each with a lens)
sp. (plural: spp.) [abbrev.]	species
species	the basic unit of **taxonomic** classification that describes a group of similar organisms that share similar genes and are capable of interbreeding and producing viable offspring
spermatheca (plural: spermathecae)	a sac or cavity in female spiders, used for the reception and storage of sperm
spiderling	the early immature **instars** of a spider
spinnerets	paired appendages at the rear of the **abdomen**, connected to the underlying silk glands and through which silk strands emerge (sometimes abbreviated to 'spinners')

spiracles	openings of **tracheae** on the **ventral** surface of the **abdomen**
stabilimentum (plural: stabilimenta)	conspicuous band or bands of dense silk decoration across the orb webs of some spider species (see *page 6*)
sternum (plural: sterna; adj.: sternal)	the heart-shaped or oval exoskeletal shield covering the undersurface of the **cephalothorax**
striae	parallel or radiating stripes, streaks, ridges or grooves
subadult	almost adult; the **penultimate instar** before maturity
synanthropic	living in, or close to, human habitation
synonym	each of two or more scientific names used to name the same **taxon** (of these, the first established takes precedence)
tarsus (plural: tarsi; adj.: tarsal)	the segment of a leg or **pedipalp** farthest from the body
taxon (plural: taxa)	a general term for a unit of biological classification (*e.g.* a **family**, **genus** or **species**)
taxonomy (adj.: taxonomic)	the theory and practice of classifying organisms
thermophilous	heat-loving
thorax	the part of the **cephalothorax** behind the **head area** and separated from it by a shallow groove
thoracic area	see **thorax**
tibia (plural: tibiae)	the fifth segment of the leg or **pedipalp**, counting from the body
trachea (plural: tracheae; adj.: tracheal)	tubes through which air is carried around the body and which open at a spiracle
trochanter	the second segment of the leg or **pedipalp**, counting from the body
tubercle	small, rounded swelling or protuberance
var. (abbrev.)	variety
ventral	on the lower surface (opposite of **dorsal**)
vice-county	a geographical division of Britain into similarly sized units used for biological recording

Spiracles – in the Buzzing Spider *Anyphaena accentuata* (*page 287*) they are midway up the ventral abdomen, but in most species they are very close to the spinnerets and difficult to see.

Spider biology

Newly emerged Garden Spider *Araneus diadematus* (Araneidae) spiderlings (LEFT). The young resemble the adult (RIGHT) in all ways except for functional sex organs and coloration.

Anatomy – a brief overview

Spiders do not have the larval or nymphal developmental stages shown by insects. Apart from size, the lack of functional sexual organs and often a difference in coloration (paler, translucent and with transparent legs), **spiderlings** newly emerged from their egg-sacs are morphologically identical to their parents. The essential anatomy of a spider is shown in the annotated photographs on *pages 14–15*. The body is divided into the **cephalothorax** (approximately equivalent to the combined head and thorax of an insect) and the **abdomen** (again similar to that of an insect), which are joined by a narrow stalk, the **pedicel**.

The cephalothorax is a rigid structure with a shield-like **carapace** protecting the **dorsal** (upper) side, and the **sternum** forming the equivalent on the **ventral** (lower) surface. From between these two plates emerge the four pairs of legs. At the front of the cephalothorax lie the mouthparts, which include the **chelicerae** used to bite prey and inject it with venom. Prominent at the front of the head area is a pair of sensory **pedipalps**, which resemble short legs. These are especially important in mature males which use them to transfer sperm to the female and, incidentally, provide critical structures for the unambiguous identification of species. On top of the carapace, towards the front, lie the eyes. These are simple structures, each with a single lens. Most British spiders have eight eyes, although a few families have six.

In contrast to the cephalothorax, the abdomen is a thin-walled structure which can expand and contract depending on whether the spider is starved or sated and, in females, whether or not she is **gravid**. In many species, at the front end of the dorsal surface, the heart can be seen beating in the mid-line. Depressed dots on the dorsal abdomen mark the position of internal muscle attachments. Underneath, again at the front end, are two pale patches. These indicate the positions of the internal **book lungs**, which are important components of the respiratory system. Just behind the book lungs is a transverse groove (the **epigastric furrow**). In mature female spiders, between the book lungs and immediately adjacent to the epigastric furrow lies a, usually highly complex, dark structure – the **epigyne**.

The epigyne represents the external **genitalia** of the female and is a critical feature used in identification.

Finally, all spiders have three pairs of **spinnerets** (or spinners) at the rear end of the abdomen. These flexible, finger-like structures are connected to a number of **silk glands** within the abdomen and are responsible for the production and fine-scale deployment of silk strands. Species in some families have an additional silk-producing organ (the **cribellum**) just in front of the spinnerets, with an associated comb-like structure of spines (the **calamistrum**) on **metatarsus** IV.

The importance of many of the features mentioned above will become clear when their functions are explained. A *Guide to spider families* is provided on *pages 54–72*.

Silk production

One of the defining features of spiders is that they all produce silk from a set of spinnerets at the rear of their abdomen. This silk plays a pivotal role in the lives of spiders and fulfils many and varied functions. There are six major types of silk gland recognized, each producing silks with different mechanical properties. Of these six gland types, each species of spider has a combination of at least three (males) or four (females), the number depending on the **family** to which they belong. The properties of silk are astonishing. It is incredibly flexible, elastic and strong, with one type (dragline silk) having a tensile strength comparable to that of high-grade alloy steel. It is also spun at ambient temperature, unlike synthetic fibres, making it very energy-efficient to produce. Furthermore, spiders can 'tune' the properties of a type of silk by changing the speed at which it is drawn out from their spinnerets and by combining multiple silk types to create threads with a wide range of characteristics. Spiders with a cribellum produce a type of non-sticky (**cribellate**) silk which acts rather like a 'woolly' sheet of Velcro, snagging the spines and hooks of the prey.

The manufacture of webs to catch prey is the most familiar use of silk; but spiders that do not make webs still use silk in a wide variety of other ways, as will become evident.

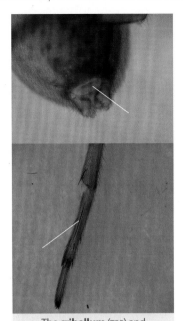

The **cribellum** (TOP) and **calamistrum** (BOTTOM) of *Amaurobius similis* (Amaurobiidae). Some spider families have an extra silk-producing organ situated in front of the **spinnerets** (the **cribellum**) with an associated comb of spines on metatarsus IV (the **calamistrum**).

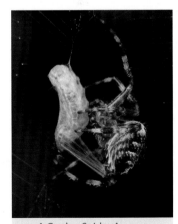

A Garden Spider *Araneus diadematus* (Araneidae) wrapping its prey, with silk 'streaming' out of its spinnerets.

Orb web of a Missing-sector orbweb spider *Zygiella x-notata* (Araneidae) – the different structural elements of the web are produced by different silk glands.

Signal thread

Radial threads

Hub

Sticky spiral

Frame thread

Glue droplets, also produced from the silk glands, are dotted equidistantly along the spirals. The larger drops are about one twentieth of a millimetre across, but the size varies with humidity.

Webs

Webs are spun by members of many spider families in order to catch aerial or crawling insect prey. Noting what sort of web (if any) a spider is associated with is a major step towards its ultimate identification. Webs can be classified approximately into eight broad types, which differ in their architectural design and the nature of the silk used in their construction. It is worth being aware that there can be variation within web-producing families; for example, some species may not produce webs at all. Additionally, some species may make webs that resemble those produced by other families. For instance, the tangled web of the Noble False Widow Spider *Steatoda nobilis* (Theridiidae) can appear similar to the sheet webs of the large house spiders (Agelenidae). A *Guide to webs* is on *pages 73–83*, with further illustrations.

Orb webs

The orb web is perhaps the iconic structure people most associate with spiders. However, members of only four families of British spiders construct webs of this type: orbweb spiders (Araneidae), long-jawed orbweb spiders (Tetragnathidae), Ray's spiders (Theridiosomatidae) and cribellate orbweb spiders (Uloboridae) – they just happen to contain a few species that are very common in urban and suburban environments. Watching the construction of an orb web is an entrancing experience, especially given that the process is entirely instinctive and completed through the sense of touch alone; vision plays no part. The web comprises three main components. The frame anchors the web to surrounding supports and serves as an attachment for the radial threads, which emanate from a central hub. These radials, in turn, act as supports for the all-important sticky spiral, which actually traps the prey. The stickiness of the spiral results either from glue droplets, which are secreted from one type of silk gland (orbweb, long-jawed orbweb and Ray's spiders) or, in the cribellate orbweb spiders, from a tangling cribellate silk. Once spun, the spider either sits at the hub or hides in a retreat, often a rolled leaf, connected to the hub by a silk line – the signal thread. Flying insects hit the web and are caught in the glue of the sticky spiral long enough for the spider to strike. These delicate orb webs are easily damaged by wind and rain, and the glue droplets lose their sticking power over time by becoming covered with pollen and dust particles in the air. Consequently, the webs are usually replaced every day or two. The spider eats the old web, recycling the silk components before making a new one.

A Garden Spider *Araneus diadematus* (Araneidae) in the final stages of dismantling a web. Most of the old web has been gathered into a ball at the hub, where it will be eaten and the silk constituents recycled.

Funnel webs

This type of web comprises a flat sheet of silk with a tubular retreat in one corner and is made by just one British family (funnelweb spiders, Agelenidae). These spiders are not to be confused with the notorious Sydney Funnelweb Spider *Atrax robustus*, which is in a different family altogether – and one not found in Britain. Funnelweb spiders build their webs both indoors and out, choosing undisturbed places such as behind furniture, in the corners of sheds and garages, under debris, in rock crevices or in low vegetation, depending on the species. These webs are not sticky and rely on the spines and bristles on the legs of prey becoming entangled in the silk-mesh sheet. The familiar cobwebs that festoon little-used places are funnel webs produced by house spiders of the **genus** *Tegenaria*.

Tangled webs

Tangled webs are built by the comb-footed spiders (Theridiidae) and comb-footed cellar spiders (Nesticidae). They are three-dimensional networks of criss-crossed silken lines, some of which, where they attach to surfaces, have glue droplets. In some theridiids, webs are reduced or absent. Rather similar looking webs are also found in the cellar spiders (Pholcidae) and the meshweb spiders (Dictynidae). In the former, the webs are larger, very open structures and, except in the very south of England, found only in buildings. Meshweb spiders produce a similar tangle to theridiids but made of cribellate silk, often connecting closely adjacent leaves in the heads of plants.

Lace webs

Laceweb spiders (Amaurobiidae) are common inhabitants of crevices in walls, fences and the corners of window frames, as well as compact conifer hedges. They produce a messy mesh of non-sticky, cribellate silk radiating out from a circular retreat. The silk of the web is lacy and, when fresh, has a distinctly bluish sheen.

Radial webs

These are minimalist webs in which the silk serves merely to alert the spider to the presence of prey; it does nothing to retain it. Tubeweb spiders (Segestriidae) live in silk-lined holes in walls and tree bark. Connected to, and radiating from, this tube are a dozen or so strands of silk which act as trip-wires. When touched by a crawling insect, the spider shoots out at high speed and overpowers it.

Sheet webs

These webs are made by lesser cobweb spiders (Hahniidae) and the largest family, the money spiders (Linyphiidae). Money spider webs are typically a domed sheet of silk strung between stems of vegetation or between twigs of trees and shrubs. In webs of the larger species, there are also many silk strands ('guy ropes') above and below the dome. These are attached to the surrounding vegetation and serve to stabilize the structure. The strands above the dome also intercept flying insects, knocking them down onto the sheet below. Characteristically, the spider lurks beneath the dome and grabs prey through the sheet. Some webs may have more simple structures than described above and, indeed, some species are so mobile that they are only rarely found with webs.

Other web types

Four other web-building families should be mentioned briefly here, three of which each contain one British species. The Purseweb Spider *Atypus affinis* (Atypidae) produces a completely closed tube of silk, part of which is buried in soft soil with the rest often extending along the ground surface. The above-ground 'sock' often becomes covered with soil particles. The spider waits within the tube and catches prey that walks on the aerial portion, pulling it through the silk wall. The very rare Ladybird Spider *Eresus sandaliatus* (Eresidae) builds a similar silk-lined retreat in the ground but with a canopy of bluish, cribellate silk radiating from the entrance. The silk becomes browner with age and is often camouflaged with the remains of prey and other debris. The Water Spider *Argyroneta aquatica* (Cybaeidae), the only truly aquatic species in Britain, builds a sheet of silk between the submerged stems of water plants. At the surface, air is repeatedly trapped in dense, water-repellent, velvety hairs on the abdomen and taken down and released beneath the sheet, creating a 'diving bell' within which the spider lives. The bell is not used to catch prey; the spider is an active underwater hunter. Finally, silk tents (nursery webs) are built in vegetation by nurseryweb spiders (Pisauridae) in order to protect their young – again, they are not used to catch prey.

The Water Spider *Argyroneta aquatica* (Cybaeidae) uses hairs on its abdomen to transport air down to its web, attached to submerged vegetation, forming a 'diving bell' (see *Guide to webs page 75*).

Many species build silken retreats in which they wait for prey, mate or house their egg-sacs. Here the orbweaver *Larinioides cornutus* (Araneidae) has fashioned a cell by binding together the tops of grasses.

Retreats

Silk is often used to construct a protected retreat in which the spider can await prey or deposit and guard egg-sacs. These retreats are often the first indication that a spider is present. *Larinioides cornutus*, an orb-weaving inhabitant of damp meadows and reedbeds, joins the tops of grass stems or the flower heads of rushes together with silk to construct a secure resting place; the retreats are often much more obvious than the spider or its web. In this case the retreat serves both as a waiting place and, ultimately, a safe haven in which to deposit egg-sacs. Ground-living spiders often make silken cells beneath debris or rocks but many species living in low-growing vegetation make retreats out of rolled leaves in order to protect their egg-sacs (see *Guide to egg-sacs, page 84*).

Courtship and mating

In web-building species, males usually abandon their webs after reaching maturity and set out to search for females. Spiders are carnivores and males have evolved often complex courtship behaviours so that females can distinguish them from potential prey and from males of other species. The nature of these courtship manoeuvres depends on the family involved. Spiders are unique amongst arthropods in that they have indirect insemination; fertilization takes place within the female's body with the sperm introduced not by a primary sex organ but by secondary structures, the pedipalps. The act of mating involves the transfer of sperm from the male's pedipalps to the female's epigyne.

The triangular sperm web of the Fen Raft Spider *Dolomedes plantarius* (Pisauridae).

Sperm induction

Sperm from the male's testes exit the body *via* **ducts** which empty into the epigastric furrow but, as mentioned, it is the pedipalps that deliver sperm to the female. Newly matured males therefore have to fill their pedipalps with sperm (sperm induction) before successful mating can take place. Depending on the species, this occurs during the courtship process itself or, more usually, before the male locates a potential partner. The male begins by making a tiny platform of silk, the sperm web, onto which he expels a drop of sperm from the epigastric furrow. The two pedipalps are alternately applied to this droplet, sucking up the sperm in the manner of a syringe.

Courtship behaviour

Even in **cursorial** species, strands of silk are continually being laid down as the spider moves around. These draglines contain chemical cues which, amongst other functions, enable males to locate potential partners. The chemicals (**pheromones**) in draglines and web silk may indicate the sex and status (mated or virgin) of a female. For web-builders, on contacting a female's web the male switches immediately to courtship mode. Web-builders have very poor eyesight and so communication between the sexes relies very much on chemical signalling and vibrations. Different species vary enormously in the details of courtship, but male web-builders may employ combinations of plucking strands of the female's web with their chelicerae, tapping a rhythm with their pedipalps or bobbing their abdomen against the silk. In families with excellent eyesight – the jumping

In species with good eyesight courtship is mostly visual and involves specific movements of often brightly coloured legs and pedipalps. Here a male (RIGHT) jumping spider *Aelurillus v-insignitus* (Salticidae) signals to a female (LEFT) with his front legs.

A male *Metellina segmentata* (Tetragnathidae) (RIGHT) cautiously explores the web of a potential mate (LEFT).

spiders (Salticidae) and the wolf spiders (Lycosidae) – the preliminaries of courtship involve visual cues. Males belonging to these families often have brightly coloured patches of hair or scales around their eyes, on their pedipalps or on their front legs, whereas females are usually a dull brown, a phenomenon called **sexual dimorphism**. The male pedipalps and legs are waved in a species-specific, semaphore-like way in

Two male jumping spiders *Evarcha arcuata* (Salticidae) fighting over a female hidden in a rolled leaf.

A male (LEFT) Nurseryweb Spider *Pisaura mirabilis* (Pisauridae) persuades a receptive female (RIGHT) to accept his wrapped fly as a nuptial gift.

front of the female, proclaiming a potential partner. Pheromones on the **cuticle** of the legs and body also play a part when the male and female are close enough to touch. In a number of spiders, vibrations *via* the substrate, for example dry leaves, alert potential partners to each other's presence. These vibrations can be produced by drumming legs and pedipalps (*e. g.* wolf spiders) or by special 'tooth and comb' mechanisms located on various parts of the spider's body (*e. g.* some money spiders).

In the Nurseryweb Spider *Pisaura mirabilis*, 'nuptial gifts' are offered to the female by a courting male. The male catches and wraps an insect which is then presented to a receptive female. While she is dealing with the gift, the male mates with her. Not only are her jaws kept busy during this process, reducing the danger to her suitor, but the male's contribution of extra energy for the female could potentially be translated into the production of more eggs carrying his genes. The males of orb-weaving *Metellina* species wait until a female has caught her own prey before attempting to court. In many spider species males mature before females, with the result that several potential mates may compete for the favours of one newly matured female. A number of males can often be observed around a female's web in *Metellina* species, where they jostle for mating opportunities. Often the largest of the males wins the contest.

Copulation

If the male's courtship is successful, the female will become quiescent and allow the male to insert his pedipalps into her epigyne. The details of the copulatory position vary between species. In some, the female leans her body to one side to allow the male access. In others, the male climbs onto the female's back and reaches round to her ventral side with his pedipalps. In the stretch spiders *Tetragnatha* species, the male locks jaws with the female and they mate with their ventral sides facing. The male pedipalps and the female

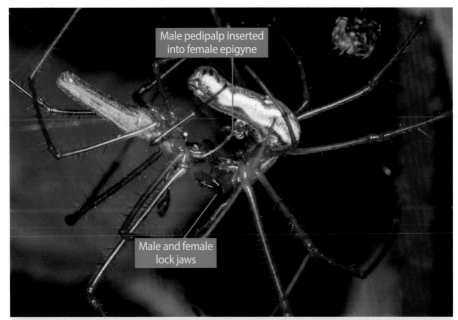

Male pedipalp inserted into female epigyne

Male and female lock jaws

During mating the male pedipalp is inserted into the female epigyne. During this process in the stretch spider *Tetragnatha montana* the jaws of the male (LEFT) lock with those of the female (RIGHT).

A male (RIGHT) Common Candy-striped Spider *Enoplognatha ovata* (Theridiidae) guards a female (LEFT) in the process of moulting to maturity.

epigyne are, in most British spiders, highly complex structures. **Processes** on the pedipalps have to engage with folds or ridges on the epigyne in order to align the structures correctly before sperm transfer can take place. Males usually apply their pedipalps alternately, each accessing different sides of the female's epigyne. The sperm entering the female is stored in paired structures called **spermathecae** until required to fertilize the eggs. Stored sperm can be utilized for multiple broods after the males have all died.

Mate guarding

When mating is over, the male may beat a hasty retreat. For the majority of species, contrary to popular belief, the male seldom falls prey to the female after mating. This is not the case, however, with the Wasp Spider *Argiope bruennichi* where males are frequently eaten. In some species, the male co-habits with the female in her web after copulation in order to minimize the chance that she will mate with other males. Conversely, in other species males may find and guard females that are just about to moult to maturity, thereby ensuring they are mating with a virgin female. Preventing other males from mating can also be achieved by sealing the orifices of the female's epigyne with secretions (*e. g.* in some theridiids) or by parts of the male pedipalp breaking off and lodging in the entrance to the spermathecae (*e. g.* in the Wasp Spider).

Egg-sacs

All spider species wrap their eggs in silk. However, the construction of egg-sacs in different species varies enormously: from the eggs being enclosed in a flimsy silk net (*e.g.* the Daddy Long-legs Spider *Pholcus phalangioides*) through to complex, multi-layered assemblies or cocoons (*e. g.* the Garden Spider *Araneus diadematus*). The functions of the egg-sac are to protect the developing eggs from desiccation, temperature extremes, predators and parasites, and in some species to make them more portable. The more elaborate structures are often found in species whose eggs overwinter, exposed to the elements and for most of the time unguarded by the female. Eggs with minimal protection, such as those of the Spitting Spider *Scytodes thoracica*, often occur within the sheltered environments of buildings. In many species the egg-sac is protected by the female for at least a while after construction. This guarding can take the form of the sac being actively transported by the female. In the Spitting Spider, for example, the eggs are supported under the body between her pedipalps and a silk band from her spinnerets, whereas in Daddy Long-legs Spiders they are carried in the chelicerae. In other cases, the female protects her offspring within an anchored structure, often a rolled leaf, or under stones. The nature of the association between female and egg-sac can be a guide to field identification. For instance, a large, cursorial female

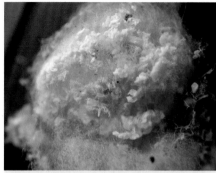

An egg-sac of the Garden Spider *Araneus diadematus* (Araneidae) opened to show the white egg shells and the pink exuviae left from the spiderlings' first moult.

lurking on vegetation and carrying a white or brown egg-sac in her chelicerae would suggest the Nurseryweb Spider *Pisaura mirabilis* or one of the even larger raft spiders (*Dolomedes* spp.). In both of these genera, the female eventually builds a nursery web in which she hangs her egg-sac and guards the hatched young until they disperse.

The egg-sacs of a very few British spiders allow identification to species without the spider being present. For example, the Wasp Spider *Argiope bruennichi* produces a large, highly characteristic flask-shaped egg-sac covered in papery brown silk, which is hung low in vegetation near the female's web. For a *Guide to egg-sacs* with characteristics that can help with the identification of species and genera see *page 84*.

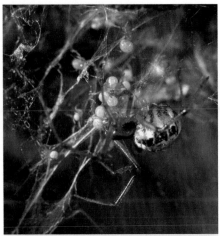

Phylloneta sisyphia (Theridiidae) feeding her young on regurgitated food.

Development and growth

The interval between copulation and egg-sac production varies enormously from a week or two (*e. g.* the Common Candy-striped Spider *Enoplognatha ovata*) to many months (*e. g.* large house spiders *Tegenaria* spp.).

Early development

The eggs hatch within the egg-sac and the young undergo one moult (see below) before the spiderlings emerge. An empty egg-sac therefore contains the remains of the egg shells, which are usually white, and the first cast skins (**exuviae**), which may be pinkish. The spiderlings exit the egg-sac as miniature versions of the adult, although they are not at this stage sexually mature. Their escape can be through a single hole made by the spiderlings themselves (*e. g. Paidiscura pallens* and the Wasp Spider *Argiope bruennichi*), or as a result of the mother teasing open the silk wall (*e. g.* the candy-striped spiders *Enoplognatha* species and wolf spiders (Lycosidae)) or even tearing it open (raft spiders *Dolomedes* species). The spiderlings may stay aggregated for a while before gradually dispersing. In a few British spiders, the female feeds the newly emerged young with regurgitated food (*e. g. Phylloneta sisyphia*). *Coelotes* (Agelenidae) females regurgitate food and also provide larger prey items for their young to share: when the mother dies, she too becomes a meal for her offspring.

Moulting

Spiders grow by moulting (**ecdysis**). The number of moults between hatching from the egg and achieving maturity varies between species. Some appear to undergo a set number of moults, whereas in others, such as large house spiders (*Tegenaria* species),

A *Neoscona adianta* (Araneidae) in the final stages of withdrawing its legs from the exuvia.

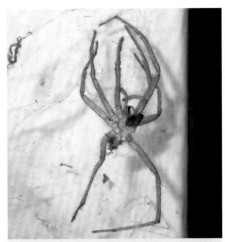

The moulted exuvia of a large house spider *Tegenaria saeva* (Agelenidae).

maturity occurs after a variable number of moults, resulting in the body sizes of mature individuals varying by a factor of two. In general, though, the larger the spider species the more moults it goes through before reaching maturity. A very tiny spider might have to moult only three times, whereas a raft spider *Dolomedes* species may go through nine or more.

Prior to a moult, the spider withdraws to a secluded place and ceases feeding for a few days. Internally, a new, soft exoskeleton is laid down at the same time as enzymes begin to dissolve the inner surface of the old one. In paler species the legs visibly darken as moulting fluid is secreted between the old and new exoskeletons. Before the moult commences the spider hangs suspended from a strand of silk, the moulting thread. Blood pressure inside the cephalothorax increases and a split appears on each side between the carapace and the sternum. The carapace flips back like a lid as the split continues around the sides of the abdomen. As the old exoskeleton peels off the abdomen, the legs start to be withdrawn. Eventually the legs are free and the spider remains attached to the moulting thread by the spinnerets alone. The spider expands in size while the new, soft exoskeleton is hardening and at the same time flexes its limbs to ensure that the joints remain supple. The whole moult can take as little as 10 to 15 minutes.

Moulting is an exacting process that can easily go wrong, leading to the spider's death. Extracting legs is often the critical stage; if prolonged for any reason, the new exoskeleton hardens before the limbs are fully withdrawn from the old one. Spiders are also extremely vulnerable to predators while they hang soft and helpless as the new exoskeleton hardens fully. In web-builders, the exuviae are often found in or near the web and can last for a very long time. They are often mistaken for dead spiders. If examined with a hand lens, all the external features of the spider can be clearly seen, including eyes, jaws and leg bristles; only the thin wall of the abdomen collapses. In all but one British species, moulting stops when maturity is reached and so no exuvia will carry the full anatomical details of the male pedipalps or female epigyne. The one exception is the female of the Purseweb Spider *Atypus affinis*. Males of this species mate and die after reaching maturity, whereas females continue to moult, becoming virgins again in the process as their spermathecae (and any stored sperm) are shed together with the rest of the exoskeleton.

Spiders often lose limbs as a result of problems during moulting or attack by a predator. If this occurs in juveniles the lost limb regenerates during subsequent moults. The replacement limb is initially smaller and paler compared to the others but can become progressively larger with successive moults so that, in the adult, all the limbs may once again be the same size.

Dispersal

Dispersal is an important process for all organisms. It reduces competition for space and food among spiderlings and ultimately lowers the chance that reproducing adults are too closely related to each other. Two major dispersal mechanisms used by many spiders involve silk: **ballooning** and **rappelling** (or rigging). These techniques are used to very different extents in different families – in some not at all and in others very frequently – and may involve either very young spiders or adults of the smaller species. Ballooning is an aerial dispersal strategy that has the potential to transport an individual hundreds or even thousands of kilometres; Charles Darwin famously observed spiders ballooning amongst the rigging of the Beagle when off the Argentine coast. However, the distances 'flown' are usually very much shorter. Rappelling on the other hand, involves short-distance movements of a few metres. Both processes are initiated by a spider moving to an elevated point (perhaps the top of a plant stem), straightening its legs and lifting its

A spider in characteristic pose prior to ballooning or rappelling.

Some spiders can move across water surfaces by raising their legs or abdomen to act as sails.

In ballooning, the strand elongates until the upward lift of the silk line is greater than the weight of the spider, which then drifts up into the air. Recent research suggests that electrostatic charges on the silk may also help the spider become airborne. Rappelling relies on the silk strand snagging adjacent vegetation. It is then pulled in, made taut, attached to the substrate and used as a bridge. The strategy employed depends on species, temperature, wind strength and local spider densities. Under some atmospheric conditions many individuals, particularly money spiders, are induced to disperse at the same time. When they land the silk strands can combine to form shrouds which festoon the vegetation. These shrouds are commonly called **gossamer**. Long-distance dispersal is also made possible by spiders clinging to debris floating in the oceans and, increasingly, as an unintended consequence of human travel and the transport of goods around the world.

Spiders also disperse on foot. In cursorial species this happens during the everyday activities involved in hunting. Wolf spiders have evolved a specific mechanism to scatter their offspring. The female carries an egg-sac attached to her spinnerets and when the young emerge they climb onto the mother's abdomen. They are transported around for a few days and gradually drop off until eventually there is none left. Males of all spiders, once mature, wander to find females and in doing so increase the chances that they will mate with unrelated females. Most bizarrely, raft spiders *Dolomedes* and other semi-aquatic species, and at least some ballooning spiders, can 'sail' short distances. Recent research has shown that they rest on the water film and raise one or more pairs of legs, or indeed the whole body, to catch the breeze which propels them across the surface. Obviously, the distances moved using these methods are relatively short compared with those potentially achieved by ballooning.

The simultaneous landing of thousands of ballooning spiders can cover vegetation in wreaths of silk called gossamer.

Longevity

In general, large spiders live longer than small ones, possibly because they need to obtain more energy over their lifetime to grow and mature, and thus take longer. Most British species are probably 'annuals', overwintering only once during their lives, although some show more flexibility. The Garden Spider *Araneus diadematus*, for example, tends to be an annual in the south of the country but requires two years to mature in the north. This might be a common pattern for some other large species. There are a few interesting exceptions to the trend that large species live longer than small ones. The Wasp Spider *Argiope bruennichi* female is one of our largest spiders (males are considerably smaller, a case of **sexual dimorphism**) and yet frequently reaches maturity and dies within a single year. This species feeds mostly on grasshoppers – large, abundant prey that clearly supply their energy needs and allow rapid growth.

Spiders can overwinter at all stages of the life-cycle, depending on the species and also on individual growth rates. For example, in the Wasp Spider it is the eggs that overwinter, with the young emerging from the egg-sac the following spring. Young of the candy-striped spiders *Enoplognatha ovata* and *E. latimana* emerge in autumn and pass the winter as second-instar spiderlings sheltering deep in the ground vegetation. Large house spiders *Tegenaria* species survive the winter in one of two stages: as half-grown juveniles (both sexes), or as mature adults (females only). Garden Spiders that take two years to mature pass their first winter as eggs and their second as half-grown juveniles.

Parasites

Spiders have a number of external parasites that may be evident in the field. Bright red mites (another arachnid) can sometimes be found clinging to the spider's legs: some of these mites are parasitic but others simply use the spider as a means of transport. Likewise, pseudoscorpions may occasionally be seen hitchhiking on spiders' legs.

Occasionally a spider looks odd and asymmetrical, and on closer examination is found to be host to a **parasitoid** wasp larva (Ichneumonidae). These off-white larvae look like fly maggots and ride on the spider's back attached by mouthparts embedded in the abdomen. They are able to survive the host moulting. The larvae initially grow slowly and seem not to affect the spider very much. Then, just before the spider is ready to moult to maturity, the entire abdominal contents are sucked out rapidly by the larva, leaving nothing but a husk. The larva pupates nearby in a silken cocoon and eventually emerges as an adult wasp.

Other wasps in the family Pompilidae specialize in hunting spiders, and may be seen carrying off paralysed prey with which they stock their burrows. A single egg is laid on the spider so that when the wasp larva hatches it has a ready source of food.

Egg-sacs can also be the target of ichneumon wasps (for example *Hemiteles similis*), whose larvae consume the eggs and then pupate within the protective silk (strictly speaking, this is predation rather than parasitism).

Finally, although dead spiders can be colonized by common moulds that grow on anything damp and decaying, other fungi (for example, *Cordyceps* species) are parasites that consume the living spider from the inside and then develop long, thin fruiting bodies, which emerge from the victim's body.

Bright red mites are occasionally seen attached to the legs and body of spiders (here the Common Candy-striped Spider *Enoplognatha ovata* (Theridiidae)).

A money spider *Neriene peltata* (Linyphiidae) acting as host for the ichneumon wasp *Acrodactyla degener* (Pimplinae). The larva is firmly attached to the spider's abdomen.

Spider infected with *Cordyceps* fungus, with fruiting bodies emerging from the host.

Zygiella x-notata (Araneidae) eggs consumed by a predatory wasp *Hemiteles similis*. Note the wasp pupae within the silk egg-sac wall.

A *Trochosa* spider (Lycosidae) caught by the spider-hunting wasp *Anoplius viaticus* (Pompilidae).

A pirate spider *Ero aphana* (Mimetidae) making short work of a *Platnickina tincta* (Theridiidae) prey.

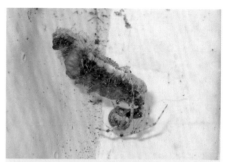

Theridion melanurum (Theridiidae) eating a hairy caterpillar.

The sit-and-wait crab spider *Misumena vatia* (Thomisidae) stays motionless on a flower until prey arrives.

The excretory products of spiders are semi-liquid and form round spots on hard surfaces.

Caught prey is swathed with silk either before or after poison is injected, depending on species and prey size.

Food capture and feeding

All British spiders are primarily carnivorous, although there is some evidence that certain orbweavers can digest pollen caught on their webs while they are recycling the silk prior to web replacement. Scavenging dead insects has occasionally been observed. Web-builders clearly use their webs to catch prey and do so in different ways, some of which have been touched on previously (*page 25*). For orbweavers, the angle and position of the web can suggest the type of prey sought. For example, the Wasp Spider *Argiope bruennichi* builds its web low down across holes in the vegetation ideally positioned to ensnare their grasshopper prey. The stretch spiders *Tetragnatha* species are often associated with water and weave an orbweb attached to emergent vegetation and frequently at an oblique angle to the water surface. These will not only catch insects flying through the air but also those emerging from the water beneath. Likewise, the cave spider *Meta menardi* (Tetragnathidae) spins an almost horizontal orbweb and feeds mostly on crawling prey that fall from the roof above. For web-spinning species it is the movement of the prey in the web, or vibration of wings, that attracts the spider's attention. Other species construct webs designed to catch much more specific prey. For example, the theridiid *Achaearanea riparia* builds a web with a number of taut vertical threads attached to the ground, the bottom parts of which have drops of gum. When an ant brushes against one, it sticks to the gum, breaks the thread and is lifted off the ground by its contraction. Some spiders, notably the pirate spiders (Mimetidae), specialize in

A Wasp Spider *Argiope bruennichi* (Araneidae) web – positioned to intercept grasshoppers and crickets.

eating other spiders. Remarkably, the Daddy Long-legs Spider *Pholcus phalangioides* is capable of tackling spider prey much more robust than itself, such as large house spiders *Tegenaria* species, as well as its normal insect diet.

Species that do not build webs have to catch their prey in more active ways. Wolf spiders (Lycosidae), for example, have good eyesight and locate prey by detecting movement. They use speed and brute strength to overpower free-running invertebrates on the ground or leaf surfaces. Jumping spiders, on the other hand, operate like a cat – they stalk prey and, when within reach, leap forward to effect a capture. Their large eyes and binocular vision enable them to assess distances accurately. Other species such as the Mouse Spider *Scotophaeus blackwalli* (Gnaphosidae) wander around slowly at night catching less mobile prey. Some species are sit-and-wait predators and remain stationary while the prey comes to them. Crab spiders, particularly the thomisids, lurk in open flowers and are able to overpower prey much larger than themselves, such as butterflies and bumblebees. Some can even change colour so as to blend in with their background. In spiders frequenting areas with open water, vibrations transmitted across the water surface, or within the water body, are used to locate prey (for example, in raft spiders *Dolomedes* species) and it seems likely that other species may use similar vibrations within terrestrial substrates.

Once caught, the prey is injected with venom. This is administered *via* the fangs of the chelicerae, which have an off-set hole at their tip (like a syringe needle) connected to poison glands located within the cephalothorax. The details of prey capture are highly variable, even within species. However, in most non-web-building spiders the prey is bitten first and then may or may not be swathed in silk. In some web-builders, such as the Garden Spider *Araneus diadematus*, larger prey items are immobilized with broad bands of silk before being bitten. Bites are often directed towards the limbs of the prey, presumably to avoid danger from mouthparts or a sting. The cribellate orbweb spiders (Uloboridae) do not produce venom but rely on wrapping the prey very tightly, eventually asphyxiating it. Some species have evolved specific techniques for dealing with potentially dangerous prey. *Segestria* species (Segestriidae), for example, seize the

Remains of food items eaten by 1) a species with teeth on its jaws – large house spider *Tegenaria saeva* (Agelenidae) (LEFT) and 2) a species with no teeth – crab spider *Misumena vatia* (Thomisidae) (RIGHT).

waist of wasps so that the hazardous extremities of jaws and sting are facing away from the spider as it hauls the prey into its tubular retreat.

Spiders cannot cope with solid food and therefore have to reduce their prey to a liquid by applying digestive juices to it before ingestion. In species with teeth on the chelicerae, such as large house spiders *Tegenaria* species (*page 246*), the prey is slowly mashed into pieces while digestive juices are added and the resulting semi-liquid 'soup' sucked back. Any solid particles of food are filtered by structures within the spider's mouth. Species without cheliceral teeth, for example crab spiders (Thomisidae), puncture the prey and secrete digestive fluids onto the surface. This fluid is drawn in by capillary action and the digested material sucked out, leaving the victim an intact but empty shell.

Waste products from the digestive process pass out of the anus, situated just above the spinnerets, at the **posterior** end of the abdomen. This waste comprises two components: faeces, which are brown, and solidified 'urine' (**guanine**), which is bright white. Small round circles of brown and white on a windowsill are a sure sign of a spider living overhead.

Coloration

While most small species are uniform brown or black, larger ones tend to exhibit various colours and/or patterns. The reason for this is probably pressure from predators. Small spiders resemble small, dark elements of their background, whereas in larger species it may be beneficial to break up their outline with patches of different colours. The patterns can be a guide to a species' identity but there are very many cases where two or more different species have identical colours and markings, as is emphasized in the species accounts later in the book. Even where patterns can be useful it is important to know which elements are constant and which are not. For example, the Garden Spider *Araneus diadematus* and the Four-spotted Orbweb Spider *Araneus quadratus* are both highly variable in background colour (ranging from pale yellow through to browns, reds and greens) and yet the white cross pattern on the former, and the four white spots on the latter, remain constant features.

Some species can change their colour according to their background or other environmental factors. The three images of Four-spotted Orbweb Spider *Araneus quadratus* (Araneidae) individuals give some indication of the range found. In all three, the four white spots on the abdomen are clear.

Spiders and people

Spiders are one of our largest, most diverse and important groups of invertebrates. Their sheer abundance makes them commercially important as crop-pest predators, while in our homes they help to control the numbers of unwelcome flies and biting insects. People have also exploited the remarkable properties of spider silk; its bio-compatibility makes it excellent for use in medicine, its extraordinary mechanical properties render it suitable for use in tough, light-weight materials, and it is both non-polluting to produce and completely biodegradable. Spider silk has been used to help heal wounds for many centuries – a use first documented by the ancient Greeks – and it continues to underpin major medical advances. These include functional replacement and regenerative repair of skin, blood vessels, tendons, joints and damaged nerve sheaths. As artificially manufactured spider silk becomes commercially viable, its many potential industrial uses include production of light-weight, bullet-proof clothing and even cosmetics.

Beyond the practical, orb webs are perhaps one of the most iconic and admired structures in the natural world – making it all the more bizarre that our relationship with spiders is so ambiguous. From time immemorial they have been both loved and loathed, but never ignored. W. S. Bristowe, in his 1956 book *World of Spiders*, gives a fascinating international overview of attitudes to spiders in literature and folklore.

Despite the fact that spiders – unlike bees and dogs – have never been known to cause a fatality in Britain, and indeed only around one percent of British spider species can even bite through human skin, fear of being bitten is rife. A bizarre fear of spiders walking into your mouth at night is also prevalent, as are much more generic feelings of fear and loathing. At worst, these constitute severe arachnophobia and may be accompanied by the physical symptoms of panic attacks, such as excessive sweating, rapid breathing and elevated pulse rate.

These fears have historically been fed by misunderstanding, propagated in literature and superstition and, more recently, in the media. This was exemplified in 2013, when an increase in the range of Noble False Widow spiders *Steatoda nobilis*, possibly as a result of climate change, hit the media spotlight. This non-native species, which established on the south coast probably in the late 19th Century, can deliver a painful bite, akin to a wasp sting at worst. Images of terrible necrotic wounds, with no verified evidence of a spider bite, and which could have been caused by bacterial infection of any bite or scratch, filled the press and unleashed a wave of arachnophobic panic. Schools and factories were closed and large numbers of spiders of many species were eradicated.

While elements in the press will always exploit such opportunities to appeal to peoples' fears, much of the irrational fear that constitutes arachnophobia can, at least, be ameliorated by a better understanding of the fascinating biology of spiders. Large house spiders (*Tegenaria* spp.) are one of the commonest triggers of arachnophobia – the reason usually given for this is their (relatively!) large size and sudden, rapid movements. However, understanding that most large house-spiders seen in homes in autumn are males in search of females hidden in nooks and crannies, and, better still, learning to distinguish males from females on the basis of their 'boxing glove' pedipalps (see *pages 14–15*), are often the first steps on the path to seeing spiders differently. The American children's book *Charlotte's Web* by E. B. White has done much to increase understanding of the lives of spiders. *Spiders – learning to love them,* recounting Australian author Lynne Kelly's personal journey from arachnophobia to arachnophilia through learning to understand spiders, is also a great read for anyone wanting to follow suit.

For those whose arachnophobia is so severe that it affects the quality of their day-to-day lives, courses run by zoos around the UK, and particularly by the Zoological Society of London through the *Friendly Spider Programme*, have a success rate of over 80%.

Spider bites – myth and reality

Although the vast majority of spiders produce venom with which to immobilize and kill their prey, there are very few British species that, if provoked, can bite and inject venom through the skin of humans and pets. This usually happens when they are trapped inside clothing or bedclothes, or picked-up clumsily. The effect of a bite is usually very mild but, as with bee and wasp stings, people's responses vary widely. Most rashes or wounds attributed to a 'spider bite' have other causes – it is almost never a spider. Many of the wounds illustrated in the media and attributed to spiders are just not consistent with the effects that genuine spider bites produce. However, if in doubt about any infected sting, bite or other wound, medical advice should be sought.

A Large house spider *Tegenaria saeva* (Agelenidae) – a species many people find threatening.

When, where and how to find spiders

Unlike many insects, spiders can be found throughout the year, although the highest diversity occurs from about mid-April through to October. Spiders are perhaps most obvious in late summer and autumn when males of large house spiders *Tegenaria* species wander round our houses, and females of the more common orbweavers, such as the Garden Spider *Araneus diadematus* and the Four-spotted Orbweb Spider *A. quadratus,* are swollen with eggs. However, different species mature at different times of the year and although this book, in general, does not rely on specimens being adult, certain key field identification features may only be present at this stage, *e. g.* the pedipalp coloration of some male jumping spiders (Salticidae). The time of year when spiders become adult and when they lay their eggs can also provide pointers to their identification. During the winter most spiders are inactive or at the egg or juvenile stage of their life-cycle.

Where in the country a spider is found is also important in narrowing down which species it might be. Although the geographical distributions of species may change with time (see *e.g.* the species accounts for the Wasp Spider (*page 204* – see also *page 422*) and *Nigma walckenaeri* (*page 262*)) this usually happens fairly slowly. So spiders found in the very north of Britain are unlikely to include the Nurseryweb Spider *Pisaura mirabilis*, the wolf spider *Pardosa prativaga* or the jumping spider *Euophrys frontalis*. The colourful crab spider *Misumena vatia* shows a very pronounced southern distribution, whereas the orbweaver *Araneus triguttatus* and the Cardinal Spider *Tegenaria parietina* are confined to the south-east. In contrast, some species have western and northern distributions and are rare or absent towards the south-east. These include the dictynid *Cryphoeca silvicola*, the agelenid *Textrix denticulata* and the linyphiid *Pityohyphantes phrygianus*. Some other species have curious distributions: for example, *Philodromus margaritatus* occurs in scattered localities in the south of England and in central Scotland, as does the Strawberry Spider *Araneus alsine*. Of course, specimens might well be found well beyond their currently known ranges but these should be checked by an expert (see *Recording Spiders, page 422*).

Spiders occur in virtually all habitats but different species have their own particular requirements in terms of macro- or micro-climate, vegetation structure and types of prey, and these too can be important pointers to identification. To give just a flavour, there is a small suite of species that are only found in dark, damp environments such as caves, culverts and under drain covers. These include the impressive cave spiders *Meta menardi* and *M. bourneti*, *Nesticus cellulanus* and *Metellina merianae*, all of which feed not only on prey that fly in but also that crawl on the cavity roof. Species that build webs need supports for their structures. Tall, grassy meadows offer abundant anchor points for orbweavers such as *Araneus quadratus* and *Larinioides cornutus*, and for many hammock webs of the money spiders (Linyphiidae). The orbweavers catch large prey such as flies, bees and butterflies, and the money spiders smaller flying and jumping insects. Bushes and trees provide stiffer supports for webs. For example, gorse bushes are favoured by the tangled web species *Phylloneta sisyphia*. Holly and oak leaves are common haunts of the tiny theridiid *Paidiscura pallens*, with its overly large spiky egg-sac, while the money spider *Drapetisca socialis* forages for flies on the trunks of trees, especially Beech. The interior of houses, sheds and garages provide protection and plenty of nooks and crannies for a whole host of species including large house spiders *Tegenaria* species, the Mouse Spider *Scotophaeus blackwalli* and the tiny pink *Oonops domesticus*. Outside, buildings, stone walls and rubble piles provide both web supports and crevices in which spiders such as *Segestria* species and the lace web weaving *Amaurobius* species can establish retreats.

Habitats offering the greatest structural diversity would be expected to have the highest species richness of spiders, but this will vary with latitude. In general, the more continental climate of south-east England is favourable to more species than the cooler, oceanic region of north-west Scotland. It is also closest to continental Europe and thus often the first area in which species new to Britain become established. In addition, our knowledge of the number of spider species known from a particular habitat type will depend upon how thoroughly the habitat has been sampled and the proportion of common *versus* rare spiders living there. Areas with a higher human population density tend to be those most thoroughly searched. If all species in a habitat are common, they will each be found after relatively little sampling. On the other hand, if a high proportion of species are rare, then a very high sampling effort would be required to record them all. However, it is important to recognize that even habitats with low species diversity are likely to be of considerable interest; spiders that have adapted to more specialist niches often represent some of our rarest and most vulnerable species. For example, the Horrid Ground Weaver Spider *Nothophantes horridus*, a linyphiid that is thought to be **endemic**, lives in subterranean crevices and is only known from just a few disused limestone quarries near Plymouth. The Midas Tree Weaver Spider *Midia midas*, another linyphiid, is found in birds' nests and squirrel dreys in ancient oak and Beech trees (neither of these rare and tiny species is covered in the *Species accounts*).

The pretty agelenid *Textrix denticulata* is largely confined to western and northern areas of Britain.

Essential equipment

The purpose of this book is to enable the identification of spiders, as far as is possible, in the field without damaging them. The following equipment is recommended:

Hand lens – A lens of ×10 magnification is the most useful in the field because it provides a sharp image when examining a spider in a collecting tube or spi-pot (see below). The hand lens can be in virtually constant use so it is advisable to have it near at hand; wearing it on a neck strap is therefore suggested. Many fairly cheap, but reasonably good, lenses with an inbuilt light are now available. These can be extremely useful when examining spiders in a spi-pot or similar as it is not always

The correct use of a hand lens. The lens should be held against the eye and the object, here a spi-pot, brought closer until the spider is in focus.

easy to position the enclosed specimen in good natural light, particularly on cloudy days. Even on sunny days, the shadows of the observer and the lens may cut out a portion of the available light.

Spi-pot – This is a simple holding device made out of readily available household materials – and can be large or small depending on the size of pot chosen. Two identical plastic or waxed-paper cups, or mini milk pots, are modified as shown below. The very bottom is cut out of Pot A and Pot B has a disc of soft packaging material or expanded polystyrene glued to its base. The cut end of Pot A is covered with cling-film and held in place, if necessary, by an elastic band. A spider is placed in Pot A (inverted from the position shown) and Pot B slid in to trap the specimen against the cling-film. In use, both the soft disc and the cling-film give a little, making it very unlikely that the specimen will be squashed and damaged. When dirty, the cling-film over the end of Pot A can easily be moved across to a new, clean area.

The construction of a simple, small spi-pot out of mini milk containers. This size is ideal for use in the field. Larger spi-pots can be made out of cardboard or plastic drinking cups.

Set up as described above, it is the ventral side of the spider that will be visible under the cling-film. To view the dorsal side of the spider, draw back Pot B a little and turn the spi-pot such that the cling-film is now uppermost. The spider will reorientate itself (encouraged with a gentle shake) with the dorsal surface next to the film. Gently push Pot B in again to immobilize. Spiders restrained in a spi-pot are easily photographed for recording purposes (see *page 422*).

An even simpler immobilization method is merely to place the spider in a clear, thin polythene bag and fold it over a few times, safely trapping the specimen and enabling both sides to be viewed with a lens.

Plastic containers – A variety of small plastic containers, tubes and pots with lids are invaluable for temporarily storing spiders. When looking under a log, for example, many spiders may be found and, as they are cannibalistic, need to be kept in individual containers. A small piece of vegetation placed in each pot maintains humidity and also serves as a 'label' that the pot is in use. In addition, a piece of paper should be inserted inside the tube on which the date, location and habitat information is written in pencil, if the spider is not to be returned immediately. Containers with spiders in should never be left in direct sunlight because the animal will quickly overheat and die.

Additional equipment

Several other simple items of equipment, although not essential, will assist with catching individual spiders and in collecting them *en masse* from tall vegetation.

Pooter – The traditional British name given to a simple mouth-operated 'vacuum cleaner', which is invaluable for catching all sorts of invertebrates. The simplest design comprises two lengths of plastic tubing, a short (approximately 8 cm) wide-bore piece and a longer (approximately 30 cm) narrow-bore length. The narrow-bore tube has a piece of fine nylon gauze (*e. g.* tights material) put over one end, which is then inserted into the wide-bore tube. It may be necessary to wrap some insulation tape around the narrow-bore tube to ensure a tight fit. In use, the wide tube is placed next to the spider and a powerful suck through the narrow tube will draw it in (but NOT into your mouth because of the gauze).

A simple pooter design.

The spider can then be viewed in the wide tube itself, retained with a finger over the end, or gently blown into a spi-pot for closer examination.

Sweep net – A device for collecting invertebrates that live in tall vegetation, such as grasses and nettles. These are readily available from many natural history equipment suppliers, but a cheap and robust version can be made from an old tennis racquet frame and a pillowcase.

Beating tray/sheet – Useful for catching spiders that live on bushes and tree branches. Beating trays are available commercially but a pale, upturned umbrella works just as well, as does a square of an old bed sheet.

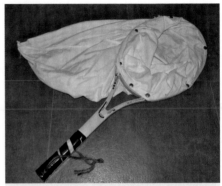

An inexpensive sweep net consisting of an old tennis racquet (with the strings removed) and a pillowcase attached to the frame with drawing pins.

Electric toothbrush (battery operated, vibrating (sonic) toothbrush) – Ideal for luring web-building, crevice-dwelling spiders out into the open (see *page 53*).

Pitfall traps – Can be made simply by sinking a smooth-sided plastic cup into the ground so that the lip is at, or slightly below, soil level. Surface-running species fall in and cannot escape.

Collecting techniques

A variety of collecting techniques is described below – this section should be read in conjunction with *Working in the Field (page 421)*.

Direct observation

The easiest way of finding spiders to identify is simply by observing them in their natural habitats or by spotting their webs. Orb webs, sheet webs and other less-structured webs may all contain spiders, either in the main web or sheltering in a retreat close by. Webs are best seen when dew-covered, but a similar effect can be achieved by spraying them with water from a plant mister. Once a web has been found, tracing silken lines back to where the spider is sitting is usually fairly easy, although extricating those living in deep holes and crevices is potentially tricky (but see *page 52*). In warm weather cursorial spiders, such as wolf spiders (Lycosidae) and the Nurseryweb Spider *Pisaura mirabilis*, frequently sit exposed on flat leaves, sunning themselves and their egg-sacs. Spiders that do not weave webs may construct some type of silken retreat, most commonly found in seed heads, in rolled-up leaves or under bark. In houses, spiders are often exposed on walls and floors and of course some end up in sinks and baths from which they cannot escape. Many species are active mainly or only at night and it can be well worthwhile going out or, indeed, looking around the inside of your house with a torch after dark.

Grubbing about

'Grubbing about' means exactly what it says; getting down on hands and knees and carefully parting grasses or other vegetation to reveal the spider inhabitants. Most of the spiders seen will probably be the 'micros', the tiny brown or black money spiders (Linyphiidae) that have too few readily observed characteristics to be included in this book. But some larger species live down at grass-roots level too, *e. g. Pachygnatha* species (Tetragnathidae) and sac spiders *Clubiona* species (Clubionidae).

Checking under stones and other objects on the ground

Many spiders live in dark, damp conditions away from sunlight: under stones, logs, bark or man-made materials that have been lying on the ground for some time. It is always worth investigating these sites, but remember to return any objects you disturb to their original positions. Bear in mind that many small spiders cling upside-down under these objects and are lifted up with them, so it is a good idea to check both the underside of the object as well as the ground beneath it.

Beating or shaking foliage

The lower branches of trees and bushes can be shaken over a sheet, upturned umbrella or commercially available beating tray to dislodge spiders living amongst the leaves. A more effective way of collecting spiders in trees is to tap the branch sharply with a stick several times, but take care not to cause damage to leaves or branches. Some spiders may initially remain stationary, curled up and playing dead; it is always worth waiting a minute or two before discarding the debris to ensure that no spiders have escaped your attention.
A sweep net can also be placed over lower branches and shaken to free attached spiders.

Beating a tree.

Sweep-netting vegetation

Spiders are often found in the upper levels of grass and other ground vegetation. They can be dislodged and collected by sweeping the net through the top of the vegetation in a figure of eight pattern such that the net is constantly billowing out behind. After a few sweeps, gently open the net and examine the contents. A slow walk through an area of long grass, for example, swinging the net as you go, can yield a large number of different invertebrates, so watch out for bees and wasps. This method is not recommended when the vegetation is wet. Sweep-net material, when wet, is heavy and can do considerable damage to the catch. Brambles and other prickly plants are best avoided as they can tear nets. One disadvantage of sweeping or beating for spiders is that they will no longer be associated with any web structures they might have built and as a result may be more difficult to identify.

After the last two techniques in particular, it is good practice to replace spiders, any other invertebrates, and debris back where it was beaten or swept from. Many invertebrates have very specific associations with particular plants and can easily be removed from their favoured environments.

Crevice sampling

Many species live in deep crevices in fences, brickwork and window frames. Luring them out of their lairs can be difficult, although they often come to the mouths of their retreats at night. One way to entice them involves 'fishing' with a maggot, although this might not appeal to everyone! Maggots can be purchased at angling shops and keep for months in a ventilated but well-lidded plastic box in a fridge. Drop a maggot into the web (flattish webs work best, *e. g.* those of the Labyrinth Spider *Agelena labrynthica* or *Tegenaria* or *Amaurobius* species) and when the occupant emerges wait for it to bite the prey. There is a split-second pause while the spider extricates the maggot from the web; this is the time to strike. Place a suitably sized container over the spider, trapping it against its web, and at the same time bring the container lid up from beneath the web to secure the spider. 'Fishing' in this way does not work very well after rain as the maggots easily squirm their way through wet silk. Maggots tethered to a piece of cotton can be used for extracting spiders from vertical crevices.

The sweep netting technique.

Traditionally, a tuning fork has been used to simulate the vibrations of prey in the web but now there is a modern alternative – the sonic toothbrush. Battery-operated sonic toothbrushes that vibrate 20,000 times a minute (about 330 Hz) in one plane are widely available from chemists and supermarkets. The vibrations set up in the web are similar to those produced by the wings of a medium-sized fly. A toothbrush is extremely effective at luring spiders from their retreats, and has the advantages of being cheaper than a tuning fork, not requiring constant striking and, unlike maggots, working well on wet webs. The brush is applied under the web (if possible) and the spiders caught as described for the 'maggot' technique above.

Pitfall-trapping

Pitfalls to catch live spiders are best deployed somewhere with little chance of disturbance and where they can be visited regularly – domestic gardens are ideal. A variety of surface-active invertebrates will be caught by this method, some of which, like spiders, are carnivorous. It is therefore important to provide structure within the trap so that organisms can hide away from each other – a ball of dried moss works well. If a pitfall trap is to be left down for a while, it is better to put one cup inside another so that, when the inner cup is lifted out for emptying, the outer cup prevents the soil-hole collapsing. A few fine holes in the bottom of both inner and outer cups will allow drainage during rain, or a cover can be placed over the top, raised off the ground so that spiders still have access. At least twice a day (to minimize risk to non-target species), empty the inner cup into a white tray and examine the catch. Checking the trap first thing in the morning and in the early evening will reveal which spiders are diurnal and which are nocturnal. Traps should be removed and the holes filled in when they are not in active use.

The 'fishing' technique using a sonic toothbrush. Here a large house spider *Tegenaria saeva* (Agelenidae) is induced out of its web in a conifer hedge.

The 'fishing' technique using a maggot demonstrated on a large house spider *Tegenaria saeva* (Agelenidae) web.

A pitfall trap set in a domestic garden.

Guide to spider families based on appearance

This guide is designed to be used with spiders for which there is no additional egg-sac or web information, such as those obtained using a sweepnet. Spiders in houses, for example, will usually be seen in an undisturbed state and here aspects of behaviour can be useful indicators (see under 'CHARACTERISTICS'). Many characteristics traditionally used to separate families are small and need a microscope to see, and even then they may not be obvious in live specimens. As a result, some families cannot be separated easily by overall appearance.

Body length indicates the approximate range for mature individuals across the family and includes both sexes. For the money spiders (Linyphiidae) the body lengths given here are just for the 11 species considered in this book.

Eyes are usually in two or three rows. Normally this is obvious but in some cases the distinction between one very curved row (usually the posterior one) and two rows is a matter of opinion. Eyes may be very small and in some species obscured by hairs, so close observation is needed. The four families with six eyes have other very obvious characteristics and so if a specimen does not match one of them, there will be eight eyes whether they are all easily visible or not. The naming of eye positions and arrangements is described on *page 14*. Descriptions of eyes and carapaces are as viewed from above. The arrangement of the eyes is indicated by an icon in the brown bar before the family name. The icons are not accurate representations but are an *aide memoire* for this section.

Similar families are included but can only serve as a rough guide. Key characteristics that help to separate families are highlighted in **bold text**.

Spiders with 6 eyes

⁙ OONOPIDAE [Goblin spiders]   **2 species** *page 109*

BODY LENGTH: **1–2 mm**   SIMILAR FAMILIES: **None**

CHARACTERISTICS: Nocturnal. Goblin spiders **move in a characteristic way** with slow walking interspersed by rapid sprints. HABITAT: Usually in houses (*Oonops domesticus*) or in dry litter, grass tussocks, under stones and tree bark (*O. pulcher*), although these habitat distinctions are by no means absolute.

CARAPACE: Almost circular but with the head area protruding. Pinkish, usually darker than the abdomen and with no pattern.

EYES: In a tight cluster.

×10

Oonops domesticus

LEGS: Pale, uniform but with the femora and trochanters darker.

ABDOMEN + SPINNERETS: **Pinkish-red with no pattern.**

::: **SCYTODIDAE** [Spitting spiders]   **1 species** *page 100*

BODY LENGTH: 3–6 mm   SIMILAR FAMILIES: **None**

CHARACTERISTICS: Nocturnal, move very slowly.
HABITAT: Inside houses, usually old ones.

EYES: Arranged in three pairs.

ABDOMEN + SPINNERETS: **Characteristic pattern** of pale brown, sometimes almost yellow, with black flecking. Almost the same size as the cephalothorax.

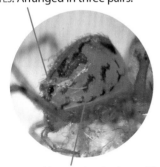

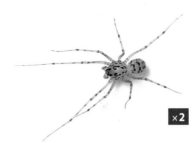

×2

CARAPACE: Almost circular but with the head area protruding. **Very domed in side view**. Pale brown, sometimes almost yellow, with distinctive black markings.

LEGS: Pale brown with black annulations.

::: **DYSDERIDAE** [Woodlouse spiders]   **4 species** *page 106*

BODY LENGTH: 6–15 mm   SIMILAR FAMILIES: **None**

CHARACTERISTICS: *Dysdera* species are common where woodlice are abundant.
HABITAT: Under stones, logs, tree bark and debris. Also indoors, in cellars and kitchens.

LEGS: Mid-brown with femora and trochanter I darker (*Dysdera*; *Harpactea ribicunda*). Paler with distinctly darker annulations (*Harpactea hombergi*).

Dysdera erythrina

CARAPACE: Dark, reddish-brown with no pattern.

EYES: In a very tight cluster.

×2

Large, pincer-like chelicerae are conspicuous and project forwards (*Dysdera*).

Dysdera crocata

ABDOMEN + SPINNERETS: **Cylindrical, orangy/ buff/slightly purple with no markings.**

::: SEGESTRIIDAE [Tubeweb spiders]   3 species *page 104*

BODY LENGTH: 6–22 mm   SIMILAR FAMILIES: None

HABITAT: Holes in walls, under bark and stones or in rubble and scree.

Segestria florentina

EYES: Arranged in three pairs.

CARAPACE: Elongated with the head area darker. *Segestria florentina* has green, iridescent chelicerae.

LEGS: Legs of *S. bavarica*, *S. senocolata* and immature *S. florentina* distinctly annulated. Uniformly coloured in adult *S. florentina*.

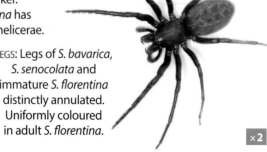

×2

Segestria bavarica

ABDOMEN + SPINNERETS: **Elongated with clear pattern of numerous dark patches (sometimes triangular) running down the midline, rather like the pattern on an Adder.**

Spiders with 8 eyes in a cluster (rows not obvious)

::: MYSMENIDAE [Dwarf cobweb spiders]   1 species *page 164*

BODY LENGTH: 1·0–1·5 mm   SIMILAR FAMILIES: Linyphiidae *p. 64*

CHARACTERISTICS: Just two records from Wales.
HABITAT: Within crevices in scree and under rocks.

LEGS: Colour as carapace with slightly darker femora.

EYES: Anterior medians small; the others, larger, are **arranged in two, tightly clustered, groups of three. Viewed from the side, the eyes of males are on a distinct turret about one third of the way from the front of the carapace.**

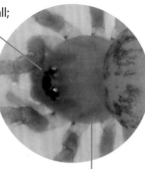

×10

ABDOMEN + SPINNERETS: Teardrop-shaped and appears to be turned through 90°, with the spinnerets pointing downwards. Off-white with darker scribble-like markings, which may be absent.

CARAPACE: Almost circular. Light brown with some diffuse darker markings.

⠿ **OECOBIDAE** [Discweb spiders]   **1 species** *page 115*

BODY LENGTH: **2–2·5 mm**   SIMILAR FAMILIES: None

CHARACTERISTICS: Run extremely fast when away from their webs. HABITAT: Confined to buildings. Apart from one (historical) breeding population, a very occasional import.

CARAPACE: Pale brown, almost circular with a dark patch in the centre, sometimes connecting to a black ocular area. The rim is marked with a thin black line above the insertion of each leg.

×10

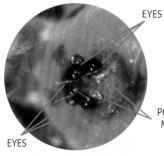

EYES

POSTERIOR MEDIANS

EYES

LEGS: Colour as carapace, varying from unmarked to distinctly annulated.

ABDOMEN + SPINNERETS: Oval. Pale yellow-brown with varying numbers of symmetrical black spots or larger fused areas over the top of white flecking. **A thin black line runs around the anterior edge. The posterior (pair of) spinnerets are long, two-segmented and with a long, central, hairy structure (tubercle) in between.**

EYES: **Appears six-eyed at first glance. The posterior medians are reduced to irregularly shaped, flat silver patches. The other eyes are loosely clustered in two pairs of three.**

⠿ **ZODARIIDAE** [Ant-hunting spiders]   **4 species** *page 308*

BODY LENGTH: **2–5 mm**   SIMILAR FAMILIES: None

CHARACTERISTICS: Ant-like when running.
HABITAT: Bare, sunny situations with clinker or stones.

×10

LEGS: Colour as carapace. Coxae and femora of legs I and II with black streaking.

CARAPACE: Medium brown with darker lines.

Zodarion rubidum (both images)

EYES: In a distinctive, clustered pattern; **anterior medians noticeably larger than the others.**

ABDOMEN + SPINNERETS: Dorsally dark brown with a few vague markings; ventrally a contrasting pale yellow. **Anterior spinnerets much larger than the others and arise from a large, pale cylindrical protrusion.**

⠶ PHOLCIDAE [Cellar spiders]   **3 species** *page 101*

BODY LENGTH: 2–10 mm   SIMILAR FAMILIES: None

CHARACTERISTICS: All species **whirl madly in their webs** when disturbed.
HABITAT: Almost always inside buildings.

`×2`

Pholcus phalangoides

EYES: Anterior medians very small; the
others are **arranged in two groups
of three and, within a group, are
very close to one another.**

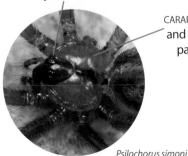

CARAPACE: **Almost circular**
and often with a darker
patch in the centre.

LEGS: **Extremely long
and thin**; coloured
as carapace.

Psilochorus simoni

ABDOMEN + SPINNERETS: Elongated and uniform buff/
grey (*Pholcus*), greenish with darker and lighter patches
(*Psilochorus*) or with a distinct, marbled pattern (*Holocnemus*).

⠶ ATYPIDAE [Purseweb spiders]   **1 species** *page 98*

BODY LENGTH: 7–15 mm   SIMILAR FAMILIES: None

HABITAT: Open habitats such as heathland, chalk
grassland or other unimproved grasslands.

EYES: **Clustered
in a tight arch.**

LEGS: Dark brown,
relatively short
and thick.

`×2`

ABDOMEN + SPINNERETS: **Two pairs of
book lungs** (see *page 16*) on the
underside. In ♂'s a hard shiny dorsal
plate (scutum) covers the anterior
two-thirds (see *page 17*).
Posterior spinnerets long with three
equal segments.

CARAPACE: **Massive, projecting jaws**, roughly
the length of the cephalothorax.

Spiders with 8 eyes in 2 rows

:::: HAHNIIDAE [Lesser cobweb spiders]   **7 species** *page 253*

BODY LENGTH: 1–3 mm   SIMILAR FAMILIES: None

HABITAT: *Hahnia* species in low vegetation, moss, leaf-litter, among stones; *Antistea elegans* in wetland habitats.

Antistea elegans

×10

CARAPACE: Thoracic area almost circular. Brown with some darker markings.

LEGS: Colour as carapace, darker segments in some species.

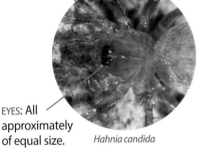

ABDOMEN + SPINNERETS: Oval, medium to dark reddish-brown with paler chevron markings.

EYES: All approximately of equal size.

Hahnia candida

The spinnerets are arranged in a row, the outer pair longer, protruding and with two segments.

:::: DICTYNIDAE [Meshweb spiders]   **17 species** *page 257*

BODY LENGTH: 1–7 mm   SIMILAR FAMILIES: None

HABITAT: Low vegetation (often dry flower heads), shrubs and trees.

×10

EYES: All approximately of equal size.

LEGS: Uniform coloration in most species, but annulated in others.

Lathys humilis

ABDOMEN + SPINNERETS: In the common species, **usually a black or reddish Christmas-tree-like pattern defined by flanking pale hairs**, but these can wear off with age. One species, *Nigma walckenaeri,* is distinctly green with lighter markings.

Nigma puella

CARAPACE: Brownish, often with darker markings or with greyish patterns of light hairs (but these can wear off). *Nigma* species are more colourful.

:::: **THERIDIIDAE** [Comb-footed spiders]   **58 species** *page 120*

BODY LENGTH: 1–14 mm   SIMILAR FAMILIES: Linyphiidae *p. 64*; Mimetidae *p. 61*; Nesticidae *p. 62*

CHARACTERISTICS: The major features distinguishing this family from the Linyphiidae are microscopic, however most linyphiids do not have a spherical abdomen and are generally found on, or close to, the ground.
HABITAT: Low vegetation, bushes, sometimes on buildings.

Steatoda grossa   ×2

CARAPACE: Round to slightly elongated, very variable in colour and pattern, but **in many species with a broad, dark median band**.

LEGS: Relatively short and in many species with darker smudges or clearer annulations.

EYES: Most are approximately equal-sized, pale or pearly and surrounded by a black ring.

Crustulina sticta

ABDOMEN + SPINNERETS: **Globular in most species, usually with a distinct pattern. In some genera, *e.g. Achaearanea* and *Cryptachea*, the abdomen is teardrop-shaped and appears to be turned through 90°, with the spinnerets pointing downwards.**

:::: **CORINNIDAE** [Ant-like sac spiders]   **2 species** *page 288*

BODY LENGTH: 2–3 mm   SIMILAR FAMILIES: Clubionidae *p. 65*; Liocranidae *p. 64*

CHARACTERISTICS: Somewhat ant-like. HABITAT: Fast-running on open ground.   ×10

LEGS: Yellow-brown with femora I and II darker.

EYES: **In straight, parallel rows** and approximately equal in size.

CARAPACE: Rather oval and dark brown.

Phrurolithus festivus
(both images)

ABDOMEN + SPINNERETS: Oval, with light brown pattern on dark brown background. Several patches of white hairs, in one species forming a chevron.

60

:::: THERIDIOSOMATIDAE [Ray's spiders]   1 **species** *page 163*

BODY LENGTH: **2–3 mm**   SIMILAR FAMILIES: None

HABITAT: Typically low down in vegetation at the water's edge.

×10

EYES: Most of the equal-sized eyes are pale or pearly and surrounded by a black ring, and form an oval.

LEGS: Rather short, light brown with a few annulations.

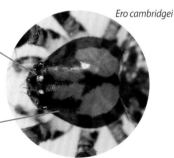

ABDOMEN + SPINNERETS: Almost spherical. **Distinctly silver background** with a dark cardiac mark and dark patches on the sides.

CARAPACE: Dark brown with lighter lateral margins.

:::: MIMETIDAE [Pirate spiders]   4 **species** *page 110*

BODY LENGTH: **2–4 mm**   SIMILAR FAMILIES: Theridiidae *p. 60*; Linyphiidae *p. 64*

HABITAT: Bushes, trees, low vegetation, sometimes in buildings.

Ero cambridgei

EYES: All approximately equal in size.

Ero cambridgei

CARAPACE: Medium brown, rather pear-shaped and with a **distinctive black rim**. Area around the eyes black.

×10

LEGS: Clearly annulated. **Metatarsi I and II appear curved** when viewed from the side and, together with their tarsi, bear a series of long, curved spines with shorter ones in beween.

ABDOMEN + SPINNERETS: **Globular with one or two pairs of small tubercles** (more obvious when viewed from the side). Pattern of white, black and red on a pale brown background.

×10

Curved metatarsus I

Ero tuberculata

:::: **THOMISIDAE** [Crab spiders]　　　　　　**27 species** *page 357*

BODY LENGTH: 2–11 mm　　　　　　　　　　SIMILAR FAMILIES: **Philodromidae** *p. 65*

CHARACTERISTICS: Very slow-moving *cf*. philodromids.
HABITAT: Low vegetation and on the ground.
Some species inhabit flower-heads.

Ozyptila praticola

LEGS: Mostly uniform in colour with **legs I and II longer
and considerably stouter than legs III and IV and
turned forwards, giving a crab-like appearance**
and an ability to walk sideways.

CARAPACE: Almost circular.
Patterns very variable.

EYES: All
approximately
equal in size.
**The eyes are
very noticeably
beady-black and
usually surrounded
by a lighter ring.
The lateral eyes
are often raised on
tubercles.**

× 10

ABDOMEN + SPINNERETS: Squat,
rather dumpy. Some species
angular and with abdominal
humps. Very variable in
colour/pattern and in some
species the colour can
change within individuals.

Thomisus onustus

:::: **NESTICIDAE** [Comb-footed cellar spiders]　　　　**1 species** *page 119*

BODY LENGTH: 3–6 mm　　　　　　　　　　SIMILAR FAMILIES: **Theridiidae** *p. 60*

HABITAT: Usually found in **dark, damp habitats** such as cellars, caves and culverts.
Can also occur in wetlands, within scree, under discarded sheet materials
(*e.g.* corrugated iron covering cavities)
and in ivy-covered walls.

LEGS: Coloured as
carapace with rather
blurry annulations.

CARAPACE: Light brown with a thin, dark border
and a wider, dark midline.

× 5

EYES: Most are pale
or pearly and usually
surrounded by a
black ring.
**The anterior median
eyes are small, the
others are larger,
approximately the
same size and in two
groups of three.**

ABDOMEN + SPINNERETS: **Pale brown,
usually with characteristic black
reticulate pattern.**

:::: ARANEIDAE [Orbweb spiders] **32 species** page 177

BODY LENGTH: **2–20 mm** SIMILAR FAMILIES: Tetragnathidae (esp. *Metellina* and *Meta*) p. 66

CHARACTERISTICS: Almost invariably clumsy walkers when away from their webs, *e.g.* on a beating tray or in a sweep net.
HABITAT: Trees, shrubs, low vegetation. Also on fences and buildings.

Larinioides cornutus ×5

CARAPACE: Head area parallel-sided. Pattern very variable. In ♀s, at least, the carapace is conspicuously smaller than the abdomen.

LEGS: **Stout and spiny**. Annulated in the majority of species.

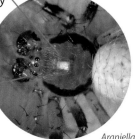

EYES: All approximately equal in size. Most are pale or pearly and usually surrounded by a black ring.

Araniella sp.

ABDOMEN + SPINNERETS: **Broad, almost spherical in some species, shield-shaped in others with the widest point about one third of the way down**. May have tubercles on the 'shoulders'. Extremely variable in colour and pattern between species. Some species easily recognizable from constant pattern elements (*e.g.* the white cross on the Garden Spider A*raneus diadematus*).

:::: ULOBORIDAE [Cribellate orbweb spiders] **3 species** page 116

BODY LENGTH: **3–6 mm** SIMILAR FAMILIES: None

HABITAT: Inside greenhouses and garden centres (*Uloborus plumipes*); low plants such as heather (*U. walckenaerius*); mainly evergreen trees and shrubs (*Hyptiotes*).

Uloborus plumipes

EYES: All approximately the same size. **The posterior row is strongly recurved and the anterior and posterior lateral eyes far apart**.

LEGS: Rather long and thin in *Uloborus* especially legs I. Legs much shorter and thicker in *Hyptiotes*.

×5

CARAPACE: Almost heart-shaped with a pattern that varies between species. In *Hyptiotes*, the ♂ pedipalps are remarkably large.

ABDOMEN + SPINNERETS: Like the carapace, variable between species. In the very common spider *Uloborus plumipes* the cephalothorax appears to attach to the middle of the abdomen, in a blunt 'T'-shape.

Uloborus plumipes

:::: **LIOCRANIDAE** [Running foliage spiders]   **12 species** *page 277*

BODY LENGTH: 3–8 mm   SIMILAR FAMILIES: Clubionidae; Corinnidae *p. 60*; Anyphaenidae

HABITAT: Nocturnal hunters at ground level in leaf-litter and low vegetation.   **×5**

LEGS: Uniformly coloured as carapace, sometimes with darker markings.

Agroeca inopina
(both images)

EYES: All approximately equal in size. Most are pale or pearly and usually surrounded by a black ring. **The eye rows take up about half of the width of the head area and in length are less than half the maximum carapace width** (*cf.* Clubionidae *p. 65*).

CARAPACE: Coloration either uniform or with a pair of darker longitudinal bands.

ABDOMEN + SPINNERETS: Usually brown with clear darker or lighter patterns, in some species as chevrons (*cf.* Anyphaenidae *p. 67*).

:::: **LINYPHIIDAE** [Money spiders]   **280 species** *page 411*

BODY LENGTH: 3–8 mm   SIMILAR FAMILIES: Theridiidae *p. 60*

CHARACTERISTICS: The major features distinguishing this family from the Theridiidae are microscopic, however most theridiids have a spherical or near-spherical abdomen (not oval) and are generally found higher in the vegetation. HABITAT: On and below the ground surface, in vegetation litter, on low plants and trees from the sea shore to mountain tops. Also frequent in agricultural crops.   **×5**

Neriene montana

EYES: Most are pale or pearly, and of equal size.

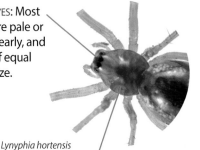

LEGS: Mostly uniformly coloured, but with annulations in some of the larger species.

Lynyphia hortensis

CARAPACE: Usually very dark brown/black and without pattern. A few of the larger genera are paler and with dark patterns. ♂'s of some species (not covered here) have spectacularly sculptured head structures.

ABDOMEN + SPINNERETS: **Usually dark brown/black and oval.** The larger genera have white flecking and sometimes distinctive patterns.

:::: **CLUBIONIDAE** [Sac spiders]   **24 species** *page 290*

BODY LENGTH: **3–10 mm**   SIMILAR FAMILIES: **Corinnidae** *p. 60*; Anyphaenidae *p. 67*; Zoridae *p. 69*

CHARACTERISTICS: A good field feature is that these species **often jump several times on a beating tray** (like Mexican jumping beans), with their legs tightly clenched together between jumps.
HABITAT: Nocturnal hunters found on the ground and higher in vegetation.

×5

CARAPACE: Brown, usually with little patterning. The head area can be lighter or darker than the thoracic area.

LEGS: Uniform coloured as carapace, but somewhat lighter in some species.

Cheiracanthium sp.

Clubiona phragmitis

EYES: All approximately equal in size. Most are pale or pearly and usually surrounded by a black ring. **The eye rows take up about three-quarters of the width of the head area and in length are approximately half the maximum carapace width** (*cf.* Liocranidae *p. 64*). **Posterior median eyes are round** (*cf.* Gnaphosidae *p. 67*).

ABDOMEN + SPINNERETS: Most *Clubiona* species are uniformly coloured but a few show a herringbone pattern. Abdomen pointed posteriorly. **Spinnerets cone-shaped and hardly separated at their base** (*cf.* Gnaphosidae *p. 67*).

:::: **PHILODROMIDAE** [Running crab spiders]   **18 species** *page 342*

BODY LENGTH: **3–12 mm**   SIMILAR FAMILIES: **Thomisidae** *p. 62*

CHARACTERISTICS: Very fast moving *cf.* thomisids.
HABITAT: Low vegetation and on the ground.

Tibellus oblongus   ×2

EYES: All ± equal in size and beady-black. Usually surrounded by a lighter ring.

LEGS: Mostly uniform in colour but in some species with clear, dark annulations. **Legs I and II are scarcely stouter than legs III and IV, and not nearly as crab-like as in the Thomisidae.**

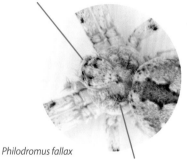

Philodromus fallax

CARAPACE: Almost circular. Patterns very variable.

ABDOMEN + SPINNERETS: **Often more elongated** *cf.* Thomisidae, especially in *Tibellus* species, and usually widest just behind the middle. Posterior rather pointed. Often with clear patterns.

:::: TETRAGNATHIDAE [Long-jawed orbweb spiders]   **14 species** *page 165*

BODY LENGTH: 3–16 mm   SIMILAR FAMILIES (especially *Metellina*, *Meta*): Araneidae *p.63*

CHARACTERISTICS: *Tetragnatha* at rest often stretch legs I and II forwards and hold them very close together. Legs III and IV may be stretched backwards but are usually not close together. In *Metellina* and *Meta*, leg I is always longer than leg II which, in turn, is longer than leg IV, whereas in Araneidae legs I, II and IV are almost equal in length.
HABITAT: Near ground level (*Pachygnatha*), in vegetation and shrubs and dark, damp places (*Metellina*), tall vegetation in damp places, often near water (*Tetragnatha*) and in caves, culverts and under manhole covers (*Meta*).

×5

EYES: Most are approximately equal-sized, pale or pearly and surrounded by a black ring.

Metellina sp.

LEGS: Long and coloured as carapace. Not annulated in *Pachygnatha*, some dark patches in *Tetragnatha* and more clearly annulated in *Metellina* and *Meta*.

Tetragnatha obtusa

CARAPACE: Shape variable. Colour usually pale to medium brown with darker marks. **In most species (except *Meta* and *Metellina*), the jaws are prominent and clearly seen from above.**

ABDOMEN + SPINNERETS: Oval in all species **except *Tetragnatha*, where the abdomen is clearly elongated. *Tetragnatha* and *Pachygnatha* have a distinctly silver background** (appearing gold when overlain by yellow pigment). *Meta* and *Metellina* more oval and could be mistaken for araneids.

:::: AMAUROBIIDAE [Laceweb spiders]   **5 species** *page 272*

BODY LENGTH: 4–15 mm   SIMILAR FAMILIES: None

HABITAT: Buildings, walls, dense hedges, under stones and tree bark.

×2

Amaurobius ferox

EYES: All approximately the same size.

LEGS: Darkish brown, some darker annulations.

CARAPACE: **Head area darker than the thoracic area.**

Amaurobius fenestralis

ABDOMEN + SPINNERETS: **Characteristic pattern of a dark cardiac mark with a paler rim.** Pale chevrons run to the posterior end. Patterns less clear in *Amaurobius ferox* and *Coelotes* spp.

:::: ANYPHAENIDAE [Buzzing spiders]   **2 species** *page 287*

BODY LENGTH: **4–7 mm**   SIMILAR FAMILIES: Clubionidae *p. 65*; Liocranidae *p. 64*

HABITAT: Branches of trees and bushes.

LEGS: Pale and vaguely annulated.   ×5

EYES: Approximately equal in size.

CARAPACE: Light brown with **two broad, dark longitudinal bands within which are paler spots**.

Anyphaena accentuata (both images)

ABDOMEN + SPINNERETS: Pale yellow with darker sides. **Distinctive pairs of dark marks resembling arrowheads occur in the midline.** On the underside, **tracheal spiracles are clearly visible mid-way between the epigastric furrow and the spinnerets** (see *p. 21*).

:::: GNAPHOSIDAE [Ground spiders]   **33 species** *page 311*

BODY LENGTH: **3–18 mm**   SIMILAR FAMILIES: Clubionidae *p. 65*

HABITAT: Nocturnal hunters. One species common in houses (*Scotophaeus blackwalli*)   ×5 but otherwise generally found on open ground and under stones.

EYES: All approximately equal in size with **posterior medians oblique and irregular in shape, often slanting ovals** (though circular in *Scotophaeus*) (*cf.* Clubionidae). Most eyes are pale or pearly and usually surrounded by a black ring.

LEGS: In most species uniformly coloured as carapace.

Zelotes electus

CARAPACE: Medium brown, distinctly narrowing anteriorly.

Scotophaeus blackwalli

ABDOMEN + SPINNERETS: Most greyish-brown to black and covered with short, dense hairs giving a sleek, furry appearance. Little patterning in most species. **Abdomen pointed. Anterior spinnerets are cylindrical and slightly longer than the posteriors. When viewed from below, the anterior spinnerets are well separated such that the median pair are clearly visible between them** (*cf.* Clubionidae).

:::: SPARASSIDAE [Huntsman spiders] — 1 species page 341

BODY LENGTH: **7–15 mm** — SIMILAR FAMILIES: None

HABITAT: Low, damp vegetation, often in scrub oak.

×2

LEGS: **Uniformly green.**

EYES: All approximately equal in size, **beady-black and ringed with white.**

CARAPACE: **Green with slightly darker central line.**

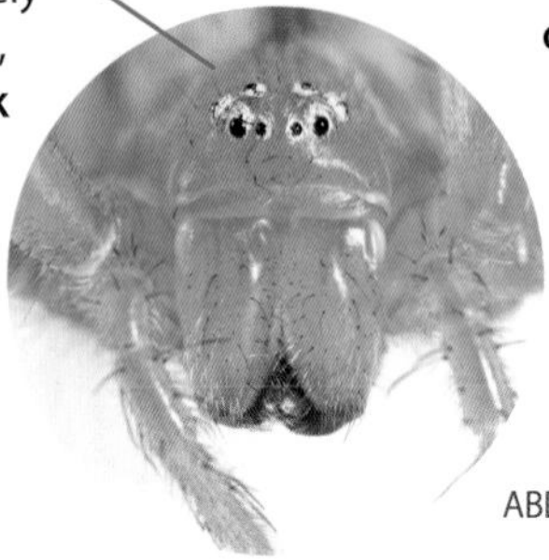

ABDOMEN + SPINNERETS: ♀ bright green with darker cardiac mark. ♂ red with two longitudinal yellow stripes and a darker cardiac mark.

:::: AGELENIDAE [Funnelweb spiders] — 11 species page 244

BODY LENGTH: **7–15 mm** — SIMILAR FAMILIES (especially *Textrix denticulata*): Lycosidae *p. 71*

CHARACTERISTICS: *Textrix denticulata* can run fast on the ground in sunny weather, resembling a lycosid. *Tegenaria* spp. and *Agelena* are more confined to their webs.

HABITAT: *Tegenaria* spp. in buildings, hedges, stone walls, vegetation; *Agelena* in low vegetation; *Textrix* in walls and between stones.

CARAPACE: The anterior part of head area is prominent and with almost parallel sides. Light brown with darker markings and a dark border.

EYES: All approximately equal in size.

LEGS: Coloured as carapace, uniform in some species and annulated in others.

Agelena labyrinthica

Tegenaria gigantea

ABDOMEN + SPINNERETS: Oval and usually with clear chevron pattern. **Posterior spinnerets are distinctly longer than the rest and in two segments.** (see *p. 14*)

×2

:::: CYBAEIDAE [Soft spiders]

1 species *page 270*

BODY LENGTH: **8–15 mm**   SIMILAR FAMILIES: None

CHARACTERISTICS: Builds an underwater silk bell which is filled with air. HABITAT: **Our only truly aquatic spider found in weedy ponds and slow-flowing water courses.** Rarely found out of water.

×2

LEGS: Colour as carapace. Legs III and IV are covered in long, fine hairs, in contrast to legs I and II.

EYES: Anterior medians smaller that the others.

CARAPACE: Medium brown with darker radial streaking. A row of very short hairs runs down the midline.

ABDOMEN + SPINNERETS: Oval, and covered with many fine hairs. Mousy-grey when out of water, silvery (when covered with air bubble) in water. **A central tracheal slit is present just behind the epigastric furrow.**

Spiders with 8 eyes in 2(3?) rows (a matter of judgement)

:::. ZORIDAE [Ghost spiders]

4 species *page 337*

BODY LENGTH: **3–7 mm**   SIMILAR FAMILIES: Clubionidae *p. 65*

HABITAT: Diurnal hunters at ground level in leaf-litter and low vegetation.

×2

EYES: All approximately equal in size.

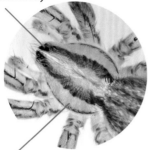

LEGS: Coloured as carapace. Patellae and tibiae usually darker.

Zora spinimana (both images)

CARAPACE: **Head area narrow in front.** Pale brown/yellowish with a pair of longitudinal brown bands.

ABDOMEN + SPINNERETS: Colour as carapace with darker, **rather diffuse markings which continue the carapace stripes.**

:::: **ZOROPSIDAE** [False wolf spiders]　　　　　**1 species**　*page 340*

BODY LENGTH: **13–20 mm**　　　　　SIMILAR FAMILIES: **None**

CHARACTERISTICS: Currently restricted to urban conurbations (mainly Greater London). HABITAT: In houses.

`×2`

EYES: All approximately equal in size.

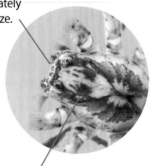

LEGS: Colour as carapace and speckled with black.

CARAPACE: Pale brown with a pair of broad longitudinal bands. **Head area dark at the edges and containing a light central oval with two dark patches.**

ABDOMEN + SPINNERETS: Oval and light/medium brown marbled. **A distinctive cardiac mark often comprising dark, diamond-shaped patches.**

Spiders with 8 eyes in 3 rows

:::: **SALTICIDAE** [Jumping spiders]　　　　　**38 species**　*page 380*

BODY LENGTH: **2–10 mm**　　　　　SIMILAR FAMILIES: **None**

HABITAT: Hunt on low vegetation in a variety of habitats. Some species frequently found on walls and fences in urban areas. Very alert.

`×5`

EYES: **The four in the front row are very large (median pair largest of all) and forward-facing.** The two in the second row are tiny and those in the third row of medium size.

Salticus sp.

LEGS: Relatively short and very variable in colour and pattern. In ♂'s leg I, or specific segments of it, are often in contrasting colours.

Euophrys frontalis

CARAPACE: **Square-fronted and clothed with coloured hairs or scales.**

ABDOMEN + SPINNERETS: Pointed oval and highly variable in colour and pattern. **Clothed with coloured hairs or scales.**

⠇⠇ LYCOSIDAE [Wolf spiders]　　38 species　page 206

BODY LENGTH: 3–20 mm　　SIMILAR FAMILIES: Agelenidae (esp. *Textrix denticulata*) p. 68; Pisauridae p. 72

CHARACTERISTICS: ♀s carry egg-sacs attached to their spinnerets and can often be seen basking. Newly-emerged young cling to the ♀'s abdomen. HABITAT: Ground-running hunters, most obvious on bare soil and leaf-litter on hot days. Also on low vegetation (*Pardosa nigriceps*).

Alopecosa barbipes ×2

EYES: Four small eyes comprise the **anterior row which is not easily seen from above** (*cf.* Pisauridae). The other **four, which are considerably larger, form an approximate square or trapezium when viewed from above.**

LEGS: Colour as carapace, sometimes annulated. ♂'s may have contrastingly coloured segments on leg I.

Arctosa perita

CARAPACE: Some genera brown with broken or continuous central and lateral yellow bands. Others have more subdued patterns. Covered in short, dense hairs.

ABDOMEN + SPINNERETS: Approximately oval. Pattern varies considerably between species. Coloration is largely a result of short, dense hairs.

⠇⠇ OXYOPIDAE [Lynx spiders]　　1 species　page 243

BODY LENGTH: 5–8 mm　　SIMILAR FAMILIES: None

CHARACTERISTICS: Rare, restricted to southern heaths. HABITAT: On south-facing slopes of dry, mature heathland, often near the top of heather.

CARAPACE: Pale brown with darker central band flanked by white.

LEGS: Coloured as carapace with dark annulations. **Armed with extremely obvious long, stout spines.**

EYES: Anterior median eyes small and not readily visible from above. The others, which are larger, **form a hexagonal pattern** when viewed from above.

×2

ABDOMEN + SPINNERETS: **Pointed oval**, pale brown with darker cardiac mark and dark and pale bands on the sides.

∴ **ERESIDAE** [Velvet spiders]

1 species *page 114*

BODY LENGTH: **6–16 mm**

SIMILAR FAMILIES: None

CHARACTERISTICS: Very rare, restricted to southern heaths.
HABITAT: Heathland.

EYES: All approximately equal in size and form a distinctive pattern – **one at each corner of the head area and the other four in a cluster at the front.**

CARAPACE: Head area large, bulbous and square-fronted. Black.

LEGS: Mature ♂, brown-black, clearly banded with white. ♀ uniformly black, sometimes with one or two white rings.

ABDOMEN + SPINNERETS: **Mature ♂ bright red with four or six black spots; mature ♀ s and juveniles, uniform black and velvety.**

×2

∴ **PISAURIDAE** [Nurseryweb spiders]

3 species *page 238*

BODY LENGTH: **10–22 mm**

SIMILAR FAMILIES: Lycosidae (*Pirata* spp. are often confused with *Dolomedes* because of their semi-aquatic habit and often pale lateral lines.) *p. 71*

CHARACTERISTICS: **Legs I and II held together when at rest**. May be seen guarding nursery web on vegetation or carrying egg-sacs, held under the body, in the chelicerae. *Dolomedes* typically hunt at the water's edge with the front legs resting on the water surface and the back legs on emergent plant stems.

×2

HABITAT: Low vegetation and bushes in meadows, hedgerows and gardens (*Pisaura*). Boggy areas and around the margins of water bodies on fens and marshes (*Dolomedes*).

Pisaura mirabilis

CARAPACE: Medium to dark brown, often with paler central band or lateral bands.

LEGS: Coloured as carapace. Not annulated.

Dolomedes sp.

EYES: **The anterior row of four small eyes is easily seen when viewed from above** (*cf*. Lycosidae). The other four are slightly larger and equal in size.

ABDOMEN + SPINNERETS: **Elongate oval**. Colour and pattern variable within and between species.

Guide to webs

Only a small number of British spider families make webs to catch prey. These come in a number of different architectural forms which provide clues as to which family is responsible. However, web design can vary enormously within families, and species of different families can produce remarkably similar webs. So care is needed. Web size is not indicated in this guide because this will inevitably vary as a spider grows, as well as between species in families. Key features which help to distinguish families within web types are shown in bold. Note that many species produce tubular retreats, although these are not used for prey capture. Names of species producing the web type shown are given or, if more than one species is concerned, that number is given in square brackets.

TENT   PISAURIDAE (Nurseryweb spiders): *Pisaura mirabilis; Dolomedes* [2]   *p. 238*

APPEARANCE: A dense, 3-dimensional structure that may appear tent-like or spherical. Spun well above the ground or water surface in grassland or wetland vegetation.
WHERE FOUND: Nursery Web Spider *Pisaura mirabilis* tents (*below*) occur in tall herbaceous vegetation in a wide variety of situations, including gardens. *Dolomedes* build their nurseries (*right*) in vegetation close to, or above, water surfaces. Webs appear from mid-summer to October.

These webs do not catch prey – they are spun as a protective retreat for young emerging from the egg-sac.

WHERE IS THE SPIDER?
♀ on the tent surface or very close by.
In *Pisaura*, sometimes inside the tent holding unhatched egg-sac.

RADIAL
SEGESTRIIDAE (Tubeweb spiders): [3] *p. 104*

APPEARANCE: Single lines of silk (trip wires) radiate from a silk-lined tube.

WHERE FOUND: Holes in walls, old beetle galleries in dead wood, under stones.

WHERE IS THE SPIDER?
Within the tube.

FUNNEL
AGELENIDAE (Funnelweb spiders): *Textrix denticulata*; *Agelena labryrinthica*; *Tegenaria* [9] *p. 244*

APPEARANCE: House spiders (*Tegenaria*) spin fairly extensive, closely-woven sheets of silk with a tubular retreat (funnel) at one edge (as do some theridiids – see Tangled web *page 83*). *Textrix denticulata* spins a similar but smaller, slightly whiter, web with a very well-defined tube. The Labyrinth Spider *Agelena labyrinthica* (LEFT) spins a web with a large tubular retreat at the rear.

WHERE FOUND: House spiders (*Tegenaria*) occupy buildings, inside and out, as well as more natural structures such as rock faces, hedges and rabbit burrows. *Textrix denticulata* occurs frequently in stone walls while the Labyrinth Spider *Agelena labyrinthica* makes its web low down in grass, gorse or heather.

WHERE IS THE SPIDER?
On top of the sheet or within the tube.

DIVING BELL
CYBAEIDAE (Soft spiders): Water Spider
Argyroneta aquatica p. 270

APPEARANCE:
A silk-encased bubble of air attached to submerged vegetation in freshwater habitats.
WHERE FOUND: The Water Spider *Argyroneta aquatica* inhabits clean, unpolluted still or slow-moving freshwater, such as ponds and lakes. Requires habitats with few predators.

WHERE IS THE SPIDER?
Usually within the bell.

LACE
AMAUROBIIDAE (Laceweb spiders): only applies to the genus *Amaurobius* [3] p. 274

APPEARANCE: the web of 'woolly' (cribellate) silk has a bluish tinge when fresh; new silk is added each night. Over time it becomes untidy, containing dust and the remains of past meals.
WHERE FOUND: Around holes in walls and fences, in dense hedges and under the loose bark of trees.

WHERE IS THE SPIDER?
Within the retreat.

TUBE

AMAUROBIIDAE (Laceweb spiders): only applies to the genus *Coelotes* [2] *p. 272*

APPEARANCE: Tubular retreat with only a collar of cribellate silk at the entrance. Can resemble an agelenid web (see *below*).

WHERE FOUND: Typically emerging from crevices under stones and logs.

WHERE IS THE SPIDER?
Within the tube.

TUBE

AGELENIDAE (Funnelweb spiders): only applies to the genus *Tegenaria* [9] *p. 246*

APPEARANCE: Some house spiders (*Tegenaria* spp.) produce a collar of silk at the entrance to holes where there are no supports for their usual web structure (see funnel web on *page 74*).

WHERE FOUND: Holes in walls and trees.

WHERE IS THE SPIDER?
Within the tube.

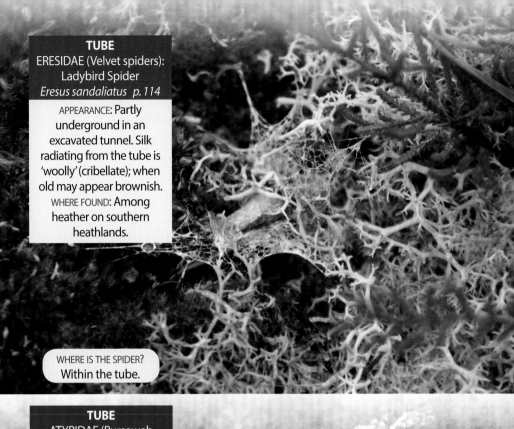

TUBE
ERESIDAE (Velvet spiders): Ladybird Spider
Eresus sandaliatus p. 114

APPEARANCE: Partly underground in an excavated tunnel. Silk radiating from the tube is 'woolly' (cribellate); when old may appear brownish.

WHERE FOUND: Among heather on southern heathlands.

WHERE IS THE SPIDER?
Within the tube.

TUBE
ATYPIDAE (Purseweb spiders): Purseweb Spider
Atypus affinis p. 98

APPEARANCE: Partly underground in an excavated tunnel. The tube is usually sealed, extends above ground and is frequently entirely covered with soil particles.

WHERE FOUND: South-facing slopes in low, unshaded vegetation.

WHERE IS THE SPIDER?
Within the tube.

ORB
TETRAGNATHIDAE (Long-jawed orbweb spiders): *Tetragnatha* [6]; *Metellina* [3]; *Meta* [2]; immature *Pachygnatha* [3] NB adult *Pachygnatha* do not spin webs *p. 165*

WHERE IS THE SPIDER?
Centre of the web or on vegetation/surface close by; some build retreats.

APPEARANCE: A circular web formed of silk threads radiating from a central point, and crossed by threads that **spiral in from the edge. There is a hole at the web hub. Can be vertical, horizontal or angles in between.**
WHERE FOUND: *Tetragnatha* spin webs on vegetation, often near water. *Meta* are found in caves, culverts and under manhole covers, while *Metellina* are common on tall vegetation, often in gardens (*M. segmentata* and *M. mengei*), or in dark, damp habitats such as rock overhangs and in woodland (*M. merianae*).

WHERE IS THE SPIDER?
Centre of the web or
in a retreat close by.

APPEARANCE: Very similar to the tetragnathid web **but usually vertical** with a **criss-cross of threads at the hub**. *Zygiella* and *Stroemiellus stroemi* webs usually have an open sector with a signal thread running through it connecting the hub with the owner's retreat (see *page 24*). *Argiope bruennichi* and *Cyclosa conica* often have an additional band of silk – the stabilimentum (see *page 6*) – spun vertically across the web through the hub (NB the stabilimentum can be a more complex design than this). WHERE FOUND: Generally in shrubs and trees. Sometimes against walls, windows *etc*. (*Nuctenea umbratica, Zygiella x-notata*).

ORB

APPEARANCE: Orb web with entangling silk applied to the spirals, spun almost horizontal (*Uloborus walckenaerius*) or at a variable angle to the horizontal (*U. plumipes*). Both often contain a stabilimentum running through the hub. The other spider in this family, *Hyptiotes paradoxus*, spins a triangle-shaped web. (see *page 118*) WHERE FOUND: On low plants, particularly heathers (*U. walckenaerius*); indoors and especially in garden centres (*U. plumipes*); in the foliage of trees, usually evergreens (*H. paradoxus*).

WHERE IS THE SPIDER? *Uloborus* spp. hang beneath the web whereas *Hyptiotes paradoxus* sits on a twig, holding a taut thread from its triangular web.

ORB
THERIDIOSOMATIDAE
(Ray's spiders):
Theridiosoma gemmosum
p. 163

APPEARANCE: Small, orb web with radial threads joining near the open hub. **The web is pulled into an umbrella shape by the spider** sitting at the centre and tensing a thread attached to a twig or leaf. WHERE FOUND: Always on vegetation close to water.

WHERE IS THE SPIDER?
Centre of the web, connected to the tension line.

Webs often difficult to see except on misty or frosty morning in autumn, when their true abundance is revealed.

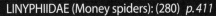

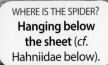

WHERE IS THE SPIDER?
Hanging below the sheet (*cf.* Hahniidae below).

APPEARANCE: Horizontal or concave sheet of silk, in larger species with supporting guy threads above and below. Small species make simple sheets in low vegetation and in soil depressions. *Drapetisca socialis* trails fine threads on tree trunks. No tubular retreat (*cf.* Agelenidae *page 76*). WHERE FOUND: Typically on low vegetation or in hedgerows, smaller species on the soil surface. Some occur on tree bark or in tree rot-holes.

SHEET
HAHNIIDAE (Lesser cobweb spiders): [7] *p. 253*

APPEARANCE:
Small sheet webs across depressions in the ground, or between stones and moss. No tubular retreat (*cf.* Agelenidae *page 76*).
WHERE FOUND: Very low down in damp places, some species are found in woodland.

WHERE IS THE SPIDER?
On top of the sheet. (*cf.* Linyphiidae above).

TANGLED
PHOLCIDAE (Cellar spiders): [3] *p. 101*

APPEARANCE: An extensive, open, three-dimensional tangle of silk. In *Psilochorus simoni* the web may, over time, develop a sheet structure. WHERE FOUND: Usually indoors. Daddy Long-legs Spider *Pholcus phalangioides* and *Holocnemus pluchei* spin webs in the corners of rooms at ceiling level, but also behind and under furniture. *Psilochorus simoni* is found in cellars, but also low down in rooms.

Spiders gyrate energetically when disturbed.

WHERE IS THE SPIDER?
Hangs upside down within the web.

TANGLED
DICTYNIDAE (Meshweb spiders): *Dictyna & Nigma* only [7] *p. 257*

APPEARANCE: **Small, tangled, 'fuzzy' mesh of cribellate silk**. Similar in appearance to those of the Theridiidae and Nesticidae but separable from the latter by size and habitat. WHERE FOUND: Commonly in the dry dead heads of plants, under leaves and amongst leaf-litter.

WHERE IS THE SPIDER?
Within the web.

APPEARANCE: Webs are a loose framework of threads usually of no recognisable structural form (*e.g. Enoplognatha ovata* (BOTTOM)). Most theridiid webs have sticky threads on the margins, or hanging vertically underneath, which snare insects. Some *Steatoda* (TOP) and *Dipoena* spp. may have a more densely woven central section which sometimes contains a tube-like retreat (resembling an agelenid funnel web – see *page 74*). In some species the web is much reduced, *e.g.* to sparse threads across pine bark in *Dipoena torva*.

WHERE FOUND: Usually in low to medium height vegetation, some species on trees. *Steatoda* generally occur under stones, in walls and garden fences and in and around houses. *Nesticus cellulanus* builds in dark, damp places such as in culverts.

WHERE IS THE SPIDER?
Within the web or on vegetation/surface close by. *Steatoda* spp. may be in a nearby retreat

83

Guide to egg-sacs

This guide covers the most recognizable and conspicuous egg-sacs, arranged according to where they are most likely to be found.

It is worth emphasising that egg-sacs from different genera/families can look almost the same. Eggs hatch and spiderlings undergo their first moult inside the egg-sac before emerging into the outside world. As a result, egg-sac colour and general appearance can change as the young within develop. Even after the young have left the egg-sac, the structure is often very persistent and at this stage may show flecks of white (egg shells) and pink (the first exuviae) within (see *page 33*).

> Egg-sacs are grouped by the typical habitat in which they are found , supplemented with any other location-related characteristics that may be helpful in identification

SIZE: The length (or other parameter if given) of the egg-sac

ATTENDING FEMALE: Whether or not a ♀ is usually on or very close to the egg-sac, although this can be subjective ✓ = always; ✓/✗ = sometimes; ✗ = never. *However, note that some attending females will die before their young emerge from the egg-sac and from then on the sac will, necessarily, be unattended.*

DESCRIPTION: Information describing the key features for identification

LOCATION: Where the egg-sac is typically found

In a small number of cases **bold text** is used to highlight instances where specific features distinguish one egg-sac from another.

INSIDE DOMESTIC BUILDINGS   **Carried by the female**

Daddy Long-legs Spider
Pholcus phalangioides
(Pholcidae: Cellar spiders)   *p. 101*

SIZE: 5–7 mm   ATTENDING FEMALE: ✓

DESCRIPTION: Eggs surrounded by a few strands of silk and carried in ♀'s chelicerae.

Spitting Spider *Scytodes thoracica*
(Scytodidae: Spitting spiders)   *p. 100*

SIZE: 4–5 mm   ATTENDING FEMALE: ✓

DESCRIPTION: Egg surrounded by a few strands of silk and supported under the body with the pedipalps and tethered with silk to the spinnerets.

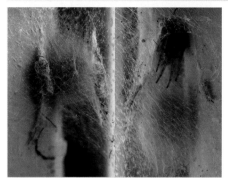 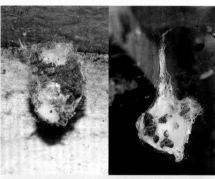

Missing-sector orbweb spider*
Zygiella x-notata
(Araneidae: Orbweb spiders) *p. 199*

SIZE: 8–10 mm ATTENDING FEMALE: ✓/✗

DESCRIPTION: Light brown, woolly silk covered egg-sac usually within a silk retreat and often with the ♀ close by.

LOCATION: Angles of walls and window frames.

Egg-sac (LEFT); with attendant female (RIGHT)

House spiders *Tegenaria*
(Agelenidae: Funnelweb spiders) *p. 246*

SIZE: 8–15 mm ATTENDING FEMALE: ✗

DESCRIPTION: White, smooth silk covering often decorated with prey remains.

LOCATION: Behind/under furniture, in garages/sheds; may be hanging near the web.

Tegenaria sp. (LEFT); *Tegenaria saeva* (RIGHT)

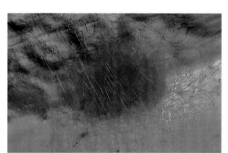 

Garden Spider* *Araneus diadematus*
(Araneidae: Orbweb spiders) *p. 178*

SIZE: 10–18 mm ATTENDING FEMALE: ✗

DESCRIPTION: Yellow-brown, woolly silk covered egg-sac stuck to a flat surface.

LOCATION: Angles of walls and window frames (only occasionally indoors); more often outside on garden vegetation (similar egg-sacs are produced by related species in other habitats.

Mouse Spider *Scotophaeus blackwalli*
(Gnaphosidae: Ground spiders) *p. 318*

SIZE: width of disc 10–12 mm
ATTENDING FEMALE: ✓

DESCRIPTION: A white, smooth disc with the eggs creating a bulge in the centre. Usually in a silken chamber together with the ♀.

LOCATION: Crevices.

* Commonly found also on the outside of buildings in similar locations

INSIDE GREENHOUSES AND GARDEN CENTRES

Achaearanea tepidariorum   p. 136
(Theridiidae: Comb-footed spiders)

SIZE: 5–7 mm   ATTENDING FEMALE: ✗

DESCRIPTION: Chocolate-brown, often pear-shaped, with a smooth, papery outer layer.

LOCATION: Hung in tangled webs or attached to surfaces (*e.g.* under staging in greenhouses), often in some numbers.

Uloborus plumipes   p. 117
(Uloboridae: Cribellate orbweb spiders)

SIZE: 11–13 mm   ATTENDING FEMALE: ✓/✗

DESCRIPTION: Variable in colour from dark brown to pale cream; flattened and smooth, the shape of a Holly leaf.

LOCATION: Attached to a surface or suspended from a mass of greyish silk (as pictured), usually in the roof of warmer sections of garden centres, sometimes on plants.

IN CAVES, CULVERTS AND SIMILAR DARK, DAMP PLACES

Hanging from the roof

Cave spiders *Meta menardi + M. bourneti*
(Tetragnathidae: Long-jawed orbweb spiders)   p. 175

SIZE: 20–26 mm   ATTENDING FEMALE: ✗

DESCRIPTION: Beautiful, large white pear-drop-shaped egg-sac suspended on a silk thread from the roof, often in some numbers.

LOCATION: Hanging from the roof.

Carried by the female

Nesticus cellulanus   p. 119
(Nesticidae: Comb-footed cellar spiders)

SIZE: 3–5 mm   ATTENDING FEMALE: ✓

DESCRIPTION: Translucent, yellowish egg-sac becoming brown and mottled with age.

LOCATION: Carried attached to the female's spinnerets.

UNDER WOOD, UNDER AND AMONG STONES AND IN GROUND DEPRESSIONS

Drassodes
(Gnaphosidae: Ground spiders)   *p. 311*

SIZE: 12–17 mm   ATTENDING FEMALE: ✓

DESCRIPTION: Thick, white egg-sacs enclosed in a silken chamber shared with the uniformly fawn ♀.

LOCATION: Under stones and logs.

Coelotes
(Amaurobiidae: Laceweb spiders)   *p. 272*

SIZE: 7–10 mm   ATTENDING FEMALE: ✓

DESCRIPTION: White, disc-shaped egg-sac attached to a surface within the ♀'s tubular, silk-lined burrow.

LOCATION: Under stones and logs, sometimes with debris incorporated.

Zelotes, *Trachyzelotes* and *Urozelotes*
(Gnaphosidae: Ground spiders)   *p. 322*

SIZE: 7–9 mm   ATTENDING FEMALE: ✓/✗

DESCRIPTION: Round, flat, nipple-shaped egg-sacs. The outer surface is smooth and papery, often pink. ♀ with sleek, black abdomen.

LOCATION: Attached to the undersides of stones or logs.

Carried at rear (attached to spinnerets)

Rugathodes bellicosus   *p. 153*
(Theridiidae: Comb-footed spiders)

SIZE: 2–3 mm   ATTENDING FEMALE: ✓

DESCRIPTION: White egg-sac, carried by free-running ♀s. The egg-sac is larger than the ♀ herself (♀ brown abdomen with paler mottling).

LOCATION: Scree slopes, rock piles and boulders on the coast.

UNDER WOOD, UNDER AND AMONG STONES AND IN GROUND DEPRESSIONS

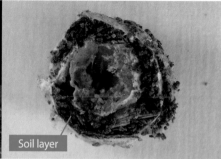

Soil layer

Tegenaria agrestis (**Agelenidae: Funnelweb spiders**)   *p. 249*

SIZE: 10–15 mm   ATTENDING FEMALE: ✓/✗

DESCRIPTION: Roughly spherical egg-sac, frequently with a bumpy surface caused by a layer of debris, often soil, incorporated beneath the outer layer of white silk (as shown in the egg-sac cross-section (RIGHT)). There may be some debris attached to the outside.

LOCATION: Under stones and debris on brownfield sites, under logs in woodland.

ATTACHED TO VEGETATION   **Unstalked**

Wasp Spider   *Argiope bruennichi*
(**Araneidae: Orbweb spiders**)   *p. 204*

SIZE: 13–18 mm   ATTENDING FEMALE: ✗

DESCRIPTION: Very large, brown, mottled, vase-shaped egg-sac (resembling a poppy seed head) with an uneven papery surface and suspended in low vegetation.

LOCATION: Coastal chalk grassland, open rough grassland, wasteland and roadside verges.

Stretch spiders   *Tetragnatha*
(**Tetragnathidae: Long-jawed orbweb spiders**)   *p. 165*

SIZE: 5–7 mm   ATTENDING FEMALE: ✓/✗

DESCRIPTION: Globular egg-sac but flattened onto a leaf or stem. The outer covering is white or grey with greenish tufts, resembling mould or a bird dropping.

LOCATION: In damp places, often close to open water.

Episinus p. 120
(Theridiidae: Comb-footed spiders)

SIZE: 3–4 mm   ATTENDING FEMALE: ✗

DESCRIPTION: White spherical or oval egg-sac. The eggs are laid in a white silk inner covering outside of which is a layer of wiry silk loops.

LOCATION: Attached by a few threads to low vegetation or the sides of stones.

Paidiscura pallens p. 151
(Theridiidae: Comb-footed spiders)

SIZE: 2–3 mm   ATTENDING FEMALE: ✓/✗

DESCRIPTION: White, spiky egg-sac considerably larger than the almost spherical ♀, which often lurks nearby.

LOCATION: Often deposited under the leaves of Holly, oak or Sycamore.

Philodromus p. 351
(Philodromidae: Running crab spiders)

SIZE: 10–25 mm   ATTENDING FEMALE: ✓

DESCRIPTION: Large round to oval, whitish egg-sac, often flattened. The sac is larger than the guarding ♀. Fragments of vegetation may be interwoven during its construction; that of the sand-dune dweller *P. fallax* is covered with sand grains.

LOCATION: Mostly attached to low vegetation; for *P. fallax* deposited in a sand depression at the base of vegetation, often Marram Grass.

Ray's Spider *Theridiosoma gemmosum* (Theridiosomatidae: Ray's spiders) *p. 163*

SIZE: egg-sac 2–3 mm, stalk **10–30 mm**

ATTENDING FEMALE: ✗

DESCRIPTION: Small, spherical egg-sac on the end of a relatively very long , thin stalk. The egg-sac is mid-brown and **smooth, not surrounded by wiry silk** (*cf.* Pirate spiders *below left*).

LOCATION: Suspended from vegetation or from a silk line.

Pirate spiders *Ero* (Mimetidae: Pirate spiders) *p. 111*

SIZE: egg-sac 2–3 mm, stalk **6–9 mm**

ATTENDING FEMALE: ✗

DESCRIPTION: Pear- or cigar-shaped egg-sac (see note below for more details) suspended from a very thin stalk. The egg-sac itself is **surrounded by a thin layer of brown, tangled, wiry silk** (*cf.* Ray's Spider *above*).

LOCATION: Attached to plant stems and rocks.

Pear-shaped egg-sac typical of *E. furcata, E. cambridgei* and *E. aphana* (LEFT); that of *E. tuberculata* can be more cigar-shaped (RIGHT).

Agroeca brunnea and *A. proxima* *p. 277* (Liocranidae: Running foliage spiders)

SIZE: bowl 7–8 mm, stalk 10–12 mm

ATTENDING FEMALE: ✗

DESCRIPTION: Pure white inverted wine-glass-shaped egg-sac. The whole sac often covered with soil particles/mud (RIGHT).

LOCATION: Usually attached to plant stems.

WITHIN ROLLED/FOLDED LEAVES

Sac spiders (some) *Clubiona*
(Clubionidae: Sac spiders) *p. 290*

SIZE: 6–9 mm   ATTENDING FEMALE: ✓

DESCRIPTION: **Silk used to bind leaf is chalky-white**. Single, somewhat flattened, **white egg-sac**; reddish-brown ♀ sealed in with it.

LOCATION: Mostly on understorey shrubs such as bramble but some also use grass leaf blades and reed heads.

Cucumber spiders *Araniella*
(Araneidae: Orbweb spiders) *p. 190*

SIZE: 6–9 mm   ATTENDING FEMALE: ✓

DESCRIPTION: Egg-sac composed of very wiry, light brown or slightly greenish silk, sometimes several laid in the same leaf.

LOCATION: Frequently on shrubs and low trees. Bright green female usually in attendance.

Common Candy-striped spider *Enoplognatha ovata* and
Scarce Candy-striped Spider *E. latimana* **(Theridiidae: Comb-footed spiders)** *p. 154*

SIZE: 6–9 mm   ATTENDING FEMALE: ✓

DESCRIPTION: **Silk used to bind leaf is white, but not chalky-white.** Single, spherical **egg-sac white or, more often, sky blue**; ♀ (yellow, with or without red-striped or red-shield patterns on abdomen) sealed in with it.

LOCATION: Mostly on tallish plants and shrubs, such as bramble.

Typical folded leaf (LEFT); female and egg-sac (RIGHT).

WITHIN WEBS/RETREATS IN VEGETATION | In webs

Egg-sacs

Dictyna
(Dictynidae: Meshweb spiders) *p. 257*

SIZE: 3–5 mm   ATTENDING FEMALE: ✓/✗

DESCRIPTION: Small, white, lens-shaped egg-sacs within a tangled, woolly silk web.

LOCATION: At the top of grass or flower stems.

Achaearanea simulans *p. 138*
(Theridiidae: Comb-footed spiders)

SIZE: 4–7 mm   ATTENDING FEMALE: ✓

DESCRIPTION: Egg-sac light brown, papery; often pear-shaped. Hung in tangled webs.

LOCATION: On bushes and small trees.

WITHIN WEBS/RETREATS IN VEGETATION | In retreats

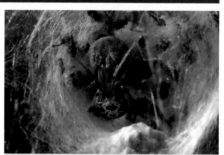

Achaearanea lunata *p. 136*
(Theridiidae: Comb-footed spiders)

SIZE: 2–4 mm   ATTENDING FEMALE: ✓

DESCRIPTION: Egg-sac light brown, papery and wrinkled. Usually contained within a leaf retreat in the upper part of a large, tangled web.

LOCATION: On bushes and small trees, occasionally on railings.

Phylloneta sisyphia and *P. impressa* *p. 140*
(Theridiidae: Comb-footed spiders)

SIZE: 3–4 mm   ATTENDING FEMALE: ✓

DESCRIPTION: Spherical, blue-green egg-sac guarded within an inverted thimble-shaped retreat, which the ♀ covers with plant debris. The ♀ regurgitates food for the emerged young.

LOCATION: Typically found on gorse bushes and heather.

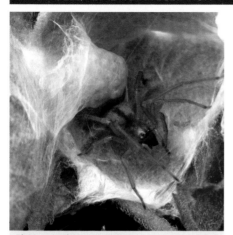

Cheiracanthium erraticum
(Clubionidae: Sac spiders)   *p. 306*

SIZE: **7–10 mm**   ATTENDING FEMALE: ✓

DESCRIPTION: Whitish egg-sac containing pink eggs in retreat constructed from two or three leaves, or grass heads, stitched together. Female with clear central abdominal red stripe flanked by yellow. Sealed in with egg-sac.

LOCATION: Leaves and grasses.

Green Huntsman Spider
Micrommata virescens
(Sparassidae: Huntsman spiders)   *p. 341*

SIZE: **10–13 mm**   ATTENDING FEMALE: ✓

DESCRIPTION: Several leaves stitched together to form a relatively large space enclosing the egg-sac. ♀ bright green, sealed in with egg-sac; eggs and young also bright green.

LOCATION: Favours lower branches of oak saplings.

Labyrinth Spider *Agelena labyrinthica* **(Agelenidae: Funnelweb spiders)**   *p. 244*

SIZE: **10–15 mm**   ATTENDING FEMALE: ✓

DESCRIPTION: Pure white, egg-sac suspended from the walls deep within the ♀'s funnel web complex or in a separate silk chamber nearby.

LOCATION: In tall grass, heather, gorse and bramble.

Egg-sac chamber on gorse (LEFT); egg-sac within dissected chamber (RIGHT).

Neottiura bimaculata p. 150
(Theridiidae: Comb-footed spiders)

SIZE: 3–4 mm   ATTENDING FEMALE: ✓

DESCRIPTION: White egg-sac, larger than the female herself (♀ reddish-brown abdomen with a broad yellow/pink central stripe).

LOCATION: Shrubs and long grass.

Otter spiders *Pirata*
(Lycosidae: Wolf spiders) *p. 233*

SIZE: 3–5 mm   ATTENDING FEMALE: ✓

DESCRIPTION: Spherical, light grey egg-sacs with conspicuous light band round equator (fast-running ♀ brown with two rows of white spots and sometimes white lateral lines on the abdomen).

LOCATION: Damp places, often on vegetation at the edge of open water.

Rugathodes sexpunctatus and *R. instabilis*
(Theridiidae: Comb-footed spiders) *p. 152*

SIZE: 2–3 mm   ATTENDING FEMALE: ✓

DESCRIPTION: Egg-sac larger than the ♀ herself (♀ brown abdomen with paler mottling); egg-sac brownish or dirty-white (see below for additional details).

R. sexpunctatus (LEFT) egg-sac dirty-white with mottling, on Ivy, Holly and other evergreens in central Scotland; *R. instabilis* (RIGHT) egg-sac brownish, in low vegetation in marshy areas.

Wolf spiders *Pardosa, Xerolycosa*
and *Hygrolycosa*
(Lycosidae: Wolf spiders) *pp. 207–220*

SIZE: 2–6 mm   ATTENDING FEMALE: ✓

DESCRIPTION: Lens-shaped, light brown/greenish-blue egg-sac, often with a distinctly lighter seam around the equator (female brown but usually with lighter patterning); fast-running spiders.

LOCATION: On leaf-litter and ground vegetation, especially on warm days.

ON VEGETATION OR BARE GROUND (CARRIED BY FREE-RUNNING FEMALES)
Carried under body (held by the chelicerae)

Nurseryweb Spider *Pisaura mirabilis*
(Pisauridae: Nurseryweb spiders) *p. 238*

SIZE: **7–9 mm** ATTENDING FEMALE: ✓

DESCRIPTION: Large, off-white egg-sac
(female 12–15 mm, elongate profile and
very variable in colour/pattern).

LOCATION: On vegetation, often basking in
the sun, or inside the nursery tent
(see *page 73*).

Raft Spider *Dolomedes fimbriatus* (bogs)
Fen Raft Spider *D. plantarius* (fens/
marshes)
(Pisauridae: Nurseryweb spiders) *p. 240*

SIZE: **6–14 mm** ATTENDING FEMALE: ✓

DESCRIPTION: Large, grey egg-sac which
becomes browner with time (♀ 13–
23 mm, cigar-shaped profile, brown or
black, and usually with white or yellow
lateral stripes along the whole body).

LOCATION: Associated with water surfaces
or emergent vegetation, often basking in
the sun.

Introduction to the species accounts

ACCOUNT ORDER

Due to layout considerations the species accounts that follow are not presented in strict **taxonomic** order, although they follow as close to the established order as possible.

FAMILY For each family there is a brief introduction that includes a summary of the number of genera recorded in Britain, and a description of the key identification features, including egg-sacs, webs, behaviour and ecology, as well as morphological characteristics.

GENERA The species accounts for each genus are prefaced by a brief introduction to the main distinguishing features of the genus as represented in Britain and giving the number of British species.

A family index is printed on the *inside back jacket flap*; a genera index on *page 480*.

SPECIES

The order in which the species within each genus are presented is based primarily on identification criteria. In most instances a species commonly encountered is first, followed by closely related and/or similar looking species.

The accounts are presented in a consistent format, as explained below. Definitions of the technical terms used are given in the *Glossary* on *pages 16–21* and the location of key identification features can be found in *Spider anatomy* on *pages 14–15*.

COMPARISON TABLES AND OTHER SPECIES INFORMATION

Page references for comparison tables, *Guide to spider families*, *Guide to webs* and the *Guide to egg-sacs* are given in green text at the head of relevant pages.

LC *Scientific name* English name ◆ 👁

♂7–9 mm ♀10–15 mm   [PAGE 105 BL]

Observation tips/habitat: Information on habitat and, where useful, tips on how to find the species.

♂♀ **Description:** A brief description is given of **key features that can be used as aids to field identification** (although these are not necessarily diagnostic). These include features of the adult cephalothorax, abdomen and legs and the expected size range of adult males and females.

Similar species: A list of species (with page references) that may be regarded as similar. Where useful, information on the key differences between the species involved is provided.

Distribution/Status: To help interpret the maps a more detailed description of the species' distribution in Britain.

The recognised symbols for male (♂) and female (♀) are used throughout the book

LEGALLY PROTECTED
Biodiversity List (En, Wa)
Nationally Scarce

UK OCCURENCE

♂
♀
J F M A M J J A S O N D

THE SPECIES ACCOUNTS

THE IDENTIFICATION ICONS

There are relatively few British spiders which can be identified with certainty without microscopic examination of the genitalia.

Careful examination in the field can often indicate the genus of a spider, but species identification is not possible in most cases. Colour depth and pattern strength can vary enormously between individual spiders both within a species as well as between members of a genus. **Identification to species level should not be based solely on the photographs – these, and the other features described, are intended only to provide good indicators as to the species involved.** In an attempt to qualify this issue, icons are given (for genus and species) that indicate the ease of identification as follows:

 Can be identified in the field (with experience), usually without capture.

 Can be identified in the field but needs careful, close examination requiring temporary capture, usually a spi-pot (see *page 48*), and a hand lens.

 Requires examination at high magnification in good light of features that are beyond the scope of this book (see *Further reading – page 463*).

In those cases where accurate identification is beyond the scope of this book the nature of the features involved is given.

NB Identification of the spiders in almost all of the images used in the species accounts was confirmed by microscopic examination of the genitalia after photography.

SCIENTIFIC AND ENGLISH NAME

Most spiders do not have generally recognized English names but those that are in common use follow the *scientific name* in the accounts of both species and, where appropriate, genera. All families have been given common names.

BODY LENGTH

Ranges of body lengths of adult ♂'s and ♀s are given as both figures and actual size bars.

IMAGE REFERENCES

The location of images on relevant pages are given in square brackets, coded as follows:
T (top); M (middle); H (higher); L (lower);
B (bottom); L (left); R (right) such that *e.g.* BL = bottom left.

SPECIES TEXTS

Follow a consistent format, covering **Observation tips/habitat**, **Description**, **Similar species** and **Distribution/Status** as detailed opposite.

LEGISLATION / CONSERVATION STATUS

If appropriate, boxes and icons indicate any relevant legislation and the species' conservation status in Britain as follows:

Left of scientific name
IUCN designation (see *page 425* for codes).

Right of name
◆ **Amber List status** (see *page 426*).

Above the map
▬ **Fully legally protected**, or
▬ **Covered by national legislation**
▬ **British Rarity Status**

Full information is detailed in *Legislation and conservation* on *page 424*.

UK OCCURRENCE

An at-a-glance summary of a species' UK occurrence based on the number of SRS 10-km square records (see *page 427*).

MAPS

Colour-coded maps show the distribution of records sent to the Spider Recording Scheme. Two levels of shading are used: ■ shows records received between 1992 and mid-2015, ■ shows earlier records.

PHENOLOGY CHARTS

Under each map a chart shows the frequency of records of adult males and females each month derived from the Spider Recording Scheme data. The darker the green monthly bars, the higher the percentage of observations. As a guide to their reliability, the number of individual spiders contributing to each chart is shown by: ● >200; ● 10–200; ● <10. If there are insufficient data no chart is presented.

Note that many species of spiders, particularly those occurring in less accessible habitats and sparsely populated areas, are under-recorded; the maps thus represent the best information available, rather than a complete picture. The distributions, and the adult seasons, of many species are also undergoing change, particularly in response to climate change; the very latest information can be found on the Spider Recording Scheme website at

srs.britishspiders.org.uk.

ATYPIDAE Purseweb spiders   **1 British genus**

The single British species in this eight-eyed family is our only representative of the sub-order Orthognatha (mygalomorphs) – the straight-jawed spiders, referring to the forward-facing chelicerae. The movement of the chelicerae is in the vertical plane and has been likened to the action of a pickaxe.

Atypus   **1 British species (illustrated)**

When viewed from above, the chelicerae can be as long as the cephalothorax. Two pairs of book lungs are present and the distinctive posterior spinners are three-segmented. *Atypus* excavates a long tunnel underground which is lined with silk. The closed end of this long tube extends above ground up to 5 cm from the tunnel entrance. The appearance of this tubular web has been likened to a sock or purse giving the genus its common name. The spider can live for up to eight years, spending much of its time in its underground burrow, generally only coming to the surface when prompted by the activity of potential prey on the exterior surface of the exposed web. ♂s are occasionally found on the ground when moving around searching for ♀s to mate.

LC *Atypus affinis* Purseweb Spider ◆

♂7–9 mm ♀10–15 mm

Observation tips/habitat: Mainly found on warm, south-facing slopes in loose chalk or sandy soils amongst short vegetation. The spider is not easy to find as the exposed web is usually covered in soil particles blending in well with its surroundings. The chelicerae are very large and can add up to 3 mm to the body length.

Description: CARAPACE Glossy greenish-brown. The head area is noticeably elevated compared to the thoracic area. ABDOMEN Brown. ♂ has darker scutum in anterior half. LEGS Glossy, coloured as carapace.

Similar species: None.

Distribution/Status: Mainly in southern England with scattered records from the west coast and from south-west Scotland.

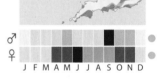

Nationally Scarce

Scarce, local

♂
♀
J F M A M J J A S O N D

the chelicerae of *Atypus affinis*

♂ *Atypus affinis* × **6**

The above ground part of the web is well camouflaged with soil and other debris (see also *p. 77*)

SCYTODIDAE Spitting spiders

1 British genus

The single British species in the genus *Scytodes* has six eyes and a highly characteristic shape and markings.

Scytodes

 1 British species (illustrated)

The cephalothorax and abdomen are of similar shape, size, coloration and pattern. The cephalothorax in side view is massively domed. *Scytodes thoracica* attacks prey by squirting sticky, venomous fluid from its chelicerae over its victim. The chelicerae are moved rapidly from side to side resulting in a zigzag pattern of gummy threads which pin the prey to the substrate.

 LC | *Scytodes thoracica* Spitting Spider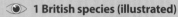

Uncommon, regional

♂3–5mm ♀4–6mm

Observation tips/habitat: A nocturnal wanderer found inside buildings (notably museums). The spider is slow moving but protects itself from predations by other spiders by using its spitting expertise as a defence.

Description: CARAPACE Pale yellow with black markings. The highly domed shape is distinctive. ABDOMEN Similar colouring and pattern to carapace. LEGS Coloured as carapace, annulated.

Similar species: None.

Distribution/Status: Widespread in the southern half of Britain.

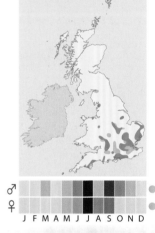

♂
♀
J F M A M J J A S O N D

♀ *Scytodes thoracica* × **6**

PHOLCIDAE Cellar spiders   **3 British genera**

The spiders in these three genera possess six eyes and very long legs. ♀s hold the egg-sacs in their chelicerae whilst sitting in the web. All are closely associated with human habitation and are thought to have been introduced to Britain with wine imports from Europe.

Pholcus   **1 British species (illustrated)**

The cylindrical yellow-grey abdomen and very long, thin legs of the single *Pholcus* species occurring in Britain often leads to confusion with harvestmen and long-legged craneflies, with which it shares its common name. Care should be taken to confirm that the body consists of just two parts (see *page 13*).

LC *Pholcus phalangioides* Daddy Long-legs Spider

♂ 7–10 mm   ♀ 8–10 mm

Observation tips/habitat: A spider found almost exclusively indoors. The loose open web, within which the spider hangs upside down, is spun in the corners of rooms, usually at ceiling level. If disturbed the spider will vibrate rapidly within the web.

Description: CARAPACE Pale yellowish-grey with central dark marking. Almost circular in shape but narrowed at the front. ABDOMEN Tubular shape. Grey in colour often with darker marks. LEGS Very long and spindly, colour as carapace; joints often with contrasting pale and dark bands.

Similar species: *Holocnemus pluchei* (*p. 103*).

Distribution/Status: Widespread throughout much of England and Wales; fewer records in northern England and Scotland.

Common, regional

♂
♀
J F M A M J J A S O N D

♀ *Pholcus phalangioides* × **2**

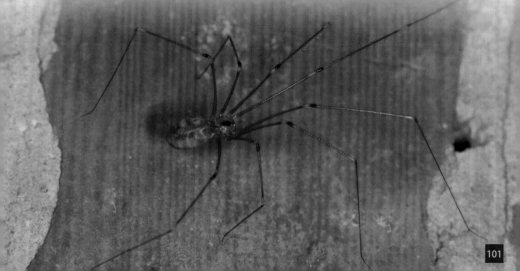

Psilochorus

 1 British species (illustrated)

Similar in appearance and habitat to *Pholcus phalangioides* (*p. 101*) but much **smaller and more delicate.**

LC *Psilochorus simoni*

Uncommon, widespread

♂ 2·0–2·5 mm ♀ 2·0–2·5 mm

Observation tips/habitat: In contrast to *Pholcus phalangioides* (*p. 101*) more often found at ground level in houses. Originally only reported from wine cellars but now recorded elsewhere indoors.

Description: CARAPACE Pale yellow with obvious darker head area and paler median band posteriorly. ABDOMEN Globular in shape and resembling a teardrop with spinners ventrally positioned. Bluish-grey in colour and covered in fine hairs. LEGS Very long, coloured as carapace; joints often with contrasting pale and dark bands.

Similar species: None.

Distribution/Status: Widespread but very scattered and infrequent in England. Very few records from Scotland and Wales.

♂
♀
J F M A M J J A S O N D

♀ *Psilochorus simoni* × **10**

Holocnemus **1 British species (illustrated)**

Similar in appearance to *Pholcus phalangioides* but is slightly **smaller and has more definite abdominal markings.**

 # Holocnemus pluchei

Rare, widespread

♂ 5–7 mm   ♀ 5·0–7·5 mm

Observation tips/habitat: Recently (2004) recorded in Britain *Holocnemus pulchei* is found amongst loose rocks in dry warm terrain and in caves and basements in Europe. In Britain the spider has been found in glasshouses and large warehouses. The web is large with a loose irregular framework of threads.

Description: CARAPACE Greyish-white with dark median line. Ventrally the sternum is black. ABDOMEN Mottled grey with an irregular jagged, dark median band edged in white, extending two thirds of abdomen length. Laterally are fine wavy bands varying from white to silver. Ventrally a broad black longitudinal line is present. LEGS Very long. Greyish-brown with alternating black and white annulations at the femur/patella and patella/tibia joints.

Similar species: *Pholcus phalangioides* (p. 101).

Distribution/Status: Restricted to just two locations in central England.

J F M A M J J A S O N D

♀ *Holocnemus pluchei* × **6**

SEGESTRIIDAE   Tubeweb spiders   **1 British genus**

Fairly large spiders with an elongate abdomen about the same width as the cephalothorax. They have six eyes arranged in three pairs.

Segestria   **3 British species (3 illustrated)**

All three species have an almost cylindrical abdomen with a distinctive lobed median band. They construct a tubular web, with lines of silk radiating from its entrance, in holes in walls, dead and dying wood, bark and cliff faces. The spider sits at the entrance to the tube with its front legs touching the radiating threads, ready to dash out and seize any prey disturbing them. Legs I, II and III are directed forwards. ♂s are very similar to ♀s but have a slimmer abdomen.

LC | ## *Segestria senoculata*

Common, widespread

♂6–9mm   ♀7–10mm   [PAGE 105 BL]

Observation tips/habitat: Smaller and paler than the rare and localised *S. bavarica*. The abdominal pattern is distinctive. It spins its tubular web in holes in walls and in decaying wood (often utilizing old galleries of wood-boring beetle larvae).

Description: CARAPACE Brown with a darker head area. ABDOMEN Pale brownish-grey with dark brown, lobed median band (similar to the dark pattern on an Adder). Some dark spotting on the margins. LEGS Brown with **darker annulations**.

Similar species: *Segestria bavarica* (*p. 105*) but that species is much larger.

Distribution/Status: Common and widespread throughout Britain.

♂
♀
J F M A M J J A S O N D

LC | ## *Segestria florentina*

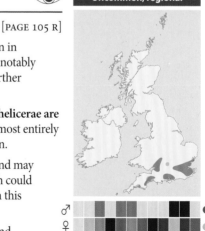

Uncommon, regional

♂10–15mm   ♀13–22mm   [PAGE 105 R]

Observation tips/habitat: The tubular web is spun in holes in **old walls where mortar has disintegrated**, notably in ports on the south coast. Recent records from further inland suggest the spider is extending its range.

Description: CARAPACE Dark brown to black. **The chelicerae are iridescent green, more obvious in ♀**. ABDOMEN Almost entirely black with indistinct median band. LEGS Dark brown.

Similar species: Immatures lack green chelicerae and may have more distinct abdominal markings, and as such could be confused with the much rarer *S. bavarica*, though this species is generally paler.

Distribution/Status: Restricted to southern England.

♂
♀
J F M A M J J A S O N D

LC *Segestria bavarica*

♂ 9–11 mm ♀ 10–13 mm [TL]

♂ ♀

Observation tips/habitat: Larger and darker than
S. senoculata. Predominantly a coastal species, spinning
its web under **stones or in cracks in cliffs**.

Description: CARAPACE Dark brown to black.
ABDOMEN Similar overall pattern to the smaller *S. senoculata*,
with a lobed median band and spotted margins, but darker.
The lobes of the median band may have paler centres.
LEGS Dark brown with **indistinct markings**.

Similar species: *Segestria senoculata* (*p. 104*) but that
species is much smaller. Immature *S. florentina*, which is
generally darker.

Distribution/Status: Very local and confined to coastal
sites in south-west England and north Wales.

Nationally Rare

Rare, local

♂
♀
J F M A M J J A S O N D

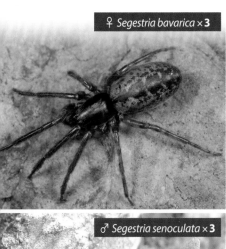

♀ *Segestria bavarica* × 3

♂ *Segestria senoculata* × 3

Iridescent green chelicerae

♀ *Segestria florentina* × 3

105

DYSDERIDAE Woodlouse spiders   **2 British genera**

Quite large spiders with six eyes which are clustered together in a circular formation.
The abdomen is narrow, oval-shaped and lacking any pattern.

Dysdera Woodlouse spiders   **2 British species (1 illustrated)**

The two species in this genus are very similar and feed almost exclusively on woodlice, utilizing
their **large, divergent chelicerae** to catch and eat their prey. They are nocturnal hunters,
sheltering during the day in silk cells.

LC *Dysdera crocata* Woodlouse Spider   **Common, regional**

♂ 9–10 mm   ♀ 11–15 mm   [T]

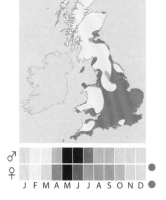

Observation tips/habitat: A distinctive spider with red
carapace and legs. It feeds almost exclusively on woodlice and
is often found in association with them. Occurs under stones
and debris in warm, slightly damp situations often in gardens
and other synanthropic habitats, but not usually in close
association with ants.

Description: CARAPACE Deep reddish brown. Large chelicerae.
ABDOMEN Light grey to beige. No pattern. LEGS Coloured as
carapace. **Femora IV have 1–3 short dorsal spines**.

Similar species: *Dysdera erythrina* (*below*), *Harpactea* (*p. 108*).

Distribution/Status: Widespread in much of southern
England, particularly near the coast. Much less common
in Wales and further north, becoming absent in northern
Scotland.

J F M A M J J A S O N D

LC *Dysdera erythrina*   **Uncommon, regional**

♂ 7–8 mm   ♀ 9–10 mm   [ILLUSTRATED ON PAGE 55]

Observation tips/habitat: Very similar to *D. crocata* in
appearance and habitat but slightly smaller. The only differences
(observable with a hand lens) are the details of spines on the
legs. In maritime and heathland habitats it is usually more
frequent than *D. crocata* and is more tolerant of ants.

Description: CARAPACE + ADBDOMEN Similar to *D. crocata*.
LEGS Similar to *D. crocata* but **no dorsal spines on femora IV**.

Similar species: *Dysdera crocata* (*above*), *Harpactea* (*p. 108*).

Distribution/Status: Widespread but very local in southern
Britain. Generally absent in the north.

J F M A M J J A S O N D

♂ *Dysdera crocata* × **6**

D. crocata has 1–3 dorsal spines on femora IV; **absent** on *D. erythrina*

Dysdera have noticeably large chelicerae for penetrating woodlouse armour

♂ *Harpactea hombergi* × **6**

DYSDERIDAE compared			
GENUS	CARAPACE COLOUR	CHELICERAE	ABDOMEN
Dysdera	Deep reddish-brown	Prominent	Wider than *Harpactea*
Harpactea	Dark/reddish brown; not as rich as *Dysdera*	Not very prominent	Narrower than *Dysdera*

Harpactea

 2 British species (1 illustrated)

The two species are similar to *Dysdera* in general appearance but the **abdomen is rather narrower**, particularly in the ♂, and the **chelicerae are not particularly prominent**. Size is helpful in distinguishing the two species but microscopic examination of the genitalia (see *page 96*) is required to confirm identification.

LC *Harpactea hombergi*

♂5–6mm ♀6–7mm [PAGE 107 B]

Observation tips/habitat: Active at night. During the day it shelters under bark and stones, often within a silk cell. It is found in ivy and accumulations of dry leaf-litter and detritus in *e.g.* the bottom of hedges, shoots emerging from a tree trunk and birds' nests.

Description: CARAPACE Dark brown, tapering towards the head area. ABDOMEN Grey, tubular, sausage-shaped. LEGS Pale brown with darker annulations.

Similar species: *Harpactea rubicunda* (*below*), *Dysdera* (*p. 106*).

Distribution/Status: Common and widely distributed in much of England and Wales. More scattered in northern England and Scotland.

Common, regional

♂
♀
J F M A M J J A S O N D

VU *Harpactea rubicunda*

♂7–8mm ♀8–12mm [NOT ILLUSTRATED]

Observation tips/habitat: Strongly resembles *Dysdera* spp. but the body colour is not as striking. It is thought to be a thermophilous (heat-loving) species in Britain. Found under stones and other ground debris.

Description: CARAPACE Reddish-brown with slight darkening towards the head area. ABDOMEN Slightly paler brown than carapace. LEGS Reddish-brown, as carapace.

Similar species: *Harpactea hombergi* (*above*), *Dysdera* (*p. 106*).

Distribution/Status: Very rare. Currently known from a single site in Essex.

Nationally Rare

Extremely rare

♂
♀ NO PHENOLOGY DATA

OONOPIDAE Goblin spiders   **1 British genus**

The two species within the genus *Oonops* are very similar in appearance being very small, pink spiders with six eyes arranged in a compact group. Another oonopid genus represented in Britain is *Orchestina*. Six females were discovered at one site in North Essex in the early 1990s; its taxonomic status is currently uncertain.

Oonops   🔍 **2 British species (1 illustrated)**

Generally nocturnal, *Oonops* are characterised by their **small size, pinkness and 'start-stop' movements**. The two species are generally found in distinctly different habitats. They can only be distinguished from each other by microscopic examination of the number of spines on tibia I.

LC *Oonops pulcher*   ♀

Common, widespread

♂ 1–2 mm ♀ 1–2 mm   [NOT ILLUSTRATED]

Observation tips/habitat:

Under bark, stones and leaves and in dry grass piles and tussocks. Occasionally found in the webs of *Amaurobius* (*p. 274*) and *Coelotes* (*p. 272*) species, where it feeds on the remains of insects abandoned by the web owners.

Description: CARAPACE Pale to dark pink. ABDOMEN As carapace. LEGS Coloured as carapace, with **four pairs of ventral spines on tibia I**.

Similar species: *Oonops domesticus* (*below*).

Distribution/Status: Widely scattered but local throughout Britain.

♂
♀
J F M A M J J A S O N D

LC *Oonops domesticus*   ♀

Uncommon, regional

♂ 1–2 mm ♀ 1–2 mm

Observation tips/habitat:
A synanthropic species generally discovered in the early hours of the morning hunting for prey. It creeps stealthily around on walls and ceilings with sudden bursts of rapid movement.

♀ *Oonops domesticus* × **10**

Description: CARAPACE + ABDOMEN Pale to dark pink, as *O. pulcher*. LEGS Coloured as carapace, with **five pairs of ventral spines on tibia I**.

Similar species: *Oonops pulcher* (*above*).

Distribution/Status: Widely scattered and uncommon in England. Few records from Wales and Scotland.

♂
♀
J F M A M J J A S O N D

109

MIMETIDAE Pirate spiders   1 British genus
The eight-eyed spiders within the single *Ero* genus are often referred to as 'pirate spiders', invading the webs of other spiders where they prey on the occupant.

LC *Ero cambridgei*   Common, widespread

♂2·5–2·8 mm ♀2·5–3·25 mm   [PAGE 111 B]

Observation tips/habitat: Occurs on bushes, trees and low vegetation in a variety of habitats, particularly where other spiders, on which it preys, are found.

Description: CARAPACE Pale brown with dark brown ocular region, and a dark brown band along the margin ranging in width from a thin to a broad line. A dark brown median line, usually dilated at the junction of the head and thoracic areas, also varies in width. Strong spines are usually present on the head area. ABDOMEN Globular shape with spinnerets pointing downwards. Creamy-brown to orange ground colour, mottled with black particularly in the anterior half which contains a pair of flattish tubercles. LEGS Pale brown with conspicuous dark annulations. Strong spines on tibiae and metatarsi I and II.

Similar species: Other *Ero* species.

Distribution/Status: Widespread and generally common throughout much of England and Wales, with fewer records in northern England and Scotland.

♂
♀
J F M A M J J A S O N D

LC *Ero furcata*   Common, widespread

♂2·5–2·8 mm ♀2·5–3·3 mm   [PAGE 111 T]

Observation tips/habitat: Found in similar situations to *E. cambridgei*. The two species often occur together.

Description: CARAPACE, ABDOMEN + LEGS Similar to *E. cambridgei* (*above*).

Similar species: Other *Ero* species.

Distribution/Status: Widespread and common throughout.

♂
♀
J F M A M J J A S O N D

Ero   Pirate spiders

🔍 **4 British species (all illustrated)**

All the four species are **attractively patterned, small spiders with an upturned, globular abdomen bearing distinctive, rounded protuberances (tubercles) on the dorsal surface.** The carapace is domed centrally. The legs have clear annulations with distinct spines on the tarsi and metatarsi of legs I and II. No web is spun and the egg-sac, covered with coarse, wiry silk and suspended on a long thin stalk, is often the first clue to the spider's presence. The genus can be split into two groups according to the number of tubercles. *E. cambridgei* and *E. furcata* have one pair of abdominal tubercles, *E. tuberculata* and *E. aphana* have two pairs. Otherwise, all four species are very similar – ♂'s and ♀ s are alike in general appearance. Microscopic examination of the genitalia (see *page 96*) is necessary to confirm identification of the species.

♀ *Ero furcata* × **10**

E. cambridgei and *E. furcata* have one pair of tubercles on the abdomen; *E. tuberculata* and *E. aphana* (both *p. 112*) have two pairs.

♀

Ero cambridgei × **10**

♀

E. cambridgei ranges from creamy-brown to orange

LC Ero tuberculata

♂ 3 mm   ♀ 3·5–4·0 mm   [PAGE 113 B]

Observation tips/habitat: Similar to, but slightly larger than, other members of the genus. Typically occurs on established heathland in heather and gorse, but has also been recorded from buildings and fenland.

Description: CARAPACE Similar to *E. cambridgei* (*p. 110*). ABDOMEN Similar to *E. cambridgei*, but has two pairs of tubercles, **the anterior pair larger and more widely separated than the posterior pair**. Ground colour ranges from cream to reddish-orange. LEGS Similar to *E. cambridgei*.

Similar species: Other *Ero* species.

Distribution/Status: Widespread but very local in south-east England with a very few records from the south-west.

Nationally Scarce
Scarce, regional

J F M A M J J A S O N D

LC Ero aphana

♂ 2·4–2·6 mm   ♀ 2·5–3·3 mm   [PAGE 113 T]

Observation tips/habitat: Occurs on dry lowland heath and increasingly recorded from dry garden and brownfield sites.

Description: CARAPACE Similar to *E. cambridgei* (*p. 110*). ABDOMEN Two pairs of tubercles (similar to *E. tuberculata* (*above*)) usually arranged to **form the four corners of a square**. LEGS Similar to *E. cambridgei*.

Similar species: Other *Ero* species.

Distribution/Status: Scarce. Widely scattered but frequent where it occurs in southern England and appears to be extending its range.

Nationally Scarce
Scarce regional

J F M A M J J A S O N D

Ero species – identification pointers			
SPECIES	CARAPACE + LEGS	ABDOMEN:TUBERCULES + OTHER FEATURES	
E. cambridgei	See *E. cambridgei* account (*p. 110*) for description	1 pair	Microscopic examination of the genitalia is necessary to confirm identification (see *page 96*)
E. furcata			
E. tuberculata		2 pairs	**Back pair larger and more separated than front**
E. aphana			**Front and back pair usually in a square formation**

♀ *Ero aphana* × **10**

E. tuberculata and *E. aphana* have two pairs of tubercles on the abdomen; *E. cambridgei* and *E. furcata* (both *p. 110*) have one pair

♂ *Ero tuberculata* × **10**

ERESIDAE Velvet spiders   **1 British genus**

The sole member of this family has eight eyes and was thought to be extinct in Britain until it was re-discovered in 1979. Since 2002 it has been successfully translocated to several new sites, although it remains extremely rare, and is fully protected by law.

Eresus   **1 British species (illustrated)**

Although having the common name Ladybird Spider only the adult ♂ of *Eresus sandaliatus* resembles a ladybird; ♀s and immature ♂s are completely black. **The two sexes differ markedly in appearance and size but cannot be mistaken for any other spider occurring in Britain.**

VU *Eresus sandaliatus* Ladybird Spider

| LEGALLY PROTECTED |
| Biodiversity List (En) |
| Nationally Rare |

Extremely rare

♂6–11 mm ♀8–16 mm

♂♀ **Observation tips/habitat:** Occurs on sheltered, south-facing slopes amongst heather and under stones. ♀ lives underground in an excavated silk-lined burrow, the entrance of which is covered with a sheet of bluish silk, which may brown with age and is often covered with debris.

Description: CARAPACE ♀ black with a covering of fine grey hairs. ♂ black with reddish hairs on margins of thoracic area. ABDOMEN ♀ velvety black with a few pale grey hairs anteriorly. ♂ Bright reddish-orange with two pairs of conspicuous black 'ladybird' spots centrally and a much smaller pair of black spots posteriorly. LEGS ♀ black with fine greyish hairs. ♂ black with rings of white hairs at the joints.

Similar species: None.

Distribution/Status: Known recently from only one site in Dorset although additional Dorset populations have been re-established by translocation.

♂   NO PHENOLOGY DATA

♀
J F M A M J J A S O N D

Eresus sandaliatus × **3**

♂   ♀

OECOBIDAE Discweb spiders   **1 British genus**
An eight-eyed family comprising a single species.

Oecobius   **1 British species (illustrated)**
Small and very fast-moving with a circular and characteristically patterned carapace.
Confined to the interior of buildings, where it spins a flat, circular web some 30 mm across.

 ## *Oecobius navus*    | **Extremely rare**

♂ 2·2–2·5 mm   ♀ 2·2–2·5 mm
♂ ♀

Observation tips/habitat: An occasional import into Britain,
although a breeding population apparently existed in the
Natural History Museum in the 1970s.

Description: CARAPACE Pale brown, almost circular with a
dark patch in the centre, sometimes connecting to a black area
incorporating the eyes. The rim of the carapace is marked with
a thin black line above the insertion of each leg. The posterior
median eyes are reduced to flat, silver plates. ABDOMEN Oval.
Pale yellow-brown with varying numbers of black spots or
larger fused areas over the top of white flecking. A thin black
line runs around the anterior edge. LEGS Colour as carapace
with some slightly darker marks.

NO PHENOLOGY DATA

Similar species: None.

Distribution/Status: Occasional import.

♀ *Oecobius navus* × **10**

ULOBORIDAE Cribellate orbweb spiders

2 British genera

This eight-eyed family is unique in having no poison glands; the spiders rely on their fuzzy, cribellate silk to entangle and immobilise their prey before wrapping it securely and feeding. The webs of the two genera are very different and can be useful aids to identification.

Uloborus

2 British species (2 illustrated)

Spiders with an unusual eye arrangement, with the two curved, almost parallel rows widely separated from each other, the anterior row close to the anterior margin of the carapace and the posterior row set back almost a third of the carapace length. The horizontal orb web usually has a stabilimentum; the spider hangs beneath this at the hub. The longish, slender egg-sac hangs vertically at the side of the web.

NT ## *Uloborus walckenaerius*

♂ 3–4 mm ♀ 3.5–6.0 mm

Nationally Rare

Rare, regional

Observation tips/habitat: Spins a web up to 20 cm in diameter low down **amongst heather or gorse on open, sunny heathland.**

Description: CARAPACE Thickly covered with white hairs and has dark longitudinal bands. ABDOMEN Greyish-white with a continuation of the linear pattern of the carapace. A brown median line has alternating whitish and brown bands on either side. Tufts of fluffy white hairs along the white bands curve upwards and are more conspicuous in profile. LEGS Dark grey-brown to red-brown and vaguely annulated with white. Legs I and II especially long.

Similar species: None.

Distribution/Status: Restricted to a few sites in central southern England.

♂
♀

J F M A M J J A S O N D

♀ *Uloborus walckenaerius* × **10**

Uloborus plumipes

NA

♂3–4mm ♀4–6mm

Observation tips/habitat: This spider has been imported
into Britain on pot plants, probably from the Netherlands.
It appears to be **restricted to hothouses and garden centres**
where the winter temperature remains well above freezing.
It spins a similar web to *U. walckenaerius* (*p. 116*).

Description: CARAPACE Thickly covered with hairs, without
pronounced longitudinal stripes. ABDOMEN Pale to dark brown
with darker median line and thick covering of hairs.
Two prominent tubercles anteriorly with two white spots
between them. LEGS Brown and hairy with bluish-white
annulations. ♀ tibia I with distinct, long, black, feathery hairs.

Similar species: None.

Distribution/Status: Widespread and increasing its range
throughout England and Scotland, with a few sites in north
Wales.

Common, widespread

♂
♀
J F M A M J J A S O N D

♀ *Uloborus plumipes* × **10**

Hyptiotes

👁 **1 British species (illustrated)**

The arrangement of the eyes is quite unlike that of any other British species. The posterior row extends in a curved line across the midline of the carapace; the anterior row is located about halfway between this and the anterior edge. *Hyptiotes paradoxus* spins a triangular web, similar to a section of orb web, with four radial threads connected by strands of cribellate silk. The web is constructed amongst foliage and is kept taut by the spider holding on to one corner of the triangle. When an insect is caught in the web the spider alternately loosens and tightens the tension of the web until the prey is fully entangled in silk before approaching to wrap it securely.

LC ## *Hyptiotes paradoxus* Triangle Spider 👁

♂ 3–4 mm ♀ 5–6 mm

Nationally Scarce

Scarce, regional

J F M A M J J A S O N D

Observation tips/habitat: Typically found on evergreen trees and shrubs, particularly Yew and Box, in mixed woodland. It is quite distinctive in appearance and is unlikely to be confused with any other British spider.

Description: CARAPACE The whole carapace is rather broad and raised up and has a dense covering of hairs. Colour ranges from ginger to dark brown. ♂ palps are conspicuous, extremely large and are similar in size to the carapace. ABDOMEN Orange-brown to red-brown with vague, black transverse bands. extending around the sides. ♀ abdomen is raised anteriorly giving the spider a hunched appearance. It may also have a pair of small tubercles in the anterior half. ♂ may be darker than ♀ and has a more cylindrical shape, lacking the raised anterior. LEGS Short and stout. Similar colour to carapace.

Similar species: None.

Distribution/Status: Widely scattered but scarce in England and Wales. Absent from Scotland.

Hyptiotes paradoxus ×6

♂ palps
as large as
the carapace

♂

CARAPACE

PALPS

♀

Hyptiotes has a distinctive web form

NESTICIDAE Comb-footed cellar spiders   **1 British genus**
The single British species in this eight-eyed family bears some resemblance to the larger theridiid spiders, but its general appearance and habitat should enable straightforward identification.

Nesticus   **1 British species (illustrated)**
The legs of *Nesticus cellulanus*, particularly leg I, are longer than those of theridiids and bear long bristles. The sexes are similar in general appearance. The ♀ carries the relatively large egg-sac attached to the spinners in a similar fashion to the theridiid *Rugathodes bellicosus* (*p.153*). However, the size difference between the two species should prevent any confusion.

LC # *Nesticus cellulanus*   **Common, local**

♂3–5mm ♀3·5–6·0mm

Observation tips/habitat: Confined to dark, damp habitats such as caves, culverts, cellars, sewers, hollow trees and thick wetland vegetation – typically **underneath manhole covers** where it spins a web of fine threads, similar to *Steatoda* (*p.129*).

Description: CARAPACE Pale yellow with a dark brown median band constricted centrally, and thin, dark marginal lines. ABDOMEN Pale yellow with distinct pattern of three or four dark rings on either side of an irregular median band. The depth of colour of the markings can vary according to light levels; the darker the habitat, the lighter the spider's colour. LEGS Pale yellow, as carapace, sometimes with distinct dark annulations.

Similar species: None.

Distribution/Status: Widespread but local throughout much of Britain.

J F M A M J J A S O N D

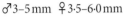
♂ *Nesticus cellulanus* × **6**

The distinctive carapace and abdomen of *Nesticus cellulanus* (♀)

119

THERIDIIDAE Comb-footed spiders   **19 British genera**

The Theridiidae are known as comb–footed spiders, but the row of serrated bristles on the tarsus of the fourth leg, giving the family this common name, is extremely small, if not completely absent, and certainly is not a feature observable in the field. Theridiids have eight eyes and show great variety in body shape and colour, and the presence or absence of abdominal patterning. The abdomen can be quite globular in shape. Three types of webs are found among this family in Britain. One is an unstructured framework of crisscross threads, at the edges of which are sticky threads; a second is a more sheet-like structure with a tubular retreat. The genus, *Episinus*, produces a simple web, spun very close to the ground. The whole family has undergone a revision recently where a number of species have been assigned to different genera. In the recent *A Revised Checklist of British Spiders* (2014) the Theridiidae include nine genera each containing just one species. Some of these genera (*e.g. Anelosimus* (*p.134*) and *Kochiura* (*p.135*)) are remarkably similar in appearance, differing principally in the structure of the male palp. A number of species within the family have only recently been recorded in Britain and knowledge of their habitat preferences and distribution is limited.

For most of these species, habitat descriptions are based on records from northern Europe, where they occur more commonly.

Episinus   🔍 **3 British species (3 illustrated)**

The three species are very similar in shape, having the **abdomen broadened and squared off posteriorly (less noticeably in ♂) and legs iii very short**. Pattern and depth of colour vary considerably and as such microscopic examination of the genitalia (see *page 96*) may be required to confirm identification of the species. Their simple webs, built very close to the ground, are hard to spot and have a few threads forming the letter 'H' or an inverted 'Y'. The spider sits upside down in the web holding onto two sticky threads which are attached to the substrate to snare crawling insects. ♂ and ♀ are fairly similar in appearance.

LC | *Episinus angulatus*   🔬   **Common, widespread**

♂3·5–4·0 mm ♀3·7–4·5 mm   [TR]

♂♀ **Observation tips/habitat:** The spider in the genus most likely to be encountered. It occurs in low vegetation in a wide variety of habitats, especially damp grassland and marshes.

Description: CARAPACE Dark brown mottled pattern centrally with pale yellow border. ABDOMEN Dark brown folium has pale yellow border. Characteristic abdominal shape, with squarish posterior, aids field identification. Spinners project beyond the posterior edge of the abdomen. LEGS Pale yellow-brown with clear dark annulations.

Similar species: Other *Episinus* species.

Distribution/Status: Widespead in southern Britain but has a very local distribution farther north.

♂
♀
J F M A M J J A S O N D

♀ *Episinus truncatus* × **6**

♀ *Episinus angulatus* × **6**

♀ *Episinus maculipes* × **6**

E. truncatus – leg III completely pale, other legs with obvious dark areas

E. angulatus – leg III pale yellow-brown with clear annulations

E. maculipes – leg III similar to, but more speckled than, *E. angulatus*

LC *Episinus truncatus*

♂3.3–4.0mm ♀3.5–4.0mm   [PAGE 121 TL]

Observation tips/habitat: Similar to *E. angulatus* (*p. 120*) but much less common. Occurs on coastal grassland and lowland heath where it spins its simple web under heather.

Description: CARAPACE **Uniform brown with no pattern**. ABDOMEN Similar to *E. angulatus* but the upper surface is almost completely covered by a brown folium apart from a white line on the posterior edge. LEGS I has a dark brown femur, patella and tibia. Legs II and IV have dark brown tibiae. **Leg III is completely greyish-white with no markings and contrasts markedly with the other legs.**

Similar species: Other *Episinus* species.

Distribution/Status: Local in southern Britain and south Wales.

Nationally Scarce
Scarce, regional

LC *Episinus maculipes*

♂4.3mm ♀4.7–5.7mm   [PAGE 121 B]

Observation tips/habitat: Similar to *E. angulatus* (*p. 120*) but often slightly larger. Occurs in woodland edge and vegetated cliff habitats near the coast. Ivy-covered areas of cliff face seem to be favoured.

Description: CARAPACE Pale brown with a dark brown median band extending the whole length. ABDOMEN Very similar to *E. angulatus*. LEGS Similar to *E. angulatus*, but appear more conspicuously speckled.

Similar species: Other *Episinus* species.

Distribution/Status: Scarce. Restricted to southern England.

Nationally Scarce
Scarce, regional

Episinus species – identification pointers			
SPECIES	CARAPACE	ABDOMEN	LEGS
E. angulatus*	Pale yellow with dark brown centre	Dark brown folium with pale yellow border	Pale yellow brown with clear dark annulations
E. maculipes*	Pale brown with dark brown centre band		As *E. angulatus* but more speckled
E. truncatus*	Uniform pale brown	As *E. angulatus* but much larger brown folium	**Distinctive colouration** with leg III unmarked greyish-white, in marked contrast to other legs - see account

* Microscopic examination of the genitalia is necessary to confirm identification (see *page 96*).

Euryopis

 1 British species (illustrated)

Unlike other theridiids, the single British *Euryopis* species does not appear to spin a web. It hunts for ants, which are trapped by wrapping them in silk threads. **The spider has a distinctive appearance** and can be identified in the field. ♀ and ♂ are similar.

LC *Euryopis flavomaculata* ◆

Nationally Scarce

Scarce, widespread

I I ♂3 mm ♀3·5–4·0 mm
♂♀

Observation tips/habitat: Occurs in damp areas, particularly moss, on heathland and moorland. Although fairly small, *E. flavomaculata* has a distinctive shape and should be identifiable in the field.

Description: CARAPACE Brown with darker head area. ABDOMEN Pointed posteriorly and rather shiny. Dark brown with four orange-brown dots centrally, and paler, whitish-yellow patches at the sides and rear. LEGS Orange-brown with tarsi and metatarsi sometimes darker.

Similar species: None.

Distribution/Status: Widespread but scarce, with very scattered distribution throughout Britain.

♂
♀

J F M A M J J A S O N D

♀ *Euryopis flavomaculata* × **10**

Dipoena

✿ **6 British species (2 illustrated)**

All six *Dipoena* species are very small and **can easily be confused with the money spiders** (Linyphiidae – *pages 411–420*). However, the **raised head area of the carapace, particularly in the ♂, helps to distinguish them**. The abdomen of all but one species is grey to black in colour, the exception being *D. melanogaster* in which the abdomen is patterned. *Dipoena* appears to feed almost exclusively on ants in a range of habitats – in low vegetation, lower branches of bushes and trees and on tree bark. All are very uncommon in Britain. All species bar one are very similar and microscopic examination of the genitalia (see *page 96*) is necessary to confirm identification.

The raised head area of the carapace helps separate *Dipoena* spp. from the linyphiids.

EN *Dipoena melanogaster* ✿

Nationally Rare
Extremely rare

I I ♂2·5mm ♀2·5–3·0mm
♂♀

Observation tips/habitat: The only *Dipoena* species with a recognisable abdominal pattern.

Description: CARAPACE Black with long bristles on head area. ABDOMEN Very globular with central indentation on anterior edge. **Distinctive pattern**; yellowish-grey with black markings forming indistinct chevrons. ♀ with scattering of black bristles, ♂ with many tiny black tubercles bearing long bristles. ♂ abdomen is smaller and darker than ♀ with just a pair of light bands in the anterior half. LEGS Orange-brown with dark annulations.

Similar species: Other *Dipoena* species, some linyphiids.

Distribution/Status: Extremely rare. Recorded from gorse and other low bushes, and in deciduous woodland at only two locations in southern England since 1990.

♂ ●
♀ ●
J F M A M J J A S O N D

Dipoena melanogaster × **10**

124

LC *Dipoena tristis*

♂ 2·5 mm   ♀ 3 mm   [NOT ILLUSTRATED]

Observation tips/habitat: Found in grassland and heathland on heather and gorse, and on low branches in both deciduous and coniferous woodland. The whole spider has a black, glossy appearance.

Description: CARAPACE Black, covered with bristles, particularly on the head area. The head area is less elevated than in others in the genus. ABDOMEN Black with a covering of hairs. LEGS Black with tarsi sometimes paler. Femora III and IV partially orange.

Similar species: Other *Dipoena* species, some linyphiids.

Distribution/Status: Scarce. Restricted to the southern counties of England.

Nationally Scarce

Scarce, regional

♂
♀
J F M A M J J A S O N D

NT *Dipoena torva*

♂ 2·5–3·0 mm   ♀ 2·8–4·0 mm

Observation tips/habitat: Restricted to Caledonian pine forest in Scotland, where it feeds on wood ants climbing up and down deeply fissured trunks of old Scots Pines.

Description: CARAPACE Dark brown with bristles in head area. ♂ carapace is distinctly elevated in a cylindrical shape, with a horseshoe-shaped indentation in the upper surface. ABDOMEN Black and shiny with many short, black bristles. LEGS Dark brown.

Similar species: Other *Dipoena* species, some linyphiids.

Distribution/Status: Rare. Recorded from a few localities in Scotland.

Biodiversity List (Sc)

Nationally Rare

Rare, regional

♂
♀
J F M A M J J A S O N D

♂ *Dipoena torva* × **10**

LC *Dipoena inornata*   🔬

I I ♂ 1·5–1·7 mm   ♀ 1·8–2·3 mm   [NOT ILLUSTRATED]
♂ ♀

Biodiversity List (En, Wa)
Nationally Scarce
Scarce, regional

Observation tips/habitat: The smallest in this genus of very small spiders. Although still uncommon, it is the most widespread *Dipoena* in Britain. It occurs amongst low vegetation, heather and under stones on lowland heath and coastal grassland, in rock and scree habitats and on sand dunes.

Description: CARAPACE Brown with raised and darkened head area bearing bristles. ABDOMEN Brown to black, covered in longish hairs giving the abdomen a glossy appearance. LEGS Yellow-brown with tibiae I and II completely black. Tibiae IV have the apical half black.

Similar species: Other *Dipoena* species, some linyphiids.

Distribution/Status: Scarce. Almost exclusively a southern species with just a single record from Scotland.

♂
♀
J F M A M J J A S O N D

VU *Dipoena erythropus*   🔬

I I ♂ 2·0–2·5 mm   ♀ 2·5 mm   [NOT ILLUSTRATED]
♂ ♀

Nationally Rare
Rare, regional

Observation tips/habitat: Recorded from rock, scree and cliff habitats, gorse on heathland and deciduous woodland.

Description: CARAPACE Greyish-yellow with some darkening at the sides. Eyes arranged in a compact group in an anteriorly projecting area. ABDOMEN Brownish-grey, covered with short hairs. LEGS Yellow-brown throughout. Metatarsus I about 1½× length of tarsus I.

Similar species: Other *Dipoena* species, particularly *Dipoena prona* (*p. 127*), some linyphiids.

Distribution/Status: Very rare. Recorded from a very few locations in southern Britain.

♂
♀
J F M A M J J A S O N D

Dipoena prona

Nationally Rare

Rare, regional

I I   ♂2mm ♀2·5mm   [NOT ILLUSTRATED]
♂♀

Observation tips/habitat: Recorded from dry heathland and limestone grassland sites, mostly in coastal areas of southern England, occasionally sand dunes.

Description: CARAPACE Similar to *D. erythropus*.
ABDOMEN Similar to *D. erythropus* but darker.
LEGS Yellow-brown suffused with black.

Similar species: Other *Dipoena* species, particularly *Dipoena erythropus* (*p. 126*), some linyphiids.

Distribution/Status: Rare. Mostly recorded in coastal areas of southern England.

♂
♀

J F M A M J J A S O N D

Dipoena species – identification pointers					
SPECIES	HABITAT		GEN. APPEARANCE	LEGS	DISTRIBUTION
D. melanogaster	Gorse, low bushes; deciduous woodland		**Distinct patterned abdomen**	Orange-brown; dark annulations	
*D. tristis**	Gorse on heathland;	+ Dec. wood + Con. wood	Black, glossy	Black; TARSI sometimes paler	
*D. erythropus**		+ Rocks/scree + Dec. wood	Yellowish-grey; CARAPACE protrudes in front of the eyes	unmarked	Southern England NB *D. prona* mainly coastal areas
*D. inornata**	Rocks/scree; coastal grassland; dunes		Brown to black, sleek	Yellow brown	TIBIAE I + II black; TIBIAE IV apical half black
*D. prona**			Brownish-grey; CARAPACE protrudes in front of the eyes		suffused with black
*D. torva**	Pine forest on tree bark		Uniform pale brown	Dark brown; unmarked	Scotland

* Distinguished by microscopic examination of the genitalia (see *page 96*).

Crustulina   🔍 **2 British species (2 illustrated)**

Both species are **very small and have the carapace covered with small 'warts'.** They have **distinctive abdominal patterns.** Small webs are constructed in low vegetation. The two species are similar.

LC *Crustulina guttata*   🔍

Uncommon, regional

♂ ♂♀ ♂1·5–2·0mm ♀1·5–2·0mm   [PAGE 129 T]

Observation tips/habitat: Occurs in leaf-litter of both deciduous and coniferous woodland and low down in grassy tussocks and ground vegetation. Most often found on dry, sandy soils.

Description: CARAPACE Dark brown with distinctive warty appearance. ABDOMEN **Distinctive pattern**; Black with clear white spots along the median line and also on the sides of the abdomen. There are four, central, reddish, impressed spots. LEGS Yellowish-brown with apices of femora, tibiae, metatarsi and tarsi of all legs darkened.

Similar species: *Crustulina sticta* (*below*).

Distribution/Status: Widespread and locally common in southern and eastern England. More scattered distribution to the west and north.

♂
♀
J F M A M J J A S O N D

LC *Crustulina sticta*   🔍

~~Nationally Scarce~~
Scarce, regional

♂ ♀ ♂2·5mm ♀2·5mm   [PAGE 129 BR]

Observation tips/habitat: Occurs in damp heathland and fenland where the web is spun at ground level. Occasionally found in coastal shingle and sand dunes.

Description: CARAPACE As *C. guttata* but less warty. ABDOMEN **Distinctive pattern**; ♀ pale yellowish-brown with anterior and median banding of white spots with two dark patches at the junction of these bands. Four red spots form a central trapezium. ♂ similar but usually with clearer markings and larger red spots. Occasionally almost completely black. LEGS ♀ pale yellowish-brown, ♂ reddish-brown without annulations.

Similar species: *Crustulina guttata* (*above*).

Distribution/Status: Scarce and local in southern and eastern England.

♂
♀
J F M A M J J A S O N D

♀ *Crustulina guttata* × **10**

Four red dots form a trapezium

♀ *Crustulina sticta* × **10**

Steatoda   False widow spiders — 🔍 **6 British species (6 illustrated)**

Robust spiders usually with a pattern of **contrasting pale and dark abdominal markings**, which varies from species to species, but **always with a white or pale band around the anterior edge of the abdomen**. The web is often large, forming a loosely woven framework of silk, with sticky threads holding it in position. Occasionally the central part of the web is a strong silken sheet; the spider sits in a tubular retreat at the edge.

LC # *Steatoda bipunctata* 🔍

♂ 4–5 mm   ♀ 4–7 mm   [PAGE 133 TL]

Observation tips/habitat: A common and widespread species found around houses. The web often occupies sheltered corners of outbuildings and garden sheds.

Description: CARAPACE Brown. Almost black in ♂.
ABDOMEN **Distinctive pattern;** A shiny, waxy appearance. Central pale brown area darkens to almost black at the margins. Median and anterior white lines are present (less obviously in ♀). **Central area often contains four small dark spots** (marking the position of internal muscle attachments). LEGS Brown with each segment darker apically, occasionally with darker annulations.

Similar species: None.

Distribution/Status: Common throughout Britain, except where *S. grossa* present.

Common, widespread

♂
♀
J F M A M J J A S O N D

LC # *Steatoda grossa*

♂4–6mm ♀6–10mm   [PAGE 132 T]

Common, regional

Observation tips/habitat: Usually found in houses or outbuildings. Occasionally recorded from other sheltered outdoor locations, *e.g.* cracks in walls.

Description: CARAPACE Pale creamy-brown to black with, occasionally, faint radiating lines. ABDOMEN Noticeably shiny. Typically a dark violet to almost black background colour with a pale crescent near the front. There are usually some cream spots, though these may be absent altogether. Some individuals can be very dark and with no discernible markings, and resemble blackcurrants. LEGS Pale creamy-brown, as carapace.

Similar species: *Steatoda nobilis* (*below*).

Distribution/Status: Widespread and scattered throughout southern Britain and extending its range elsewhere.

♂
♀
J F M A M J J A S O N D

Due to the variability in markings in many cases *S. nobilis* and *S. grossa* can only be safely identified by microscopic examination of the genitalia (see *page 96*).

LC # *Steatoda nobilis* Noble False Widow Spider

♂7–10mm ♀8–11mm   [PAGE 132 B]

Common, regional

Observation tips/habitat: The largest British *Steatoda* species, found around houses, outbuildings and gardens, especially on stone walls. It is more active at night when it sits at the entrance to its retreat on the edge of a loosely woven, scaffold-like web built of extremely strong silk (which can closely resemble a *Tegenaria* web (see *pages 74, 76*). Females have been known to bite humans but only in response to threat or disturbance. Sightings have increased dramatically over recent years.

Description: CARAPACE Dark brown to black.
ABDOMEN Noticeably shiny. Typically a white/cream crescent at the front. Distinct, dark brown patches on the 'shoulders' and sides of the abdomen bracket a paler central band which occasionally contains a smaller, dark triangle. Some individuals can be very dark with no discernible markings, and resemble blackcurrants. LEGS Reddish-orange.

♂
♀
J F M A M J J A S O N D

Similar species: *S. grossa* (*above*), especially ♂s, where abdominal markings are less clear.

Distribution/Status: Common throughout southern England and extending its range towards the north and west.

LC *Steatoda phalerata* 🔍

♂4·0–4·5mm ♀3–5mm   [PAGE 133 BR]

♂♀ **Observation tips/habitat:** Ant-like in appearance and found low down in dry grassland and heathland, often in association with ants upon which it feeds. It spins no discernible web.

Description: CARAPACE Dark brown to black with a pitted appearance. ABDOMEN **Distinctive pattern**; black background with cream/yellow markings in a band at the front of the abdomen and small lenticular markings halfway down either side. LEGS Reddish-brown with darker annulations.

Similar species: None.

Distribution/Status: Widespread throughout Britain but infrequent, and locally distributed.

Uncommon, widespread

♂
♀
J F M A M J J A S O N D

NA *Steatoda triangulosa* 🔍

♂3·5–4·0mm ♀4·0–5·2mm   [ALSO PAGE 133 TR]

♂♀ **Observation tips/habitat:** Recently (1996) recorded in Britain, *S. triangulosa* occurs around houses. The web is constructed to capture crawling insects, particularly ants. **The clear abdominal pattern is easily recognizable.**

Description: CARAPACE Dark brown. ABDOMEN **Distinctive pattern**; Two distinct, dark, longitudinal, dentate bands contrast clearly with the creamy-white ground colour. LEGS Pale brown (orange-brown in ♂) with faint, darker annulations.

Similar species: None.

Distribution/Status: Possibly an introduced species, it is not yet clear whether it is established in Britain. Further records are most likely to occur in populated areas in southern Britain.

Rare, local

♂ NO PHENOLOGY DATA
♀
J F M A M J J A S O N D

♀ *Steatoda triangulosa* ×**6**

Dark examples of *S. grossa* (ABOVE) and *S. nobilis* (BELOW) illustrating the difficulty in assigning many individuals to species in the field

♀ *Steatoda grossa* ×**6**

♀ *Steatoda nobilis* ×**6**

LC # *Steatoda albomaculata* 🔍

♂4–5mm ♀3–6mm   [BL]

Observation tips/habitat: Found in dry, sandy heathland, especially when recently burnt, or on shingle, under stones and amongst debris. The web is spun in low vegetation or between large stones.

Description: CARAPACE Pale brown to black. ABDOMEN **Distinctive pattern**; typically front edge of abdomen and sides cream/yellow. Central section dark, almost black, with a lobed edge and a double row of pale spots on the midline, sometimes suffused with yellow or pink; occasionally the pattern is indistinct or absent. LEGS Reddish-brown with darker annulations.

Similar species: None.

Distribution/Status: Rare and locally distributed in southern and south-east England.

Nationally Rare

Rare, regional

♂
♀
J F M A M J J A S O N D

♀ *Steatoda bipunctata* ×**6**

Four small dark spots usually present

♀ *Steatoda triangulosa* ×**6**

♂ *Steatoda albomaculata* ×**6**

♂ *Steatoda phalerata* ×**8**

133

Due to the small size and variability in appearance of both *Anelosimus* and *Kochiura* (*p. 135*) microscopic examination of the genitalia (see *page 96*) is necessary to confirm identification.

Anelosimus

♀ **1 British species (illustrated)**

The single species in this genus is small and differs from other theridiids except *Kochiura aulica* (*p. 135*) in having a **dark median band on both the carapace and the abdomen**. The web is a loose framework of threads.

LC | *Anelosimus vittatus* ♀

Common, regional

♂ 2·5–3·5 mm ♀ 3·0–3·5 mm

Observation tips/habitat: Occurs on the foliage of trees, particularly oak, where it constructs its web in the lower branches. Also on bushes and tall plants.

Description: CARAPACE Light brown with a **thin dark border**. A broad, dark chocolate-brown, median band often tapers slightly towards the posterior. ♂ palp is elongated. ABDOMEN Pale creamy-brown with a dark brown median band with dentate edging. Occasionally there are two pairs of darkened lobes in the posterior half. The median band is sometimes reddish. LEGS Light brown, sometimes with faint annulations.

Similar species: *Kochiura aulica* (*p. 135*).

Distribution/Status: Widespread and common in much of England, less so elsewhere.

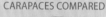

♂
♀

J F M A M J J A S O N D

♀ *Anelosimus vittatus* × **10**

CARAPACES COMPARED

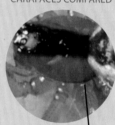

Anelosimus vittatus
thin dark border

Kochiura aulica
more obvious border

Kochiura

☿ **1 British species (illustrated)**

This genus contains one species formerly included in the *Anelosimus* genus (p. 134). The general appearance of the spiders and their webs in the two genera is very similar but *Kochiura* tends to have a **more conspicuous carapace border**.

LC | ## *Kochiura aulica* | ☿

♂2·5–3·0mm ♀3·0–3·5mm

Observation tips/habitat: Similar to *Anelosimus vittatus* but much rarer. Occurs on lowland heaths and coastal grassland, where it can be found with its web near the tips of gorse branches. It is also known from brownfield sites with heathland characteristics.

Description: CARAPACE Similar to *A. vittatus* but the **dark border may be more conspicuous**. The median band also tapers more strongly towards the posterior. ♂ palp is very distinctive. ABDOMEN Similar to *A. vittatus* but the median band is more regular in width and paler, sometimes absent. Very dark specimens occur occasionally. LEGS Medium brown with all segments having darkened apices.

Similar species: *Anelosimus vittatus* (p. 134).

Distribution/Status: Scarce. Confined to southern England.

Nationally Scarce

Scarce, regional

♂ | J F M A M J J A S O N D
♀ |

Colour intensity and pattern details vary between individuals

♀ *Kochiura aulica* × **10**

Achaearanea

🔍 **4 British species (4 illustrated)**

The abdomen of the genus *Achaearanea* is highly characteristic and can be clearly recognized in the field. **It has a teardrop shape and is distinctly upturned so that the anterior section appears much higher relative to the carapace and the spinners point downwards.** The pattern and colouring of the abdomen is extremely variable between and within the different species. Sexes have similar appearance, with ♂'s usually smaller. Webs are unstructured, loose frameworks of silken threads, often referred to as 'scaffold' webs. Habitat preferences, web structure and location, and method of egg-sac protection can help in suggesting species although microscopic examination of the genitalia (see *page 96*) is necessary to confirm identification.

LC ## *Achaearanea tepidariorum* 🔬

Uncommon, local

♂ 3–4 mm ♀ 5–7 mm   [PAGE 137 B]

Observation tips/habitat: A synanthropic species occurring in houses and more often in heated greenhouses. Occasionally found outdoors.

Description: CARAPACE Medium to light brown.
ABDOMEN Variable pattern sometimes similar to *A. lunata* (*p. 138*) but usually more subdued, giving a mottled appearance. LEGS Pale yellow-brown with dark annulations.

Similar species: *Achaearanea simulans* (*below*), *Cryptachaea veruculata* (*p. 139*).

Distribution/Status: Widespread throughout much of England, less so in Scotland and Wales.

♂
♀
J F M A M J J A S O N D

LC ## *Achaearanea simulans* 🔬

Common, regional

♂ 2–3 mm ♀ 3–5 mm   [PAGE 137 TR]

Observation tips/habitat: Indistinguishable from *A. tepidariorum* in both general appearance and microscopic structure of the genitalia. However *A. simulans* is slightly smaller and never found indoors. It typically occurs on the lower branches of trees and bushes in a wide range of habitats including gardens, woodland edge, hedges and scrub.

Description: CARAPACE, ABDOMEN + LEGS
As *A. tepidariorum*.

Similar species: *Achaearanea tepidariorum* (*above*), *Cryptachaea veruculata* (*p. 139*).

Distribution/Status: Widespread but infrequent in southern and central England.

♂
♀
J F M A M J J A S O N D

Achaearanea lunata × **10**

Achaearanea riparia × **10**

♀ *Achaearanea simulans* × **10**

♀ *Achaearanea tepidariorum* × **10**

LC *Achaearanea lunata*

I I ♂2·5mm ♀2·5–3·0mm   [PAGE 137 TL]
♂♀

Observation tips/habitat: Spins extensive web amongst low branches of trees and on bushes 1–2 metres above ground level, usually in shaded, sheltered locations. Also, found in deep crevices in the bark of tree trunks. In the upper section of the web dead, curled-up leaves are utilized to form a retreat.

Description: CARAPACE Ranges from light brown to black. ABDOMEN Colour and pattern varied. Usually darker underside, sometimes with striking reddish patches interspersed with black and white oblique markings on the 'shoulders' of the abdomen. Some can be pale brown with less obvious markings. LEGS Light, brownish-yellow, with all segments (except tarsi) darker in the apical half.

Similar species: *Achaearanea riparia* (*below*).

J F M A M J J A S O N D

Distribution/Status: Widespread but uncommon in the southern half of England. Absent from much of Wales and the south-west.

LC *Achaearanea riparia*

Scarce, local

I I ♂3·0–3·3mm ♀3·0–3·5mm   [PAGE 137 ML]
♂♀

Observation tips/habitat: Similar to *A. lunata* but slightly larger and much less common. Web is spun close to the ground hanging from low vegetation and attached to ground by sticky threads amongst which crawling insects, particularly ants, become entangled. Mainly found on heathland in low vegetation or under overhanging banks.

Description: CARAPACE Dark brown to black. ABDOMEN As *A. lunata* but usually less distinct patterning. LEGS Similar to *A. lunata*.

Similar species: *Achaearanea lunata* (*above*).

Distribution/Status: Rare with very scattered distribution in England and Wales.

J F M A M J J A S O N D

Cryptachaea

 2 British species (1 illustrated)

The two species known from Britain were formerly in the genus *Achaearanea* (*p. 136*) having a similar upturned, teardrop-shaped abdomen, but **differing in the microscopic structure of their genitalia**. Both are cosmopolitan spiders; *Cryptachaea veruculata* is recorded only from the Isles of Scilly, introduced from Australasia in the early 20th century. *C. blattea* also is a common Australasian species and may well have arrived in Britain via imported house plants from Europe.

NA *Cryptachaea veruculata*

♂2·5–3·5 mm ♀3·7–5·2 mm   [NOT ILLUSTRATED]

Observation tips/habitat: Spins scaffold webs on trees and bushes.

Description: CARAPACE Pale brown. ABDOMEN Dark, elongated, diamond-shaped median band outlined in white and flanked by mottled, reddish-brown sides. LEGS Pale yellow-brown with dark annulations.

Similar species: *Achaearanea tepidariorum*, *A. simulans* (both *p. 136*)).

Distribution/Status: Known only from the Isles of Scilly.

Extremely rare

dark and white tubercle

♂ NO PHENOLOGY DATA
♀
J F M A M J J A S O N D

♀ *Cryptachaea blattea* × **10**

NA *Cryptachaea blattea*

♂1·7-2·4 mm ♀2·2-3·2 mm

Observation tips/habitat: Found in trees and bushes, in similar situations to *C. veruculata* (*above*).

Description: CARAPACE Dark yellow to dark brown or black. ABDOMEN Mottled black and white pattern. **About halfway along is a central small tubercle which is dark anteriorly and white posteriorly**. LEGS Yellow-white with dark brown annulations.

Similar species: None, though a high magnification is required to see the diagnostic tubercle on the abdomen.

Distribution/Status: Known from two sites in southern England.

Extremely rare

♂
♀
J F M A M J J A S O N D

Phylloneta

 2 British species (2 illustrated)

The two spiders within this genus are very similar in appearance and web structure. **The abdominal pattern is distinctive.**

LC *Phylloneta sisyphia*

Abundant, widespread

♂2·5–3·0 mm ♀3–4 mm

Observation tips/habitat: Typically found on gorse and heather in open habitats where it spins an inverted, cone-shaped silken retreat, covered with plant debris. Beneath this it spins a typical theridiid tangled web. (see *p. 83*) It also occurs in less open habitats on oak, Blackthorn and Juniper, and on herbaceous plants such as nettles and thistles.

Description: CARAPACE Pale brown with darker median band and borderline (thinner than that of *P. impressa*). ABDOMEN Two bands of broad, black patches, separated by three oblique white lines, flank a reddish-brown median stripe with white edging. Ventrally the abdomen has a black patch **immediately in front of the spinnerets**. LEGS Pale brown with all segments darkened apically.

J F M A M J J A S O N D

Similar species: *Phylloneta impressa* (*p. 141*).

Distribution/Status: Abundant and widespread throughout much of southern Britain but less so in the north.

♀ *Phylloneta sisyphia* × **10**

dark areas of legs paler than those of *P. impressa*

ABDOMEN – VENTRAL VIEWS COMPARED

Phylloneta sisyphia
Almost all with one dark patch, a few with a second patch like *P. impressa*

Phylloneta impressa
Two dark patches; the anterior patch is not always present *i.e.* resembles *P. sisyphia*

Phylloneta and the following six genera, *Theridion*, *Platnickina*, *Simitidion*, *Neottiura*, *Paidiscura* and *Rugathodes* (collectively referred to here as the *Theridion* group) were all formerly included in the one genus *Theridion*. Most of the 18 species are fairly small spiders, 1·5–3·5 mm in length, and the majority spin typical theridiid tangled webs (see *page 83*) in a range of habitats. Abdominal colouring and pattern vary greatly within and between all the species. Both sexes are of similar appearance but with ♂'s having a slightly smaller abdomen and often a more distinct pattern. **Ventral abdominal markings can be useful in species determination.**

LC *Phylloneta impressa* 🔍

Common, widespread

♂ 2·5–3·5 mm ♀ 4·0–4·5 mm

♂♀ **Observation tips/habitat:** Very similar in appearance and web to *P. sisyphia* and often found in similar habitats, although perhaps occurring more often on lower vegetation.

Description: CARAPACE As *P. sisyphia* but with a **thicker borderline.** ABDOMEN As *P. sisyphia* but, ventrally, often with an **additional dark, roughly triangular patch centrally positioned.** LEGS As *P. sisyphia* but dark areas more pronounced.

Similar species: *Phylloneta sisyphia* (p. 140).

Distribution/Status: Widespread and common in southern central England. Scattered elsewhere.

♂
♀
J F M A M J J A S O N D

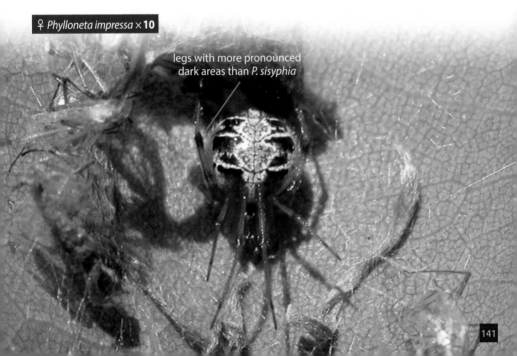

♀ *Phylloneta impressa* ×**10**

legs with more pronounced dark areas than *P. sisyphia*

141

Theridion 🔍 **9 British species (9 illustrated)**

Contains nine species having **distinct dorsal patterns on the abdomen** which show a wide variation of colour contrast, tone and depth. *T. blackwalli* has a fairly distinctive carapace markings; *T. pinastri* has a distinct abdomen pattern; *T. pictum, T. hemerobium* and *T. varians* have a paler carapace background colour; *T. melanurum, T. mystaceum* and *T. familiare* have a darker carapace background colour, as does *T. hannoniae* but that species occupies a very specific habitat. Beyond these broad groupings, abdomen patterns are highly variable within and between species and as such microscopic examination of the genitalia (see *page 96*) is necessary to confirm identification of the species.

LC *Theridion pictum* 🔬

Uncommon, widespread

♂ 2·3–3·5 mm ♀ 3·5–4·8 mm   [PAGE 143 TL]

♂♀ **Observation tips/habitat:** Occurs on bushes, herbaceous plants and other structures including post and rail fencing, mainly in wetland and other damp, lowland habitats.

Description: CARAPACE Yellow-brown, with a dark median band and a dark borderline. ABDOMEN Red-brown median band with lateral spikes and white edging. The remaining area is whitish and mottled with brown, black or grey. LEGS Light brown with dark annulations.

Similar species: *Theridion hemerobium*, (*p. 144*), *T. varians* (*below*).

Distribution/Status: Widespread and locally common in England and Wales, less so in Scotland.

♂
♀
J F M A M J J A S O N D

LC *Theridion varians* 🔬

Common, widespread

♂ 2·25–2·75 mm ♀ 2·5–3·5 mm   [PAGE 143 ML]

♂♀ **Observation tips/habitat:** Highly variable in abdominal colour and pattern, *T. varians* occurs mainly on shrubs and trees but is also found on lower vegetation, walls and fences. Prefers lowland habitats; much less common at higher altitudes.

Description: CARAPACE Pale yellow with a dark median band and borderline. ABDOMEN Dark to light grey with a whitish dentate median band edged with black. Ventrally the abdomen is yellowish-brown with some white spots. ♂ has a swollen epigastric area. LEGS Pale with dark annulations.

Similar species: *Theridion hemerobium* (*p. 144*), *T. pictum* (*above*).

Distribution/Status: Common and widespread in lowland England apart from the south-west. Far less common in Wales and Scotland.

♂
♀
J F M A M J J A S O N D

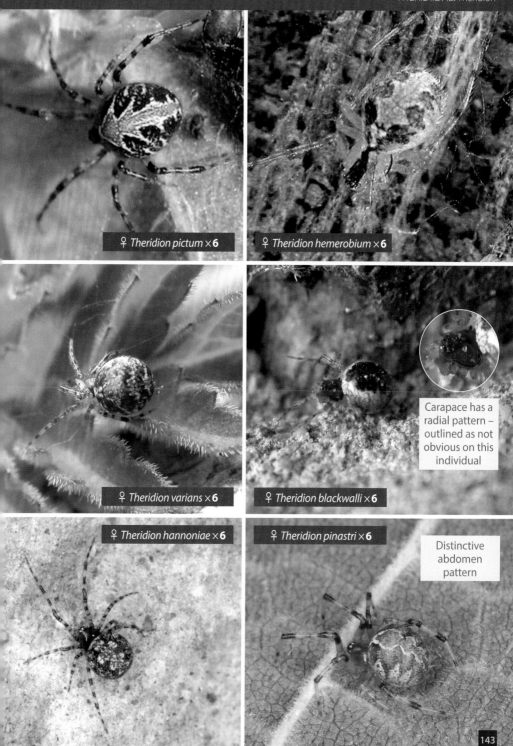

♀ *Theridion pictum* × **6**

♀ *Theridion hemerobium* × **6**

♀ *Theridion varians* × **6**

♀ *Theridion blackwalli* × **6**

Carapace has a radial pattern – outlined as not obvious on this individual

♀ *Theridion hannoniae* × **6**

♀ *Theridion pinastri* × **6**

Distinctive abdomen pattern

143

NA *Theridion hemerobium*

♂ 3·0–3·5 mm ♀ 3·0–4·5 mm   [PAGE 143 TR]

♂♀ **Observation tips/habitat:** First recorded in Britain in 1982, *Theridion hemerobium* has always been found near open water, particularly on canal margins. Very variable in abdominal pattern and can resemble *T. pictum* or *T. varians*.

Description: CARAPACE Whitish-yellow with a broad, dark median band and a dark borderline. ABDOMEN Often with a whitish median band serrated at the edges. LEGS Pale yellowish-brown with dark annulations.

Similar species: *Theridion pictum*, *T. varians* (both *p. 142*).

Distribution/Status: Although apparently scarce, it has been found in widely distributed localities in England and may have been overlooked in the past.

♂
♀
J F M A M J J A S O N D

LC *Theridion blackwalli*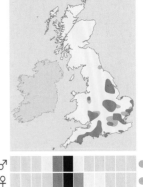

♂ 2·0–2·5 mm ♀ 2·5–3·0 mm   [PAGE 143 MR]

♂♀ **Observation tips/habitat:** Found in a variety of habitats. It builds its web in and around buildings, in grass tussocks and on other low plants and tree trunks. In some areas it seems to favour church walls and gravestones.

Description: CARAPACE Brown with a black head area and typically **a distinctive pattern of inward-facing, thin, triangular, black wedge-shapes emanating from a black borderline**. ABDOMEN Conspicuous black area in the anterior half with black spots on a white, reticulated posterior part. The sides are also reticulated white. Occasionally the whole abdomen is black. Ventrally, two small, white spots occur midway between the epigastric furrow and the spinnerets. LEGS Yellow-brown with faint dark annulations. Ventrally there are some dark spots on the femora, tibiae and metatarsi.

♂
♀
J F M A M J J A S O N D

Similar species: None.

Distribution/Status: Widespread but local in central and southern England but infrequent elsewhere and absent from Scotland.

LC *Theridion pinastri* $\mathcal{Q}$

Nationally Scarce

Scarce, regional

♂2·2–2·8 mm   ♀2·5–3·5 mm   [PAGE 143 BR]

Observation tips/habitat: First recorded in Britain in 1977, *T. pinastri* appears to favour mature broadleaved trees in open situations in wood pasture, acid grassland and heathland.

Description: CARAPACE Brownish-yellow with a darker edge. ABDOMEN **Distinctive pattern**; brick-red median band with wavy white edging and sides with a reticulated brown and white pattern that extends to the ventral surface. The area around the spinnerets is darkened. ♂ has swollen epigastric area. LEGS Pale yellow with dark annulations.

Similar species: None.

Distribution/Status: Widely recorded in south-east England but absent elsewhere.

♂

♀

J F M A M J J A S O N D

NA *Theridion hannoniae*   🔬

Very rare

♂1·6–2·1 mm   ♀1·6–2·4 mm   [PAGE 143 BL]

Observation tips/habitat: Recently (2007) recorded in Britain, *Theridion hannoniae* occurs amongst piles of rocks or large stones.

Description: CARAPACE Brown to dark brown with a darkened borderline. ABDOMEN Highly variable in pattern and depth of colour. Usually grey with a white dentate median band, edged with black. Sometimes the abdomen is dark grey and marked with a number of bright spots. Ventrally dark grey with two white spots in front of the spinnerets. LEGS Yellow-brown with dark annulations.

Similar species: No other *Theridion* species likely in habitat.

Distribution/Status: Extremely rare. Only recorded from one site in South Wales; its status in Britain is uncertain.

♂

♀

J F M A M J J A S O N D

LC *Theridion mystaceum* ♀

♂♀ ♂1·5–2·5mm ♀1·5–2·5mm [PAGE 147 TR]

Observation tips/habitat: Usually found away from buildings on the foliage and bark of trees and shrubs, and also on rock faces close to the sea.

Description: CARAPACE Dark brown with a darker median band and a dark margin of variable width. ABDOMEN Typically dark grey with a whitish dentate median band, but highly variable. ♂ has a swollen epigastric area. LEGS Pale yellow with dark annulations.

Similar species: *Theridion familiare* (*p. 147*), *T. melanarum* (*below*).

Distribution/Status: Widespread in southern Britain but more scattered in the north.

♂
♀
J F M A M J J A S O N D

T. mystaceum, T. melanurum and *T. familiare* can only be safely identified by microscopic examination of the genitalia (see *page 96*).

LC *Theridion melanurum* ♀

♂♀ ♂2·2–3·8mm ♀2·5–3·8mm [PAGE 147 B]

Observation tips/habitat: Generally found in and around buildings. Occasionally it strays to nearby vegetation where it can easily be confused with the near identical *Theridion mystaceum*.

Description: CARAPACE, ABDOMEN + LEGS Similar to *T. mystaceum*.

Similar species: *Theridion mystaceum* (*above*), *T. familiare* (*p. 147*).

Distribution/Status: Widespread in much of England but less so in the south-west and Wales and very restricted in Scotland.

♂
♀
J F M A M J J A S O N D

LC *Theridion familiare*

♂ 1·5 mm ♀ 1·5–2·0 mm

Observation tips/habitat: Mainly found in and around buildings, but occasionally in gardens, on walls, gorse and other bushes.

Description: CARAPACE Brownish-orange sometimes with a dark 'V'-shaped patch around the eyes. ABDOMEN Similar to *T. mystaceum* but a more reddish overall appearance and the anterior part of the median band is wider. LEGS Pale yellow with faint, dark annulations.

Similar species: *Theridion mystaceum*, *T. melanurum* (both *p. 146*).

Distribution/Status: Scarce and very local in southern England. Very rare elsewhere.

Nationally Scarce

Scarce, local

♂ J F M A M J J A S O N D
♀ J F M A M J J A S O N D

♀ *Theridion familiare* × **10**

♀ *Theridion mystaceum* × **10**

Typical individual

♀ *Theridion melanurum* × **10**

Pale individual (*cf. T. mystaceum* (ABOVE)) showing the extent of variation found in both of these closely related species

147

Platnickina

♁ **1 British species (illustrated)**

Best distinguished from other *Theridion* group species by microscopic examination of the genitalia.

LC *Platnickina tincta*   ♁   **Common, regional**

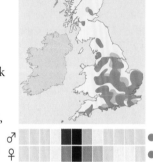

I⟂ ♂2·5mm ♀2·5–3·5mm
♂♀

Observation tips/habitat: Usually found on low vegetation, shrubs, and the lower branches of trees, particularly Yew. Often occurs in the webs of other small spiders (theridiids and araneids) feeding on them or on items already trapped in the web.

Description: CARAPACE Yellowish-grey with a dark borderline and a dark triangular marking on the head area. Sometimes dark radiating streaks are present. ABDOMEN Colouring and pattern very variable, particularly in the extent of the dark area in the anterior half. The remainder is mottled grey and reddish-brown, sometimes forming a vague median band. Ventrally equally variable in depth of colour but, if pale, a triangular dark patch is often present between the spinnerets and the epigastric region. LEGS Yellowish-grey with numerous dark annulations and spots.

♂
♀

J F M A M J J A S O N D

Similar species: Others in the *Theridion* group.

Distribution/Status: Widespread throughout much of southern and central England. Much less common in Wales and the south-west and rare in Scotland.

♀ *Platnickina tincta* ×**10**

Simitidion

🔬 **1 British species (illustrated)**

Best distinguished from other *Theridion* group species by microscopic examination of the genitalia.

LC ## *Simitidion simile* 🔬

Uncommon, regional

♂2·0–2·5 mm ♀2·0–2·5 mm

Observation tips/habitat: Most often found on heathland where it spins its web in gorse, heather and other low vegetation.

Description: CARAPACE Medium to light brown with no discernible pattern. Sometimes margins slightly darker. ABDOMEN Very variable in pattern and depth of colour. Usually a median band is recognizable, containing, midway, a pale triangular mark extending across the width of the abdomen. LEGS Coloured as carapace usually with dark annulations and spots, particularly on apices of segments.

Similar species: Others in the *Theridion* group.

Distribution/Status: Widespread in southern England but much less so elsewhere, with very few records from Scotland.

♂
♀
J F M A M J J A S O N D

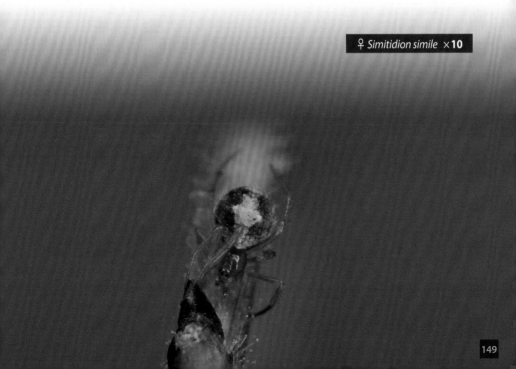

♀ *Simitidion simile* ×**10**

Neottiura 🔍 **1 British species (illustrated)**

The **distinctive abdominal stripe** of the one species in this genus makes field recognition of the ♀ fairly straightforward.

LC | *Neottiura bimaculata* 🔍

Abundant, regional

♂ 2·5–3·0 mm   ♀ 2·5–3·3 mm

Observation tips/habitat: Occurs in low vegetation and bushes, occasionally on low tree branches. The ♀ carries her egg-sac around attached to the spinnerets.

Description: CARAPACE Light brown with a darker head area. Sometimes darker striations are present. ♂ has a raised eye area and relatively large palps, which are held out in front of the spider when running. ABDOMEN Reddish-brown and globular with a **conspicuous, cream (sometimes pink) median stripe tapering towards the spinnerets.** In ♂ the median band is reduced to a few white spots. LEGS Light yellow.

Similar species: None.

Distribution/Status: Abundant and widespread in much of Britain but rather local in the north, particularly in upland areas.

♂
♀

J F M A M J J A S O N D

♀ *Neottiura bimaculata* × **10**

Paidiscura

 1 British species (illustrated)

Although extremely small the ♀ of the single species in this genus is easily detected in the field as **the very distinctive spiky, white egg-sac is commonly found on the underside of leaves (particularly oak and Holly) usually with the ♀ in attendance or very close by.** The spikes of the egg-sac, which is appreciably larger than the accompanying spider, all point in the same direction.

LC

Paidiscura pallens

♂ 1·2–1·5 mm   ♀ 1·7–1·8 mm

Observation tips/habitat: Typically occurs amongst the foliage of trees. Both sexes are very variable in their markings.

Description: CARAPACE Pale yellow sometimes with faint radial striations. Head area is greyish-black, in ♂ sometimes darker. ABDOMEN ♀ globular, almost spherical, with colour and pattern very variable. It can match the carapace colour with an indistinct pattern or have the anterior area darkened with a pale transverse band or cross. ♂ has a dorsal surface which is usually dark brown to black, sometimes with paler mottling. LEGS Pale, sometimes with dark annulations.

Similar species: Individual *P. pallens* found away from the egg-sac are easily confused with other members of the *Theridion* group and in these cases microscopic examination of the genitalia is necessary for identification (see *page 96*).

Distribution/Status: Abundant and widespread throughout Britain although more scattered in upland areas and the north.

Abundant, widespread

♂
♀

J F M A M J J A S O N D

♀ *Paidiscura pallens* × 10

Paidiscura has a distinctive egg-sac

151

Rugathodes

♔ **3 British species (3 illustrated)**

All three species are very small and have a similar appearance to each other and other members of the *Theridion* group. **Habitat preferences and distribution are helpful in suggesting species** though microscopic examination of the genitalia (see *page 96*) is necessary for confirmation.

NA # *Rugathodes sexpunctatus* ♔

Extremely rare

♂2·3–2·4mm ♀2·2–2·6mm [PAGE 153 T]
♂♀

Observation tips/habitat: *R. sexpunctatus* has only recently (2012) been added to the British list. It was first recorded from a cemetery in Glasgow where large numbers were discovered in Ivy hanging from old walls and has since been found in other evergreen species in the area, including Holly, Juniper, pine and Yew. ♀ carries the egg-sac attached to her spinnerets.

Description: CARAPACE Pale yellow-brown with a dark median band usually extending the full length of the carapace. ABDOMEN Similar to *R. instabilis* (*below*) with equally variable pattern. Three pairs of white spots within grey patches reflected in the specific name *sexpunctatus*. LEGS Pale yellow with dark annulations in ♀, paler annulations in ♂.

Similar species: Other *Rugathodes* species.

Distribution/Status: Restricted to a few localities in and around Glasgow.

J F M A M J J A S O N D

LC # *Rugathodes instabilis* ♔

Nationally Scarce

Scarce, regional

♂1·7–2·3mm ♀2·0–2·5mm [PAGE 153 BL]
♂♀

Observation tips/habitat: Occurs in wetland habitats including fens, carr woodlands and saltmarshes, where it spins its web amongst low vegetation. The ♀ carries her pinkish brown egg-sac attached to her spinnerets.

Description: CARAPACE Pale yellow with a darker median band. ♂ has enlarged chelicerae. ABDOMEN Pattern very variable. Pale yellow ground colour with longitudinal bands of dark markings flanking a pale median area. Dark markings may form complete bands, or in ♂ the whole dorsal area may be dark. Ventrally, the area round the spinnerets is usually dark. LEGS Pale yellow.

Similar species: Other *Rugathodes* species.

Distribution/Status: Generally scarce but widespread in East Anglia and south-east England. Much more local elsewhere and absent north of Derbyshire.

J F M A M J J A S O N D

Rugathodes bellicosus

LC

♂ 1·7 mm ♀ 1·5–2·0 mm [BR]

Nationally Rare

Rare, regional

Observation tips/habitat: Occurs amongst rocks on high ground. Flimsy webs are constructed in cavities within rock and boulder scree. The egg-sac, when carried by the ♀, is relatively large compared to the size of the body.

Description: CARAPACE Similar to *R. instabilis* (p. 152). Dark median band extends only half the length of the carapace. ♂ has enlarged chelicerae. ABDOMEN Similar to *R. instabilis* and equally variable in the extent of patterning. LEGS Pale yellow.

Similar species: Other *Rugathodes* species.

Distribution/Status: Restricted to uplands of north Wales and northern England and Scotland. Locally abundant within its habitat.

♂
♀
J F M A M J J A S O N D

♂

Rugathodes sexpunctatus × **10**

♀ with egg-sac

Abdomen of ♂ varies considerably in depth of colour from very pale (as here) to almost black

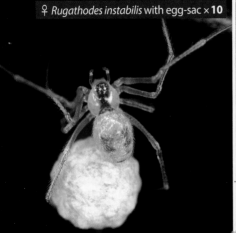

♀ *Rugathodes instabilis* with egg-sac × **10**

♀ *Rugathodes bellicosus* with egg-sac × **10**

Enoplognatha ⚥ [*E. ovata + E. latimana*] **6 British species (4 illustrated)**

Enoplognatha ovata and *E. latimana* are very similar to each other and are easily recognized in the field. Both are long-legged and occur in three colour forms. The other four species are very different from this pair and from each other. However, **all have a more oval, less globular abdomen than many other theridiids.**

LC *Enoplognatha ovata* Common Candy-striped Spider ⚥

	Abundant, widespread

♂ 3–5mm ♀ 4–6mm   [PAGE 155 TL, ML, BL]

Observation tips/habitat: Occurs in open habitats on low vegetation where the ♀ creates a retreat for its bluish egg-sac by rolling a leaf and securing it with lines of silk.

Description: CARAPACE Pale with an dark median band and a thin dark borderline. ♂ chelicerae enlarged.
ABDOMEN Three colour forms all often with two lateral rows of black dots. Commonest form is completely yellowish-white (form *lineata*), others either have two, red longitudinal bands (form *redimita*) or a single broad red band (form *ovata*) covering most of the dorsal area. LEGS Relatively long, pale and yellow with apices of tibiae I darkened.

Similar species: *Enoplognatha latimana* (*below*).

Distribution/Status: Very common and widespread throughout Britain.

♂
♀
J F M A M J J A S O N D

E. ovata and *E. latimana* can only be safely identified by microscopic examination of the genitalia (see *page 96*).

LC *Enoplognatha latimana* Scarce Candy-striped Spider ⚥

	Common, local

♂ 3–5mm ♀ 4–6mm   [PAGE 155 TR, MR]

Observation tips/habitat: Habitat similar to *E. ovata* but in Britain appears to prefer more open, drier and sunnier sites.

Description: CARAPACE Very similar to *E. ovata*. ♂ chelicerae enlarged. ABDOMEN Very similar to *E. ovata* but the form with a single broad red band is much rarer. LEGS As *E. ovata*.

Similar species: *Enoplognatha ovata* (*above*).

Distribution/Status: Common in coastal habitats in southern and western England and Wales. Only common inland in the south-east. Almost absent from Scotland.

♂
♀
J F M A M J J A S O N D

♀ *Enoplognatha ovata* ×**6**

♀ *Enoplognatha latimana* ×**6**

form *lineata*

form *redimita*

form *ovata*

The rolled leaf egg-sac retreat made by
E. ovata and *E. latimana*

VU ***Enoplognatha tecta*** ♀

♂ 4·0–4·5 mm ♀ 4·5–6·0 mm [NOT ILLUSTRATED]

Observation tips/habitat: Found in vegetation by water courses near the coast. Only two known sites and three British records, the most recent from East Anglia in 2009. It is thought to be extinct at the second site, in Dorset.

Description: CARAPACE Similar to *E. mordax*. ♂ chelicerae enlarged. ABDOMEN Similar to *E. mordax*. The dark midline is flanked by white spots with a pair of dark patches anteriorly and a central dark patch posteriorly. **Ventrally there are scattered white spots which do not form a square and longitudinal white lines are absent.** LEGS Similar to *E. mordax*.

Similar species: *Enoplognatha mordax* (below), *E. oelandica* (p. 157).

Distribution/Status: Extremely rare.

Nationally Rare

Extremely rare

♂ NO PHENOLOGY DATA
♀
J F M A M J J A S O N D

LC ***Enoplognatha mordax*** ♀

♂ 3·0–3·5 mm ♀ 3·5–4·5 mm

Observation tips/habitat: Restricted to saltmarsh habitats where it occurs at ground level.

Description: CARAPACE Yellow-brown with few markings. ♂ chelicerae enlarged. ABDOMEN Leaf-like pattern with dark edging and a central dark line flanked by white spots. **Ventrally black with a pair of longitudinal white lines.** LEGS Yellow-brown, relatively long but thinner than in *E. ovata*.

Similar species: *Enoplognatha tecta* (above), *E. oelandica* (p. 157).

Distribution/Status: Scarce; confined to coastal sites in the south and east of England, and in Wales.

Nationally Scarce

Scarce, local

♀ *Enoplognatha mordax* × 6

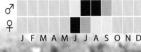
♂
♀
J F M A M J J A S O N D

CR *Enoplognatha oelandica*

♂ 2·5–3·0 mm   ♀ 3–5 mm   [NOT ILLUSTRATED]

Observation tips/habitat: Occurs on sand dunes, dry sandy heaths and grassland, under stones or among vegetation.

Description: CARAPACE Mid- to dark brown. ♂ chelicerae enlarged. ABDOMEN Brown with numerous white spots and a ring of small black patches edging the dorsal area. The dark, median stripe sometimes appears as two patches. **Ventrally there are four white spots forming a central square.** LEGS Brown with darkened apices to all segments.

Similar species: *Enoplognatha tecta*, *E. mordax* (both *p. 156*).

Distribution/Status: Very rare; recorded from a few sites in mid-south and south-east England, most recently in 1997.

Nationally Rare

Extremely rare

♂
♀
J F M A M J J A S O N D

LC *Enoplognatha thoracica*

♂ 2·5–3·0 mm   ♀ 3·5–4·0 mm

Observation tips/habitat: Very different from other *Enoplognatha* species and can be mistaken for a linyphiid (*pp. 411–420*). It occurs in a variety of habitats under stones and plant debris on the ground.

Description: CARAPACE Brown to dark brown. ♂ chelicerae enlarged. ABDOMEN Black, occasionally with small white spots. LEGS Brown, rather robust.

Similar species: Some linyphiids.

Distribution/Status: Widespread and locally common in the south, becoming scarcer farther north and west.

Common, regional

♂
♀
J F M A M J J A S O N D

♀ *Enoplognatha thoracica* × **6**

157

Pholcomma
 1 British species (illustrated)

A very small spider with **short legs and a distinctly globular abdomen, giving it a squat appearance**. It can easily be mistaken for a linyphiid (*pages 411–420*) and microscopic examination of the genitalia (see *page 96*) is necessary to confirm identification of the species.

LC *Pholcomma gibbum* ♀

Common, widespread

♂ 1·25–1·5 mm ♀ 1·2–1·5 mm [PAGE 159 TL]

Observation tips/habitat: Occurs at ground level amongst moss and leaf-litter in a variety of habitats. Spins a typical theridiid scaffold web with sticky threads attached to the ground.

Description: CARAPACE Orange-brown and broad.
ABDOMEN ♀ greyish-brown with four, reddish, impressed spots.
♂ has reddish-brown scutum both dorsally and ventrally.
LEGS Orange-brown.

Similar species: *Theonoe minutissima* (*below*), some linyphiids.

Distribution/Status: Widespread and generally common.

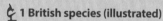

♂
♀
J F M A M J J A S O N D

Theonoe
 1 British species (illustrated)

Very similar to and even smaller than *Pholcomma gibbum*, having the appearance of a small linyphiid (*pages 411–420*). Microscopic examination of the genitalia (see *page 96*) is necessary to confirm identification of the species.

LC *Theonoe minutissima* ♀

Uncommon, local

♂ 1·0–1·3 mm ♀ 1·0–1·3 mm [PAGE 159 TR]

Observation tips/habitat: Occurs in similar habitats to *Pholcomma gibbum*.

Description: CARAPACE Yellowish-brown to deep brown.
ABDOMEN Grey to black with four reddish impressed spots.
LEGS Colour as carapace.

Similar species: *Pholcomma gibbum* (*above*), some linyphiids.

Distribution/Status: Uncommon but widespread throughout much of northern and western Britain. Apparently absent from much of the south-east.

♂
♀
J F M A M J J A S O N D

♀ *Pholcomma gibbum* × **10**

♂ *Theonoe minutissima* × **10**

Coleosoma

🔬 **1 British species (illustrated)**

The single British species in this genus appears to have been introduced into this country with the import of exotic plants. **It is confined to tropical glasshouses.**

NA *Coleosoma floridanum* 🔬

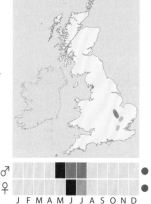

Rare, local

♂ 1·7–2·0 mm   ♀ 1·3–2·0 mm

Observation tips/habitat: The spider occupies crevices in walls and under stones, as well as on vegetation in garden centres and botanic gardens. It spins tiny webs less that 8 mm in diameter.

Description: CARAPACE Uniform yellowish-brown with a narrow dark margin. ABDOMEN ♀ very pale, oval and with two dark bands either side of the midline anteriorly with another pair towards the rear end. Scattered white flecking. ♂ an ant mimic. Similar coloration to ♀ but abdomen more that twice as long as wide. A distinct protrusion in the midline overhangs the rear of the carapace. LEGS Colour as carapace, sometimes with dark patches.

♂
♀

J F M A M J J A S O N D

Similar species: None, but the spider's very small size necessitates the use of a microscope to confirm identification.

Distribution/Status: Just a few records in the east Midlands and in Lancaster.

Coleosoma floridanum × **10**

Robertus

 5 British species (3 illustrated)

All five species are small, dark spiders with no discernible pattern and can easily be mistaken for a Linyphiid (*pages 411–420*). They can usually be **distinguished from the Linyphiidae in the field by examination of the tarsi with a hand lens; they are distinctly darker than the femora** – a feature not present in the majority of the Linyphiidae. The species most likely to be encountered is *Robertus lividus*. Microscopic examination of the genitalia (*see page 96*) is necessary to identify the species.

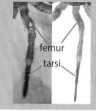

Robertus (LEFT) tarsi are obviously darker than the femora, unlike most Linyphiids (RIGHT)

LC ## *Robertus lividus*   ♀

Abundant, widespread

♂ 2·5–4·0 mm   ♀ 2·5–4·0 mm   [PAGE 161 B]

Observation tips/habitat: Occurs in a variety of habitats ranging from woodland to open moorland. It is found amongst leaf-litter, in moss and grass and under stones.

Description: CARAPACE Dark brown and shiny. ABDOMEN Greyish-black with four reddish, impressed spots. LEGS Orange-brown with darker tarsi.

Similar species: Other *Robertus* species.

Distribution/Status: Abundant and widespread throughout Britain.

♂
♀
J F M A M J J A S O N D

LC ## *Robertus arundineti*   ♀

Uncommon, widespread

♂ 2·0–2·25 mm   ♀ 2·2–2·5 mm   [PAGE 161 TR]

Observation tips/habitat: Occupies similar habitats to *R. lividus*, but may favour slightly damper conditions. Generally smaller than *R. lividus* (*above*).

Description: CARAPACE Yellowish-brown to brown. ABDOMEN + LEGS Similar to *R. lividus* but usually slightly paler.

Similar species: Other *Robertus* species.

Distribution/Status: Widespread throughout, but generally uncommon.

♂
♀
J F M A M J J A S O N D

CR *Robertus scoticus*

Biodiversity List (Sc)
Nationally Rare
Extremely rare

♂ 1·7–2·0 mm ♀ 2 mm　　　　　　　[TL]

Observation tips/habitat: Only known from Caledonian pine forest amongst moss and pine litter in damp areas.

Description: CARAPACE Brown with darker radial striae. ABDOMEN + LEGS Similar to *R. lividus* (*p. 160*) but usually slightly paler.

Similar species: Other *Robertus* species.

Distribution/Status: Extremely rare: only recorded from two Perthshire woodlands.

♂
♀
J F M A M J J A S O N D

♀ *Robertus scoticus* × **10**

♀ *Robertus arundineti* × **10**

♀ *Robertus lividus* × **10**

`DD` # *Robertus insignis* 🔬

I I ♂2·5mm ♀2·5mm [NOT ILLUSTRATED]
♂♀

Observation tips/habitat: Just one recent (1988) specimen recorded from a fen in the Norfolk Broads amongst Great Fen-sedge.

Description: CARAPACE Brown.
ABDOMEN +LEGS Similar to *R. lividus* (*p. 160*).

Similar species: Other *Robertus* species.

Distribution/Status: Extremely rare.
Only recorded from two sites in north-east Norfolk.

Nationally Rare
Extremely rare

NO PHENOLOGY DATA

`LC` # *Robertus neglectus* ◆ 🔬

I I ♂1·7–2·0mm ♀2·0–2·25mm [NOT ILLUSTRATED]
♂♀

Observation tips/habitat: Occurs in similar habitats to *R. lividus* and *R. arundineti* (both *p. 160*) but is smaller than both.

Description: CARAPACE Brown to orange-brown.
ABDOMEN + LEGS Similar to *R. lividus*.

Similar species: Other *Robertus* species.

Distribution/Status: Widespread but scarce and localized.

Nationally Scarce
Scarce, widespread

♂
♀
J F M A M J J A S O N D

Robertus species – identification pointers			
SPECIES	CARAPACE	OTHER FEATURES	HABITAT
R. lividus*	Dark brown and shiny	2·5–4·0 mm	Woodland, open moorland NB *R. arundineti*, may prefer damper conditions
R. arundineti*	Yellowish-brown to brown	Smaller than *R. lividus*; slightly paler	
R. neglectus*	Brown to brown-orange	Smaller than *R. lividus* + *R. arundineti*	
R. insignis*	Brown	Size as small *R. lividus*;	**Norfolk Broads fenland**
R. scoticus*	Brown with darker radial striae	Smaller; slightly paler than *R. lividus*	**Caledonian Pine Forest**

* Distinguished by microscopic examination of the genitalia (see *page 96*).

THERIDIOSOMATIDAE　Ray's spiders　　1 British genus

This eight-eyed family contains just one genus containing a single species which is similar to a small theridiid but differs from that family in constructing a small orb web which lacks a recognizable hub.

Theridiosoma　　🔍 1 British species (illustrated)

The one spider in this genus has a **spherical abdomen covered with large silver patches**. It sits at the hub of a small orb web on a taut thread of silk, distorting the web to resemble the shape of an umbrella. When prey comes into contact with the web this suspension thread is released with a jerk, entangling the potential meal.

LC | *Theridiosoma gemmosum*　Ray's Spider　🔍

♂ 1·5–2·0 mm　♀ 2–3 mm

Nationally Scarce

Scarce, regional

Observation tips/habitat: Occurs among low herbage, grass, *etc.*, in a variety of wet habitats. It spins a small orb web low down among vegetation. The egg-sac is attached by a long stalk to bushes and trees at a some distance above the web.

Description: CARAPACE ♀ dark around the eyes, the remainder pale brown occasionally with dark streaking. ♂ similar but with more definite darker markings. ♂ palps are large compared with the body size. ABDOMEN Very globular and overhanging the carapace. Silvery patches occur dorsally, with dark patches at the sides and a dark, wedge-shaped patch posteriorly. May have a thin, dark median line with horizontal branching. LEGS Pale yellow.

Similar species: None.

Distribution/Status: Widespread but very local in southern Britain. Absent from the north.

♂
♀
J F M A M J J A S O N D

♀ *Theridiosoma gemmosum* × **10**

163

MYSMENIDAE Dwarf cobweb spiders   **1 British genus**

This eight-eyed family of minute orb web spinning spiders is a very recent (2012) addition to the British spider list and is represented by just one species in a single genus.

Trogloneta   ⚲ **1 British species (illustrated)**

The spider spins a tiny three-dimensional orb web which, when viewed from above, resembles the web of some of the smaller araneids.

 NA

Trogloneta granulum   ⚲

Extremely rare

♂ ♀ ♂ 0·9 mm ♀ 1·1 mm

Observation tips/habitat: Appears to favour moist, dark spaces in slopes of scree often in wooded areas. Only two records exist for *T. granulum*; due to its minute size it may well be under-recorded.

Description: CARAPACE Brownish-yellow. ♂ has elevated head area. ABDOMEN Greyish-white, sometimes with vague black spots. Globular in shape and upturned so that spinnerets point downwards when viewed in profile. LEGS Brownish-yellow.

Similar species: None, though its tiny size means that microscopic examination of the genitalia is required to distinguish it from juveniles of other families.

Distribution/Status: Rare. Known from two sites in Wales.

♂ NO PHENOLOGY DATA
♀
J F M A M J J A S O N D

♀ *Trogloneta granulum* ×**40**

×**10**

TETRAGNATHIDAE Long-jawed orbweb spiders   **4 British genera**

Within this eight-eyed family, spiders in the genus *Tetragnatha* are characterized by a cylindrical abdomen, large elongated chelicerae and long legs. *Pachygnatha* (*p. 170*) also has enlarged chelicerae (particulary in ♂s). *Metellina* (*p. 172*) and *Meta* (*p. 175*) do not have enlarged chelicerae. Orb webs with a small hole in the hub are spun by all species except for adult *Pachygnatha*, which hunt their prey at ground level and spin no web.

Tetragnatha Stretch spiders

6 British species (6 illustrated)

TETRAGNATHA compared: *p. 168*

All species have enlarged chelicerae, long legs and a very elongated abdomen which usually has a silvery/metallic sheen. They spin fairly simple, rather delicate orb webs with few radii, widely spaced spirals and an empty space at the hub. There is no retreat and spiders can be found sitting in the centre of the web, which is often spun at an angle, or even horizontally, near water. When disturbed the spider will leave the web and stretch its body and legs out along a grass or reed stem, providing extremely effective camouflage. The appearance of *Tetragnatha* spp. in the field enables the genus to be easily recognized. *T. extensa* and *T. montana* are by far the commonest species and the most likely to be encountered. However, microscopic examination of the genitalia (see page 96) is necessary to separate the species safely.

Typical pose of a *Tetragnatha* spider when disturbed

LC *Tetragnatha extensa* Common Stretch Spider ⚷

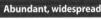

Abundant, widespread

♂6–9 mm ♀6·5–11·0 mm   [PAGE 166 B]

Observation tips/habitat: In wetland habitats where it spins its web in grasses and low vegetation close to, or over, open water.

Description: CARAPACE Yellowish-brown, sometimes with slightly darker markings radiating from the fovea. Ventrally, the sternum has at the anterior end a central, yellow, triangular patch (see *p. 167*). ABDOMEN Silvery-grey with two sinuous longitudinal stripes varying from yellowish-green to reddish-brown. Centrally, a thin, black branched line runs the length of the abdomen. Ventrally, a narrow dark band flanked by thin silvery lines runs from the epigastric furrow to the spinnerets. LEGS Coloured as carapace, some darkening at joints.

Similar species: *Tetragnatha montana, T. pinicola* (both *p. 167*).

Distribution/Status: Abundant and widespread throughout much of Britain.

♂
♀

J F M A M J J A S O N D

♀ *Tetragnatha montana* × **4**

♀ *Tetragnatha extensa* × **4**

LC
Tetragnatha montana

♂6–9 mm　♀6.5–11.0 mm　　　　　　　　　　[PAGE 166 T]

Observation tips/habitat: Similar habitat to *T. extensa* but sometimes slightly farther away from open water. Web is spun in low vegetation and also bushes and trees.

Description: CARAPACE Similar to *T. extensa* but sometimes darker. The sternum is all brown, with no yellow patch (see *below*). ABDOMEN Very similar to *T. extensa* but usually darker. LEGS Yellowish-brown, as carapace, some darkening at joints.

Similar species: *Tetragnatha extensa* (*p. 165*), *T. pinicola* (*below*).

Distribution/Status: Abundant and widespread in southern Britain, less so in the north.

Abundant, widespread

♂
♀
J F M A M J J A S O N D

LC
Tetragnatha pinicola

♂4.5–5.0 mm　♀5–6 mm

Observation tips/habitat: Webs usually found on trees, occasionally on lower plants. Not as closely associated with water as *T. extensa* and *T. montana*. Similar to *T. extensa* but smaller.

Description: CARAPACE Pale brown sometimes with darker striae. Sternum has pale central patch like *T. extensa* (see *below*). ABDOMEN Similar to *T. extensa* but much more silvery in appearance. Ventrally, a dark longitudinal line sometimes has silvery patches. LEGS Pale brown, as carapace.

Similar species: *Tetragnatha montana* (*above*), *T. extensa* (*p. 165*).

Distribution/Status: Widespread but local in southern England.

Uncommon, regional

♂
♀
J F M A M J J A S O N D

Tetragnatha sternum patterns

yellow triangle

T. extensa,
T. pinicola

plain

Other
Tetragnatha

♀ *Tetragnatha pinicola* × **4**

LC *Tetragnatha obtusa*

♂3.5–5.0 mm ♀5–7 mm   [PAGE 169 TL]

♂♀ **Observation tips/habitat:** Occurs on trees in woodland and also on heathland pines.

Description: CARAPACE Pale with a darker triangular area covering the head area; this is very conspicuous in the field. Sternum is a uniform dark brown. ABDOMEN Ranges in colour from silvery green to brown. The distinct folium pattern has dark margins and is noticeably constricted at midpoint. LEGS Pale brown with darker annulations at joints.

Similar species: *Tetragnatha nigrita* (*below*).

Distribution/Status: Widespread but local in England and Wales. Rare in Scotland.

♂
♀
J F M A M J J A S O N D

LC *Tetragnatha nigrita*

♂5–8 mm ♀7–10 mm   [PAGE 169 TR]

♂♀ **Observation tips/habitat:** Generally much darker than other tetragnathids but recorded from similar habitats, particularly trees.

Description: CARAPACE Dark brown with a black head area. Dark brown sternum. ABDOMEN Similar to *T. obtusa* but the folium broader anteriorly and tapering towards the spinnerets. It has lobed edges posteriorly. LEGS As *T. obtusa* but darker.

Similar species: *Tetragnatha obtusa* (*above*).

Distribution/Status: Widespread but uncommon in southern England and Wales. Rare in northern England and Scotland.

♂
♀
J F M A M J J A S O N D

Tetragnatha species – identification pointers			
SPECIES	CARAPACE	STERNUM	ABDOMEN PATTERN (V-LINE = VENTRAL LINE)
*T. pinicola**	Pale brown	Yellow triangle at front end	As *T. extensa* but much more silvery V-LINE: dark; sometimes with silvery patches
*T. extensa**	Yellowish-brown		Silver grey with two longitudinal stripes V-LINE: dark; flanked by silvery lines
*T. montana**	(NB *T. montana* sometimes darker)	All brown	As T. extensa but sometimes darker V-LINE: As *T. extensa*
*T. striata**			FOLIUM: Dark brown; ± light median line
*T. obtusa**	Pale; HEAD AREA: dark triangle	All dark brown	FOLIUM: Dark margins; constricted at midpoint
*T. nigrita**	Dark brown; HEAD AREA: black		FOLIUM: Dark; tapering to rear

* Microscopic examination of genitalia (see *page 96*) is required for safe identification.

♀ *Tetragnatha obtusa* × **4**

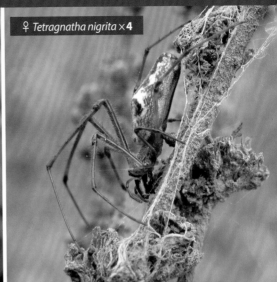

♀ *Tetragnatha nigrita* × **4**

♂

Tetragnatha striata × **4**

♀

LC *Tetragnatha striata* 🔍

♂8–10mm ♀8·5–12·0mm   [PAGE 169 B]

♂♀

Observation tips/habitat: Primarily a specialist of reedbed habitats, spinning its web close to open water. May be commoner than records suggest as a consequence of its inaccessible habitat.

Description: CARAPACE Yellowish-brown. Brown sternum. ABDOMEN Dark brown folium sometimes with a light median line. LEGS Coloured as carapace.

Similar species: None.

Distribution/Status: Widespread but very local in southern England and Wales. Rare in northern England and Scotland.

♂
♀
J F M A M J J A S O N D

Pachygnatha   🔍 **3 British species (3 illustrated)**

The three species have **enlarged chelicerae but do not have the elongated abdomen of** *Tetragnatha* (p. 165). They are generally found at ground level during the day. Orb webs are only spun by young spiderlings, although adults can be found trailing lines of silk high up in vegetation at night. All three species vary in markings, particularly in the depth of colour of the carapace and microscopic examination of the genitalia (see page 96) is necessary to confirm identification.

LC *Pachygnatha clerki* 🦗

♂5–6mm ♀6–7mm   [PAGE 171 BL]

♂♀

Observation tips/habitat: This is the largest member of the genus and usually occurs in fairly wet habitats, such as marshes and bogs and on river, stream and pond margins, where it can be fairly common.

Description: CARAPACE Brown with a darker median band and less distinct submarginal stripes. Glossy appearance with faint punctuations on the margins and sometimes also in lines radiating from the fovea. Chelicerae similar colour to carapace. ABDOMEN ♀ reticulated, olive-brown appearance with a dark folium containing a cream median band. ♂ similar but showing a greater contrast of light and dark areas. LEGS Light brown.

Similar species: Other *Pachygnatha* species.

Distribution/Status: Widespread and very common in much of Britain.

♂
♀
J F M A M J J A S O N D

LC *Pachygnatha listeri*

♂3·0–4·5 mm ♀3·5–5·0 mm [T]

Uncommon, widespread

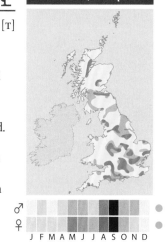

Observation tips/habitat: Unlike others in the genus, *P. listeri* is more habitat-specific. It is almost always found amongst leaf-litter in mature or ancient broad-leaf and mixed woodland. A similar spider to *P. clerki*, but smaller.

Description: CARAPACE Similar to *P. clerki* but dark markings are sometimes absent and punctuations are more pronounced. Chelicerae are very dark brown, sometimes almost black and generally much darker than the carapace. ABDOMEN Similar to *P. clerki* but the folium varies in its depth of colour and has a more irregular design. The median band is sometimes broken up into a series of paired, white spots or, occasionally, may be completely absent. LEGS Light brown.

Similar species: Other *Pachygnatha* species.

Distribution/Status: Uncommon but widespread in much of Britain but very infrequent in northern Scotland, Wales, and the south-west.

♂
♀
J F M A M J J A S O N D

Pachygnatha listeri × **6**

♂ ♀

♀ *Pachygnatha clerki* × **6**

♀ *Pachygnatha degeeri* × **6**

LC *Pachygnatha degeeri*

Abundant, widespread

♂2·5–3·0 mm ♀3·0–3·8 mm [PAGE 171 BR]

Observation tips/habitat: By far the commonest species in the genus, occurring close to ground level in a wide variety of habitats ranging from woodland rides to derelict industrial sites.

Description: CARAPACE Very dark brown with a distinctly pitted surface. Chelicerae similar colour to carapace. ABDOMEN Brown folium with darker edges, occasionally with white spots along the median line. Whitish sides contrast strongly with the dorsal surface. LEGS Light brown.

Similar species: Other *Pachygnatha* species.

Distribution/Status: Abundant and widespread throughout Britain.

♂
♀

J F M A M J J A S O N D

Metellina

👁 **3 British species (3 illustrated)**

All three species in this genus are common; *M. segmentata* and *M. mengei* together are probably the most frequently seen orb web spiders in Britain. The webs are superficially similar to those of the Araneidae (see *page 79*) but differ in having more closely set, radial threads and spirals. *M. segmentata* and *M. mengei* are almost indistinguishable in the field but the season of maturity is different and can be a useful guide to species determination. **The oval, tapering shape of the abdomen is characteristic of the genus**, although superficially these species could be mistaken for araneids (*p. 177*). All three species vary in appearance, colour and pattern depth and microscopic examination of the genitalia (see page 96) is necessary to confirm identification.

LC *Metellina segmentata*

Abundant, widespread

♂4–6 mm ♀4–8 mm [PAGE 173 B]

Observation tips/habitat: Occurs in a wide variety of habitats on vegetation and other structures up to a height of around two metres. Adults usually found during **late summer and autumn**.

Description: CARAPACE Pale brown with a dark median marking in shape of a tuning fork which is easily seen in the field. ABDOMEN Ranges from pale yellowy-green to dark brown in general colouring. The abdominal pattern is usually darker in the anterior half where two triangular marks are usually fairly distinct with a tapering folium extending posteriorly from the rear point of each triangle. **Ventrally, there is a dark median band between the spinnerets and the epigastric furrow.** LEGS Pale brown, sometimes with faint annulations.

Similar species: Other *Metellina* species.

Distribution/Status: Very common throughout Britain.

♂
♀

J F M A M J J A S O N D

LC

Metellina mengei

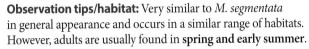

♂3·5–5·0 mm   ♀3·5–6·0 mm

Observation tips/habitat: Very similar to *M. segmentata* in general appearance and occurs in a similar range of habitats. However, adults are usually found in **spring and early summer**.

Description: CARAPACE As *M. segmentata*. ABDOMEN As *M. segmentata*. **Ventrally, the dark median band usually extends beyond the epigastric furrow**. LEGS As *M. segmentata*.

Similar species: Other *Metellina* species.

Distribution/Status: Very common throughout Britain.

♂
♀
J F M A M J J A S O N D

♀ *Metellina mengei* × **4**

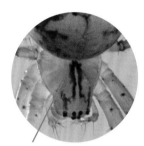

Metellina sp. showing the 'tuning fork' marking on the carapace

♀ *Metellina segmentata* × **4**

173

LC *Metellina merianae* + var. *celata* ⚲

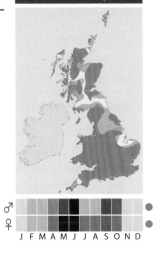

Abundant, widespread

♂ 4·5–7·0 mm ♀ 5·5–9·0 mm

Observation tips/habitat: Occurs in dark, secluded sites which are often fairly damp. Webs can be found under vegetation overhanging steep-sided ditches and stream banks, under bridges, at cave entrances and in damp woodland.

Description: CARAPACE Pale brown with dark triangular marking covering the head area and tapering towards the posterior of the carapace. Dark marginal line and radiating dark streaks present in the thoracic area. ABDOMEN Similar pattern to *M. segmentata* (*p. 172*) but usually rather vague. General colour varies considerably. Some individuals have a conspicuous yellow median band running the full length of the abdomen (var. *celata*). LEGS Pale brown with dark spots on femora I and II and often dark annulations throughout.

♂
♀

J F M A M J J A S O N D

Similar species: Other *Metellina* species.

Distribution/Status: Common and widespread throughout Britain.

♀ *Metellina merianae* × 4

The dark abdomen with a conspicuous yellow band gives var. *celata* a strikingly different appearance

Meta Cave spiders **2 British species (2 illustrated)**

Both species are **large, glossy, long-legged spiders living in conditions of total darkness.**
Often referred to as cave spiders but also occurring in other dark locations, such as under
manhole covers. Appearance, size and habitat enable identification of the genus in the field, but
microscopic examination of the genitalia (see *page 96*) is necessary to confirm identification of
the species.

LC ## *Meta menardi*

♂10–11 mm ♀12–15 mm   [PAGE 176 B]

Uncommon, widespread

Observation tips/habitat: Occurs in damp conditions deep
inside caves, mines, sewers, ice-houses, damp cellars and railway
tunnels. A large orb web is produced but usually the spider
sits on a vertical surface slightly away from the web. A large,
white, teardrop-shaped egg-sac is suspended from the roof of
the habitat and may remain in place long after the young have
emerged.

Description: CARAPACE Reddish-brown with black median
band, more pronounced posteriorly, and darkened margins.
ABDOMEN Chestnut brown with pair of dark patches anteriorly
and dark banding posteriorly. LEGS Chestnut brown with
darker blotches.

Similar species: *Meta bourneti* (*below*).

Distribution/Status: Widespread but local throughout Britain.

♂
♀
J F M A M J J A S O N D

LC ## *Meta bourneti*

♂10–13 mm ♀13–16 mm   [PAGE 176 T]

Nationally Scarce

Scarce, regional

Observation tips/habitat: Very similar to *M. menardi* in
appearance and habitat requirements. It has been recorded
from ancient woodland sites where it may be associated with
large, ancient trees with hollow trunks. *M. bourneti* has also
been recorded from the interior of abandoned WW2 pillboxes
and burial vaults in Highgate Cemetery, London, and also
underground culverts and inspection chambers.

Description: CARAPACE + ABDOMEN Very similar to *M. menardi*.
LEGS Very similar to *M. menardi* but usually lacking the darker
markings.

Similar species: *Meta menardi* (*above*).

Distribution/Status: Widespread but scattered
distribution in southern England.

♂
♀
J F M A M J J A S O N D

♀ *Meta bourneti* × **2**

♀ *Meta menardi* × **2**

ARANEIDAE Orbweb spiders   **16 British genera**

All members of this eight-eyed family spin orb webs which, apart from one species, have closed hubs. In two species a wavy band of silk, the stabilimentum, is an additional feature of the web. Many araneids are brightly coloured and have distinctive abdominal patterns which allow for field identification to at least generic level. Legs are relatively short and stout and in most species are covered in numerous spines. Some species exhibit great variety in colour but the pattern of abdominal markings usually remains constant. ♂'s usually have a much smaller abdomen than ♀s but otherwise are similar in pattern and colouring.

Araneus   **7 British species (7 illustrated)**

Mature ♀s of **five of the seven** species in this genus are large, conspicuous spiders with a distinctively patterned globular abdomen. The spider can often be found sitting in the hub of its orb web, waiting for incoming prey. **The other two species (A. sturmi and A. triguttatus) are smaller and have a more triangular-shaped abdomen with darkened 'shoulders'.**

Araneus species – abdomen dorsal patterns		
A. diadematus	Cross-like pattern of pale spots and markings in anterior half	
A. quadratus	Pale yellow to bright orange, cherry-red or chocolate-brown with four white spots in anterior half	
A. marmoreus	var. *marmoreus*: yellowish-green to dark brown; resembles A. quadratus but folium more distinct with darker edging	var. *pyramidatus*: plain yellow with red-brown wedge in posterior half
A. angulatus	Pale brown, with a pair of distinct humps on the 'shoulders'	
A. alsine	Reddish-orange to deep violet with white speckling	
A. sturmi	Variable; folium usually pointed at front, broadening at the 'shoulders' and tapering towards rear	
A. triguttatus	Similar to A. sturmi but folium often does not extend beyond 'shoulders'	

LC

Araneus quadratus Four-spotted Orbweb spider   **Common, widespread**

♂6–8 mm ♀9–20 mm   **[PAGE 179 TL]**

Observation tips/habitat: Size, and the distinctive abdominal pattern of the mature ♀ help in field identification. Occurs on undisturbed herbaceous vegetation and shrubs, such as rushes and sedges, and heather and gorse, which provide a sufficiently robust structure to support a large web of up to 40 cm diameter. The ♀ constructs a sizeable retreat at the margin of the web.

Description: CARAPACE Pale brown with darker lateral bands separated from the margin by a pale area. Broad, dark median band of varying width; sometimes reduced to a thin line in ♂. A covering of white hairs is usually present. ABDOMEN Very variable in colour, ranging from pale yellow to bright orange, cherry-red or chocolate-brown (see *page 43*). **It has four white spots in the anterior half** and a vague folium edged with white markings. Whole abdomen can have distinctly circular shape in gravid ♀s. LEGS Pale brown with darker annulations in ♀. ♂ has less distinct markings. Numerous spines.

Similar species: *Araneus marmoreus* var. *marmoreus* (p. 182).

Distribution/Status: Common and widespread throughout Britain.

♂
♀
J F M A M J J A S O N D

LC *Araneus angulatus*   Angular Orbweb Spider   👁

Nationally Scarce

Scarce, regional

♂10–12 mm   ♀12–19 mm   [PAGE 179 TR]

Observation tips/habitat: This is the largest British spider to have **prominent abdominal tubercles**. It occurs in deciduous woodland often close to the woodland edge. The web may be spun high up in trees suspended from a very long frame-thread.

Description: CARAPACE Reddish-brown with a darker border and a covering of long white hairs. ♂ is sometimes much darker overall. Ventrally, the sternum is dark brown with an irregular yellow median band. ABDOMEN **Pale brown with a pair of distinct humps on the 'shoulders' of the abdomen**, behind which a deeper brown folium tapers towards the spinnerets. Sometimes a series of white markings may run down the median area. LEGS Pale brown with darker annulations.

Similar species: None, though immatures could possibly be confused with *Gibbaranea gibbosa* (p. 186).

J F M A M J J A S O N D

Distribution/Status: Infrequent, very local and largely confined to southern coastal counties of England.

LC *Araneus diadematus*   Garden Spider   👁

Abundant, widespread

♂4–8 mm   ♀10–18 mm   [PAGE 179 B]

Observation tips/habitat: The best known and commonest of the orb web spiders, *A. diadematus* is also known as the Cross Spider or the Diadem Spider. It occurs in a wide range of habitats wherever the structure can accommodate an orb web up to 40 cm diameter at heights of up to 2·5 m. The ♂ is much smaller than the ♀.

Description: CARAPACE Light brown usually with some darker markings. ♂ markings less distinct. A covering of white hairs is usually present. ABDOMEN Extremely variable ground colour ranging from pale yellowy-green through to dark brown, usually with a darker, white-edged folium. **Centrally, a cross-like pattern of pale or white spots and markings is almost always present anteriorly**. The 'shoulders' of the abdomen are sometimes angular and occasionally observable as small humps. LEGS Pale brown with darker annulations in ♀. ♂ with less distinct markings. Numerous spines.

J F M A M J J A S O N D

Similar species: None.

Distribution/Status: Very common and widespread throughout Britain.

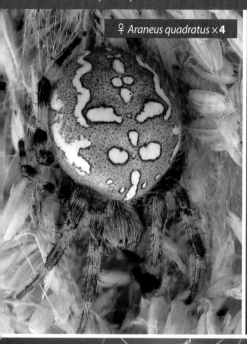

♀ *Araneus quadratus* × **4**

♀ *Araneus angulatus* × **4**

♀ *Araneus diadematus* × **4**

Araneus sturmi

Uncommon, local

♂ 3–4 mm   ♀ 3–5 mm

♂♀ **Observation tips/habitat:** Usually on evergreen trees and bushes in mature woodland. It has also been recorded from mature Yew and other evergreens in urban churchyards.

Description: CARAPACE Pale reddish-brown with the head area lighter. ♂ can be darker. ABDOMEN Slightly triangular in shape. Darkened 'shoulders' with conspicuous white edging posteriorly. The remainder of the abdomen varies from yellow to reddish-brown, sometimes containing a folium edged in white. LEGS Reddish-brown. In ♂ usually darker with faint annulations.

Similar species: *Araneus triguttatus* (*below*).

Distribution/Status: Generally uncommon with a scattered distribution in much of Britain, but absent in some areas.

♂
♀
J F M A M J J A S O N D

A. *sturmi* and A. *triguttatus* can only be identified by microscopic examination of the genitalia.

Araneus triguttatus

Uncommon, regional

♂ 3·0–4·5 mm   ♀ 4·5–6·0 mm

♂♀ **Observation tips/habitat:** Similar to, but slightly larger than, A. *sturmi*. Occurs in deciduous woodland where, in contrast to A. *sturmi*, the web is spun amongst the foliage of broadleaved trees, particularly oak.

Description: CARAPACE Similar to A. *sturmi*. ABDOMEN More triangular in shape than A. *sturmi* but with similar darkened 'shoulders'. Folium rarely present in the remaining area, which usually has a pinkish coloration. LEGS Similar to A. *sturmi*.

Similar species: *Araneus sturmi* (*above*).

Distribution/Status: Generally restricted to south-east England where it can be fairly common.

♂
♀
J F M A M J J A S O N D

♀ *Araneus sturmi* × **4**

♀ *Araneus triguttatus* × **4**

LC *Araneus alsine* Strawberry Spider

Nationally Scarce

Scarce, local

♂5–6mm ♀7–13mm

Observation tips/habitat: Occurs in two different habitats in different parts of Britain. In northern Scotland it is found in bog areas whereas in southern England it favours damp woodland clearings. The web is spun in low vegetation and the retreat usually consists of one or two dried leaves forming an inverted cone suspended in the upper part of the web. **The spider has an unmistakable appearance** but can be easily overlooked in the field.

Description: CARAPACE Orange-brown with a sparse covering of white hairs. ABDOMEN Generally reddish-orange, but can vary to a deep violet, with white speckling and glossy overall appearance. LEGS As carapace, with no annulations.

Similar species: None.

Distribution/Status: Scarce and very local in specific habitats in Scotland and south-east England.

♂
♀
J F M A M J J A S O N D

♀ *Araneus alsine* × **4**

181

♀ *Araneus marmoreus* × **4**

Araneus marmoreus var. *marmoreus* (LEFT), *A. marmoreus* var. *pyramidatus* (CENTRE),
A. marmoreus var. *marmoreus* reddish colour form (RIGHT)

LC *Araneus marmoreus* vars. *marmoreus* + *pyramidatus* 👁   **Uncommon, regional**

♂5–7mm ♀5–14mm

■ var. *pyramidatus*
■ var. *marmoreus*

Observation tips/habitat: Two distinct, genetically
determined, colour forms *A. marmoreus* var. *marmoreus*
and *A. marmoreus* var. *pyramidatus* are found in Britain.
They occur in damp woodland and heathland on tall plants
and on the lower branches of trees. Occasionally they may be
found in the same place, together with intermediate forms.
Webs are spun amongst foliage often at higher levels than
both *A. diadematus* and *A. quadratus*.

Description: CARAPACE Closely resembles *A. quadratus* but
the median line is thin and two dark patches are usually
present anteriorly, on either side of median line.
ABDOMEN *A. marmoreus* var. *marmoreus* can resemble
A. quadratus but usually has a **more distinct folium with
dark edging**. The ground colour and general appearance is
very variable, ranging from yellowish-green to dark brown.
A. marmoreus var. *pyramidatus* has a **reddish-brown wedge-like marking in the posterior
half, with the rest of the dorsal area plain yellow**. LEGS Pale brown with distinct,
darker annulations.

♂
♀

J F M A M J J A S O N D

Similar species: *Araneus quadratus* (*p. 177*).

Distribution/Status: *A. marmoreus* var. *marmoreus* is rare, occuring mainly on fen and
heathland sites in eastern England. *A. marmoreus* var. *pyramidatus* is uncommon but
widespread throughout south-east England.

Larinioides

 3 British species (3 illustrated)

These species have **some association with water** and have **patterns of conspicuous white hairs on the carapace.** They all have a similarly patterned abdomen. ♂s are similar to ♀s, but have a smaller abdomen with more distinctive patterns.

 LC *Larinioides cornutus*

Abundant, widespread

♂5–8 mm ♀6–9 mm

Observation tips/habitat: The commonest species of the genus, *L. cornutus* spins its large web on tall grasses, reeds and other vegetation close to both freshwater and the sea. Also frequent in damp meadows. A substantial retreat is constructed high up in vegetation adjacent to the web.

Description: CARAPACE Pale brown with darker streaks radiating from the fovea and a covering of white hairs. ABDOMEN Ground colour very variable, ranging from cream through to orange-brown. The folium consists of two dark, dentate bars, **often with thin, white transverse lines, converging posteriorly.** A pale cardiac area contains a central dark patch. LEGS Pale brown, as carapace, sometimes with dark annulations.

Similar species: Other *Larinioides* species.

Distribution/Status: Very common and widespread in much of England and Wales. More scattered distribution in Scotland.

♂
♀
J F M A M J J A S O N D

♀ *Larinioides cornutus* × **6**

normal colour form

orange-brown colour form

Larinioides sclopetarius Bridge Orbweb Spider 🔍

LC

Common, local

♂ 8–9 mm ♀ 10–14 mm

Observation tips/habitat: Appreciably larger than *L. cornutus* (*p. 183*) and *L. patagiatus* (*p. 185*) and with a distinct, velvety appearance. Occurs close to water where webs are spun on bridges, buildings and fencing, rarely on vegetation.

Description: CARAPACE Black, with white hairs around the carapace margin and also **along the edge of the head area, where they form a conspicuous 'V-shape'**. ABDOMEN Generally quite dark with the edges of the folium picked out in white. ♂'s smaller abdomen concentrates the white markings. LEGS Colour varies from cream to dark brown. Annulations present on paler specimens.

Similar species: Other *Larinioides* species.

Distribution/Status: Locally distributed throughout England and Wales. Rarer in Scotland.

♂
♀
J F M A M J J A S O N D

♀ *Larinioides sclopetarius* ×**6**

LC *Larinioides patagiatus*

♂ 5–6 mm ♀ 5–7 mm

Observation tips/habitat: Spins web on trees and shrubs often with a retreat under loose bark. It usually prefers drier habitats than other members of the genus but occasionally can be found alongside *L. cornutus* (*p. 183*) near water.

Description: CARAPACE Dark brown to black with a covering of white hairs around the head area. ABDOMEN Ground colour pale to dark brown. A similar pattern to *L. cornutus* but the **folium has no transverse white lines and often is only clearly defined in the posterior half of the dorsal area.** LEGS Brown with darker annulations.

Similar species: Other *Larinioides* species.

Distribution/Status: Scarce with a widely scattered distribution throughout Britain.

Nationally Scarce

Scarce, local

♂
♀

J F M A M J J A S O N D

♀ *Larinioides patagiatus* × **6**

185

Gibbaranea

 🔍 **1 British species (illustrated)**

The single species in this genus is **distinctive in colour and shape, with greenish sides and a prominently humped abdomen** (a second species, *G. bituberculata*, was last recorded in 1950 and is now considered extinct in Britain).

LC *Gibbaranea gibbosa* Humped Orbweb Spider 🔍

♂ 4–5 mm ♀ 5–7 mm

Observation tips/habitat: Occurs in the foliage of trees, particularly evergreens. **Two prominent humps on the 'shoulders' of the abdomen are clearly visible with a hand lens and, when combined with the greenish appearance and size of the spider,** enable fairly straightforward identification in the field.

Description: CARAPACE Brown with darker streaks and light hairs. ♂ somewhat darker than ♀. ABDOMEN General appearance usually greyish-green but can vary to darker shades. Conspicuous tubercles are often paler than the rest of the dorsal area. LEGS Pale brown with darker annulations. Spines are white with brown bases.

Similar species: Possible confusion with immature *Araneus angulatus* (p.178).

Distribution/Status: Widespread and fairly frequent in southern and eastern England. Rare in the remainder of Britain.

Common, regional

J F M A M J J A S O N D

♀ *Gibbaranea gibbosa* × **6**

Nuctenea

 1 British species (illustrated)

The single species in this genus found in Britain has, unusually for the family, a **quite distinctive, flattened appearance and is almost black at first glance.** ♀s and ♂s are similar but the latter are smaller.

LC *Nuctenea umbratica* Walnut Orbweb Spider

Abundant, widespread

♂ 8–9 mm ♀ 11–14 mm

Observation tips/habitat: Commonly found in a wide range of habitats. The spider hides away during the day under bark or squeezed into narrow cracks in fenceposts, door and window frames. Away from buildings it is associated with dead wood. It emerges at night and spins a large orb web. Sitting at its hub, it catches moths and other nocturnal flying insects.

Description: CARAPACE Dark brown to black. ABDOMEN Distinctly flattened with a leathery appearance. Mottled brown with a wide, black, white-edged folium containing four pairs of small depressions on either side of the centre line. Ventrally a pair of white spots is present. LEGS Dark brown to black.

Similar species: None.

Distribution/Status: Abundant and widespread throughout much of England and Wales, rather scattered in Scotland.

♂
♀

J F M A M J J A S O N D

♀ *Nuctenea umbratica* × **4**

Agalenatea

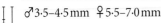 **1 British species (illustrated)**

♀s of the British species in this genus appear to have an **almost rounded abdomen if viewed from above.** The ♂ abdomen is more triangular. **The abdominal pattern in both sexes is usually one of three distinct colour forms.**

LC *Agalenatea redii*

Common, regional

♂ 3·5–4·5 mm ♀ 5·5–7·0 mm

Observation tips/habitat: Occurs amongst heather and gorse, and in rough grassland, often in rather damp situations, where it spins its web fairly low down amongst the stems. A retreat is often constructed in an adjacent dead flower head.

Description: CARAPACE Yellow-brown head area with darker thoracic area which includes a pair of light patches posteriorly. The whole is covered with white hairs. ABDOMEN Three colour/pattern forms are commonly found. A dark cardiac mark edged with white is usually present and can be quite conspicuous in some individuals. LEGS Variable shades of brown with darker, often incomplete, annulations.

Similar species: None.

Distribution/Status: Widespread but local in much of England and Wales. Rare in north-west England and absent from Scotland apart from one coastal record in the south-west.

♂
♀

J F M A M J J A S O N D

Agalenatea redii × **6**

The three forms of *Agalenatea redii* – form α (left), form δ (centre), form ζ (right)

Neoscona **1 British species (illustrated)**

The British species in this genus differs from other araneid genera in the noticeably slimmer shape of the abdomen. **The abdominal pattern has clear and distinctive markings readily recognisable in the field.**

LC ## *Neoscona adianta*

♂4–5mm ♂ 5–7mm ♀

Common, regional

Observation tips/habitat: Occurs mainly on heather and gorse and occasionally on low grass in a variety of open habitats including heathland, coastal grasslands, saltmarsh and fen. The web is spun at a low level and the spider constructs an adjacent silk platform on which it sits.

Description: CARAPACE Pale brown with thin darker median and lateral bands and a covering of white hairs. ABDOMEN The ground colour is variable, ranging from greyish-brown to reddish-brown. **A distinct pattern comprises a thin, irregular, brown median band flanked by pairs of black-edged, white triangular patches decreasing in size towards the spinnerets.** Thinly covered with long silky hairs. LEGS Pale brown with dark annulations at the joints. Relatively thin but bearing numerous dark spines.

J F M A M J J A S O N D

Similar species: None.

Distribution/Status: Widespread but only locally frequent in south-east England. Elsewhere more uncommon and favouring coastal sites with only a few records inland.

♀ *Neoscona adianta* ×**6**

> ## *Araniella*   Cucumber spiders   **5 British species (2 or 3 illustrated)**
>
> Four of the British *Araniella* species have a **bright, apple-green abdomen** and the fifth has a distinctively patterned abdomen; all are recognizable in the field as belonging to the genus. The commonest two species, *A. cucurbitina* and *A. opisthographa*, are indistinguishable in general appearance and size. The remaining species are rare and, apart from *A. displicata*, microscopic examination of the genitalia (see *page 96*) is necessary to separate them. All spin small orb webs amongst plant foliage. Sometimes the web is spun within the margins of a single leaf and consequently the typical structure of the orb web may be compromised.

LC   ## *Araniella cucurbitina*   Common Cucumber Spider   ☍   **Common, widespread**

♂3·5–4·0 mm   ♀4–6 mm   [PAGE 191 B]

♂♀ **Observation tips/habitat:** Occurs in a range of habitats mainly on trees (particularly oak) and bushes in woodland and hedgerows. Often found in similar habitats to *A. opisthographa*.

Description: CARAPACE ♀ yellow-brown and glossy. ♂ similar but with broad black marginal bands. ABDOMEN Apple green with paler whitish sides. Centrally, two pairs of black, depressed spots and posteriorly, at the sides, usually four or five pairs of black spots converging towards the spinnerets. There is a conspicuous red spot immediately above the spinnerets, only visible from below. LEGS ♀ as carapace. ♂ darker with black annulations around joints.

Similar species: Other *Araniella* species except *A. displicata*.

Distribution/Status: Common and widespread throughout much of England and Wales. More scattered in the west and less common in Scotland.

♂
♀
J F M A M J J A S O N D

LC   ## *Araniella opisthographa*   Cucumber spider   ☍   **Common, widespread**

♂3·5–4·0 mm   ♀4–6 mm   [SEE *A. cucurbitina*]

♂♀ **Observation tips/habitat:** Very similar to *A. cucurbitina* in general appearance and habitat preference.

Description: CARAPACE + ABDOMEN + LEGS
Very similar to *A. cucurbitina* (*above*).

Similar species: Other *Araniella* species except *A. displicata*.

Distribution/Status: Widespread and common in much of England, but less so than *A. cucurbitina*. Scarcer in Wales and Scotland.

♂
♀
J F M A M J J A S O N D

♀ *Araniella displicata* × **6**

Araniella cucurbitina or *opisthographa* × **6**

♂

♀

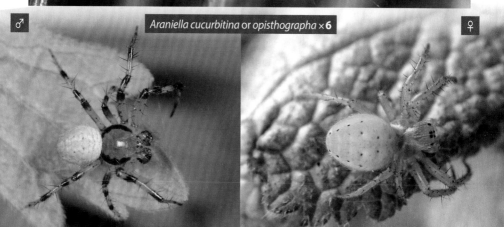

Araniella alpica Cucumber spider

♂ 4–5 mm ♀ 5–6 mm [NOT ILLUSTRATED]

Observation tips/habitat: Very similar to *A. cucurbitina* and *A. opisthographa* in general appearance. Occurs on trees and shrubs, typically Yew, Beech and Dogwood.

Description: CARAPACE + ABDOMEN + LEGS
Very similar to *A. cucurbitina* / *A. opisthographa* (*p. 190*).

Similar species: Other *Araniella* species except *A. displicata*.

Distribution/Status: Rare, only recorded from a few sites in southern England.

Nationally Rare

Rare, regional

♂ NO PHENOLOGY DATA
♀
J F M A M J J A S O N D

LC *Araniella inconspicua* Cucumber spider

♂ 4·0–4·5 mm ♀ 5 mm   [NOT ILLUSTRATED]

♂♀ **Observation tips/habitat:** Very similar to *A. cucurbitina* and *A. opisthographa* in general appearance. Occurs mostly on trees, especially oak and pine.

Description: CARAPACE + ABDOMEN + LEGS
Very similar to *A. cucurbitina* / *A. opisthographa* (*p.190*).

Similar species: Other *Araniella* species except *A. displicata*.

Distribution/Status: Scattered and very local distribution in southern England.

Nationally Scarce

Scarce, regional

♂
♀
J F M A M J J A S O N D

NT *Araniella displicata* 🔍

♂ 4–5 mm ♀ 5–11 mm   [PAGE 191 T]

♂♀ **Observation tips/habitat:** Differs from other *Araniella* species in its abdominal coloration and pattern. ♀ s can also be much larger. Occurs on trees, particularly pine.

Description: CARAPACE Reddish-brown. ABDOMEN Slightly pointed in front. Ground colour at sides varies from green to red. A dentated, white median band contains a series of markings, usually green anteriorly but becoming redder and decreasing in size towards the spinnerets. The whole dorsal area usually has a white border. LEGS Coloured as carapace, sometimes with darker annulations.

Similar species: None.

Distribution/Status: Rare, confined to a few sites in south-east England.

Nationally Rare

Rare, regional

♂
♀
J F M A M J J A S O N D

Zilla

🔍 **1 British species (illustrated)**

The single member of this genus is among the smaller araneids occurring in Britain. It has a **distinctively marked abdomen** which overhangs and sometimes completely obscures the carapace when the spider is seen hanging in the centre of the web awaiting prey. ♂ is similar to ♀.

LC ## *Zilla diodia* 🔍

Common, regional

♂ 2·0–2·5 mm ♀ 3–4 mm

Observation tips/habitat: Often occurs in rather dark, shaded situations amongst heather and the lower branches of trees and shrubs at the edge of clearings or rides in mixed woodland. Also found in old hedgerows, scrub near the coast and, occasionally, gardens. The web has a large, finely interwoven hub.

Description: CARAPACE Pale brown with darker 'V'-shaped mark delineating the head area, which has sparse covering of white hairs. ABDOMEN **Distinctive shape and markings**; triangular in shape and rather shiny. Anteriorly, a white, flattened, triangular shape is set against a dark background. Behind this is a pair of dark lozenge shapes and then a dark folium with white edging posteriorly. The whole is set against a silvery, reticulated background. LEGS Femora light brown with darker annulations. Other segments are darker with similar markings.

Similar species: None.

Distribution/Status: Restricted to southern England where it is frequent in parts of the south-east.

♂
♀
J F M A M J J A S O N D

♀ *Zilla diodia* × **6**

Hypsosinga

🔍 **4 British species (4 illustrated)**

All four *Hypsosinga* species are relatively small orb web spinners with a **shiny, oval abdomen marked with conspicuous, broad, longitudinal bands**. Webs are spun close to the ground. All the species are uncommon or rare; *H. pygmaea* is the one most likely to be encountered.

LC ## *Hypsosinga pygmaea*   🔍

Common, widespread

♂ 2·5–3·0 mm   ♀ 3·5–4·5 mm   [PAGE 195 T]

♂♀ **Observation tips/habitat:** *H. pygmaea* has a **very distinctive appearance** which can help with field identification. Occurs on low vegetation, often on chalk grassland and occasionally on damp areas of heathland and acid grassland.

Description: CARAPACE Brown to black. ABDOMEN **Dark brown to black with creamy-white longitudinal bands giving a conspicuous stripy appearance**. There is some variation in the amount of white colouring and some individuals, particularly ♂s, are completely black. LEGS Orange-brown with darkened femora I in ♂.

Similar species: None.

Distribution/Status: Widespread in much of southern Britain. Rarer in the north.

♂
♀
J F M A M J J A S O N D

H. albovittata, *H. sanguinea* and *H. heri* are very variable in pattern and colour. Even though there are certain pattern traits that give a good indication as to the species, microscopic examination of the genitalia (see *page 96*) is necessary to be completely sure of identification.

LC ## *Hypsosinga albovittata*   ⚲

Nationally Scarce

Scarce, widespread

♂ 2·2–3·0 mm   ♀ 2·5–3·0 mm   [PAGE 195 ML]

♂♀ **Observation tips/habitat:** Usually occurs on heathland but also recorded from chalk grassland. Web constructed less than 20 cm from ground level and has widely spaced spirals.

Description: CARAPACE Dark brown with paler head area and a white median band widening posteriorly. ABDOMEN Distinctive pattern comprising a white, reticulated median band (seemingly a continuation of the carapace median band when viewed from above) surrounded by a dark, broad, 'U'-shaped band with uneven edges. The sides of the abdomen are the same colour as the median band. LEGS Reddish-brown. ♂ femora I and II sometimes darker.

Similar species: *Hypsosinga sanguinea*, *H. heri* (both *p. 196*).

Distribution/Status: Scarce but widespread throughout Britain.

♂
♀
J F M A M J J A S O N D

♀ *Hypsosinga pygmaea* × **10**

♀ *Hypsosinga albovittata* × **10**

♀ *Hypsosinga sanguinea* × **10**

♀ *Hypsosinga heri* × **10**

LC *Hypsosinga sanguinea* 🔬

♂2·5–3·0mm ♀3–4mm [PAGE 195 MR]

♂♀ **Observation tips/habitat:** Very similar in appearance to
H. albovittata. Usually occurs on heathland in damp areas of
fairly mature heather.

Description: CARAPACE Similar to *H.albovittata* but perhaps
slightly paler. ABDOMEN Similar to *H. albovittata* but may
have greater contrast between the longitudinal bands.
LEGS Reddish-brown with all femora darkened to some
extent in ♂.

Similar species: *Hypsosinga albovittata* (p. 194), *H. heri* (below).

Distribution/Status: Uncommon and almost entirely
restricted to south-east England with just a few records
from the south-west and the Midlands.

Nationally Scarce

Scarce, regional

♂
♀
J F M A M J J A S O N D

VU *Hypsosinga heri* 🔬

♂2·0–2·5mm ♀3·5–4·5mm [PAGE 195 B]

♂♀ **Observation tips/habitat:** Thought to be extinct in Britain
but recently (2014) rediscovered at a wetland site on the
south coast where it occurs on low vegetation close to water.
Similar in appearance to *H. albovittata* and *H. sanguinea*.

Description: CARAPACE Reddish with dark markings centrally
and at the junction between the head and thoracic areas.
The head area can appear almost black, especially in ♂s.
ABDOMEN Similar general pattern to *H. albovittata* and
H. sanguinea but dark bands may be reddish-orange, and
white areas may also have an orange tinge. LEGS Reddish-brown.

Similar species: *Hypsosinga albovittata* (p. 194), *H. sanguinea*
(*above*).

Distribution/Status: Extremely rare.

Nationally Rare

Extremely rare

♂ NO PHENOLOGY DATA
♀
J F M A M J J A S O N D

Singa

🔍 **1 British species (illustrated)**

Similar to *Hypsosinga* (*p.194*) in general appearance and habitat but the webs are spun slightly higher above ground level. Also, compared to *Hypsosinga*, the single species that occurs in Britain has a **distinctive, more complex abdomen pattern.**

LC *Singa hamata* 🔍

Nationally Scarce

Scarce, local

♂3–4mm ♀5–6mm

Observation tips/habitat: Occurs on low vegetation in damp habitats. The spider spins a pinkish retreat for its egg-sacs close to the orb web.

Description: CARAPACE Dark brown with the head area often the darkest part. ABDOMEN **Distinctive pattern**; usually dark brown ground colour with a thin, white median line, strongly branched in the anterior half. The pattern and the extent of the white varies between individuals. LEGS Yellow-brown with darkening at joints.

Similar species: None.

Distribution/Status: Widely scattered throughout Britain but rather scarce.

♂
♀
J F M A M J J A S O N D

♀ *Singa hamata* ×**6**

Cercidia

🔍 **1 British species (illustrated)**

The general shape and reddish colouring of the single British species make the spider easily recognisable in the field. The vertical orb web has a hole at the hub where the spider sits, awaiting prey. Any slight disturbance of the web will cause the spider to fall to the ground.

LC *Cercidia prominens* 🔍

♂ 3–4 mm ♀ 3·5–5·0 mm

♂♀ **Observation tips/habitat:** Occurs on heathland and chalk grassland, often in sparsely vegetated areas. As with species in the *Hypsosinga* (*p. 194*) and *Singa* (*p. 197*) genera, the orb web is spun very close to the ground.

Description: CARAPACE Brown (of a darker shade than the abdomen) and covered with white bristles. ABDOMEN Orange to rusty-red but the depth of colour can vary. May have a vague pattern and, in darker specimens and ♂s, a pale, median stripe. The abdomen is oval in shape with the anterior noticeably pointed and overhanging the carapace. The anterior edge carries three or four short, stout spines on either side of the central point. A dorsal scutum is present (more obvious in ♂s). LEGS Coloured as carapace. ♂s have stout spines on tibiae II.

Similar species: None.

Distribution/Status: Generally scarce though widespread in central and southern Britain. Far fewer records from the south-west, Wales and Scotland.

Nationally Scarce

Scarce, widespread

♂
♀

J F M A M J J A S O N D

♂ | *Cercidia prominens* × **6** | ♀

Zygiella　Missing-sector orbweb spiders　 **2 British species (2 illustrated)**

These species spin **distinctive orb webs recognisable in the field**. One section in the upper part of the web is usually, but not always, open (*i.e.*. it does not contain spiral threads). Running through the centre of this empty section is a single thread leading from the hub to the spider's retreat at the edge of the web. The spider, sitting in this retreat, senses any prey caught in the web by holding onto this 'signal' line with the front legs. ♂s are similar to ♀s but slightly smaller. The two species are similar in appearance but have distinctly different habitats.

LC ## *Zygiella x-notata*　Missing-sector orbweb spider

Abundant, widespread

♂3·5–5·0 mm　♀6–7 mm

Observation tips/habitat: Almost always in association with human habitation, commonly spinning its web in the upper corners of door and window frames. Also found under gutters and on fences and sometimes ventures onto garden shrubs.

Description: CARAPACE Pale brown with darker head area. ABDOMEN Oval in shape with a large silvery-grey folium that has dark edges. Sides reddish-brown, though colour depth is variable. The **'shoulders' of the abdomen are slate grey**. LEGS Pale brown with faint darker markings.

Similar species: *Zygiella atrica* (*p. 200*), *Stroemiellus stroemi* (*p. 201*).

Distribution/Status: Very common and widespread.

♂
♀
J F M A M J J A S O N D

STROEMIELLUS + *ZYGIELLA* compared: *p. 201*

♀ *Zygiella x-notata* ×**6**

LC *Zygiella atrica*   Missing-sector orbweb spider   🔍

♂3·0–3·5 mm   ♀6·0–6·5 mm

Observation tips/habitat: Similar in appearance to *Z. x-notata* but not usually associated with buildings, although occasionally recorded from gardens. Occurs commonly on open ground, spinning its web in thorn bushes and gorse, but also recorded from heathland, on pine trunks and heather, and on rocks close to the sea.

Description: CARAPACE Pale brown with darker head area, similar to *Z. x-notata*. ♂ palpal segments are extremely long; the femur is almost as long as the carapace and very noticeable in the field. ABDOMEN Similar to *Z. x-notata* in shape and in having the sides a variable reddish-brown. The large, dark-edged **folium has a striking silvery inner area.** The 'shoulders' of the abdomen are distinctly pinkish-red. LEGS Similar to *Z. x-notata*.

Similar species: *Zygiella x-notata* (p. 199), *Stroemiellus stroemi* (p. 201).

Distribution/Status: Common and widespread.

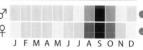

♂
♀
J F M A M J J A S O N D

♀ *Zygiella atrica* ×**6**

Stroemiellus

 1 British species (illustrated)

Until recently (2014) the single British *Stroemiellus* species was assigned to the genus *Zygiella* (*p. 199*) and is very similar to *Z. atrica* in appearance. It also spins the same type of orb web with an open section. **Habitat and abdominal pattern differences aid identification.**

NT *Stroemiellus stroemi*

Nationally Rare

Rare, regional

♂3.0–3.5mm ♀4.0–4.5mm

Observation tips/habitat: This seems to be one of the few British spiders exclusively associated with ancient trees. It spins its small, delicate web amongst fissures on the bark of ancient oak and pine and can be quite abundant in this specialized habitat.

Description: CARAPACE Similar to *Z. atrica*.
ABDOMEN Similar to *Z. atrica* but differs in the folium having a broader dark edge and a **central area that is brownish with pale patches.** The 'shoulders' of the abdomen are dark brown. LEGS Yellow with faint, darker annulations.

Similar species: *Zygiella x-notata* (*p. 199*), *Z. atrica* (*p. 200*).

Distribution/Status: Rare and very local in southern Britain and central Scotland.

♂ NO PHENOLOGY DATA
♀
J F M A M J J A S O N D

♀ *Stroemiellus stroemi* × **10**

Zygiella and *Stroemiellus* species – identification pointers				
SPECIES	ABDOMEN			HABITAT
	FOLIUM EDGES	FOLIUM CENTRE	'SHOULDERS'	
Z. x-notata	Dark	Silver-grey	Slate grey	Primarily buildings, can be in gardens
Z. atrica		Silver	Pinkish-red	Not buildings; primarily open ground, but occasionally in gardens
S. stroemi	Dark, broader than *Zygiella*	**Brownish with pale patches**	**Dark brown**	Ancient trees

Mangora

🔍 **1 British species (illustrated)**

The species found in Britain has a **distinctive appearance and should be recognizable in the field**. Sexes are similar but the ♂ is smaller.

LC *Mangora acalypha* 🔍

Common, regional

♂ 2·5–3·0 mm ♀ 3·5–4·0 mm

♂♀ **Observation tips/habitat:** Occurs on heathland and in open woodland, where it spins a densely woven orb web amongst low vegetation such as heather and gorse.

Description: CARAPACE Pear-shaped. Pale brown with a thin black border and thin black median band. ABDOMEN Reticulated greyish-white (can vary to pink) with a thin black median line in the anterior half. Posteriorly, three longitudinal bars often coalesce to form a dark rectangle, with the whole dark mark resembling a cricket bat. A curved, reddish band is often present crossing the anterior half of the abdomen. LEGS Pale yellow-brown, sometimes with darker annulations/spotting.

Similar species: None.

Distribution/Status: Widespread but patchy distribution in southern England (where it can be numerous) and south Wales.

♂
♀

J F M A M J J A S O N D

♀ *Mangora acalypha* × **6**

Cyclosa

👁 **1 British species (illustrated)**

The British species is **easily recognized in the field by the elongated hump at the rear of the abdomen. No other British spider has this abdominal shape.** The orb web often includes a stabilimentum which appears to provide camouflage for the spider sitting in the centre. This camouflage is further enhanced by the posture of the spider; with the legs folded up against the carapace edge it resembles a piece of detritus or discarded food.

.c *Cyclosa conica* 👁

Common, widespread

♂ 3·0–4·5 mm   ♀ 4·5–7·0 mm

Observation tips/habitat: Occurs on shrubs and trees, especially evergreens, in dark moist woodland and, surprisingly, also on heathland. The web is spun in dark, shady situations. Both ♂ and ♀ are very variable in pattern and colour; it is the abdominal shape that provides the most useful diagnostic feature.

Description: CARAPACE Black with white hairs, but normally covered by legs (see above). ABDOMEN Protuberance at rear of abdomen very conspicuous in ♀s, less so in ♂'s and absent in immatures. Pattern and colour are very variable but the general appearance is often quite attractive, particularly when bright colours such as orange, red or green are present. LEGS Fairly short, pale creamy-yellow. They may or may not have darker annulations.

♂
♀

J F M A M J J A S O N D

Similar species: None.

Distribution/Status: Widespread but fairly local in much of Britain. Rather more scattered in the west and north.

♂ | *Cyclosa conica* × **6** | ♀

Argiope

 1 British species (illustrated)

The ♀ of the *Argiope* species occurring in Britain is **large and has an unmistakable appearance.** It should not present any problems for field identification. The ♂, however, is much smaller and far less striking in appearance. The large orb web includes a zigzag band of silk – the stabilimentum. A substantial range extension of *A. bruennichi* in Britain during the present century is generally thought to be a result of climate change.

LC *Argiope bruennichi*   Wasp Spider

Common, regional

♂ 4·0–4·5 mm   ♀ 11–15 mm

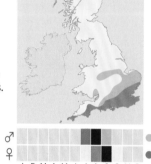

Observation tips/habitat: Occurs in areas of unmanaged grassland, wasteland and roadside verges. The large orb web is spun just above ground level in grass and other low vegetation and the adult spider is easily hidden by the surrounding herbage. The main food item is grasshoppers. A large urn-shaped egg-sac is positioned higher up in the vegetation.

Description: CARAPACE Pale yellow with faint, darker markings. The whole carapace is thickly covered with fine, grey, silky hairs. ABDOMEN ♀ has transverse yellow and white bands edged in black with additional black horizontal bars – the whole giving a distinctly striped, wasp-like appearance. ♂ has no stripes but instead is pale brown with two vague, longitudinal bands. LEGS Pale yellow-brown with darker annulations.

♂
♀

J F M A M J J A S O N D

Similar species: None.

Distribution/Status: Widespread along the south coast and in south-east England, with recent scattered records as far north as the east Midlands. Northward spread may well continue.

♂ *Argiope bruennichi* × **6**

♀ *Argiope bruennichi* ×**6**

LYCOSIDAE Wolf spiders

8 British genera

Spiders in this family are commonly known as wolf spiders. The arrangement of their eight eyes is quite distinctive. When viewed from in front, they can appear as three rows; a line of four small eyes anteriorly, a pair of larger eyes above these on the vertical front of the head area, and farther back a pair of posterior eyes widely spaced on each side of the head area. They do not spin webs to catch prey but, instead, use their well-developed eyesight to hunt their prey down, running rapidly across the ground, often in warm sunny conditions.

The females of many species carry their egg-sac around with them attached to the spinnerets at the rear of the abdomen. When the young emerge they climb onto their mother's back and are carried around with her for a few days before they disperse. Some lycosid genera, particularly *Pardosa* and *Trochosa*, contain species that are very similar to each other. This and the variability of appearance within individual species make field identification almost impossible. Even with the use of a microscope, identification can be extremely difficult.

Pardosa species – identification pointers

SPECIES	LEG ANNULATION	CARAPACE MEDIAN BAND	LATERAL BAND	TYPICAL HABITAT
P. prativaga*		Yellowish brown (ill-defined in ♀); dilated behind eyes and tapering towards posterior	Yellowish brown (ill-defined in ♀); usually broken	WIDE RANGE
P. saltans**	Clear	Whitish-grey; broad around eyes and tapering towards posterior	Two narrow bands on each margin - inner broken, outer continuous	Overmature woodland
P. lugubris**				Ancient woodland
P. amentata*	Clear on ♀; less so on ♂	Yellowish-brown; dilated behind eyes and tapering towards posterior	Broken and/or with dentate inner edge	WIDE RANGE
P. agricola*	Clear on femora and tibiae; less so on other segments	Yellow; well defined, generally narrow but dilated behind the eyes and midway in ♀	Broken	Shingle on coasts, stream and river banks
P. hortensis*		Pale brown, broad around eyes and tapering towards posterior		Open habitats
P. proxima*	Very vague on inner segments	Yellow, rather short and tapering at each end	Yellow broken into three sections	Moist habitats near streams and on coast
P. agrestis*		Yellowish, narrow	Yellowish, continuous	Thinly vegetated dry areas
P. monticola**	Present but sometimes obscure	Yellowish-brown, broad	Yellowish-brown, continuous	Open grassland, heath
P. palustris**				Dry grassland, heath
P. pullata*		Yellowish-brown (ill-defined in ♀) dilated behind eyes and tapering towards posterior	Yellowish brown (ill-defined in ♀) Either continuous or broken	WIDE RANGE
P. trailli*		Very obscure (whole spider very dark)		Mountains – loose scree
P. paludicola*		Greyish-brown, broad around eyes and tapering towards posterior	Continuous, dentated	Long grass – woodland glades and fenland
P. nigriceps*	None	Yellow, dilated behind eyes and tapering towards posterior	Yellow, continuous	Low vegetation and bushes
P. purbeckensis*		Yellowish, narrow	Yellowish, continuous	Saltmarsh, tidal habitat

* Microscopic examination of genitalia (see *page 96*) is required for safe identification.

** Can only be distinguished by microscopic examination of the genitalia (see *page 96*).

Pardosa

 15 British species (15 illustrated)

Probably the commonest lycosid and certainly the most likely to be seen. **Head elevated and, when viewed from the front, has almost vertical sides**. Generally brown in colour with darker or paler markings, but variable between individuals of the same species. **Legs IV noticeably longer than the others**. Females carry eggs around in an egg-sac that is **greenish-blue with a whitish seam**.

LC *Pardosa monticola*

Common, widespread

♂ 4·0–5·5 mm ♀ 4–6 mm   [PAGE 208 TL]

Observation tips/habitat: *P. monticola* is usually found in well-established open areas of grassland and heath, often sparsely vegetated. Its general colouring can be very variable, ranging from light brown to black but contrasting colours on the carapace are distinctive.

Description: CARAPACE Similar to the form of *P. agrestis* with a thin yellowish-brown median band. The thin lateral bands have a similar colour and are usually clearly defined. The whole carapace is edged with a thin, dark line. ABDOMEN Variable in depth of colour and pattern but usually with a clear cardiac mark which is paler than the rest of the abdomen. LEGS As with other members of the genus, the legs are pale to mid-brown with black streaks and mottling, more so on femora than other segments.

Similar species: All other *Pardosa* species, particularly *P. palustris* (*below*), *P. agrestis*, *P. purbeckensis* (both *p. 210*).

Distribution/Status: Widespread but locally distributed.

♂
♀
J F M A M J J A S O N D

LC *Pardosa palustris*

Common, widespread

♂ 4·5–5·5 mm ♀ 4·5–6·0 mm   [PAGE 208 MR]

Observation tips/habitat: *P. palustris* is often indistinguishable in general appearance from *P. monticola* in the field and is found in similar habitats, although it seems to prefer drier, heathland conditions.

Description: CARAPACE Very similar to *P. monticola*. Median band sometimes dilated as in the *P. agrestis* form. ABDOMEN + LEGS Very similar to *P. monticola*.

Similar species: All other *Pardosa* species, particularly *P. monticola* (*above*), *P. agrestis*, *P. purbeckensis* (both *p. 210*).

Distribution/Status: Common and widespread.

♂
♀
J F M A M J J A S O N D

♀ *Pardosa monticola* with egg-sac × **4**

♀ *Pardosa nigriceps* × **4**

♀ *Pardosa agrestis* with egg-sac × **4**

♀ *Pardosa palustris* × **4**

♀ *Pardosa purbeckensis* × **4**

♀ *Pardosa pullata* with egg-sac × **4**

♀ *Pardosa prativaga* with egg-sac × **4**

♂   *Pardosa amentata* × **4**   ♀

♂   *Pardosa trailli* × **4**   ♀

LC *Pardosa agrestis*

♂4.5–7.0 mm ♀6–9 mm [PAGE 208 ML]

Nationally Scarce

Scarce, local

Observation tips/habitat: Occurs in a variety of habitats, ♂♀ predominantly on thinly vegetated substrates and in clay pits and chalk pits, but also on dry banks above saltmarshes and flood-plain meadows.

Description: CARAPACE In both ♀ and ♂ the yellowish median and lateral bands contrast strongly with a dark brown ground colour. Median band is often dilated as in *P. agricola* (*p. 215*) but occasionally is uniformly thin. ABDOMEN ♀ and ♂ both brown with a paler cardiac mark. Obscure patterns may be present. The posterior half may have two rows of indistinct white spots converging towards the spinnerets. LEGS In ♀ slightly paler colour than abdomen with black streaking on femora; other segments annulated. ♂ femora similar to ♀ but other segments not annulated.

♂
♀
J F M A M J J A S O N D

Similar species: All other *Pardosa* species, particularly *P. purbeckensis* (below), *P. palustris, P. monticola* (both *p. 207*).

Distribution/Status: Largely restricted to southern England but with scattered records elsewhere.

LC *Pardosa purbeckensis*

♂6–7 mm ♀7–9 mm [PAGE 208 B]

Uncommon, local

Observation tips/habitat: Occurs on saltmarsh and other ♂♀ tidal habitats. Until recently *P. purbeckensis* and *P. agrestis* were thought to be varieties of the same species. However habitat and courtship behaviour preferences suggest not.

Description: CARAPACE Very similar to the form of *P. agrestis* with thin median band and lateral bands contrasting with the ground colour. ABDOMEN Similar to *P. agrestis*. The rows of white spots may be clearer. LEGS Similar to *P. agrestis*.

Similar species: All other *Pardosa* species, particularly *P. agrestis* (*above*), *P. palustris, P. monticola* (both *p. 207*).

Distribution/Status: Widespread on coasts of Britain.

♂
♀
J F M A M J J A S O N D

LC *Pardosa nigriceps* ♀

Abundant, widespread

♂4–5mm ♀5–7mm   [PAGE 208 TR]

Observation tips/habitat: This is the only *Pardosa* species found above ground level, frequenting low vegetation and bushes. It occurs in a wide variety of habitats including grasslands, heathland, woodland clearings and road verges.

Description: CARAPACE Longer than other *Pardosa* species. ♀ dark brown with clear yellow median and lateral bands. ♂ is similar with white hairs on the head area and with the median and lateral bands less striking. ♂ palps are densely covered with black hairs. ABDOMEN ♀ has a typical *Pardosa* pattern, dark brown on yellowish-brown background. ♂ is generally darker. LEGS ♀ & ♂ yellowish-brown with some dark streaking on the femora.

Similar species: All other *Pardosa* species.

Distribution/Status: Abundant and widespread.

♂
♀
J F M A M J J A S O N D

LC *Pardosa pullata* ♀

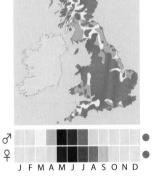

Abundant, widespread

♂4–5mm ♀4–6mm   [PAGE 209 TL]

Observation tips/habitat: One of the commonest *Pardosa* species in Britain. Often found running over sunlit ground in a wide variety of habitats including grasslands, heathland, moorland, woodland rides and brownfield sites.

Description: CARAPACE ♀ dark brown with ill-defined yellowish-brown median and lateral bands. ♂ dark brown with a clear, yellowish-brown median band. ABDOMEN ♀ & ♂ ground colour as carapace. Ill-defined pattern may be present in ♀. ♂ has a pale cardiac mark with a slightly clearer pattern. LEGS ♀ & ♂ very pale brown apart from slightly darker femora. No annulations, though sometimes with dark speckles.

Similar species: All other *Pardosa* species, particularly *P. prativaga*, *P. amentata* (both *p. 212*), *P. trailli*, *P. hortensis* (both *p. 213*).

Distribution/Status: Abundant and widespread.

♂
♀
J F M A M J J A S O N D

LC *Pardosa prativaga*

♂4–5mm ♀4–6mm　　　　　　　　[PAGE 209 TR]

♂♀ **Observation tips/habitat:** A common *Pardosa* species very similar to *P. pullata* in appearance (though *P. pullata* lacks leg annulations) and often occurring with it in suitable habitats.

Description: CARAPACE + ABDOMEN Very similar to *P. pullata*. LEGS Clearly annulated in both sexes.

Similar species: All other *Pardosa* species, particularly *P. pullata* (*p. 211*), *P. amentata* (*below*), *P. trailli*, *P. hortensis* (both *p. 213*).

Distribution/Status: Common and widespread, though much more localized in Scotland.

♂
♀
J F M A M J J A S O N D

LC *Pardosa amentata*

♂5·0–6·5mm ♀5·5–8·0mm　　　　　　[PAGE 209 M]

♂♀ **Observation tips/habitat:** *P. amentata* is similar to *P. pullata* and *P. prativaga* and is equally common in a wide range of habitats. Usually the commonest *Pardosa* species found in gardens.

Description: CARAPACE ♀ with a dark brown ground colour and a paler yellow-brown median band of variable width. Lateral bands of same colour have dentate inner edges. ♂ is much darker than ♀ and has palps thickly covered with black hairs. ABDOMEN ♀ & ♂ olive-brown with a slightly paler median band, edged with black marks and tapering towards the spinnerets. LEGS ♀ clearly annulated, ♂ less so.

Similar species: All other *Pardosa* species, particularly *P. pullata* (*p. 211*), *P. trailli*, *P. hortensis* (both *p. 213*), *P. prativaga* (*above*).

Distribution/Status: Abundant and widespread.

♂
♀
J F M A M J J A S O N D

VU *Pardosa trailli*

Nationally Rare

Rare, regional

♂6·5–7·0 mm ♀7·0–8·5 mm   [PAGE 209 B]

Observation tips/habitat: This is a montane species particularly favouring areas of loose scree. It is similar to *P. amentata* in general appearance but is usually darker and larger.

Description: CARAPACE Very dark in both sexes with very obscure banding, often impossible to see. ABDOMEN Similar to carapace with typical *Pardosa* abdominal pattern very obscure. LEGS ♀ dark brown with random black markings on femora and faint annulations on remaining segments. ♂ generally light brown, apart from dark femora, with very indistinct markings.

Similar species: All other *Pardosa* species, particularly *P. amentata*, *P. prativaga*, (both *p. 212*), *P. pullata* (*p. 211*), *P. hortensis* (*below*).

Distribution/Status: Rare and very local in mountainous areas of Wales, the Lake District and Scotland.

♂
♀
J F M A M J J A S O N D

LC *Pardosa hortensis*

Uncommon, regional

♂3·5–4·5 mm ♀4·5–6·0 mm   [PAGE 214 TR]

Observation tips/habitat: This is the smallest member of the genus in Britain and occurs in open habitats such as woodland clearings, heathland, sand pits and the seashore. The spider is similar to *P. amentata* but the markings are less distinct.

Description: CARAPACE ♀ greyish-brown with paler median band which is deeply indented in the anterior third and tapers to a point at the rear. The lateral bands are broken and rather obscure. ♂ is darker. ABDOMEN ♀ typical *Pardosa* pattern but very indistinct. ♂ darker. LEGS ♀ rather pale with clear, dark annulations on the femora and tibiae, less so on other segments. ♂ similar but less distinct.

Similar species: All other *Pardosa* species, particularly *P. pullata* (*p. 211*), *P. prativaga*, *P. amentata* (both *p. 212*), *P. trailli* (*above*).

Distribution/Status: Most frequent in southern England; occurs throughout but rare in Scotland.

♂
♀
J F M A M J J A S O N D

213

♀ *Pardosa agricola* × **4**

♀ *Pardosa hortensis* × **4**

♂   *Pardosa saltans* × **4**

♀ with egg-sac in chelicereae

♀ *Pardosa lugubris* with egg-sac × **4**

♀ *Pardosa proxima* × **4**

Pardosa agricola

♂4·5–6·5mm ♀5·5–8·0mm   [PAGE 214 TL]

Uncommon, widespread

Observation tips/habitat: Favours shingle in coastal areas and on the banks of streams and rivers. Occasionally also recorded from sand dunes.

Description: CARAPACE ♀ brown with a pale median band of varying width (widest behind eyes and midway) and broken lateral bands. ♂ is darker with less clear markings. ABDOMEN ♀ greyish–brown with a vague pattern. A paler cardiac mark is usually present within an ill-defined median band which usually runs along the whole length. ♂'s generally darker with the markings less clear. LEGS ♀ clearly annulated. ♂ less so.

Similar species: All other *Pardosa* species.

Distribution/Status: Widespread in northern England and Scotland but less so farther south, with very few records away from the coast in southern England.

♂
♀
J F M A M J J A S O N D

Pardosa proxima

♂4·5–5·0mm ♀5·5–6·5mm   [PAGE 214 BR]

Nationally Scarce

Scarce, regional

Observation tips/habitat: A species favouring damp habitats, typically along stream-sides and at coastal sites.

Description: CARAPACE ♀ dark brown with yellow median and lateral bands, the latter broken into three sections. The median band tapers at both ends and is rather short. ♂ is similar but darker. ABDOMEN ♀ ground colour as carapace with a distinct yellow cardiac mark. ♂ is similar but darker. LEGS ♀ yellowish with annulations outwards to the tibiae. In ♂ usually only the femora are annulated.

Similar species: All other *Pardosa* species.

Distribution/Status: Locally distributed in southern England and Wales.

♂
♀
J F M A M J J A S O N D

Pardosa saltans LC

♂4–5mm ♀5–6mm   [PAGE 214 M]

Observation tips/habitat: Very much a woodland spider largely restricted to over-mature and ancient woodland sites and occasionally nearby grassland and hedgerows. It can be numerous, running over the ground in open clearings as well as amongst litter within the shade of the wood.

Description: CARAPACE ♀ dark brown to black with a fairly broad whitish median band which tapers towards rear. In ♂'s the median band of thick white hairs is almost parallel-sided and very conspicuous in living spiders – similar to that of *Xerolycosa nemoralis*. ABDOMEN Dark brown in both ♀ & ♂ with a typical *Pardosa* pattern similar to *P. amentata* (*p. 212*), but often quite obscure. LEGS Pale brown. ♀ has distinct annulations, ♂ has darkened femora.

Similar species: All other *Pardosa* species, particularly *P. lugubris* (*below*), *Xerolycosa nemoralis* (*p. 219*).

Distribution/Status: Common and widespread throughout England and Wales, less so in Scotland.

Common, widespread

♂
♀

J F M A M J J A S O N D

Pardosa lugubris LC

♂4–5mm ♀5–6mm   [PAGE 214 BL]

Observation tips/habitat: A rare spider associated with ancient woodland sites where it can be quite abundant. Indistinguishable in general appearance from *P. saltans* in the field. Until 2000, it was identified, together with *P. saltans,* as one species – *Pardosa lugubris.*

Description: CARAPACE + ABDOMEN + LEGS Very similar to *P. saltans.*

Similar species: All other *Pardosa* species, particularly *P. saltans* (*above*), *Xerolycosa nemoralis* (*p. 219*).

Distribution/Status: Scarce. Largely restricted to Caledonian pine forest in Scotland. One record from northern England.

Nationally Scarce

Scarce, regional

♂
♀

J F M A M J J A S O N D

EN *Pardosa paludicola*

Nationally Rare

Extremely rare

♂7 mm ♀8–9 mm

Observation tips/habitat: The largest of the *Pardosa* species found in Britain and probably the rarest. Similar to *P. amentata* (*p. 212*) but much darker and larger. Associated with long grass in woodland glades and around wooded areas on fens.

Description: CARAPACE ♀ dark brown to black with lighter bands. The median band is wider behind the head area and the narrow lateral bands are dentated without breaks. ♂ is similar to ♀, but paler. ABDOMEN ♀ dark brown with a very obscure pattern. A darker edging to the cardiac mark is sometimes present. At first glance the whole abdomen can appear black. ♂ is similar to ♀, but paler. LEGS ♀ similar colour to rest of body with scattered dark marks. ♂ much paler than ♀ with slightly darker femora.

Similar species: All other *Pardosa* species.

Distribution/Status: Extremely rare. Widely scattered records in southern England and Wales but found at only two of these sites in the last 30 years.

♂
♀
J F M A M J J A S O N D

♀ *Pardosa paludicola* ×**4**

Hygrolycosa

🔍 **1 British species (illustrated)**

The *Hygrolycosa* genus is represented by just one species in Europe. It is similar to *Pardosa* (p. 207) but the **legs are less spiny** and both **legs and carapace have a glossy appearance**. Like *Pardosa*, the head is elevated but, when viewed from the front, **has more sloping sides**. In contrast to *Pardosa*, the egg-sac is **beige with a white seam**.

EN *Hygrolycosa rubrofasciata* 🔍

Nationally Rare

Extremely rare

♂5·0–5·5mm ♀5·5–6·0mm

Observation tips/habitat: Both sexes have an unmistakable appearance with distinctly contrasting dark and pale markings. Usually found on the ground in damp areas of woodland and fenland.

Description: CARAPACE ♀ median, pale brown band extends the whole length of carapace and is flanked by wide, dark brown parallel bands. Outside these are wide, lateral, pale brown bands each containing a line of dark spots. The whole carapace is edged with a thin dark line. ♂ is similar to ♀ but darker. ABDOMEN ♀ reddish-brown with a faint pattern containing a paler cardiac mark and pairs of white spots in the posterior half. ♂ is similar to ♀ but darker. LEGS ♀ inner segments, outwards to the patellae, are pale yellow with distinct, dark brown mottling. The outer segments are darker with no mottling. ♂ inner segments, outwards to the patellae, are very dark brown with obscure markings; the remainder are pale brown.

Similar species: None.

Distribution/Status: Very rare and locally distributed.

J F M A M J J A S O N D

♂ | *Hygrolycosa rubrofasciata* × **6** | ♀

Xerolycosa

🔍 **2 British species (2 illustrated)**

Xerolycosa spiders are similar in appearance to *Pardosa* (*p. 207*) but the **head area is not as elevated or straight-sided**. The carapace bands partly consist of white hairs; with lateral bands only present in the rear half. The ♂ is paler and more clearly marked than the ♀. Both species favour dry habitats. Microscopic examination of the genitalia (see *page 96*) is required to identify the species.

LC

Xerolycosa nemoralis

Nationally Scarce

Scarce, regional

♂ 4·5–6·0 mm   ♀ 4·5–7·5 mm

Observation tips/habitat: Occurs on sparsely vegetated ground, including in woodland clearings, chalk grassland, burnt heathland and brownfield sites. Both sexes are of a pinkish hue.

Description: CARAPACE Both sexes almost black with a clear median band of pinkish-white hairs, widest behind the eyes, similar to *Pardosa saltans*. Lateral bands are also composed of white hairs, which can wear away. ABDOMEN ♀ mottled pinkish-grey with dark patches on the 'shoulders' and a conspicuous tuft of white hairs at the apex of the abdomen. The whole abdomen is covered with patches of white hair. ♂ similar to ♀ apart from a pale brown ground colour and two rows of white spots converging towards the spinnerets in the rear half.
LEGS ♀ dark pinkish-brown with clear annulations on femora. ♂ pale grey with a conspicuous covering of white hairs on the tibiae of the forelegs.

♂
♀

J F M A M J J A S O N D

Similar species: *Xerolycosa miniata* (*p. 219*), *Pardosa saltans* and *P. lugubris* (both *p. 216*).

Distribution/Status: Scarce, but can be locally abundant. Mainly in south-east England.

♀ *Xerolycosa nemoralis* × **6**

219

LC *Xerolycosa miniata*

Nationally Scarce

Scarce, local

♂4·5–5·5mm ♀5·5–6·5mm

Observation tips/habitat: Almost exclusively a coastal species in Britain. Its speckled, sandy appearance gives it excellent camouflage in its favoured habitat of dry, fixed sand dunes.

Description: CARAPACE ♀ brown with a paler median band covered in white hairs and constricted at the midpoint. The paleness of the lateral bands is partly a result of being covered with white hairs. ♂ is similar to ♀ but lighter and with clearer markings. ABDOMEN Paler than the carapace. A lighter central band has, on either side, a row of widely spaced dots composed of white hairs, with a faint white line connecting each pair. ♂ as ♀. LEGS ♀ brown; the femora and tibiae have darker annulations. ♂ is similar to ♀ but with white hairs on tibiae I & II.

Similar species: *Xerolycosa nemoralis* (*p. 219*), *Pardosa saltans* and *P. lugubris* (both *p. 216*).

Distribution/Status: Local in coastal dune systems throughout Britain.

♂
♀

J F M A M J J A S O N D

♂ *Xerolycosa miniata* × **4** ♀

Alopecosa

🔍 **4 British species (4 illustrated)**

These are all fairly large, robust spiders. The **clear median band on the carapace and the distinctive abdominal cardiac mark** are characteristic of the genus. The female digs a burrow where she remains with her egg-sac. *Alopecosa* species are variable and, aside from the generally larger size of *A. fabrilis* and the swollen dark tibia I of *A. cuneata*, microscopic examination of the genitalia (see *page 96*) is necessary to separate the species.

LC *Alopecosa pulverulenta* 🔬

Abundant, widespread

♂5–8mm ♀6·5–10·0mm   [PAGE 223 TL]

Observation tips/habitat: In a range of open habitats including heathland, grassland, cultivated land and urban gardens.

Description: CARAPACE Dark brown to black with a clear, pale, median band (almost white in ♂). Pale lateral bands are faint and may be absent. ABDOMEN Reddish-brown with a paler central band which tapers and darkens towards the spinnerets. Within this band is a dark cardiac stripe edged with black. In ♂ the pattern is clearer. LEGS ♀ brown with faint annulations on the femora. ♂ is similar to ♀ apart from legs I & II, which have the femora and tibiae dark brown to black, with the remainder pale yellow.

Similar species: *Alopecosa cuneata* (*below*), *A. barbipes* (*p. 222*).

♂
♀
J F M A M J J A S O N D

Distribution/Status: Abundant and widespread throughout Britain.

LC *Alopecosa cuneata* 🔬

Nationally Scarce

Scarce, regional

♂6·0–7·5mm ♀6–8mm   [PAGE 223 TR]

Observation tips/habitat: Similar to *A. pulverulenta* but more closely associated with old grassland and dunes, often in calcareous areas.

Description: CARAPACE Similar to *A. pulverulenta* but the lateral bands are more clearly defined. ABDOMEN A similar pattern to *A. pulverulenta* but the contrast between the dark and light areas is much more obvious and distinct. LEGS Yellowish-brown with far fewer dark markings than *A. pulverulenta*, apart from ♂, **which has clearly swollen dark tibiae on leg I. These are obvious in the field.**

Similar species: *Alopecosa pulverulenta* (*above*), *A. barbipes* (*p. 222*).

♂
♀
J F M A M J J A S O N D

Distribution/Status: Scarce and local in lowlands of southern England.

LC *Alopecosa barbipes* ◆

Uncommon, widespread

♂7·5–9·0mm ♀8–12mm   [PAGE 223 M]

Observation tips/habitat: Similar to *A. pulverulenta* but larger. Favours thinly vegetated ground on open heathland and unimproved chalk grassland.

Description: CARAPACE ♂ and ♀ dark brown with light median band of uneven width, in ♂ covered in white hairs. Pale brown lateral bands extend round sides of ocular area. ABDOMEN Pale median band contains distinct dark cardiac stripe on either side of which are two thin black lines extending obliquely backwards. LEGS ♀ brown with clear annulations on femora. ♂ brown with no annulations but tibia and metatarsus of forelegs black with dense covering of black hairs on underside.

Similar species: *Alopecosa fabrilis* (below), *A. pulverulenta*, *A. cuneata* (both *p. 221*).

Distribution/Status: Widely distributed throughout Britain but rather local.

♂
♀

J F M A M J J A S O N D

CR *Alopecosa fabrilis*

Biodiversity List (En)
Nationally Rare

Extremely rare

♂10–12mm ♀13–16mm   [PAGE 223 B]

Observation tips/habitat: The largest of the *Alopecosa* species in Britain, distinguishing it from other *Alopecosa*. It is also the rarest, having been found at only three dry heathland sites in southern England, and last recorded in 1990. The general pattern of *A. fabrilis* is similar to *A. barbipes* but the spider itself is usually darker and sometimes has a greyish appearance. The ♂ has lighter areas covered with white hairs.

Description: CARAPACE Both ♂ and ♀ are dark brown with clear, paler, greyish median and lateral bands. ABDOMEN Similar to *A. barbipes* but with clearer white markings and darker ground colour. LEGS ♀ femora with faint annulations, sometimes with large dark spots; the remainder are unmarked. Noticeably long in ♂ and covered with white hairs apart from the outer segments.

Similar species: *Alopecosa pulverulenta*, *A. cuneata* (both *p. 221*) and *A. barbipes* (*above*), which is noticeably smaller.

Distribution/Status: Extremely rare.

NO PHENOLOGY DATA

♀ *Alopecosa pulverulenta* × **6**

♂ *Alopecosa cuneata* × **6**

♀ *Alopecosa barbipes* × **4**

♀ *Alopecosa fabrilis* × **4**

General appearance can vary from light brownish-grey (as illustrated) to a much darker shade

223

Trochosa

 4 British species (4 illustrated)

Large, robust spiders which are generally brown in colour (never black). **The pale brown median band is wider in the anterior half of the carapace and contains two short, dark stripes.** *Trochosa* are nocturnal spiders actively hunting for prey on the ground. Females excavate a short burrow where they remain during the day with their egg-sacs. Males can occasionally be found moving amongst the undergrowth during daylight hours.

LC *Trochosa ruricola* ♀

Common, widespread

♂7–9mm ♀9–14mm [PAGE 225 T]

Observation tips/habitat: Often under logs and stones in damp grassland, marshland and ditch margins.

♂♀ **Description:** CARAPACE ♀ dark brown with a paler median band containing dark streaks. The lateral bands are thin and pale. In ♂, very dark brown with thinner lateral bands than ♀. ABDOMEN ♀ grey-brown with paler cardiac mark contrasting clearly with the rest of the abdomen. The cardiac mark can appear as a continuation of the median carapace band. ♂ similar to ♀ but darker, making the pale cardiac mark more obvious. LEGS Greyish-brown apart from the tibiae, tarsi and metatarsi I of ♂, which are dark brown and are used in courtship.

Similar species: *Trochosa robusta* (*below*).

Distribution/Status: Widespread and common throughout southern Britain, generally at low altitudes. Less frequent in the north.

♂
♀
J F M A M J J A S O N D

VU *Trochosa robusta* ♀

Nationally Rare

Rare, regional

♂9–18mm ♀11–20mm [PAGE 225 B]

Observation tips/habitat: Very similar to *T. ruricola* though much rarer. It is found mainly on stony, chalk grassland, particularly on cliff tops and undercliffs. **It differs from *T. ruricola* in its size and habitat.**

♂♀ **Description:** CARAPAC + ABDOMEN + LEGS Both sexes very similar to *T. ruricola*.

Similar species: *Trochosa ruricola* (*above*).

Distribution/Status: Rare, restricted to a few sites in southern England.

♂
♀
J F M A M J J A S O N D

The four species are very similar and microscopic examination of the genitalia (see *page 96*) is is essential for reliable identification. However, they can be separated into two groups according to the colour of the cardiac mark. The groups are: *Trochosa ruricola/T. robusta* (cardiac mark paler than rest of abdomen); and *Trochosa terricola/T. spinipalpis* (cardiac mark same colour as rest of abdomen). Habitat preferences are also helpful in determining species.

♀ *Trochosa ruricola* × **4**

♀ *Trochosa robusta* × **4**

☒ *Trochosa terricola* ☽

♂7–9mm ♀7–14mm [PAGE 227 TL]

Abundant, widespread

Observation tips/habitat: The commonest species in the genus. Occurs in a wide range of habitats including woodland, grassland, heathland and brownfield sites under logs and stones. In contrast to *T. ruricola* (*p. 224*) it prefers drier conditions and can be common in upland areas.

Description: CARAPACE Dark brown with reddish-brown median and lateral bands, the latter slightly wider than in *T. ruricola*. ABDOMEN Reddish brown with indistinct markings. The cardiac mark is the same colour as the rest of the abdomen. LEGS Reddish-brown with faintly annulated femora. In ♂ the tibiae and metatarsi are darker.

Similar species: *Trochosa spinipalpis* (*below*).

Distribution/Status: Abundant and widespread throughout Britain.

♂
♀
J F M A M J J A S O N D

☒ *Trochosa spinipalpis* ◆ ☽

♂8–10mm ♀9–11mm [PAGE 227 TR]

Nationally Scarce

Scarce, widespread

Observation tips/habitat: Very similar in appearance to *T. terricola* but favours much damper habitats, such as bogs, wet heathland, damp meadows, fens and marshland. Much less common than *T. terricola* but past misidentifications may be responsible for some dubious records.

Description: CARAPACE Very similar to *T. terricola*. ABDOMEN Very similar to *T. terricola* but **abdomen is coloured a deeper brown, often with a reddish tinge**. LEGS Very similar to *T. terricola*.

Similar species: *Trochosa terricola* (*above*).

Distribution/Status: Widespread but scarce with a scattered distribution.

♂
♀
J F M A M J J A S O N D

♀ *Trochosa terricola* × **4**

♀ *Trochosa spinipalpis* × **4**

Aulonia

🔍 **1 British species (illustrated)**

The single species of *Aulonia* is superficially similar to other lycosid genera, but its **characteristic appearance** allows identification in the field. The sexes are similar.

CR *Aulonia albimana* 🔍

Nationally Rare

Extremely rare

♂ 3·0–3·5 mm ♀ 3·5–4·5 mm

Observation tips/habitat: Occurs in grassland in sheltered spots exposed to the sun. Known from only one site in Britain.

Description: CARAPACE Dark brown with black mottling and thin white marginal bands. The white patellae of the pedipalps contrast markedly with remaining black pedipalp segments and with the femora of the forelegs. Without the white patellae rather similar to *Pirata latitans*. ABDOMEN Dark brown, almost black in ♂, with a thin, light cardiac stripe. LEGS Yellowish-brown apart from the black femora of the forelegs.

Similar species: Could be confused with *Pirata latitans* (p. 233).

Distribution/Status: Extremely rare. Known only from the Isle of Wight, where it was last recorded in the 1980s.

J F M A M J J A S O N D

♀ *Aulonia albimana* × **6**

The white patella of the pedipalp readily separates *Aulonia albimana* from *Pirata latitans*

227

Arctosa

🔍 **5 British species (5 illustrated)**

Arctosa species differ from other lycosids in having **no clearly defined median band on the carapace**. The legs are usually marked with black annulations or spots and differences between the sexes are very slight. Habitat preferences are helpful in suggesting species.

LC *Arctosa perita* 🔍 **Common, widespread**

♂ 6·5–9·0 mm ♀ 6·5–9·0 mm

♂♀ **Observation tips/habitat:** By far the commonest species in the genus. Its colouring can be made up of a mixture of black, brown, pink, yellow and cream markings – aiding its camouflage, particularly on a sandy substrate. It usually occurs on dry, sandy soils on heathland or coastal dunes, where it makes a burrow. On burnt areas of heathland the spider may be almost completely black. Both sexes can frequently be seen moving around rapidly, particularly in sunny conditions.

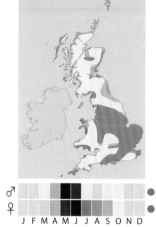

Description: CARAPACE Ground colour varies from brown to grey, occasionally to black. The posterior eyes have small patches of white hairs to the sides and the rear. White hairs also make up broken lateral bands in the rear half of the carapace. Centrally, dark streaks radiate from the fovea. ABDOMEN The background colour is brown, with paler sides. Usually a greyish cardiac mark is present, flanked by two pinkish-white patches with smaller white spots behind. This pattern is repeated in the posterior half of the abdomen on either side of a pale brown median band. LEGS Pale with very clear, dark annulations.

♂
♀
J F M A M J J A S O N D

Similar species: None.

Distribution/Status: Widespread in coastal areas throughout Britain. Its inland distribution is scattered according to suitable habitat.

♀ *Arctosa perita* × **4**

LC *Arctosa cinerea* 🔍

♂12–14mm ♀12–17mm

♂♀

Observation tips/habitat: One of Britain's largest spiders, *Arctosa cinerea* has a very specialized habitat among stones in riverbeds and lakes. Here it constructs a silk-lined burrow under stones where it may be submerged for long periods during flooding. The whole animal is covered with fine hairs and often has a greyish overall appearance. The size of *A. cinerea* means there is little likelihood of confusion with other species.

Description: CARAPACE Dark brownish-grey with paler patches behind the posterior eyes and darker streaks radiating from the fovea. ABDOMEN Brownish-grey with a cardiac mark, edged in black, which is dilated slightly around the midpoint. Two rows of white spots in the posterior half converge towards the spinnerets. LEGS Brown with darker annulations.

Similar species: None.

Distribution/Status: Scattered distribution in the north and west of Britain is partly limited by availability of its habitat.

Nationally Scarce

Scarce, local

♂
♀
J F M A M J J A S O N D

♀ *Arctosa cinerea* × **4**

NT *Arctosa fulvolineata* ♀

♂7·5–8·5 mm ♀10–12 mm [PAGE 231 T]

Observation tips/habitat: Very similar to *A. leopardus* but larger. This rare spider is confined to saltmarsh habitats where it is found under debris, stones and mud fragments. Coastal protection work seriously threatens its habitat.

Description: CARAPACE Dark brown with a very indistinct, paler median area more obvious towards the rear. Light lateral bands are very indistinct. Dark streaks radiate from the fovea. ABDOMEN Clear yellow cardiac mark, with the rest of the abdomen brown with mottled black markings forming an obscure pattern. LEGS Similar colour to the carapace with faint, darker annulations.

Similar species: *Arctosa leopardus* (*below*) is smaller.

Distribution/Status: Rare. Confined to the coasts of East Anglia and southern England.

Biodiversity List (En)
Nationally Rare
Rare, local

♂
♀
J F M A M J J A S O N D

LC *Arctosa leopardus* ♀

♂6·5–7·0 mm ♀8·5–9·5 mm [PAGE 231 B]

Observation tips/habitat: Occurs in a variety of damp habitats including wet heathland, dune slacks, fens and marshes. Unlike *A. perita* (*p. 228*) it seems not to dig a burrow but instead spins a silken cell amongst litter or vegetation. Depth of colouring can vary.

Description: CARAPACE Dark brown with darker streaks radiating from the fovea. Often has a glossy appearance and may be covered with fine pubescence. Sometimes lateral bands of white hairs present. ABDOMEN Dark brown to black with paler (sometimes conspicuous yellow in ♂) cardiac mark. Posterior half contains two pairs of dark spots and the whole covered with fine hairs. LEGS Pale brown with distinctly darker annulations.

Similar species: *Arctosa fulvolineata* (*above*) is larger.

Distribution/Status: Widespread in Wales and southern England. Scattered distribution elsewhere.

Uncommon, regional

♂
♀
J F M A M J J A S O N D

♀ *Arctosa fulvolineata* × **4**

♀ *Arctosa leopardus* × **4**

Arctosa alpigena 🔍

♂7–8mm ♀9–10mm

Observation tips/habitat: A rare spider in Britain. It is only found at altitudes above 1,000 metres on **high mountain plateaux**. This, and its **distinct markings**, make *A. alpigena* identifiable in the field. It spins silk tubes in matted vegetation and is only rarely seen actively running about.

Description: CARAPACE Reddish-brown with darker streaks radiating from the fovea. Two of these radiating marks form more distinct dark bars where they delimit the boundary between the head and thoracic areas. The head area is thickly covered with greyish hairs. ABDOMEN Brown with a conspicuous, white cardiac stripe edged in black and blunt at the rear end. In the posterior half, paler transverse bars may be present. LEGS Similar colour to carapace with alternating pale and dark annulations on legs III and IV.

Similar species: None.

Distribution/Status: Rare. Restricted to mountainous areas in Scotland.

♂
♀
J F M A M J J A S O N D

♀ *Arctosa alpigena* ×**4**

Pirata   Otter spiders   🔍 **6 British species (6 illustrated)**

Similar in appearance to *Pardosa* (*p.207*) but a **'Y'-shaped median mark on the carapace, and pairs of white spots on the abdomen of most species**, are characteristic of *Pirata*. Five of the six species favour wet and marshy habitats where they run rapidly over vegetation and the water surface hunting for prey. They spin tubular webs, with openings occasionally at water level. Females carrying white egg-sacs on their spinnerets can be very conspicuous as they move around. The sexes are very similar in general appearance.

LC

Pirata latitans   🔍   **Common, regional**

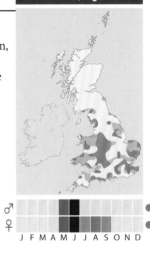

♂ 2·5–4·0 mm   ♀ 4–5 mm

Observation tips/habitat: The smallest *Pirata* species in Britain, *P. latitans* lacks the distinctive patterning of other species in the genus. It occurs at ground level in fens and marshes, often at the edge of open water and sometimes in damp grassland. It is less associated with acidic habitats that the other *Pirata* species.

Description: CARAPACE Dark brown with little, if any, indication of a median band and no lateral bands. Fine white hairs on the sides. ABDOMEN Dark brown with a velvety appearance. White hairs on the sides and two rows of white spots converging towards the spinnerets. LEGS Brown (darker in ♂) with faint annulations.

Similar species: Could be confused with *Aulonia albimana* (*p.227*)

♂ | J F M A M J J A S O N D

Distribution/Status: Widespread in southern Britain, less so northwards. Absent from Scotland.

♀ *Pirata latitans* with egg-sac × **6**

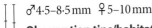

| LC | *Pirata piscatorius* ◆ |

♂4·5–8·5mm ♀5–10mm

Observation tips/habitat: Usually in very wet areas, often near open water. ♀s have been known to spin a vertical tube half submerged in water from which they may attack passing insects. If the tube is disturbed the spider may well descend below the water surface. Both sexes can appear almost black.

Description: CARAPACE Very dark reddish-brown to black with clear white marginal bands. ABDOMEN Similar colour to carapace with two lines of clear white spots running longitudinally down the abdomen. The colour of the cardiac mark usually matches the rest of the abdomen, but occasionally it can be paler.
LEGS Very dark reddish-brown to black with streaks on the femora.

Similar species: None.

Distribution/Status: A scarce spider that is relatively widespread in Wales but patchily distributed elsewhere.

Nationally Scarce

Scarce, local

♂
♀

J F M A M J J A S O N D

♀ *Pirata piscatorius* ×**6**

The carapace ranges in colour from black to reddish-brown

Pirata piraticus   ♀

Abundant, widespread

♂ 4·0–6·5 mm   ♀ 4·5–9·0 mm   [PAGE 236 T]

Observation tips/habitat: Found in a wide range of wetland habitats including pond and stream edges, marsh, fen and blanket bog. Active on the surfaces of vegetation and water in sunny conditions, but hides away in cooler weather.

Description: CARAPACE Brown, usually with a paler 'Y'-shaped median band. The arms of the 'Y' contain a pair of dark streaks separated by a thin pale line. Light lateral bands are more obvious in the posterior half. Marginal lines of white hairs are often noticeable in the field. ABDOMEN Yellow cardiac mark edged with white hairs is obvious in ♀, sometimes white hairs less clear in ♂. Two lines of white spots converge towards the spinnerets in the posterior half. A band of white hairs covers each side of the abdomen. LEGS Greenish-brown.

♂
♀
J F M A M J J A S O N D

Similar species: *Pirata tenuitarsis, P. uliginosus* (both *p. 237*), *P. hygrophilus* (*below*).

Distribution/Status: Widespread throughout Britain.

Pirata hygrophilus   ♀

Common, widespread

♂ 4·5–5·5 mm   ♀ 5·0–6·5 mm   [PAGE 236 B]

Observation tips/habitat: Similar to *P. piraticus* but usually darker, sometimes appearing almost black in the field. Occurs in damp woodland and other shaded wetland habitats. It tends to be more active at night, hiding amongst ground vegetation during the day.

Description: CARAPACE Similar to *P. piraticus* but a dark band is present at the carapace margin and lateral white hairs are indistinct or absent. ABDOMEN Similar to *P. piraticus* with the lines of white spots usually distinct. However, the cardiac mark is very indistinct and lacks the edging of white hairs. The whole abdomen often has a reddish tinge. White hairs on the sides are not obvious. LEGS Brown with darker annulations on the femora.

♂
♀
J F M A M J J A S O N D

Similar species: *P. piraticus* (*above*), *Pirata uliginosus, P. tenuitarsis* (both *p. 237*).

Distribution/Status: Widespread in southern Britain, more scattered in the north.

♀ *Pirata piraticus* ×**6**

♀ *Pirata tenuitarsis* ×**6**

♀ *Pirata uliginosus* ×**6**

♀ *Pirata hygrophilus* with egg-sac ×**6**

c *Pirata tenuitarsis* ♂

Nationally Scarce

Scarce, local

♂4–6 mm   ♀4·5–8·0 mm   [PAGE 236 ML]

Observation tips/habitat: Very similar to *P. piraticus* in general appearance. Appears to have specific habitat requirements of acid bog, particularly *Sphagnum* mosses.

Description: CARAPACE Similar to *P. piraticus*. The lateral bands are wider but can be hidden by white hairs. ABDOMEN Similar to *P. piraticus* but lacking the white edging to a less obvious cardiac mark. Lines of white spots are very conspicuous. LEGS As *P. piraticus*.

Similar species: *P. piraticus*, *P. hygrophilus* (both *p. 235*), *Pirata uliginosus* (*below*).

Distribution/Status: Local but may be common in acidic bogs and on wet heaths.

♂

♀

J F M A M J J A S O N D

c *Pirata uliginosus* ♂

Uncommon, widespread

♂4–5 mm   ♀5–6 mm   [PAGE 236 MR]

Observation tips/habitat: Very similar to *P. hygrophilus* but occurring in drier habitats than other *Pirata* species, particularly unimproved chalk grassland as well as drying, rank and grassy bogs.

Description: CARAPACE Similar to *P. hygrophilus* but markings are less distinct. ABDOMEN Similar to *P. hygrophilus*. LEGS As *P. hygrophilus* but annulations are less obvious.

Similar species: *P. hygrophilus*, *P. piraticus* (both *p. 235*), *P. tenuitarsis* (*above*).

Distribution/Status: Widespread but scattered distribution throughout Britain.

♂

♀

J F M A M J J A S O N D

Pirata piraticus | *P. tenuitarsis* | *P. hygrophilus* | *P. uliginosus* – identification pointers				
SPECIES	CARAPACE		ABDOMEN	LEGS
	LATERAL BANDS	LATERAL WHITE HAIRS	CARDIAC MARK	
P. piraticus*	Light; more obvious in posterior half	often apparent	Yellow; **edged with white hairs**	Greenish-brown
P. tenuitarsis*	As *P. piraticus* but wider	can hide lateral band		
P. hygrophilus*	As *P. piraticus* but with dark band	indistinct/absent	Yellow; indistinct **no white hairs**	Brown; FEMORA: dark annulations (less obvious in *P. uliginosus*)
P. uliginosus*	As *P. hygrophilus* but less distinct			

* Microscopic examination of genitalia (see *page 96*) is required for safe identification.

PISAURIDAE   Nurseryweb spiders   2 British genera

The pisaurid species are all fairly large, long-legged, eight-eyed spiders with a tapering abdomen. ♀s carry their egg-sacs, held by the chelicerae, underneath the body. ♀s guard their hatched young in large, tent-like 'nursery' webs, constructed in herbaceous vegetation, for the first few days after they emerge from the egg-sac.

Pisaura   1 British species (illustrated)

The 'nursery web' of *Pisaura mirabilis* (see also *page 73*) is frequently seen during May and June but can be found even as late as September. **Although the colour pattern is extremely variable there is always colour/pattern co-ordination between the carapace and the tapering abdomen.** The spider hunts on low vegetation but the ♀ can often be seen within the nursery holding her white, unhatched egg-sac. Later, when the spiderlings have hatched, the guarding ♀s are conspicuous on the outside of the nursery. Uniquely amongst British spiders, the ♂ presents the ♀ with a nuptial gift of wrapped prey as a distraction before mating, possibly to avoid being eaten. The sexes are similar in appearance and size. **Not associated with open water.**

Pisaura mirabilis nursery web

LC   *Pisaura mirabilis*   Nurseryweb Spider   **Abundant, widespread**

♂10–13mm   ♀12–15mm

Observation tips/habitat: A distinctive spider found in a variety of habitats including grassland, heathland and open woodland. Nursery webs often occur on the verges of rides and paths. Occasionally spiders can be observed 'sunbathing' on leaves, typically with the first and second legs outstretched and held together at an angle to the body.

Description: CARAPACE Extremely variable in depth of colour and pattern. Greyish-brown ground colour with a darker median band containing a conspicuous, thin yellow or white midline running the whole length (this median line is obvious even in immature specimens). ABDOMEN Pale yellowish-grey to darker brown at the sides and usually with a wavy-edged folium covering whole length of the abdomen, tapering towards the spinnerets. The depth of colour and patterning within the folium varies considerably. The folium is very indistinct or completely absent in some specimens and the abdomen is then a greyish-brown with a vague darker pattern. LEGS Uniform brown, sometimes with black or white mottling.

J F M A M J J A S O N D

Similar species: None.

Distribution/Status: Abundant and widespread in much of England and Wales. Less so in the north and Scotland.

♀ *Pisaura mirabilis* ×**3**

Pisaura mirabilis ♀ with egg-sac and silk dragline

Dolomedes　Raft spiders　　　　　👁 **2 British species (2 illustrated)**

The two species in this genus are very similar and usually **occupy permanently wet habitats**. Their large size and predominantly dark brown appearance, **usually with contrasting whitish or yellow submarginal stripes on the carapace and abdomen**, makes the genus easily recognisable in the field but microscopic examination of the genitalia (see *page 96*) is necessary to separate the species. An ambush hunter, the spider sits on emergent vegetation with its forelegs resting on the water surface; sensory hairs on the legs detect vibrations created by potential predators and prey. It can also go underwater to hunt, or if threatened. Prey items are largely invertebrate but vertebrates – both fishes and amphibians – are also taken.

Although superficial, the similarity in the wetland habitat and white marginal bands of some *Pirata* species (*p. 233–237*), and in the appearance, posture and nursery webs of *Pisaura mirabilis* (*p. 238*), often cause confusion with *Dolomedes* species.

VU
VU

Dolomedes plantarius　Fen Raft Spider　🔬

LEGALLY PROTECTED
Biodiversity List (En, Wa)
Nationally Rare
Extremely rare

♂ 10–16 mm　♀ 13–22 mm

Observation tips/habitat: Semi-aquatic, and until recently, recorded from just three wetland sites. New populations now established in East Anglia as part of a conservation programme to reduce its vulnerability. Very similar to *D. fimbriatus* in general appearance and size, but differs in its specific habitat requirements; restricted to lowland sites with a permanent supply of neutral to alkaline, base-rich, unpolluted water. Nursery webs are built in stiff-leaved, marginal emergent vegetation and in floating rosettes of Water Soldier; it is not a reedbed species.

Description: CARAPACE Dark brown to black, with two yellow or white broad longitudinal stripes close to the margins; occasionally the stripes are absent from both carapace and abdomen. ABDOMEN Dark brown to black (slightly more so than carapace) with two lateral, longitudinal yellow or white stripes appearing as continuations of the carapace stripes (often narrower than in *D. fimbriatus*). Usually no obvious cardiac mark. LEGS Uniform brown.

♂
♀

J F M A M J J A S O N D

Similar species: *Dolomedes fimbriatus* (*p. 242*). Can be confused with some *Pirata* species, *Pisaura mirabilis* (see *above*).

Distribution/Status: Very rare and, until recently, apparently confined to three sites; in East Anglia, East Sussex and south Wales.

♂ *Dolomedes plantarius* × **2**

Dolomedes plantarius ♀ at water's edge with forelegs checking for movement of the water surface indicating possible prey activity

LC *Dolomedes fimbriatus* Raft Spider

Nationally Scarce

Scarce, local

♂9–16mm ♀13–22mm

Observation tips/habitat: Found on acid mires, usually in association with *Sphagnum* mosses. Occurs on wet, lowland heaths and in upland mires, often constructing its nurseries in Bog Myrtle or heather. Rather less closely associated with open water than *D. plantarius*, with juveniles often found in drier habitats, including in tree branches.

Description: CARAPACE Dark brown to black, with two yellow or white broad longitudinal stripes close to the margins. ABDOMEN Dark brown to black (slightly more so than carapace) with two lateral, longitudinal yellow or white stripes appearing as continuations of the carapace stripes. The stripes are often slightly broader than in *D. plantarius*; occasionally the stripes are absent. A faint, lighter, cardiac mark is usually present. LEGS Uniform brown.

♂
♀
J F M A M J J A S O N D

Similar species: *Dolomedes plantarius* (p. 240). Can be confused with some *Pirata* species, *Pisaura mirabilis* (see p. 240).

Distribution/Status: Widespread on wet heaths in southern England. Very scattered throughout the rest of Britain.

♂ *Dolomedes fimbriatus* ×**2**

OXYOPIDAE Lynx spiders   **1 British genus**

The Oxyopidae are eight-eyed hunting spiders which run around rapidly on low vegetation, such as heather, chasing and occasionally jumping on their prey. In common with the Salticidae and the Lycosidae, oxyopids have very well-developed eyesight and they are able to recognise prey from some centimetres away. They have long, slender legs enabling them to negotiate the undergrowth with ease. ♀s can sometimes be seen guarding their flattish, disc-like egg-sac in the upper levels of low vegetation. Both sexes have a similar appearance.

Oxyopes Lynx spiders   🔍 **1 British species (illustrated)**

Readily identifiable in the field by its **abdominal shape and general appearance**. However, some care is needed to avoid confusion with the running crab spider *Philodromus histrio*.

Oxyopes heterophthalmus Lynx Spider 🔍

Nationally Rare

Rare, local

♂ 5·5–6·5 mm ♂ 5–8 mm ♀

Observation tips/habitat: On established, dry heathland where it is usually found on south-facing slopes amongst heather.

Description: CARAPACE Dark brown ground colour with two white bands flanking a dark median band, tapering towards the posterior. Thinner, white bands extend round the front of the head area which also has a thin median line. ♂ palps each have a conspicuous, thin, chitinous protuberance which is directed inwards. ABDOMEN Distinctive cardiac mark (black in ♂, brown in ♀), edged in white. This edging continues through to the spinnerets as a thin line, all contained within a brown median band. Sides are darker and interspersed with white streaks. Tapering abdominal shape is noticeable in the field and differs from *P. histrio*. LEGS Pale brown with numerous long dark spines, which are conspicuous in the field (absent in *P. histrio*).

♂
♀
J F M A M J J A S O N D

Similar species: *Philodromus histrio* (page 351).

Distribution/Status: Rare. Recorded only from a few heathland sites in Surrey in the last 100 years.

♀ *Oxyopes heterophthalmus* × **4**

♀ *Oxyopes heterophthalmus*
showing conspicuous leg spines

243

AGELENIDAE　Funnelweb spiders

3 British genera

All agelenids have eight eyes and conspicuously long posterior spinnerets, which provide a key pointer for field identification. In all genera the cephalothorax is rather long and narrowing at the front, and the abdomen has chevron-like markings. Their funnel webs are typically large, horizontal sheets of silk with a tubular retreat at one edge.

Agelena

 1 British species (illustrated)

The distinctive sheet web is a significant clue to the presence of the single species in this genus.

LC　*Agelena labyrinthica*　Labyrinth Spider

Common, regional

♂ 8–9 mm　♀ 8–12 mm

Observation tips/habitat: Spins a large funnel web low down in vegetation – often brambles, heather and gorse. In late summer the female constructs a chamber, within the web, made up of a complex maze of dense silken tubes (hence the specific name *labyrinthica*). Within this structure she constructs her egg-sac and can often be found on guard at the entrance.

Description: CARAPACE Distinct banding, laterally pale, then dark brown on either side of a pale central section. This pattern runs the whole length of the carapace. ABDOMEN Dark grey with a paler longitudinal median band bisecting white chevron-like markings. LEGS Covered in long hairs. Pale brown with some darker markings.

Similar species: None.

Distribution/Status: Widespread in southern England and Wales with scattered records from farther north. Not recorded in Scotland.

J F M A M J J A S O N D

♀ *Agelena labyrinthica* × 4

Textrix

 1 British species (illustrated)

The single member of this genus is often seen running around very quickly on the ground in hot weather where it can be mistaken for a wolf spider. However, the **long spinnerets and characteristic pattern** are sufficiently obvious to avoid confusion.

LC

Textrix denticulata

Common, widespread

♂6–7mm ♀6–7mm

Observation tips/habitat: An attractively marked spider which spins a small sheet web containing a tubular retreat amongst stones, stone walls and low shrubs.

Description: CARAPACE Dark brown to almost black with a pale median band. The head area is elevated and narrowed. ABDOMEN Dark-grey to black with a pale ∩-shaped marking in the anterior half. The 'arms' of this shape extend backwards as lines of white spots containing a pinkish-red median section. **Long spinnerets are very conspicuous.** LEGS Brown with black annulations and occasionally rings of white hairs at joints.

Similar species: None.

Distribution/Status: Widespread but scattered distribution throughout much of Britain apart from the south-east where it is much less frequent.

♂
♀
J F M A M J J A S O N D

♂ *Textrix denticulata* × **6**

Tegenaria   House spiders

👁 **9 British species (8 illustrated)**

Large, robust spiders with relatively long legs and, usually, a chevron pattern on the abdomen. Most *Tegenaria* species are synanthropic but can also be recorded from the wider countryside. *T. gigantea*, *T. saeva* and *T. atrica* are collectively known as large house spiders. It has recently been suggested that the three species should be regarded as just one species, *Eratigena atrica*. Although the new genus is valid, this approach is certainly not justified in Britain, at least.

♀

Tegenaria saeva × **3**

♂

♂ *Tegenaria atrica* × **3**

LC

Tegenaria gigantea Large house spider

Common, widespread

♂ 10–14 mm ♀ 11–16 mm

Observation tips/habitat: Spins a tubular retreat spreading out into a sheet web which can be very large in undisturbed locations indoors and in outbuildings (the classical 'cobweb'). In holes in walls, the web can be reduced to a collar with a few radiating threads. Extremely long legs, particularly in the ♂, are characteristic of this group of large house spiders.

Description: CARAPACE Brown with darker markings on the margins of the raised head area, running back as dentate bands. This is more marked in ♂. Thin, dark border. ABDOMEN Pale brown with mottling of darker markings, creating a series of pale chevrons. The pattern is quite variable. LEGS Very long – up to 2× body length in ♀, up to 3× body length in ♂. Uniformly coloured as carapace, without annulations.

♂
♀
J F M A M J J A S O N D

Similar species: All other *Tegenaria* species, apart from *T. domestica*, *T. silvestris* and *T. picta*.

Distribution/Status: Widespread across much of eastern and central England but with only scattered records from the West Country and Wales. Common across northern England but more scattered in Scotland.

♀ *Tegenaria gigantea* × 3

LC *Tegenaria saeva* Large house spider

Common, regional

♂10–14mm ♀11–16mm   [PAGE 246 T]

Observation tips/habitat: As *Tegenaria gigantea* but with a much more western distribution in Britain. It hybridises with *T. gigantea* where the two species meet.

Description: CARAPACE + ABDOMEN +LEGS
Similar to *Tegenaria gigantea*.

Similar species: All other *Tegenaria* species, apart from *T. domestica, T. silvestris* and *T. picta*.

Distribution/Status: Widespread across the West Country and Wales but largely absent from eastern and central England. Common across northern England but more scattered in Scotland.

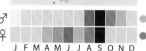

J F M A M J J A S O N D

LC *Tegenaria atrica* Large house spider ✄

Scarce, local

♂10–14mm ♀11–16mm   [PAGE 246 B]

Observation tips/habitat: As *Tegenaria gigantea*. Previously thought to be represented only by rare imports from the Republic of Ireland or the continent until a very extensive population was reported from the Newcastle upon Tyne area in 2014.

Description: CARAPACE + ABDOMEN + LEGS
Similar to *Tegenaria gigantea*.

Similar species: All other *Tegenaria* species, apart from *T. domestica, T. silvestris* and *T. picta*.

Distribution/Status: Very scattered distribution in Britain but common in and around Newcastle upon Tyne.

J F M A M J J A S O N D

Tegenaria I – carapace with **strong pattern** (*gigantea* group) – identification pointers				
SPECIES	ABDOMEN	LEG	LEG/BODY LENGTH	HABITAT
T. gigantea*	Pale brown; darker 'chevrons'	Not annulated	♂3×; ♀2×	Houses, outbuildings. waste ground
T. saeva*				
T. atrica*				
T. agrestis*				Waste ground
T. silvestris	As *T. gigantea* but chevrons may be less distinct	Annulated; pale brown		Woodland
T. parietina	Pale brown; darker mottling; central stripe bordered by darker bands with whitish spots	Annulated; brown	♂3–5×; ♀>2×	Outbuildings, houses
T. ferruginea	As *T. parietina* but tinged rusty	Annulated; rusty	♂+♀1·5×	Tree holes, walls

* Distinguished by microscopic examination of the genitalia (see *page 96*).

LC *Tegenaria agrestis*

Uncommon, regional

♂7–10 mm ♀10–15 mm   [PAGE 250 T]

Observation tips/habitat: Not commonly found in houses, preferring scrubby grassland on waste ground, brownfield sites and railway margins. The retreat is often under stones or in crevices, with the web extended onto nearby vegetation.

Description: CARAPACE + ABDOMEN +LEGS
Similar to *Tegenaria gigantea*.

Similar species: All other *Tegenaria* species, apart from *T. domestica*, *T. silvestris* and *T. picta*.

Distribution/Status: Uncommon. Widespread but scattered distribution throughout England and Wales.

J F M A M J J A S O N D

LC *Tegenaria parietina* Cardinal Spider

Scarce, local

♂10–17 mm ♀11–20 mm   [PAGE 250 B]

Observation tips/habitat: As *Tegenaria gigantea*. Sometimes found in houses but more often in particularly old buildings. There are some records of it living in dense hedgerows and ivy, well away from buildings.

Description: CARAPACE Similar to *Tegenaria gigantea*.
ABDOMEN Ground colour pale brown with darker mottling. Flanking a less mottled central stripe are two darker bands incorporating a number of distinct, whitish spots which are large anteriorly but reduce in size towards the spinnerets. LEGS Even longer than *Tegenaria gigantea*, particularly in ♂ where they can be up to 5× the body length. Brown, as carapace and with distinctly darker annulations.

Similar species: All other *Tegenaria* species, apart from *T. domestica*, *T. silvestris* and *T. picta*.

Distribution/Status: Restricted to the southern counties of England.

J F M A M J J A S O N D

Tegenaria II – carapace with **weak/no pattern** – identification pointers				
SPECIES	GENERAL	CARAPACE	ABDOMEN	LEGS
T. domestica	House dwelling; much smaller than other *Tegenaria* found in houses	Yellowish-brown, occasionally with faint dentate markings	Yellowish-brown, with very faint 'chevron' pattern	Yellowish-brown; often faint annulations
T. picta	Chalk pits; much smaller than any other *Tegenaria*	Dark brown; no markings	Dark-brown, with reddish 'chevron' pattern	Dark brown

♀ *Tegenaria agrestis* × **3**

♀ *Tegenaria parietina* × **3**

NA

Tegenaria ferruginea

Extremely rare

♂9–11 mm ♀11–14 mm   [PAGE 251 L]

Observation tips/habitat: Recorded from a single Yorkshire churchyard, where it occupies tree holes, dense vegetation and the external wall of the church.

Description: CARAPACE Similar to *Tegenaria gigantea*. The thin border is interrupted and the whole carapace is tinged rusty-red. ABDOMEN Similar to *Tegenaria parietina* but **the whole spider has an overall rusty-red tinge, especially the central stripe**. LEGS Similar to *Tegenaria parietina* but the dark annulations are even more pronounced. Overall coloration is a rusty-red. Leg length 1·5× the body length in both sexes.

Similar species: All other *Tegenaria* species, apart from *T. domestica*, *T. silvestris* and *T. picta*.

Distribution/Status: Recorded only from a single site in central Yorkshire.

♂
♀

J F M A M J J A S O N D

♀ *Tegenaria ferruginea* × **3**

♀ *Tegenaria silvestris* × **3**

♀ *Tegenaria domestica* × **3**

LC *Tegenaria silvestris* 🔍

Common, regional

♂ 5–6 mm　♀ 5–7 mm　　　　　　　　[TR]

Observation tips/habitat: Very similar colouring and markings to other members of the genus but **a much smaller spider**. Commonly found in woodlands in damp situations under stones, fallen logs and tree bark. Rarely ventures into houses.

Description: CARAPACE Similar pattern to *Tegenaria gigantea*. ABDOMEN Similar pattern to *Tegenaria gigantea* but the chevrons may be less distinct. LEGS Pale brown with **distinct, darker annulations**.

Similar species: All other *Tegenaria* species, apart from *T. domestica* and *T. picta*.

Distribution/Status: Widespread throughout central and southern England and Wales. Much less so farther north.

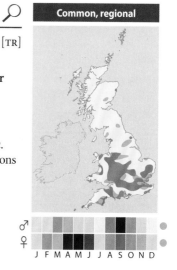

♂
♀
J F M A M J J A S O N D

LC *Tegenaria domestica* Common House Spider   **Common, widespread**

♂6–9mm ♀9–10mm   [PAGE 251 BR]

Observation tips/habitat: Differs from other house-dwelling ♂♀ *Tegenaria* in being smaller and paler in colour, sometimes almost completely lacking the darker abdominal markings. Almost exclusively confined to houses.

Description: CARAPACE Yellowish-brown, occasionally with faint markings in a pattern similar to that of *Tegenaria gigantea*. ABDOMEN Similar yellowish-brown ground colour to carapace with mottled darker markings that create a series of pale chevrons (similar to *Tegenaria gigantea* but fainter). Markings sometimes almost absent. LEGS Coloured as carapace and often with faint, darker annulations.

Similar species: None.

Distribution/Status: Widespread throughout Britain but with a more scattered distribution to the west and north.

♂
♀
J F M A M J J A S O N D

VU *Tegenaria picta*   Nationally Rare

Extremely rare

♂5–6mm ♀6–7mm   [NOT ILLUSTRATED]

Observation tips/habitat: Around half the size of most other ♂♀ *Tegenaria*. Only recently recorded from a few chalk pit sites in south-east England where it spins small sheet webs under stones.

Description: CARAPACE Dark brown with no markings. ABDOMEN Dark brown with reddish markings creating a series of pale chevrons similar to the pattern of *Tegenaria gigantea*. LEGS Dark brown.

Similar species: None, but could be mistaken for immatures of other *Tegenaria* species.

Distribution/Status: Very localized in the south-east.

♂
♀
J F M A M J J A S O N D

HAHNIIDAE Lesser cobweb spiders   **2 British genera**

All of the species are small and make sheet webs at ground level. They have eight eyes and the spinnerets arranged in a transverse row — the two outer spinnerets have two segments — all features discernible with a hand lens. Once this has been confirmed it is a matter of which genus. On the ventral side of the abdomen a thin linear slit containing the tracheal spiracles (respiratory openings) should be observable with a hand lens. Its position is helpful in determining the different genera within the family.

Antistea   🔍 **1 British species (illustrated)**

The single British species has a glossy appearance and a rounded carapace with the head area (carrying the eyes) projecting forward. The tracheal spiracles are about **halfway between the spinnerets and the epigastric furrow. The carapace and the legs are distinctly reddish-orange.**

LC *Antistea elegans*   🔍

Common, widespread

♂ 2·5–3·0 mm   ♀ 2·5–3·0 mm

Observation tips/habitat: Spins a small sheet web across depressions in the ground, typically beneath plants, in a variety of damp habitats such as reedbeds, marshes, bogs and the margins of woodland ponds.

Description: CARAPACE Very glossy, orange-brown with a black midline and fovea. Bristles are present around the eyes and also in a line back to the fovea. ABDOMEN Dark grey with pale brown chevrons in the posterior half. LEGS Orange-brown, as carapace.

Similar species: None.

Distribution/Status: Common and widespread throughout Britain.

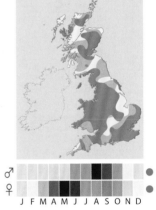

♂
♀
J F M A M J J A S O N D

♀ *Antistea elegans* × **10**

253

Hahnia

🔍 **6 British species (5 illustrated)**

Three of the six species are very uncommon or rare. In contrast to *Antistea* (*page 253*) the tracheal spiracles are slightly closer to spinnerets than to the epigastric furrow, and the carapace and the legs are not orange. All *Hahnia* species are very small and microscopic examination of the genitalia (see *page 96*) is necessary to confirm identification of the species.

LC *Hahnia montana* 🔬

Common, widespread

⚲ ⚲
♂♀ ♂1·5–1·8mm ♀1·8–2·0mm [PAGE 255 TL]

Observation tips/habitat: The commonest species of the genus. Typically occurring in leaf-litter in damp woodland habitats. Also occasionally recorded from grassland, heathland, fens and sand dunes.

Description: CARAPACE Brownish-grey with a darker foveal area and radiating streaks. ABDOMEN Dark brown to black. Faint, pale chevrons may be visible in the posterior half. LEGS Brown with paler patellae.

Similar species: All other *Hahnia* species.

Distribution/Status: Common and widespread but scattered distribution throughout Britain.

♂
♀

J F M A M J J A S O N D

LC *Hahnia nava* 🔬

Common, widespread

⚲ ⚲
♂♀ ♂1·5–2·0mm ♀1·5–2·0mm [PAGE 255 TR]

Observation tips/habitat: Has a dullish-black appearance in the field and is superficially similar to *H. montana* (*above*). It occurs away from woodland in low vegetation in grassland, heathland and amongst stones on open ground.

Description: CARAPACE Dark brownish-black. ABDOMEN Black, covered with long hairs. LEGS Dark brown to black, occasionally with bases of segments yellow.

Similar species: All other *Hahnia* species.

Distribution/Status: Widespread and local in the southern half of Britain, more scattered in the west and north.

♂
♀

J F M A M J J A S O N D

♀ *Hahnia montana* × **10**

♀ *Hahnia nava* × **10**

DD *Hahnia microphthalma*

♂? ♀1·4mm   [NOT ILLUSTRATED]

Observation tips/habitat: Only a few specimens of this species are known to science. The British finds from the 1970s suggest that it may live in soil fissures; adult ♀s have only been found in the winter season. Consequently low numbers of records may be due to under-recording. ♂s are not known.

Description: CARAPACE Pale yellow.
ABDOMEN Pale yellowish-grey. LEGS As carapace.

Similar species: All other *Hahnia* species.

Distribution/Status: Extremely rare. Recorded from only two sites in southern England in the 1970s.

Nationally Rare

Extremely rare

NO PHENOLOGY DATA

LC *Hahnia helveola*

♂2·2–2·5mm ♀2·5–3·0mm   [PAGE 256 R]

Observation tips/habitat: Usually occurs in woodland amongst leaf-litter, moss and ground detritus. Sometimes recorded from more open grassland, moorland and heathland sites.

Description: CARAPACE Pale yellow, sometimes with a darker foveal area and radiating streaks. ABDOMEN Yellowish with broad dark chevrons. LEGS Coloured as carapace.

Similar species: All other *Hahnia* species, especially *Hahnia candida* and *H. pusilla* (both *p. 256*).

Distribution/Status: Widespread and fairly common in south-east England, local and scattered elsewhere.

Uncommon, widespread

♂
♀
J F M A M J J A S O N D

♀ *Hahnia candida* × **10**

♂ *Hahnia pusilla* × **10**

♀ *Hahnia helveola* × **10**

LC # *Hahnia pusilla*

	Nationally Scarce
	Scarce, local

♂♀ ♂1·3–1·5mm ♀1·3–1·5mm [c]

Observation tips/habitat: Similar in appearance to *H. helveola* but without the dark markings. Occurs in low vegetation and under stones, often in damp habitats.

Description: CARAPACE Typically pale yellow-brown with no darker markings. ABDOMEN Typically pale yellow without dark markings but covered in fine hairs. Occasionally the body colour of the whole spider can be a much darker brown (as specimen shown). LEGS Pale brown.

Similar species: All other *Hahnia* species, especially *Hahnia candida* (*below*) and *H. helveola* (*p. 255*).

Distribution/Status: Generally very uncommon. Distribution concentrated in south-east England and in a band from north Wales to Yorkshire.

J F M A M J J A S O N D

VU # *Hahnia candida*

	Nationally Rare
	Extremely rare

♂♀ ♂1·3–1·4mm ♀1·3–1·4mm [L]

Observation tips/habitat: Typically occurs under stones on coastal cliffs and shingle but has also been found amongst heather. Similar in appearance to *H. helveola* and *H. pusilla*.

Description: CARAPACE + ABDOMEN Very similar to *H. pusilla*. LEGS Very similar to *H. pusilla* but sometimes darker.

Similar species: All other *Hahnia* species, especially *Hahnia pusilla* (*above*) and *H. helveola* (*p. 255*).

Distribution/Status: Very rare. Most records from the Isle of Portland; other locations also close to the south coast.

J F M A M J J A S O N D

DICTYNIDAE Meshweb spiders

9 British genera

Contains 17 eight-eyed species in nine genera. All but two of the species are less than 3·5 mm in length and many are extremely small indeed. Over two-thirds of the species are uncommon or rare, the commonest members of the family being those in the genus *Dictyna*. Apart from species in the genus *Cicurina* (*p. 261*) and *Nigma* (*p. 262*), microscopic examination of the genitalia is required to determine the majority of species. The genus *Dictyna* should be identifiable in the field with the use of a hand lens but the species within it require more detailed inspection to confirm their identity.

Dictyna

◯ **5 British species (4 illustrated)**

All the species are **small with characteristic patterns of light hairs on both carapace and abdomen.** *Dictyna* spin small, intricately woven webs of fleecy (cribellate) silk on plants and amongst leaf-litter on the ground. The nature of the silk causes the web to gather dust and debris and as a consequence may appear 'untidy'. Typically the spider can often be discovered hiding in its **silk retreat spun in the dead flower heads of plants.** The similar abdominal patterns and small size of all the *Dictyna* species means that microscopic examination of the genitalia (see *page 96*) is necessary to confirm identification of the species.

LC ## *Dictyna latens*

Common, regional

♂ 2·0–2·5 mm   ♀ 2·5–3·5 mm

Observation tips/habitat: Differs from other *Dictyna* species in having a much darker appearance, even when the covering of white hairs is still present. Favours heathland habitat where it frequently occurs on heather and gorse.

Description: CARAPACE Dark brown to black with a covering of white hairs. ABDOMEN Dark brown to black and covered with white hairs. There is no definite pattern other than a dark central band with lobed edges. LEGS Dark brown to black.

Similar species: All other *Dictyna* species.

Distribution/Status: Scattered distribution in England and Wales with concentration of records in south-east. Absent from Scotland.

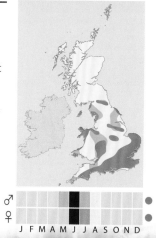

♂
♀
J F M A M J J A S O N D

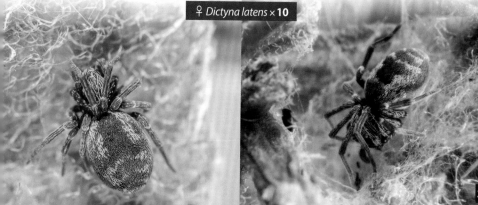

♀ *Dictyna latens* × **10**

257

LC *Dictyna arundinacea* ♀

Abundant, widespread

♂ ♀ ♂2–3mm ♀2·5–3·5mm [PAGE 259 TL]

Observation tips/habitat: By far the commonest member of the genus. Occurs on low vegetation in rough grassland at the edges of fields, hedges and woodland rides. Favoured web locations are in the dead heads of plants such as umbellifers, docks and thistles and, on heathland, in mature heather and gorse.

Description: CARAPACE Dark brown to black with five longitudinal rows of white hairs. ABDOMEN Dark brown ground colour with a covering of short, conspicuous white hairs, apart from the cardiac area, which extends and widens towards the spinnerets and sides. The posterior dark area may contain thin, transverse bands of white hairs. The dark cardiac area sometimes has a thin, longitudinal, central line of white hairs. LEGS Pale brown sometimes with faint annulations. **Apical ends of tarsi I, II and III darker than the remaining segments.**

♂
♀
J F M A M J J A S O N D

Similar species: All other *Dictyna* species.

Distribution/Status: Abundant and widespread in much of Britain, a more scattered distribution in the north and west.

LC *Dictyna uncinata* ♀

Common, regional

♂ ♀ ♂2·0–2·5mm ♀2·2–2·8mm [PAGE 259 TR]

Observation tips/habitat: Very similar to *D. arundinacea*, often occurring in the same habitats but usually at a higher level in the vegetation. Spins its web across the surface of leaves of bushes and trees. It is commonly found in scrub, hedgerows and woodland, particularly on the margins of rides and clearings. It has also been recorded from gardens.

Description: CARAPACE Very similar to *D. arundinacea*. ABDOMEN Very similar to *D. arundinacea*. The cardiac mark is possibly less well defined. LEGS Pale brown sometimes with faint annulations – very similar to *D. arundinacea* but with **no darkening of the apical ends of the tarsi.**

♂
♀
J F M A M J J A S O N D

Similar species: All other *Dictyna* species.

Distribution/Status: Common and widespread in much of England but much less so in the south-west, Wales and Scotland.

♀ *Dictyna arundinacea* × **10**

♀ *Dictyna uncinata* × **10**

♀ *Dictyna pusilla* × **10**

LC *Dictyna pusilla* 🔬

♂♂ ♂1·5–2·5mm ♀1·5–2·5mm   [PAGE 259 B]
♂♀

Observation tips/habitat: Smaller but very similar in
appearance and habitat to *D. arundinacea*; particularly
abundant on Juniper, gorse, Yew and pine, making its web
in the angles between the needles or spines.

Description: CARAPACE Similar to *D. arundinacea*.
ABDOMEN Similar to *D. arundinacea* but dark cardiac mark
may be thinner, and the dark marking at the posterior may
be completely absent. LEGS Pale brown with dark annulations
on the apices of all segments.

Similar species: All other *Dictyna* species.

Distribution/Status: Scarce. Mainly recorded in central-
eastern Scotland with just a few widely scattered records from
the rest of Britain.

♂
♀
J F M A M J J A S O N D

CR *Dictyna major* 🔬

♂♂ ♂2·5–3·0mm ♀3·0–3·5mm   [NOT ILLUSTRATED]
♂♀

Observation tips/habitat: Similar to *D. arundinacea*
but slightly larger. Recorded from ground vegetation and
detritus on coastal sites and the margins of lochs in Scotland.
The whole spider appears lighter than others in the genus.

Description: CARAPACE Similar to *D. arundinacea*.
ABDOMEN Similar to *D. arundinacea* but smaller dark cardiac
area has three distinct spikes posteriorly. Remainder of
abdomen with thick covering of white hairs with some dark
markings posteriorly. LEGS Pale brown.

Similar species: All other *Dictyna* species.

Distribution/Status: Extremely rare. Only a few records
from Scotland.

NO PHENOLOGY DATA

Cicurina

🔍 **1 British species (illustrated)**

The single species of this genus has a similar general appearance to some of the clubionids (*p. 290*), but **differs in having a glossy carapace which lacks any covering of hairs**. It spins a small sheet web in damp habitats with a retreat where the female sits guarding her egg-sac which is often covered with the remains of prey and other debris. ♂s and ♀s are similar.

LC *Cicurina cicur* ◆

🔍

Nationally Scarce

Scarce, regional

♂5–7mm ♀5–7mm

Observation tips/habitat: The largest representative of the family Dictynidae in Britain. Occurs in dark damp habitats in woodland, under stones and logs and in moss and low vegetation. Also in cellars, caves and drains.

Description: CARAPACE Yellow-brown and glossy. ABDOMEN Uniform pinkish-brown without a pattern. LEGS Femora coloured as carapace, remaining segments slightly darker. Apart from the tarsi, all segments have fairly long spines.

Similar species: None.

Distribution/Status: Widespread but very local in central and south-east England. Very scattered elsewhere and almost completely absent from Scotland and Wales.

♂
♀
J F M A M J J A S O N D

♀ *Cicurina cicur* × **6**

Nigma

⌕ **2 British species (2 illustrated)**

Both species are quite distinctive in appearance. They spin small, insubstantial webs, often within a curled leaf, in bushes and trees. ♀s and ♂s of the two species are quite different from each other and should be identifiable in the field with the use of a hand lens.

LC *Nigma walckenaeri*   ⌕   **Uncommon, regional**

♂3–4mm ♀4–5mm   [PAGE 263 T]

♂♀ **Observation tips/habitat:** Similar habitat to *N. puella* (*below*), favouring Ivy, Holly and other garden shrubs. Appears to prefer slightly larger leaves in which to spin its web than *N. puella*. General green appearance of ♀ is a useful diagnostic feature in the field.

Description: CARAPACE ♀ greenish thoracic area with slightly paler head area and thin marginal lines of white hairs. ♂ reddish-brown with paler margins. ABDOMEN ♀ green with light hairs forming a vague pattern of lines and chevrons. ♂ similar to ♀. LEGS ♀ pale green. ♂ similar to ♀ but legs I and II sometimes brownish-yellow.

Similar species: None.

Distribution/Status: Recorded from central-eastern England and the Thames and Severn valleys where it can be frequent. Almost completely absent elsewhere.

♂
♀

J F M A M J J A S O N D

LC *Nigma puella*   ⌕   Nationally Scarce

                                          Scarce, regional

♂2·0–2·8mm ♀2·5–3·0mm   [PAGE 263 B]

♂♀ **Observation tips/habitat:** Occurs in the foliage of trees and bushes often in suburban gardens and parks, also occasionally in scrub and woodland.

Description: CARAPACE ♀ greyish-brown median band flanked by darker bands with semicircular white patches along the posterior margins. Long white hairs on the head area point forwards. ♂ reddish-brown with paler margins. ABDOMEN ♀ creamy-white with conspicuous red cardiac mark. ♂ pinkish-red, sometimes with deeper red median band. LEGS Pale yellowy-brown.

Similar species: None.

Distribution/Status: Local and scattered distribution in southern England and Wales.

♂
♀

J F M A M J J A S O N D

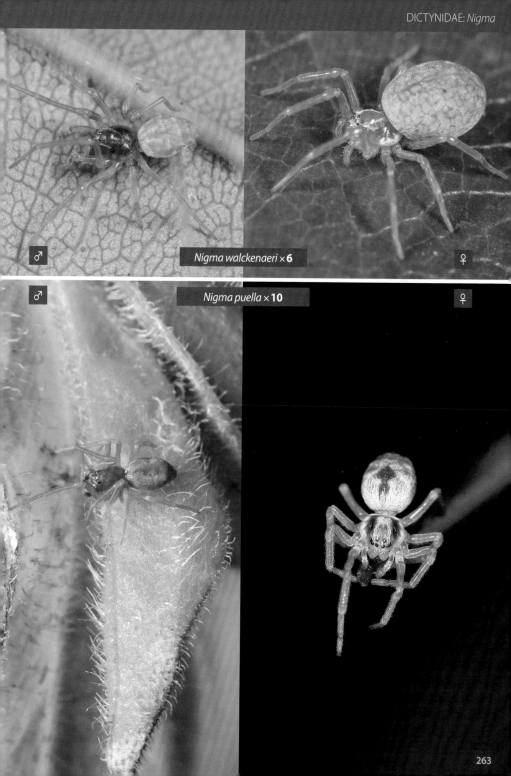

♂   *Nigma walckenaeri* × **6**   ♀

♂   *Nigma puella* × **10**   ♀

Cryphoeca
⚥ 1 British species (illustrated)

The single British species sometimes spins a small sheet web but often there is just a simple tubular retreat, typically hidden in leaf-litter and other concealed locations. ♂s and ♀s are similar, **with a characteristic pattern of white hairs on the abdomen.**

LC *Cryphoeca silvicola* ⚥

Common, regional

♂2·5–3·0mm ♀2·5–3·0mm   [PAGE 265 TL]

Observation tips/habitat: Occurs in woodlands amongst leaf-litter, under loose bark and in holes and crevices in bark. Also, on higher ground, amongst stones and rubble. ♂ usually darker than ♀.

Description: CARAPACE Brown, the head area usually darker than the thoracic area, which may have darker streaks radiating from fovea. ABDOMEN Dark grey to black with a pattern of lighter chevrons. The posterior spinnerets are conspicuous in ♂. LEGS Pale brown with darker annulations.

Similar species: *Tuberta maerens* (*below*).

Distribution/Status: Widespread and common in western and northern Britain, but is absent from East Anglia and south-east England.

♂
♀
J F M A M J J A S O N D

Tuberta
⚥ 1 British species (illustrated)

The single British species in this genus is extremely rare and appears to be restricted to trees in warm, dry microhabitats. It is **very similar to *Cryphoeca silvicola* in general appearance, but is slightly darker and smaller** and best separated by microscopic examination of the genitalia.

EN *Tuberta maerens* ⚥

Nationally Rare

Extremely rare

♂2mm ♀2mm   [PAGE 265 TR]

Observation tips/habitat: Recorded from fissures in the bark of tree trunks, particularly oak, in warm and sunny open woodland habitats.

Description: CARAPACE Very similar to *Cryphoeca silvicola* with vague radiating streaks on a yellow-brown background. ABDOMEN Black ground colour with a pale pattern similar to that of *C. silvicola*. LEGS Pale yellow-brown, sometimes with darker markings.

Similar species: *Cryphoeca silvicola* (*above*).

Distribution/Status: Very rare; recorded from sites in Oxfordshire and southern England, but not since the mid-1990s.

♂
♀   NO PHENOLOGY DATA

♀ *Cryphoeca silvicola* × **10**

♀ *Tuberta maerens* × **10**

Altella

ﾊ **1 British species (illustrated)**

The single British species is an extremely rare **minute, yellowish-brown spider**. Due to its extremely small size microscopic examination is required to confirm identification.

PE # *Altella lucida*

Biodiversity List (En)
Nationally Rare

Extremely rare

♂ 1·3–1·5 mm ♀ 1·5–1·8 mm

Observation tips/habitat: Occurs on dry heathland under stones. General coloration is yellowish-brown.

Description: CARAPACE Yellowish-brown with a slightly darker head area. ABDOMEN Grey, sometimes with a faint longitudinal central stripe. LEGS Yellowish-brown.

Similar species: None.

Distribution/Status: Extremely rare and possibly extinct in Britain; only two localities known and last recorded over 40 years ago.

♀ *Altella lucida* × **20**

NO PHENOLOGY DATA

× **10**

Argenna   🔬 **2 British species (2 illustrated)**

The two species within this genus are very similar. They are both **extremely small and have no distinctive features**. Both sexes have a similar appearance. Microscopic examination of the genitalia (see *page 96*) is necessary to confirm identification of the species.

LC *Argenna subnigra*   🔬

Nationally Scarce

Scarce, regional

⚥ ♂1·5–1·8mm ♀1·7–2·5mm   [PAGE 267 TL]
♂♀

Observation tips/habitat: Occurs under stones and amongst vegetation at ground level, usually in open, thinly vegetated areas of grasslands, dune systems, and waste ground. Occasionally occurs on bushes. Most frequently found near the coast.

Description: CARAPACE Pale to dark brown, sometimes with a dark margin. Darker streaks radiate from the fovea. ♂ often much darker. ABDOMEN Dark grey to black with three longitudinal lines of white hair tufts. LEGS Lighter shade than carapace with no markings.

Similar species: *Argenna patula* (*below*).

Distribution/Status: Scarce. Widely scattered throughout England and Wales with a concentration of records in the south-east.

♂
♀
J F M A M J J A S O N D

LC *Argenna patula*   🔬

Nationally Scarce

Scarce, regional

⚥ ♂2·5–2·8mm ♀2·7–3·0mm   [PAGE 267 TR]
♂♀

Observation tips/habitat: Very similar to, but slightly larger than *A. subnigra*. Restricted to coastal locations where it occurs amongst strandline detritus and under stones on the banks of tidal rivers.

Description: CARAPACE + ABDOMEN + LEGS Similar to *A. subnigra*.

Similar species: *Argenna subnigra* (*above*).

Distribution/Status: Scarce. Restricted to coastal sites in England and Wales, concentrated in East Anglia and the Thames estuary.

♂
♀
J F M A M J J A S O N D

♀ *Argenna subnigra* ×**10**

♀ *Argenna patula* ×**10**

Lathys

🔬 **3 British species (3 illustrated)**

Of the three species occurring in Britain only one, *L. humilis*, with **characteristic markings on its carapace and abdomen**, is likely to be encountered; the others are very rare. They are all small and have a similar appearance; sexes are similar. Microscopic examination of the genitalia (see *page 96*) is necessary to confirm identification of the species.

LC

Lathys humilis

🔬

Common, regional

♂1·7–2·0mm ♀2·0–2·5mm [PAGE 268 L]

Observation tips/habitat: Typically occurs in woodland and scrub amongst the foliage of Holly, Yew, pines and gorse. Appears to favour evergreens with small, sturdy leaves but has also been recorded from oak. Ornamental evergreens and privet hedges in parks and gardens are also a favoured habitat.

Description: CARAPACE Pale brown with darker streaks in the head area and dark, wedge-shaped markings radiating from the fovea in the thoracic area. ABDOMEN Light greenish-brown, mottled with white. A median band of paired dark patches widens towards the spinnerets. This pattern can vary but is usually clear against the paler background. The sides are usually dark with less white mottling. ♂'s similar but occasionally much darker. LEGS Yellowish-brown with very conspicuous dark annulations.

Similar species: Other *Lathys* species.

Distribution/Status: Widespread in southern Britain, scattered elsewhere and almost completely absent from Scotland and Wales.

♂
♀
J F M A M J J A S O N D

Lathys nielseni VU

♂ 1·6–2·0 mm ♀ 1·6–2·0 mm [C]

♂♀

Observation tips/habitat: Similar to *L. humilis* (*p. 267*) but paler in general appearance. Occurs in damp situations under stones or amongst litter at ground level on heathland.

Description: CARAPACE Similar to *L. humilis* but paler. ABDOMEN Similar to *L. humilis* but paler. LEGS Yellowish-brown but only faint apical darkening of segments.

Similar species: Other *Lathys* species.

Distribution/Status: Rare. Seemingly restricted to a small area of heathland in southern England.

Nationally Rare
Rare, regional

NO PHENOLOGY DATA

Lathys stigmatisata VU

♂ 2 mm ♀ 2·2–2·8 mm [R]

♂♀

Observation tips/habitat: Similar to *L. humilis* (*p. 267*) but not as strongly patterned. Appears to be restricted to coastal habitats where it occurs under stones and amongst low vegetation on areas of shingle.

Description: CARAPACE Similar to *L. humilis* but markings not as clear. ABDOMEN Greyish-brown with little or no pattern. LEGS Brown with no markings.

Similar species: Other *Lathys* species.

Distribution/Status: Rare. Only recorded from a few coastal sites in south-east and south-west England and south-west Wales.

Nationally Rare
Extremely rare

♂
♀
J F M A M J J A S O N D

♀ *Lathys humilis* × **10**

♀ *Lathys nielseni* × **10**

♂ *Lathys stigmatisata* × **10**

Mastigusa $\mathcal{P}$[♂] | ξ [♀] **1 British species (illustrated)**

The single British species in this genus is closely associated with ants' nests in ancient woodlands, often in the vicinity of old oak trees and stumps. **Specific habitat and appearance (particularly the ♂) allow for recognition with a hand lens.** The almost identical *Mastigusa arietina* was last recorded in the early 1900s but is now thought to be extinct in Britain.

Mastigusa macrophthalma $\mathcal{P}$[♂] | ξ [♀]

VU

Nationally Rare

Extremely rare

♂ 3.0–3.5 mm ♀ 3.0–3.5 mm

Observation tips/habitat: Occurs in ant nests, living with the ants and placing egg-sacs in galleries deep within the nest. Occasionally single individuals may be found away from ant nests under bark and within the hollow trunks of ancient trees.

Description: CARAPACE Pale yellow-brown and shiny. ♂ palps are very distinctive and enormous (compared to the size of the spider), having a whip-like extension which curves back over the carapace. ABDOMEN Ranges in colour from pale reddish-brown to dark grey with pairs of paler patches running longitudinally. At the posterior end these patches can resemble chevrons. Overall ♂ is slightly darker. LEGS Coloured as carapace.

Similar species: None.

Distribution/Status: Very rare. Recorded from just a few sites in Britain, always in areas of ancient woodland.

♂
♀

J F M A M J J A S O N D

♂ has a whip-like extension that curves back over the carapace

Mastigusa arietina [macrophthalma] ×6

The images above are of *Mastigusa arietina*. *M. macrophthalma* and *M. arietina* are virtually identical and some scientists consider them to be one species

CYBAEIDAE Soft spiders

1 British genus

The single British species in this eight-eyed family is the well-known Water Spider — the only spider known to live almost entirely under water. It spins a web in submerged vegetation which resembles a diving bell when filled with air, which is gathered at the surface and transported underwater on the hairy body and hind legs of the spider. The spider catches and consumes prey, mates and produces young in this aquatic environment and usually only comes to the surface to collect air, moult and disperse. Unusually amongst spiders, when the two sexes are found together the ♂ is often bigger than the ♀.

Argyroneta

 **1 British species (illustrated)**

Has a **very distinctive appearance underwater where a bubble of air, trapped by hairs on the abdomen, gives the spider a silvery sheen.** They are occasionally found wandering around on waterside plants where they appear dark brown with a velvety grey abdomen, their long, powerful legs make them look rather ungainly. Their identity can be confirmed by placing them on the water surface and seeing them immediately dive down.

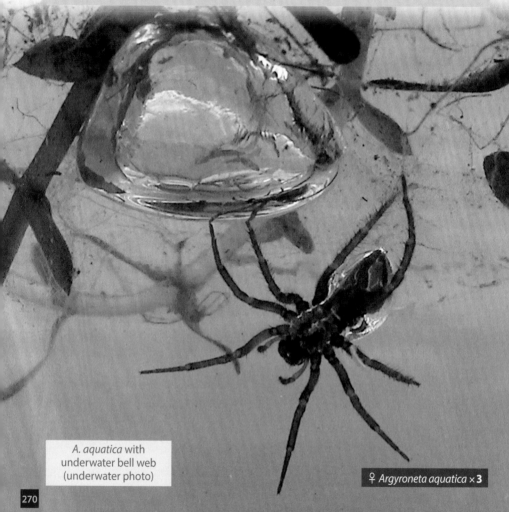

A. aquatica with underwater bell web (underwater photo)

♀ *Argyroneta aquatica* × **3**

LC *Argyroneta aquatica* Water Spider

Common, widespread

♂ 9–12 mm ♀ 8–15 mm

Observation tips/habitat: Occurs in clean, well-vegetated freshwater in ponds and streams with little or no current. It is often very difficult to find amongst aquatic vegetation.

Description: CARAPACE Pale to medium reddish-brown with indistinct darker streaks radiating from the fovea. There is a row of short fine hairs along the midline. ABDOMEN Fairly uniform, dark mousy-grey but thickly covered with short, velvety hair. LEGS Coloured as carapace. Legs III and IV covered with conspicuous, long, fine hairs; hairs largely absent on legs I and II.

Similar species: None.

Distribution/Status: Widespread and scattered in much of eastern England. More local in the west and Scotland. Can often be abundant in appropriate habitat. Probably under-recorded.

♂
♀
J F M A M J J A S O N D

Dorsal view of *A. aquatica* with air bubble surrounding the abdomen and showing the carapace features (underwater photo)

AMAUROBIIDAE Laceweb spiders   **2 British genera**

Comprises five species in two genera. All are eight-eyed, fairly large, robust spiders with swollen chelicerae which are clearly visible from above. The anterior section of the cephalothorax is broad and rounded.

LC *Coelotes atropos*

Common, regional

♂7–9mm ♀9–13mm   [PAGE 272 T]

Observation tips/habitat: Occurs in woodland, moorland and scrubby heathland under logs, and amongst leaf-litter at the bases of tree trunks. In woodland sites *C. atropos* can also be found living in rot-holes in the trunks of mature trees.

Description: CARAPACE Dark reddish-brown. The head area is darker with the chelicerae sometimes almost black. ABDOMEN Greyish-brown with a darker wedge-shaped, median stripe tapering towards the posterior. Scattered dark markings occur on either side. LEGS Coloured as carapace.

Similar species: *Coelotes terrestris* (*below*).

Distribution/Status: Common and widespread in Wales and the western half of England. Rare in south-east England and almost completely absent from Scotland.

♂
♀
J F M A M J J A S O N D

♀ *Coelotes atropos* ×**4**

Coelotes

 2 British species (2 illustrated)

Both species construct a **tubular, silk-lined burrow with a collar of cribellate silk** around the entrance. **The head area of the carapace is darker than the rest and the abdomen has a clear median stripe.** The depth of abdominal colour varies in both spiders and therefore microscopic examination of the genitalia (see *page 96*) is necessary to correctly identify the species.

LC *Coelotes terrestris* 🔎

♂7–10 mm ♀9–13 mm [PAGE 272 B]

Observation tips/habitat: Similar to *C. atropos* in the field and occurs in similar habitats.

Description: CARAPACE As *Coelotes atropos*.
ABDOMEN As *Coelotes atropos*, apart from a pale cardiac marking in the anterior half of the median stripe.
LEGS As *Coelotes atropos*.

Similar species: *Coelotes atropos* (*above*).

Distribution/Status: Generally confined to south-east England with only a few records from elsewhere.

Nationally Scarce

Uncommon, regional

J F M A M J J A S O N D

♀ *Coelotes terrestris* × 4

273

Amaurobius

 3 British species (3 illustrated)

Amaurobius webs, when fresh, have a lace-like appearance with a bluish tinge. The spider is active at night and, with a torch, can be observed adding to the web – drawing out fresh silk from the spinnerets with rapid movements of the hind legs. **The head area of the carapace is distinctly darker than the rest and the abdomen has a characteristic dark-brown, wedge-shaped marking edged with yellow.**

LC *Amaurobius similis*   ♀   **Common, widespread**

♂ 6–8 mm   ♀ 9–12 mm

♂ ♀ **Observation tips/habitat:** Found on buildings where its web is spun around holes in walls, fences and window frames, in which the spider lurks during the day. Can also occur away from houses where it may replace *A. fenestralis*.

Description: CARAPACE Dark reddish-brown. The head area is darker. ABDOMEN The dorsal surface has a dark brown, wedge-shaped marking edged with yellow in the anterior half. A pattern of pale chevrons occurs towards the rear. LEGS Coloured as carapace with darker annulations.

Similar species: *Amaurobius fenestralis* (*p. 276*).

Distribution/Status: A common and widespread species throughout much of Britain, more scattered in the north.

♂
♀

J F M A M J J A S O N D

A. similis and A. fenestralis can only be safely identified by microscopic examination of the genitalia (see *page 96*).

♀ *Amaurobius similis* ×**6**

♂ *A. ferox* showing
a white patch on
each pedipalp

♀ *Amaurobius ferox* × **6**

♀ *Amaurobius fenestralis* × **6**

LC *Amaurobius fenestralis* ⚲   Abundant, widespread

♂4–7mm ♀7–9mm   [PAGE 275 B]

Observation tips/habitat: Similar web to *A. similis*.
♂♀ Found under the bark of trees, under stones and in dense
vegetation such as gorse. Occasionally found on fences but
not regarded as a spider associated with gardens and buildings.

Description: CARAPACE + ABDOMEN + LEGS As *A. similis*.

Similar species: *Amaurobius similis* (*p. 274*).

Distribution/Status: Abundant and widespread, probably
commoner than *A. similis* in Scotland.

♂
♀
J F M A M J J A S O N D

LC *Amaurobius ferox* 🔍   Common, regional

♂8–10mm ♀11–15mm   [PAGE 275 T]

Observation tips/habitat: The largest, and darkest, member
of the genus found in the UK. Females, particularly, are often
almost black in appearance. Similar web and habitat to
♂♀ *A. similis*. Much less common than other *Amaurobius* spp.

Description: CARAPACE Dark brown with darker, almost black,
head area. The mature ♂ has a diagnostic, bright white patch on
each pedipalp. ABDOMEN ♀ Almost black with faint, sometimes
invisible, paler median markings in the anterior half. ♂ has
more distinct markings similar to *A. similis*, with a dark wedge
shape containing a pale central stripe. LEGS Dark with no
annulations.

Similar species: None.

Distribution/Status: Widely distributed in England, mainly
near the coast in Wales and with a few records from Scotland.

♂
♀
J F M A M J J A S O N D

276

LIOCRANIDAE Running foliage spiders

5 British genera

Closely resembling the Clubionidae (*p. 290*), the Liocranidae are eight-eyed nocturnal hunters that do not spin a web. The notable difference between these families is in eye position (see *pp. 64-65*). In most species both the abdomen and carapace have clear markings, which are fairly similar throughout the family. The principal differences between the genera are the number of pairs of ventral spines on metatarsus I and II and tibia I and II, which are usually discernible with a good-quality hand lens (see table *below*). Sexes are generally similar. The two spiders most likely to be encountered are within the genus *Agroeca*; the national status of all other members of the Liocranidae varies from uncommon to extremely rare.

Liocranidae: pairs of ventral spines by genera					
	Liocranum	*Agraecina*	*Agroeca*	*Apostenus*	*Scotina*
METATARSI I	1	2	3	3	♂3; ♀5–7
METATARSI II	1	2	3	3	♂3; ♀3–6
TIBIAE I	4	2	2	5	♂6–7; ♀7–10
TIBIAE II	4	2	2	5	♂5–7; ♀7–9

Agroeca

⬭ **6 British species (5 illustrated)**

The six species are very similar in general appearance; the depth of colour and strength of markings on both carapace and abdomen provide the principal differences. **Metatarsi I and II have three pairs of ventral spines; tibiae I and II have two** (see table *above*). All species occur amongst low vegetation, moss and leaf-litter. The two commonest, *A. brunnea* and *A. proxima*, produce a distinctive, stalked egg-sac which is suspended upside down in low vegetation, resembling an upturned wineglass. The egg-sac, which is seen more often than the spider, is covered in grains of soil brought up from the ground. Microscopic examination of the genitalia (see *page 96*) is necessary to confirm identification of the species.

♀ *Agroeca brunnea* ×**6**

LC *Agroeca brunnea*

Uncommon, widespread

♂5–6 mm ♀7–8 mm [PAGE 277 B]

Observation tips/habitat: The largest *Agroeca* species in Britain, found mainly in woodland at ground level amongst leaf-litter, grasses or other low vegetation. It is also recorded from grassland and heathland habitats. Its presence is usually betrayed by its distinctive egg-sac hanging in low vegetation.

Description: CARAPACE Pale brown with darker streaks radiating from the fovea but stopping short so as to leave a clear gap before a thin dark border. ABDOMEN Reddish-brown, with an indistinct darker cardiac mark and chevrons towards the posterior. LEGS Reddish-brown.

Similar species: Other *Agroeca* species, *Agraecina striata* (*p. 282*) which has two pairs of ventral spines on metatarsus I.

Distribution/Status: Widespread but scattered in much of England. Less so in the north, Scotland, Wales and the south-west.

LC *Agroeca proxima*

Uncommon, widespread

♂4·0–4·5 mm ♀5·5–7·5 mm [PAGE 281 T]

Observation tips/habitat: Similar to *A. brunnea* (*p. 277*) but perhaps more pinkish-grey. Prefers drier habitats in low vegetation and is probably one of the commonest species found on heathland. As with *A. brunnea* the egg-sac is usually conspicuous and maybe the only clue to the spider's presence.

Description: CARAPACE Similar to *A. brunnea* but the radiating dark streaks often reach the margin. ABDOMEN Similar to *A. brunnea* but the pattern is possibly clearer. LEGS Similar to *A. brunnea*.

Similar species: Other *Agroeca* species, *Agraecina striata* (*p. 282*) which has two pairs of ventral spines on metatarsus I.

Distribution/Status: Widespread and fairly common throughout Britain.

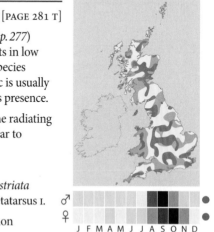

Agroeca inopina ♀

♂3·0–4·5mm ♀4·5–7·5mm   [PAGE 281 M]

Observation tips/habitat: Similar to *A. proxima* (*p. 278*) but darker overall. Occurs amongst grass clumps and other low vegetation typically in dry, open habitats such as chalk grassland. It is also occasionally found on sand dunes and in open, stony areas of heathland.

Description: CARAPACE Similar to *A. proxima* but dark streaks more distinct and reaching the margin. ABDOMEN Darker than *A. proxima*. LEGS Brown with faint annulations.

Similar species: Other *Agroeca* species, *Agraecina striata* (*p. 282*) which has two pairs of ventral spines on metatarsus I.

Distribution/Status: Widespread but local in south-east and south-central England. Very scattered elsewhere in the southern half of Britain.

♂
♀
J F M A M J J A S O N D

Agroeca lusatica ♀

♂5–6mm ♀6–7mm   [PAGE 281 B]

Observation tips/habitat: Similar in general appearance to *A. proxima* (*p. 278*) and in Britain only recorded from two sand dune habitats.

Description: CARAPACE Similar to other *Agroeca* species, but the dark radiating streaks do not reach the thin dark margin. ABDOMEN As other *Agroeca* species. LEGS Brown with femora and patellae noticeably lighter.

Similar species: Other *Agroeca* species, *Agraecina striata* (*p. 282*) which has two pairs of ventral spines on metatarsus I.

Distribution/Status: Rare. Currently known from two coastal locations in south-east England.

♂
♀
J F M A M J J A S O N D

Agroeca dentigera

♂4·5mm ♀5·5–6·0mm [NOT ILLUSTRATED]

♂♀ **Observation tips/habitat:** Similar to *A. lusatica* (*p. 279*) in its sand dune habitat preference. Recorded in Britain from a single location. Appearance similar to *A. brunnea* (*p. 278*) but the ground colour and markings are rather lighter.

Description: CARAPACE Similar to other *Agroeca* species but with a thin, dark borderline. ABDOMEN Similar to other *Agroeca* species. The central dorsal stripe is not well defined and on either side is an irregular pattern of dark bars and blotches. LEGS Sometimes with faint annulations on the tibiae.

Similar species: Other *Agroeca* species, *Agraecina striata* (*p. 282*) which has two pairs of ventral spines on metatarsus I.

Distribution/Status: Extremely rare, only known from one site on the coast of west Wales.

Nationally Rare — Extremely rare

♂ NO PHENOLOGY DATA
♀
J F M A M J J A S O N D

Agroeca cuprea

♂3·5–4·0mm ♀4–5mm

♂♀ **Observation tips/habitat:** Predominantly a coastal spider with only one known inland area. It occurs in dry sandy habitats on heathland, coastal grassland and dunes. Although similar in appearance to other *Agroeca* species it is usually much darker. The whole spider is covered with coppery-coloured hairs.

Description: CARAPACE Similar to other *Agroeca* species, but much darker. Radiating streaks are often more diffuse and indistinct, and may be completely hidden. ABDOMEN Similar to other *Agroeca* species. LEGS Pale brown with darker femora.

Similar species: Other *Agroeca* species, *Agraecina striata* (*p. 282*).

Distribution/Status: Widespread but very scattered records from coastal sites in the south-east, south-west and north-west. Also recorded inland from the Brecklands of East Anglia.

Biodiversity List (En) — Nationally Rare — Rare, local

♂
♀
J F M A M J J A S O N D

♀ *Agroeca cuprea* ×6

AGROECA CARAPACE STREAKS

A. brunnea – clear gap
before thin dark margin

A. proxima –
often reach margin

A. inopina –
reach dark margin

♀ *Agroeca proxima* ×**6**

♀ *Agroeca inopina* ×**6**

♂ *Agroeca lusatica* ×**6**

Agraecina

🔍 **1 British species (illustrated)**

The genus is very similar to *Agroeca* (*page 277*) but differs in having **three pairs of ventral spines on metatarsus I** (two in *Agraecina* – see table *page 277*), accounting for its designation as a separate genus. It also **prefers much damper habitats** than *Agroeca* species.

LC *Agraecina striata* 🔍

♂3·0–3·5mm ♀4·5–5·5mm

Observation tips/habitat: Occurs at ground level in a variety of fresh and brackish wetland habitats, including wet heathland, bogs, marshes, fens, and wet, broadleaved woodland.

Description: CARAPACE Similar markings to *Agroeca* species. ♀ has a yellowish ground colour with no borderline; ♂ is darker, sometimes with a greyish-black borderline. ABDOMEN Similar pattern to *Agroeca* but often more pronounced, although variable in the depth of colour. Usually a dark brown ground colour with a thin, pale, irregular median band flanked by five or six pairs of light spots and with a pair of lighter bands on each side of the abdomen. LEGS Light brown with faint annulations.

Similar species: *Agroeca* species (*pp. 277–281*), which have three pairs of spines on metatarsus I.

Distribution/Status: Occasional northern records but mainly confined to the southern half of Britain where it is predominantly found near the coast.

Nationally Scarce

Scarce, local

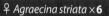

♂
♀
J F M A M J J A S O N D

♀ *Agraecina striata* ×**6**

Apostenus

 1 British species (illustrated)

Similar in general appearance to members of the genus *Scotina* (*page 284*). *Apostenus* differs principally in having **five pairs of ventral spines on tibiae I and II and three pairs on metatarsi I and II** (see table *page 277*).

VU *Apostenus fuscus*

Nationally Rare

Extremely rare

♂2·8–4·0mm ♀3–4mm

Observation tips/habitat: Only recorded from a single area of coastal shingle where a thin soil layer supports a sparse vegetation of grasses, mosses and lichens.

Description: CARAPACE Brown with a thin, darker borderline; no other pattern. ABDOMEN Dark grey with an indistinct longitudinal pattern of pairs of white spots. LEGS Pale brown, with five pairs of ventral spines on tibiae I and II and three pairs on metatarsi I and II.

Similar species: None.

Distribution/Status: Very rare. Known only from the Dungeness area in south-east England.

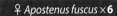

♂
♀

J F M A M J J A S O N D

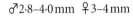

Apostenus has five pairs of spines on the ventral side of tibiae I and II

1 2 3 4 5

♀ *Apostenus fuscus* ×**6**

283

Scotina

🔎 **3 British species (3 illustrated)**

All three species are **similar in general appearance to the** *Agroeca* genus (*page 277*). However, they differ **in having 6–10 pairs of ventral spines on tibiae I, 5–9 on tibiae II, 3–7 on metatarsi I and 3–6 on metatarsi II which are quite conspicuous when viewed with a hand lens** (see table *page 277*). They are small spiders, occurring in leaf-litter and plant detritus under vegetation. All are uncommon and similar to one another. Microscopic examination of the genitalia (see *page 96*) is necessary to confirm identification of the species.

LC *Scotina celans* ♀

Nationally Scarce
Scarce, widespread

♂2·5–3·0mm ♀4·0–4·8mm [PAGE 285 T]

♂♀ **Observation tips/habitat:** Generally a woodland species, occurring in damp conditions amongst moss and ground debris. Also recorded from heathland but usually only from damper areas; *S. gracilipes* (*below*) is the commoner heathland species.

Description: CARAPACE Dark brown to black with **thin, lighter median and lateral bands.** ABDOMEN Reddish-brown with paler chevrons and spots in ♂. These markings are less obvious in ♀ and may disappear altogether under a covering of fine hairs. LEGS In ♀ the colour darkens outwards from the body, from pale yellowish-brown femora to dark brown tarsi, but less so on tibiae and tarsi III and IV. In ♂ similar, but paler.

Similar species: Other *Scotina* species.

Distribution/Status: Widespread but uncommon in south-east England. Much more scattered elsewhere.

♂
♀
J F M A M J J A S O N D

LC *Scotina gracilipes* ♀

Nationally Scarce
Scarce, widespread

♂2·5–3·5mm ♀2·5–3·5mm [PAGE 285 BL]

Observation tips/habitat: Typically in dry, open heathland habitats at ground level amongst heather roots, favouring more mature heather areas. Also occasionally recorded from woodland and raised bog.

Description: CARAPACE Dark brown, without the light banding of *S. celans*. ABDOMEN Dark sides with central, paler band widening towards the spinnerets and containing five dark, flattened, W-shaped markings posteriorly forming a clear pattern. LEGS Clear distinction between yellowish-brown femora and dark brown tibiae and metatarsi of legs I, II and III. Less clear on leg IV.

Similar species: Other *Scotina* species.

Distribution/Status: Widespread but scattered distribution throughout Britain. Generally scarce but can be common on some southern heathlands.

♂
♀
J F M A M J J A S O N D

Scotina palliardii

♂2·5–3·5 mm ♀2·5–3·5 mm   [BR]

Observation tips/habitat: Occurs in wet heathland amongst moss and heather litter. Also recorded from chalk grassland. **Description:** CARAPACE Dark brown, as in *S. gracilipes*, occasionally with lighter streaking. ABDOMEN **Darker than other *Scotina* species with a less distinct pattern, if any.** LEGS Similar to *S. gracilipes*, particularly in legs I and II.

Similar species: Other *Scotina* species.

Distribution/Status: Rare. Recorded from only a very few sites in recent years. Confined to south-east and south-central Britain.

Nationally Rare

Rare, regional

♂
♀
J F M A M J J A S O N D

♀ *Scotina celans* × **6**

♀ *Scotina gracilipes* × **6**

♀ *Scotina palliardii* × **6**

285

Liocranum

🔍 **1 British species (illustrated)**

The single species in this genus is **larger than most other liocranids, and has a clear abdominal pattern** in both sexes. **Metatarsi** I and II have one pair of ventral spines; tibiae I and II four pairs (see table *page 277*).

LC *Liocranum rupicola* 🔍

Nationally Scarce

Scarce, regional

♂5·5–6·0mm ♀6·0–8·5mm

Observation tips/habitat: Favours a much drier habitat than most other liocranids and occurs under and amongst stones in, for example, quarries and dry-stone walls. Occasionally recorded in houses.

Description: CARAPACE Irregular, pale brown, median band flanked by a pair of darker lateral bands with paler sub-marginal bands and a dark borderline. ABDOMEN Dark brown ground colour with a conspicuous lighter pattern: anteriorly, a diamond-shaped area with a thin, dark, median line; posteriorly, a series of pale chevrons diminishing in size towards the spinnerets. LEGS Greyish-brown with faint annulations.

Similar species: None.

Distribution/Status: Locally distributed in south Wales and south-west England.

J F M A M J J A S O N D

♀ *Liocranum rupicola* ×6

ANYPHAENIDAE   Buzzing spiders   **1 British genus**

The single British genus has eight eyes and is superficially similar to the Clubionidae (*p. 290*) in appearance and body shape.

Anyphaena   **2 British species (1 illustrated)**

The spiders in this genus are easily identified in the field by their **conspicuous abdominal markings**. Ventrally, **the tracheal spiracle is easily seen, positioned halfway between the spinnerets and the epigastric furrow**. The sexes are similar. Microscopic examination of the genitalia (see *page 96*) is necessary to distinguish between the species.

LC   *Anyphaena accentuata*   Buzzing Spider   ⚲   **Common, regional**

♂ 4·0–6·5 mm   ♀ 4·5–7·0 mm

Observation tips/habitat: Occurs in the foliage of trees and bushes. Where found it can be quite numerous.

Description: CARAPACE Two dark brown lateral bands flank a pale yellow-brown median band which has a pair of dark spots behind the eyes. The lateral bands have dentate outer edges and contain small pale streaks. ABDOMEN Pale yellow-brown with darker sides. Centrally the dark markings resemble two arrowheads pointing forwards. LEGS Yellow-brown with numerous small, dark marks, sometimes amounting to annulations.

Similar species: *Anyphaena sabina* (*p. 288*).

Distribution/Status: Widespread and common in much of southern Britain. Much less so north of a line drawn between the Humber and Mersey estuaries.

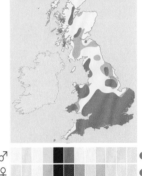

♂
♀
J F M A M J J A S O N D

♂ *Anyphena accentuata* × **6**

Anyphaena sabina 🔬

Extremely rare

♂5·5–6·5mm　♀7·0–9·5mm　　　　　[NOT ILLUSTRATED]

Observation tips/habitat: A recent (2014) addition to the British spider fauna *A. sabina* occurs in similar habitats to *A. accentuata* within small, neglected urban sites of overgrown rubble with rough, tussocky grass patches. It is indistinguishable from *A. accentuata* in general appearance and the spider can only be identified by microscopic examination of the genitalia (see *page 96*).

Description: CARAPACE + ABDOMEN + LEGS Similar to *A.accentuata*.

Similar species: *Anyphaena accentuata* (*p.287*).

Distribution/Status: Confined to the London area where it appears to be well established.

♂
♀

J F M A M J J A S O N D

CORINNIDAE Ant-like sac spiders　　　1 British genus

The single genus in this eight-eyed family is similar to the Liocranidae (*p.277*) but has recently been regarded as a separate family because of differences in the structure of the male pedipalp.

Phrurolithus　　　🔍 2 British species (1 illustrated)

The two species are small and very similar. They have **an ant-like appearance** and, unlike the Liocranidae, are **active during the day**. They run around rapidly in warm, sunny conditions hunting prey. *Phrurolithus festivus* is by far the most likely species to be encountered. The genus has a **characteristic appearance enabling recognition in the field**. In the ♂ the abdomen is completely covered with a shiny scutum.

♀ *Phrurolithus festivus* × **10**

.c *Phrurolithus festivus*

Common, regional

♂2·5–3·0 mm   ♀2·5–3·0 mm   [PAGE 288]

Observation tips/habitat: Occurs in a wide variety of habitats including under stones, in leaf-litter, grasslands and gardens, often in association with ants, in both dry and damp conditions.

Description: CARAPACE Dark brown with a black head area and covered with fine hairs. ABDOMEN Dark grey to black with distinctive patches of white hairs, one on each 'shoulder' of the abdomen and, centrally, a curved row of three, sometimes joining to form a chevron. Another small, white patch is present just above the spinnerets. LEGS Pale brown with darker femora I and II.

Similar species: *Phrurolithus minimus* (*below*).

Distribution/Status: Widely scattered and fairly common in much of southern England. Less so in the west, north and Scotland.

J F M A M J J A S O N D

NB The visual differences described in the accounts may not be present in all individuals and microscopic examination is necessary to confirm identification of the two species.

.LC *Phrurolithus minimus*

Nationally Scarce

Scarce, regional

♂2·0–2·5 mm   ♀2·5–3·0 mm   [NOT ILLUSTRATED]

Observation tips/habitat: Occurs mainly on chalk grassland in open stony areas. Occasionally recorded from open woodland on bare, stony ground or on dry leaf-litter. General appearance is similar to *P. festivus*, but the spider seems to prefer drier conditions.

Description: CARAPACE Reddish-brown. ABDOMEN Similar to *P. festivus* but the white markings are usually less clear and the central ones may be completely absent. LEGS Similar to *P. festivus* but often slightly darker.

Similar species: *Phrurolithus festivus* (*above*).

Distribution/Status: Very local and mainly confined to south-east England with just a few scattered records elsewhere.

J F M A M J J A S O N D

CLUBIONIDAE Sac spiders

2 British genera

Contains 25, eight-eyed species in two genera. The majority are greyish-brown in colour with a mousy appearance, but lacking any distinctive pattern. They are predominantly nocturnal hunters. The ♀s are often found guarding their egg-sacs in silk cells hidden amongst vegetation, commonly within folded leaves, under loose bark or in ground debris.

Clubiona

21 British species (19 illustrated)

The **carapace usually has no clear markings** and apart from two species (*C. corticalis* and *C. comta*) **the abdomen has no distinct pattern. Generally the chelicerae are a darker shade than the rest of the body**, sometimes quite distinctly so. **Leg ɪᴠ is the longest.**

With the exception of *C. corticalis* and *C. comta*, the *Clubiona* spp. are extremely similar to each other and features such as abdomen and carapace colour, hairiness, and strength and depth of markings are variable, highly subjective, and overlap both within and between species. Consequently, members of the genus are not distinguishable in the field, even with the use of a hand lens, and microscopic examination of the genitalia is necessary to determine the identification of individual species.

♀ *Clubiona corticalis* × **4**

♀ *Clubiona comta* × **4**

LC

Clubiona corticalis 🔍

♂6–10mm ♀7–10mm   [PAGE 290 T]

Observation tips/habitat: Typically occurs under loose bark of ancient and dead trees, but also found under stones and in leaf-litter in a variety of habitats including mixed woodland, heathland, marsh vegetation and scrubby grassland. Sometimes found in birds' nests and squirrel dreys.

Description: CARAPACE Brown, sometimes with a darker head area. ABDOMEN ♀ brown with a clear yellowish-brown median band containing a dark brown cardiac streak which extends halfway to the spinnerets. Posteriorly, the median band is broken into four or five chevrons. ♂ has a similar pattern but the abdomen is narrower. LEGS Coloured as carapace.

Similar species: *Clubiona comta* (*below*).

♂
♀
J F M A M J J A S O N D

Distribution/Status: Common and widespread in southern and central England. Scattered in Wales, the south-west and northern England. Absent from Scotland.

LC

Clubiona comta 🔍

♂3–5mm ♀3.5–6.0mm   [PAGE 290 B]

Observation tips/habitat: The commonest of the smaller clubionids, *C. comta* is typically found in the foliage and under loose bark of trees and bushes. Its small size and characteristic appearance should enable field identification with a hand lens.

Description: CARAPACE ♀ pale brown, sometimes with a thin, dark borderline. ♂ is darker with a broader borderline. ABDOMEN A very similar pattern to *C. corticalis* but the spider itself is much smaller. The pattern is usually quite distinct but more reddish-brown than in *C. corticalis*. LEGS Coloured as carapace.

Similar species: *Clubiona corticalis* (*above*).

Distribution/Status: Common and widespread in much of England but more scattered in the west and north, Wales and Scotland.

♂
♀
J F M A M J J A S O N D

LC *Clubiona terrestris*   🔬

Common, widespread

♂5–6mm   ♀6–7mm   [PAGE 296 BL]

♂♀ **Observation tips/habitat:** Typically found at ground level in leaf-litter and detritus in fairly dry conditions. Occurs in a wide variety of habitats, including on trees and shrubs, in gardens and in and around buildings. It is also sometimes found under loose bark or stones.

Description: CARAPACE Light yellowish-brown, with dark chelicerae. ABDOMEN Paler than most other clubionids, varying from yellow to reddish-brown, and with a dark cardiac stripe tapering posteriorly. LEGS Pale yellow.

Similar species: All other *Clubiona* species (apart from *C. comta* and *C. corticalis*).

Distribution/Status: Common and widespread in the southern half of Britain. Scattered farther north.

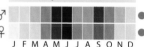

♂
♀
J F M A M J J A S O N D

LC *Clubiona neglecta*   🔬

Common, widespread

♂4–6mm   ♀6–8mm   [PAGE 296 ML]

♂♀ **Observation tips/habitat:** Occurs in thinly vegetated, open habitats such as short grassland, sand dunes, brownfield sites, abandoned quarries and brick pits. It is usually found amongst scrub and under stones.

Description: CARAPACE Similar to *C. terrestris* (*above*) but with a darker head area particularly in ♂. Dark chelicerae. ABDOMEN Reddish-brown with a slightly darker, but often rather vague, cardiac stripe. LEGS Very pale yellow.

Similar species: All other *Clubiona* species (apart from *C. comta* and *C. corticalis*).

Distribution/Status: Widespread but very local and scattered throughout Britain.

♂
♀
J F M A M J J A S O N D

Clubiona pseudoneglecta

♂5·3–5·5mm ♀5·3–6·8mm [PAGE 296 MR]

Observation tips/habitat: Very similar in general appearance to *C. neglecta* (*p. 292*) and only recently (2000) recognized as a separate species. It appears to be restricted to sand dune habitats in Britain.

Description: CARAPACE + ABDOMEN + LEGS
Very similar to *C. neglecta*.

Similar species: All other *Clubiona* species (apart from *C. comta* and *C. corticalis*).

Distribution/Status: Rare. Apparently restricted to just one coastal site in mainland Britain but also recorded from the Channel Isles and the Isles of Scilly.

Nationally Rare

Extremely rare

♂
♀
J F M A M J J A S O N D

Clubiona lutescens

♂4–6mm ♀6–8mm [PAGE 296 T]

Observation tips/habitat: Similar to both *C. terrestris* and *C. neglecta* (both *p. 292*) in general appearance and care needs to be taken in species determination. Found in a wide variety of habitats including woodland, grassland, wetland, gardens, allotments, brownfield sites and coastal areas, usually in fairly damp situations.

Description: CARAPACE + ABDOMEN + LEGS Similar to *C. neglecta*.

Similar species: All other *Clubiona* species (apart from *C. comta* and *C. corticalis*).

Distribution/Status: Common and widespread in much of England. More scattered in Wales and the south-west and uncommon in Scotland.

Common, widespread

♂
♀
J F M A M J J A S O N D

LC *Clubiona reclusa*

Abundant, widespread

♂5–6mm ♀6–9mm   [PAGE 296 BR]

Observation tips/habitat: Occurs amongst low vegetation and detritus in a wide range of habitats, most often in damp, marshy situations but also scrub grassland, nettle beds, rubbish tips and heathland. Its appearance is uniform and typical of the genus. It is probably the commonest species of the genus in Britain.

Description: CARAPACE Reddish-brown, with a darker borderline. ABDOMEN Dark brown, sometimes a vague dorsal stripe may be discernible. LEGS Coloured as carapace, may be slightly lighter in ♂.

Similar species: All other *Clubiona* species (apart from *C. comta* and *C. corticalis*).

Distribution/Status: Abundant and widespread throughout Britain.

♂
♀

J F M A M J J A S O N D

LC *Clubiona brevipes*

Common, regional

♂4–6mm ♀4·5–7·0mm   [PAGE 297 TL]

Observation tips/habitat: Found in similar habitats to *C. comta* but is markedly different in appearance. Appears to favour oaks, where it can be abundant.

Description: CARAPACE Dark brown with almost black chelicerae. ABDOMEN Reddish-brown, occasionally with an indistinct, darker cardiac stripe. LEGS Yellowish-brown, much lighter than the carapace.

Similar species: All other *Clubiona* species (apart from *C. comta* and *C. corticalis*).

Distribution/Status: Common and widespread in southern half of England. More scattered in the south-west, Wales and as far north as central Scotland.

♂
♀

J F M A M J J A S O N D

LC *Clubiona trivialis* ♀

♂ 3·5–4·0 mm ♀ 4–4·5 mm [PAGE 297 TR]

Common, widespread

♂♀ Observation tips/habitat: Occurs amongst low vegetation such as heather and gorse and under stones, frequently on high ground in moorland and heathland habitats. It has also been recorded from sea level. The spider has an overall reddish appearance.

Description: CARAPACE Yellowish-brown. ABDOMEN Usually a uniform reddish-brown, occasionally with a faint cardiac mark. LEGS Pale yellow, slightly darker in ♂.

Similar species: All other *Clubiona* species (apart from *C. comta* and *C. corticalis*).

Distribution/Status: Widespread and fairly frequent in the north and west of Britain. Very scattered in south-east England.

♂
♀
J F M A M J J A S O N D

NT *Clubiona juvenis* ♀

♂ 4–5 mm ♀ 5–6 mm [PAGE 297 ML]

Nationally Rare

Rare, regional

♂♀ Observation tips/habitat: Restricted to reedbeds and fens in Britain where ♀s have been recorded from silken retreats spun in reed heads.

Description: CARAPACE Yellowish-brown with darker chelicerae and head area. It is noticeably oblong in shape when viewed from above. ABDOMEN Pale yellow with a reddish cardiac mark and a covering of silky hairs. Coloration is darker in ♂. LEGS Pale yellow.

Similar species: All other *Clubiona* species (apart from *C. comta* and *C. corticalis*).

Distribution/Status: Rare, recorded from a very few sites in East Anglia, the Thames estuary and Dorset.

♂
♀
J F M A M J J A S O N D

♂   *Clubiona lutescens* ×**6**   ♀

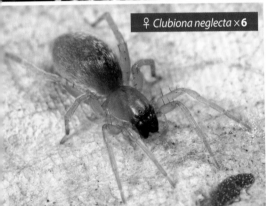

♀ *Clubiona neglecta* ×**6**

♀ *Clubiona pseudoneglecta* ×**6**

♀ *Clubiona terrestris* ×**6**

♀ *Clubiona reclusa* with egg-sac ×**6**

♀ *Clubiona brevipes* ×**6**

♀ *Clubiona trivialis* ×**6**

♀ *Clubiona juvenis* ×**6**

♀ *Clubiona subsultans* ×**6**

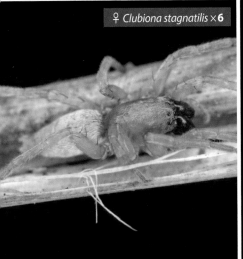

♀ *Clubiona stagnatilis* ×**6**

♀ *Clubiona norvegica* ×**6**

NT *Clubiona subsultans*

♂4–7mm ♀5–7mm   [PAGE 297 MR]

Biodiversity List (Sc)
Nationally Rare
Rare, regional

Observation tips/habitat: Occurs in native pine forest, on the ground under stones and amongst pine needle litter and moss. Also recorded underneath bark.

Description: CARAPACE Yellowish-brown.
ABDOMEN Pale yellow-brown with a conspicuous, dark cardiac mark extending halfway down the abdomen.
LEGS Yelowish-brown, as carapace.

Similar species: All other *Clubiona* species (apart from *C. comta* and *C. corticalis*).

Distribution/Status: Restricted to Caledonian pine forest in central and northern Scotland where it can be common.

♂
♀
J F M A M J J A S O N D

LC *Clubiona stagnatilis*

♂5–7mm ♀6–8mm   [PAGE 297 BL]

Common, widespread

Observation tips/habitat: A wetland species mainly occurring in fens, bogs and coastal habitats.

Description: CARAPACE As *C. subsultans* (*above*).
ABDOMEN Reddish-brown, sometimes with slightly darker cardiac mark. LEGS As *C. subsultans*.

Similar species: All other *Clubiona* species (apart from *C. comta* and *C. corticalis*).

Distribution/Status: Widespread but scattered in England and Wales. Less common in Scotland.

♂
♀
J F M A M J J A S O N D

LC *Clubiona norvegica* ◆

Nationally Scarce
Scarce, regional

♂4–5mm ♀5–8mm   [PAGE 297 BR]

Observation tips/habitat: Occurs mainly at high altitudes in wet moorland amongst *Sphagnum* and other mosses. General appearance very similar to *C. stagnatilis* (*p. 298*).

Description: CARAPACE As *C. stagnatilis*.
ABDOMEN As *C. stagnatilis* but slightly more greyish-brown.
LEGS As *C. stagnatilis*.

Similar species: All other *Clubiona* species (apart from *C. comta* and *C. corticalis*).

Distribution/Status: Widespread in the Welsh uplands, widely scattered elsewhere but mainly in the uplands of northern England and Scotland.

♂
♀
J F M A M J J A S O N D

LC *Clubiona subtilis*

Uncommon, regional

♂2·5–3·0mm ♀3·0–4·5mm   [PAGE 301 TL]

Observation tips/habitat: Typically a wetland species, occurring mainly in fens, bogs and coastal habitats, but occasionally recorded from tidal litter on sand dunes.

Description: CARAPACE Pale yellowish-brown with a darker head area. Sometimes ♂s can be a much darker brown.
ABDOMEN Similar to *C. diversa* (*p. 300*) but usually slightly darker and with the midline markings more apparent. LEGS Yellow in ♀, darker shade in ♂.

Similar species: All other *Clubiona* species (apart from *C. comta* and *C. corticalis*).

Distribution/Status: Widespread in East Anglia, south-east England and coastal Wales. Much more scattered elsewhere and absent from large areas of the north and Scotland.

♂
♀
J F M A M J J A S O N D

299

LC *Clubiona diversa* ♀

♂ ♂ ♂3–4mm ♀4–5mm   [PAGE 301 TR]

Common, widespread

♂♀ **Observation tips/habitat:** Occurs amongst low vegetation in dryish habitats on chalk grassland in the south of Britain, but in wetter, boggy and marshy areas in the north, where it can be quite common. It is nocturnally active, but ♀s can be found during the day guarding their egg-sacs, contained within white, silken cells, under logs and stones.

Description: CARAPACE Pale yellowish-brown, sometimes slightly darker in ♂. Darkened ♂ palps contrast markedly with the rest of the body. ABDOMEN Pale yellow with reddish midline markings which are variable in their depth of colour but usually discernible in living spiders. LEGS Pale yellowish-brown, as carapace.

Similar species: All other *Clubiona* species (apart from *C. comta* and *C. corticalis*).

Distribution/Status: Widespread and scattered throughout Britain.

♂
♀

J F M A M J J A S O N D

VU *Clubiona rosserae* Rosser's Sac Spider ♀

♂ ♂ ♂4–5mm ♀5.5–6mm   [PAGE 301 M]

Biodiversity List (En)
Nationally Rare
Extremely rare

♂♀ **Observation tips/habitat:** An extremely rare spider in Britain. It is only recorded from two fenland sites where it occurs in sedge tussocks and amongst sedge and reed litter. Very similar in appearance to *C. lutescens* (*p. 293*).

Description: CARAPACE As *C. lutescens*. ABDOMEN As *C. lutescens*. The cardiac stripe may be more definite. LEGS As *C. lutescens*.

Similar species: All other *Clubiona* species (apart from *C. corticalis* and *C. comta*).

Distribution/Status: Extremely rare. Known from only two East Anglian fens.

♂
♀

J F M A M J J A S O N D

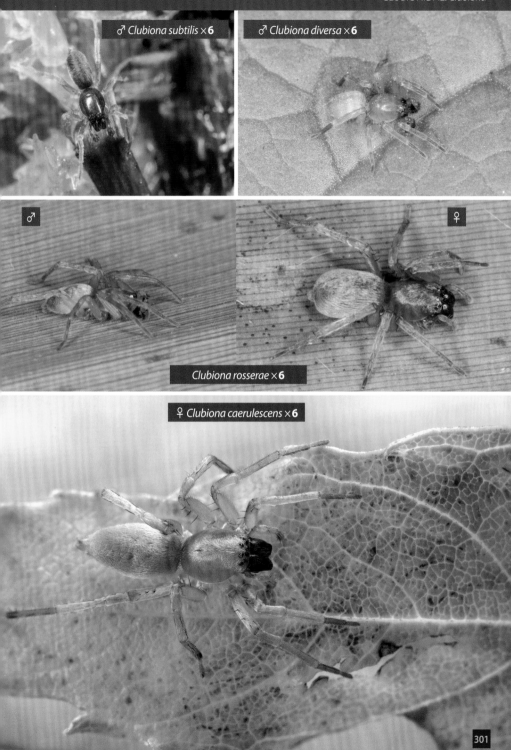

♂ *Clubiona subtilis* ×**6**

♂ *Clubiona diversa* ×**6**

♂

♀

Clubiona rosserae ×**6**

♀ *Clubiona caerulescens* ×**6**

VU *Clubiona caerulescens* 🔬

♂5–7mm ♀6–9mm   [PAGE 301 B]

Observation tips/habitat: Occurs on low vegetation in
♂♀ woodland and scrub, particularly in fairly dry conditions.

Description: CARAPACE Yellow-brown. ABDOMEN Pale brown
with a **covering of long, silky hairs that are more conspicuous
than in other *Clubiona* species**. A very indistinct darker cardiac
mark is sometimes present. LEGS Light brownish-yellow.

Similar species: All other *Clubiona* species (apart from
C. comta and *C. corticalis*).

Distribution/Status: Very rare but widely scattered
throughout Britain.

Nationally Rare
Rare, local

♂
♀   NO PHENOLOGY DATA

LC *Clubiona pallidula* 🔬

♂6–8mm ♀7–11mm   [PAGE 303 BL]

Observation tips/habitat: One of the larger members of the
genus, this spider typically inhabits the foliage of trees and
♂♀ shrubs but also regularly occurs in gardens, grassy areas and
under stones. Occasionally found inside houses, outhouses and
derelict buildings.

Description: CARAPACE Greyish-brown, sometimes with a
darker head area. ABDOMEN Dark brown but covered with
pale, silky hairs giving the live spider a silvery appearance.
LEGS Yellow-brown.

Similar species: All other *Clubiona* species (apart from
C. comta and *C. corticalis*).

Distribution/Status: Local and widespread in central and
southern England, more scattered elsewhere and almost
completely absent from Scotland.

Common, regional

♂
♀
J F M A M J J A S O N D

Clubiona phragmitis

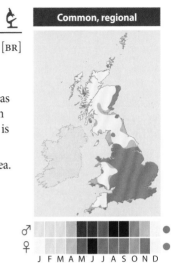

♂5–10 mm ♀7–11 mm   [BR]

Observation tips/habitat: Principally favours wetland habitats, particularly in emergent vegetation at the water margins, also occasionally recorded from sand dunes. In areas of open water the spider can be seen lying in wait for prey on stems just above the water surface. A folded reed leaf retreat is often a clue to the presence of the ♀.

Description: CARAPACE Yellow-brown with a darker head area. The chelicerae are large and dark. ABDOMEN Greyish-brown with a covering of silky hairs. LEGS Yellow-brown.

Similar species: All other *Clubiona* species (apart from *C. comta* and *C. corticalis*).

Distribution/Status: Widespread and locally common in much of central and southern England. Less so in the south-west, the north and Wales. Almost completely absent from inland Scotland.

♂
♀
J F M A M J J A S O N D

♀ *Clubiona pallidula* ×**6**

♀ *Clubiona phragmitis* ×**6**

303

NT *Clubiona frisia*

♂5–6mm ♀5–7mm   [NOT ILLUSTRATED]

♂♀ **Observation tips/habitat:** Restricted to a few coastal sand dunes where it occurs in tussocks of Marram Grass.

Description: CARAPACE Yellowish-brown.
ABDOMEN Reddish-brown with a slightly darker cardiac stripe.
LEGS Coloured as carapace.

Similar species: All other *Clubiona* species (apart from *C. comta* and *C. corticalis*).

Distribution/Status: Rare. Occurs at a few coastal sites in East Anglia and south-east England.

♂
♀
J F M A M J J A S O N D

NT *Clubiona genevensis*

♂3·0–3·5mm ♀3·5–4·5mm

♂♀ **Observation tips/habitat:** In Britain, occurs in coastal grassland and heath, under stones and amongst low vegetation. Only found in coastal locations very close to the sea.

Description: CARAPACE Reddish-brown, slightly darker in the head area. ABDOMEN Yellow-brown with a reddish pattern similar to that of *C. comta* (*p. 291*). LEGS Pale yellowish-brown.

Similar species: All other *Clubiona* species (apart from *C. comta* and *C. corticalis*).

Distribution/Status: Rare. Recorded from a very few locations on the west and south coast.

♂
♀
J F M A M J J A S O N D

♂ *Clubiona genevensis* ×**6**

Cheiracanthium

 3 British species (3 illustrated)

The three species are **similar in general appearance to** *Clubiona* (*pp. 290–304*) but have a more **robust body, thinner legs and are paler in colour. Leg I is the longest.** ♂s are quite similar to ♀s but have a narrower abdomen and noticeably longer chelicerae. *Cheiracanthium erraticum* is the species most likely to be encountered and has a distinctive abdominal pattern, allowing fairly easy recognition in the field, though care should be taken to avoid confusion with *C. pennyi.*

LC ## *Cheiracanthium virescens*

Nationally Scarce

Scarce, regional

♂ 5–7 mm   ♀ 5–9 mm

♂♀ **Observation tips/habitat:** Occurs under stones and ground vegetation in dry, sandy areas in open habitats such as heathland, waste-ground and dunes. Similar to, but less colourful than, other members of the genus. Usually the species found on heathland.

Description: CARAPACE Yellowish-brown. ABDOMEN Grey-green with a **darker cardiac stripe in the anterior half of the abdomen.** LEGS Vary from pale yellow to brown; very similar to *C. erraticum* (*p. 306*).

Similar species: Other *Cheiracanthium* species.

Distribution/Status: Uncommon and scattered throughout Britain.

♂
♀
J F M A M J J A S O N D

central stripe only in the front half

♀ *Cheiracanthium virescens* × **6**

LC *Cheiracanthium erraticum*

♂ 5·0–6·5 mm ♀ 6–9 mm

Observation tips/habitat: Occurs on low vegetation in a variety of grassy habitats and also heathland and marsh. The ♀ binds a few leaves or grass heads together to form a retreat for herself and her egg-sac. This can be quite conspicuous and is often the most obvious clue to the spider's presence.

Description: CARAPACE Usually pale brown, but sometimes more greyish with a pair of lighter patches in the head area. ♂ palpal tibiae are noticeably long. ABDOMEN Clear pattern comprising a distinct, reddish central stripe within a broad, yellowish median band flanked by greenish-grey sides. LEGS Vary from pale yellow to brown.

Similar species: *C. pennyi* (*p. 307*).

♂
♀

J F M A M J J A S O N D

Distribution/Status: Widespread and local in the southern half of Britain. More scattered elsewhere.

♂ *Cheiracanthium erraticum* ×**6**

Cheiracanthium species – identification pointers			
SPECIES	*C. virescens*	*C. erraticum*	*C. pennyi***
CARAPACE	yellowish-brown	pale brown, sometimes greyish	
ABDOMEN	grey-green, darker **anterior cardiac stripe**	yellow with reddish **full central stripe** and grey sides	as *C. erraticum* – NB **full central stripe** sometimes thin
LEGS	variable in colour, ranging from pale yellow to brown		

* Distinguished from *C. erraticum* by microscopic examination of the genitalia (see *page 96*).

Cheiracanthium pennyi ♀

♂5–6mm ♀6–7mm

Nationally Rare

Extremely rare

Observation tips/habitat: Very similar to *C. erraticum* (*p. 306*) but much rarer. Microscopic examination of the genitalia (see *page 96*) is required to confirm identification of the species. Occurs on mature dry heathland where it is closely associated with heather.

Description: CARAPACE Very similar to *C. erraticum*. ABDOMEN Very similar to *C. erraticum*. Sometimes the central, reddish stripe is quite thin. LEGS Very similar to *C. erraticum*.

Similar species: *C. erraticum* (*p. 306*).

Distribution/Status: Extremely rare. Present at just two sites in southern England.

♂
♀

J F M A M J J A S O N D

♀ *Cheiracanthium pennyi* with egg-sac × **6**

307

ZODARIIDAE Ant-hunting spiders   **1 British genus**

Often referred to as 'ant spiders' this eight-eyed family is represented by just one genus containing four species, which have all been added to the British fauna since 1985.

Zodarion Ant spiders   🔍 **4 British species (2 illustrated)**

All four species are ant mimics, living in association with ants and feeding on them exclusively. They are small, dark spiders, often moving around rapidly, closely resembling each other, and are all rare. **The anterior spinnerets are much larger than the rest and emanate from a cylindrical projection**, discernible with a hand lens. The dorsal surface of the abdomen is dark and the ventral surface pale. Habitat requirements of all *Zodarion* species are quite specific; loose stones in warm, dry, sunny situations are particularly favoured. The two sexes have a similar appearance. All four British species build small debris-covered retreats ('igloos').

LC # *Zodarion italicum*   ♀

Nationally Scarce

Scarce, regional

⚲ ⚲   ♂1·6–2·9 mm   ♀2·1–4·3 mm

♂♀ **Observation tips/habitat:** Occurs with ants in open grassland, waste ground and abandoned quarries. The spider makes a characteristic retreat ('igloo'), decorated with grit and other detritus, on or in the substrate.

Description: CARAPACE Brown with thin black striations radiating from the fovea. ABDOMEN Dorsally, shiny black; ventrally and laterally, pale yellow. LEGS Brown with black markings on femora I and II.

Similar species: Other *Zodarion* species, particularly *Z. rubidum* (*p. 309*).

Distribution/Status: Well established in the Thames Gateway where it is widespread and common. A few scattered records come from elsewhere in south-east England.

♂
♀
J F M A M J J A S O N D

♂ *Zodarion italicum* × **10**

Zodarion debris-covered
'igloo' (×4)

Zodarion species – identification pointers				
SPECIES	CARAPACE	ABDOMEN DORSAL SURFACE	LEGS	FEMORA
Z. italicum*	brown with black striations	shiny black	brown	dark markings on FEMORA I and II
Z. vicinum*				
Z. rubidum*		dark maroon		no markings on FEMORA I and II
Z. fuscum*				dark markings on FEMORA I–IV

* Microscopic examination of the genitalia is necessary to confirm identification (see *page 96*).

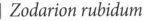 # *Zodarion rubidum*

Nationally Rare

Extremely rare

♂2·2–4·7 mm ♀3·2–4·5 mm

Observation tips/habitat: Recorded from a brownfield site in old, abandoned rail marshalling yards. Occurs alongside communities of the common black ant *Lasius niger*.

Description: CARAPACE As *Z. italicum* (*p. 308*).
ABDOMEN As *Z. italicum* but the dorsal colour is dark maroon. LEGS Brown, as *Z. italicum*, but femora I and II lack the dark markings.

Similar species: Other *Zodarion* species.

Distribution/Status: Extemely rare; known from a single site in the Thames Gateway.

♂
♀
J F M A M J J A S O N D

♀ *Zodarion rubidum* ×**10**

Zodarion vicinum

♂2·4–2·8mm ♀2·7–3·8mm   [NOT ILLUSTRATED]

♂♀ **Observation tips/habitat:** Occurs amongst rock debris at the base of a cliff in an area of chalk grassland, where it is closely assocated with the ant *Lasius alienus*.

Description: CARAPACE+ABDOMEN + LEGS As *Z. italicum* (*p. 308*).

Similar species: Other *Zodarion* species, particularly *Z. italicum*.

Distribution/Status: Very rare; known from a single site on the Kent coast.

Nationally Rare

Extremely rare

♂   NO PHENOLOGY DATA
♀

J F M A M J J A S O N D

Zodarion fuscum

♂2·2–3·2mm ♀3·2–4·0mm   [NOT ILLUSTRATED]

♂♀ **Observation tips/habitat:** As with other members of the genus, *Z. fuscum* favours sparsely vegetated areas with a broken substrate of rough stony debris such as gravel or clinker on open sunny sites. Like *Z. italicum* The spider makes a characteristic retreat (decorated with grit and other detritus) under or in the substrate.

Description: CARAPACE As *Z. italicum* (*p. 308*).
ABDOMEN As *Z. italicum* but the dorsal colour is dark maroon.
LEGS Brown with dark markings on all femora.

Similar species: Other *Zodarion* species.

Distribution/Status: Very rare. Known from three locations in England.

Nationally Rare

Extremely rare

♂
♀

J F M A M J J A S O N D

GNAPHOSIDAE Ground spiders   **11 British genera**

The majority are greyish-brown to black with little or no abdominal pattern. Exceptions to this are the genera *Phaeocedus* (*p. 320*), *Callilepis* (*p. 321*) and *Micaria* (*p. 333*), which all have pale abdominal markings. The anterior spinnerets are conspicuously cylindrical. Of their eight eyes, the posterior median pair often have a slit-like or oval appearance whilst the anterior median pair are usually darker than the others. Gnaphosids are ground-dwelling spiders, occurring under stones and amongst low vegetation and, apart from *Micaria, Phaeocedus* and *Callilepis*, are nocturnally active. The sexes are generally similar.

Drassodes   🔍 **3 British species (3 illustrated)**

The three spiders in this genus have a **greyish-brown appearance** and are rather like some clubionids (*pp. 290–304*). However, *Drassodes* species have **longer spinnerets and distinctly oval posterior median eyes**. They are all fairly aggressive nocturnal hunters of ground insects and are similar in appearance. The smaller size of *D. pubescens* usually separates it from the other two species. Microscopic examination of the genitalia (see *page 96*) is necessary to distinguish between the species.

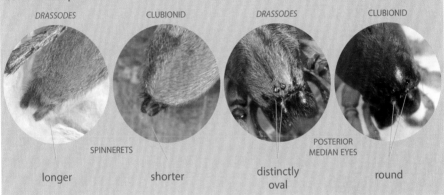

DRASSODES   CLUBIONID   DRASSODES   CLUBIONID

SPINNERETS   POSTERIOR MEDIAN EYES

longer   shorter   distinctly oval   round

LC

Drassodes cupreus   ♀   Common, widespread

♂ 9–18 mm   ♀ 9–18 mm   [PAGE 313 B]

Observation tips/habitat: The commonest spider of the genus. It occurs under scattered stones and ground debris and in grass tussocks, typically on heathland (especially in the south) and old grasslands. It also occurs low down in the foliage of gorse and heather. The spider has a coppery appearance in the field.

Description: CARAPACE Reddish-brown, covered with short hairs. ABDOMEN Colour similar to carapace but slightly greyer, sometimes with a vague cardiac mark. LEGS As carapace.

Similar species: Other *Drassodes* species.

Distribution/Status: Fairly common and widespread throughout Britain.

♂
♀
J F M A M J J A S O N D

311

LC # *Drassodes lapidosus*

♂9–18 mm ♀9–18 mm   [PAGE 313 T]

Observation tips/habitat: Very similar to *D. cupreus* (*p. 311*) but less common and preferring much drier conditions. Typically found amongst stones and scree but is also synanthropic, being found in unkempt gardens and on waste ground, particularly amongst abandoned piles of rubble.

Description: CARAPACE + ABDOMEN + LEGS Very similar to *D. cupreus*.

Similar species: Other *Drassodes* species.

Distribution/Status: Widespread in the southern half of Britain, scattered and sporadic elsewhere.

J F M A M J J A S O N D

LC # *Drassodes pubescens*

♂4–6 mm ♀6–9 mm

Observation tips/habitat: Much smaller than *D. cupreus* (*p. 311*) and *D. lapidosus* (*above*) and may have a paler general appearance and prefer slightly damper conditions. Occurs in grassland and heathland, under stones and at the base of grass tussocks. Also recorded from tussocks in woodland.

Description: CARAPACE + ABDOMEN + LEGS Very similar to *D. cupreus*.

Similar species: Other *Drassodes* species.

Distribution/Status: Widespread in southern England but rapidly becomes much scarcer towards the north.

J F M A M J J A S O N D

♀ *Drassodes pubescens* ×4

♀ *Drassodes lapidosus* with egg-sac × **4**

♀ *Drassodes cupreus* × **4**

Haplodrassus 🔍 **6 British species (6 illustrated)**

Only one species, *H. signifer*, is likely to be encountered. The other five are scarce or threatened in Britain. The genus *Haplodrassus* was formerly included with *Drassodes* (*p. 311*) and there are close similarities between the two. *Haplodrassus* species are darker and occasionally have vague abdominal patterns. ♀s are similar to ♂s. **Habitat preferences offer some help in narrowing down the choice of species** in the *Haplodrassus* and *Drassodes* genera (see table *p. 316*). Microscopic examination of the genitalia (see page 96) is necessary to confirm identification of the species.

LC *Haplodrassus signifer*   🔬

Common, widespread

♂6–8mm ♀8–9mm   [PAGE 316 TL]

♂♀ **Observation tips/habitat:** Variable in colour. Typically occurs on heathland and grassland under stones, low down in grass tussocks and amongst moss and leaf-litter. It favours dry conditions but may be found on raised, drier areas within boggy habitats.

Description: CARAPACE Varies from pale to dark brown. Darker lines radiating from the fovea are present on some lighter individuals. ABDOMEN Very variable, from brown to almost black, often with a coppery sheen. Lighter chevrons are usually present posteriorly. LEGS Pale brown.

Similar species: Other *Haplodrassus* species.

Distribution/Status: Common and widespread in suitable habitat throughout Britain.

♂
♀
J F M A M J J A S O N D

LC *Haplodrassus dalmatensis*   🔬

Biodiversity List (En, Wa)
Nationally Scarce

♂4·0–4·5mm ♀4·5–6·5mm   [PAGE 316 TR]

Scarce, regional

♂♀ **Observation tips/habitat:** Occurs on dry heathland at ground level amongst heather and under stones. Also recorded from coastal sand dunes and shingle. Generally similar to *H. signifer* but noticeably smaller.

Description: CARAPACE Similar to *H. signifer* (*above*). ABDOMEN Similar to *H. signifer*, but the pattern is usually much clearer and sometimes the whole abdomen is paler. LEGS Similar to *H. signifer*.

Similar species: Other *Haplodrassus* species.

Distribution/Status: Rare. Main concentration is on heathland sites in southern England and on coastal sites in East Anglia.

♂
♀
J F M A M J J A S O N D

Haplodrassus umbratilis

♂ 5–6 mm   ♀ 6·0–7·5 mm   [PAGE 316 BL]

Observation tips/habitat: Recorded from dry, stony areas on heathland.

Description: CARAPACE + ABDOMEN + LEGS
Similar to *H. signifer* (*p. 314*).

Similar species: Other *Haplodrassus* species.

Distribution/Status: Rare. Recorded from only six sites in southern and south-east England, most recently in 1990.

 Haplodrassus soerenseni

♂ 4·5–5·5 mm   ♀ 6–7 mm   [PAGE 316 BR]

Observation tips/habitat: Occurs exclusively in native pine forest in Britain where it is found at ground level amongst pine litter and moss. The spider has a similar appearance to *H. signifer* but is smaller.

Description: CARAPACE + ABDOMEN + LEGS Similar to *H. signifer* (*p. 314*).

Similar species: Other *Haplodrassus* species.

Distribution/Status: Rare. Restricted to two areas of Caledonian pine forest in Scotland.

♀ *Haplodrassus signifer* × **4**

♀ *Haplodrassus dalmatensis* × **4**

♀ *Haplodrassus umbratilis* with egg-sac × **4**

♀ *Haplodrassus soerenseni* × **4**

Drassodes and *Haplodrassus* species – identification pointers					
SPECIES	SIZE (mm)	CARAPACE	ABDOMEN	LEGS	HABITAT PREFERENCES
*D. cupreus**	9–18	Reddish-brown; covered with short hairs	Greyish-brown	Reddish-brown	Heathland and old grassland
*D. lapidosus**	9–18				Stony places, scree, waste ground
*D. pubescens**	**4–9**				Heathland, grassland, woodland,
*H. signifer**	6·0–9·0	Pale to dark brown; radial lines on some paler individuals	Brown to black, often with coppery sheen; lighter chevrons usually present toward the rear	Pale brown	Drier areas on heathland and grassland
*H. umbratilis**	5·0–7·5				Dry stony areas on heathland
*H. soerenseni**	4·5–7·0				**Caledonian pine forest**
*H. silvestris**	6·5–10·0				Woodland
H. minor	**3·5–4·0**				Strandline litter and sparse shingle
*H. dalmatensis**	4·0–6·5		As above but with pattern usually clearer		Heathland; sand dunes; shngle

* Only safely distinguished by microscopic examination of the genitalia (see *page 96*).

LC *Haplodrassus silvestris*

♂6·5–7·5mm ♀8–10mm

Observation tips/habitat: Very similar to *H. signifer* (*p. 314*) but typically occurring in woodland where it can be found in leaf-litter, under stones and the loose bark of trees.

Description: CARAPACE + ABDOMEN + LEGS Similar to *H. signifer*.

Similar species: Other *Haplodrassus* species.

Distribution/Status: Widespread, but scarce and very locally distributed throughout Britain.

Nationally Scarce

Scarce, local

♂ | J F M A M J J A S O N D
♀ |

♂ *Haplodrassus silvestris* × **4**

LC *Haplodrassus minor*

♂3·5mm ♀4mm

Observation tips/habitat: Similar to *H. signifer* (*p. 314*) but is the smallest member of the genus in Britain. A coastal spider typically occurring amongst strandline litter and sparse shingle vegetation.

Description: CARAPACE + ABDOMEN + LEGS Similar to *H. signifer*.

Similar species: Other *Haplodrassus* species.

Distribution/Status: Scarce. Restricted to coastal sites in East Anglia, southern England and west Wales.

Nationally Scarce

Scarce, regional

♂ | J F M A M J J A S O N D
♀ |

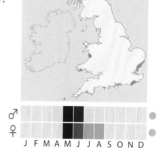

♀ *Haplodrassus minor* with egg-sac × **4**

317

Scotophaeus   Mouse spiders   **2 British species (2 illustrated)**

These two very similar **nocturnally active** species are quite large and usually found **closely associated with houses**. They are commonly known as mouse spiders because of their **greyish, hairy appearance**. The sexes are similar but ♂s **have a small scutum on the dorsal surface of the abdomen**.

LC ## *Scotophaeus blackwalli*   Mouse Spider   🔬   **Common, widespread**

♂8–9mm ♀10–12mm   [PAGE 319 B]

♂♀ **Observation tips/habitat:** Very often found in houses, particularly in the north of Britain. Farther south, the spider has also been recorded from outhouses and gardens. It is typically seen wandering around indoors at night.

Description: CARAPACE Reddish-brown and covered with dark hairs. The head area is narrower than in *Drassodes* (*p. 311*) and *Haplodrassus* (*p. 314*). ABDOMEN Brownish-grey with a thick covering of hairs, giving it a greasy appearance. LEGS Noticeably short and robust, coloured as carapace.

Similar species: *Scotophaeus scutulatus* (*below*).

Distribution/Status: Widespread and relatively common in much of England, more scattered in Wales and Scotland.

♂
♀
J F M A M J J A S O N D

S. blackwalli is by far the species most likely to be encountered throughout the whole of Britain. *S. scutulatus* is very rare and microscopic examination of the genitalia is essential to confirm identification (see *page 96*).

NA ## *Scotophaeus scutulatus*   🔬   **Extremely rare**

♂7–11mm ♀8–16mm   [PAGE 319 T]

♂♀ **Observation tips/habitat:** Very similar to *S. blackwalli* in appearance but can be larger. A synanthropic species, assumed to be introduced, and recorded from one location in Britain.

Description: CARAPACE + ABDOMEN + LEGS Similar to *S. blackwalli*.

Similar species: *Scotophaeus blackwalli* (*above*).

Distribution/Status: Very rare. Recorded from just one small area in south-east England.

♂
♀
J F M A M J J A S O N D

♀ *Scotophaeus scutulatus* × **4**

♀ *Scotophaeus blackwalli* × **4**

Phaeocedus

 1 British species (illustrated)

The single species is rather **ant-like in appearance** and is **active during the day.** There are **conspicuous white markings on the abdomen.** The sexes are similar but the ♂ **has an abdominal scutum.**

VU *Phaeocedus braccatus*

Nationally Rare

Rare, regional

♂4–5mm ♀4·5–6·5mm

Observation tips/habitat: Occurs mainly on chalk grassland, especially near the coast. It is found under stones or in areas of sparse vegetation where it can be seen running around in sunny conditions. Also recorded from dry heathland and coastal shingle. The movement of the ♂s, in particular, can be very ant-like.

Description: CARAPACE Ranges from reddish-brown to black, sometimes with small patches of white hairs. ABDOMEN Black with a covering of fine hairs and a conspicuous pattern of three pairs of white spots. One pair is at the anterior margin and two further pairs are central, on either side of the midline; the posterior pair is smaller. This pattern is usually quite faint in ♀s. LEGS Pale brown with dark femora I and II, providing a distinct contrast.

Similar species: None.

Distribution/Status: Rare. Mainly confined to southern England with one site on the East Anglian coast.

♂
♀
J F M A M J J A S O N D

♂ *Phaeocedus braccatus* × **6**

Callilepis

$\mathcal{P}$ **1 British species (illustrated)**

The British species feeds on ants and is **rather ant-like in appearance** and movement. It has a **distinctive abdomen pattern** and the **strong legs have conspicuous spines, particularly on the darker legs I and II.**

Callilepis nocturna

$\mathcal{P}$

Nationally Rare

Rare, regional

♂ 3·0–4·5 mm ♀ 3·5–6·0 mm

Observation tips/habitat: In Britain it occurs on coastal grassland and cliffs, but it is known from coniferous woodland in Europe. The spider runs around rapidly over bare ground in sunny conditions, hunting for ants.

Description: CARAPACE Dark brown and covered in pale hairs. The posterior median eyes have a narrow, slit-like appearance. ABDOMEN Brown, with a distinct, curved patch of white hairs across the anterior part, a pair of small white spots centrally and another larger pair above the spinnerets. LEGS Reddish-brown. Legs I and II are darker and more robust than the others. All furnished with conspicuous spines.

Similar species: None.

Distribution/Status: Known from three coastal sites in southern England and south-west Wales.

♂
♀
J F M A M J J A S O N D

♀ *Callilepis nocturna* ×**6**

Zelotes

🔍 6 British species (6 illustrated)

This genus used to included species now placed in the genera *Trachyzelotes* (*p.325*), *Urozelotes* and *Drassyllus* (both *p.328*), primarily on the basis of the similarities in general appearance. They all have **a very dark glossy carapace which is noticeably narrowed anteriorly with the eyes grouped closely together** and, apart from *Urozelotes rusticus*, have a sleek blackish abdomen. **They are the only group of British spiders with a body length of 4mm or more that are predominantly black**; variations in the colouring of the leg segments help to distinguish the different species. The sexes are similar, but ♂'s have a slimmer abdomen with a small scutum dorsally. Typically these spiders are found at ground level amongst detritus and under stones where the ♀ can often be discovered with a domed, papery egg-sac. The recent splitting of the genus into four rests on microscopic diagnostic differences in the structure of the male pedipalp. In the following pages the descriptions for the four genera of *Zelotes*, *Trachyzelotes*, *Urozelotes* and *Drassyllus* are grouped together. Microscopic examination of the genitalia (see *page 96*) may be necessary to confirm identification of the species.

Zelotes, Uroyzelotes, Trachyzelotes, Drasyllus species – identification pointers

SPECIES	HABITAT	CARAPACE	BRANCHIAL OPERCULA	LEGS I + II FEMUR	PATELLA	TIBIA	METATARSUS	TARSUS
*Z. latreillei**	Dry, open chalk grassland + sandy heath	Black	Orange	Black				
*Z. longipes**	Heathland, especially recently burnt areas	Black	Orange	Black				
*Z. subterraneus**	Dry vegetation in variety of habitats	Black	Orange	Black				
*Z. apricorum**		Black	Orange	Black				
*Z. petrensis**		Black	Orange	Black				
Z. electus	Coastal dunes	Reddish-brown	Orange	Yellow	Dark brown	Dark brown	Orange-brown	
U. rusticus	Houses	Reddish-brown	Orange	Orange-brown				
T. pedestris	Dry, open chalk grassland	Black	Orange	Black	Medium brown			
D. praeficus	Dry, open chalk grassland	Black	Yellow-orange	Black				Yellow
*D. pusillus**	NB *D. pusillus* also on sandy heath	Dark brown	Brown	Dark brown/black			Light brown	
*D. lutetianus**	Plant litter in marshes, dunes + coastal strandline	Dark brown	Brown	Dark brown/black			Light brown	

* Microscopic examination of the genitalia is necessary to confirm identification (see *page 96*).

LC *Zelotes latreillei*

Common, widespread

♂4·5–7·5mm ♀7–8mm   [PAGE 326 TL]

Observation tips/habitat: Typically a lowland species and probably the commonest of the *Zelotes*-type group in Britain. It prefers open areas of heathland and chalk grassland where it occurs under stones and ground debris. It may also be seen running rapidly in sunny conditions. The whole spider has a glossy black appearance.

Description: CARAPACE Black. ABDOMEN Black. ♂'s have a small dorsal scutum. Ventrally the branchial opercula are orange. LEGS Black. The tarsi are sometimes slightly paler.

Similar species: Other *Zelotes* except *Z. electus* (p. 325), *Trachyzelotes pedestris* (p. 327), *Urozelotes rusticus* (p. 328).

Distribution/Status: Widespread in much of Britain. Less so in the north and in Scotland.

♂
♀

J F M A M J J A S O N D

LC *Zelotes apricorum*

Uncommon, regional

♂5–6mm ♀6·5–9·0mm   [PAGE 326 HMR]

Observation tips/habitat: Occurs in a variety of habitats under stones and ground debris. Has similar habits to other *Zelotes* species. Often seen running in sunshine.

Description: CARAPACE + ABDOMEN + LEGS Very similar to *Z. latreillei* (*above*).

Similar species: Other *Zelotes* except *Z. electus* (p. 325), *Trachyzelotes pedestris* (p. 327), *Urozelotes rusticus* (p. 328).

Distribution/Status: Widespread and scattered in western Britain and south-east England.

♂
♀

J F M A M J J A S O N D

323

`LC` *Zelotes subterraneus*

♂5–6mm ♀6·5–9·0mm   [PAGE 326 HML]

Observation tips/habitat: Very closely related to ♂♀ *Z. apricorum* (*p. 323*) and occupying similar habitats; until recently the two species were confused. Typically occurs under stones.

Description: CARAPACE + ABDOMEN + LEGS
Very similar to *Z. latreillei* (*p. 323*).

Similar species: Other *Zelotes* except *Z. electus* (*p. 325*), *Trachyzelotes pedestris* (*p. 327*), *Urozelotes rusticus* (*p. 328*).

Distribution/Status: Scarce. Apart from a few inland records in central England and Scotland, predominantly a coastal species.

Nationally Scarce

Scarce, local

♂
♀
J F M A M J J A S O N D

`LC` *Zelotes petrensis*

♂5–6mm ♀6–7mm   [PAGE 326 LML]

Observation tips/habitat: Occurs in a variety of dry ♂♀ open habitats in similar situations as other *Zelotes* species.

Description: CARAPACE + ABDOMEN + LEGS
Very similar to *Z. latreillei* (*p. 323*).

Similar species: Other *Zelotes* except *Z. electus* (*p. 325*), *Trachyzelotes pedestris* (*p. 327*), *Urozelotes rusticus* (*p. 328*).

Distribution/Status: Rare in scattered locations predominantly in south-east England.

Nationally Rare

Rare, regional

♂
♀
J F M A M J J A S O N D

Zelotes longipes

VU

Nationally Rare

Rare, regional

♂5–6mm ♀6–8mm [PAGE 326 TR]

Observation tips/habitat: Generally restricted to heathland habitats where it occurs on recently burnt areas, decreasing in numbers as the recovering vegetation becomes more dense. Occasionally occurs on dry coastal sites.

Description: CARAPACE + ABDOMEN + LEGS
Very similar to *Z. latreillei* (*p. 323*).

Similar species: Other *Zelotes* except *Z. electus* (*below*), *Trachyzelotes pedestris* (*p. 327*), *Urozelotes rusticus* (*p. 328*).

Distribution/Status: Rare. Very much a species of appropriate habitats in southern England.

♂
♀
J F M A M J J A S O N D

Zelotes electus

LC

Nationally Scarce

Scarce, regional

♂3.5–4.5mm ♀4.0–5.5mm [PAGE 326 LMR]

Observation tips/habitat: Generally restricted to coastal habitats, particularly dunes, where it is found under stones and amongst low vegetation. Also recorded from sandy Breckland sites and lowland heath. Particularly active in bright sunny conditions.

Description: CARAPACE Reddish-brown to dark brown. ABDOMEN Brownish-black. Ventrally the branchial opercula are orange. LEGS Quite stout relative to other species in this group. The femora are pale brown, darker apically. The patellae, tibiae and metatarsi are all dark brown, the tarsi paler.

Similar species: None.

Distribution/Status: Scarce but widely distributed around the coasts of Britain.

♂
♀
J F M A M J J A S O N D

♀ *Zelotes latreillei* × **4**

♀ *Zelotes longipes* × **4**

♀ *Zelotes subterraneus* × **4**

♀ *Zelotes apricorum* × **4**

♀ *Zelotes petrensis* × **4**

♀ *Zelotes electus* × **4**

♀ *Urozelotes rusticus* × **4**

Trachyzelotes

🔍 **1 British species (illustrated)**

C *Trachyzelotes pedestris* 🔍

♂4–6mm ♀7–8mm   [BL]

Observation tips/habitat: Typically occurs in and under loose stones in dry and open chalk grassland, where it can be common. It is occasionally recorded from open, sandy areas on Breckland heaths. It has a similar body appearance to *Zelotes* species but **conspicuously different leg coloration.**

Description: CARAPACE + ABDOMEN Black, similar to *Z. latreillei*. LEGS Coxae, trochanters and femora black with the remaining segments medium brown.

Similar species: None.

Distribution/Status: Widespread in southern England south of a line from the Wash to the Severn estuary.

Uncommon, regional

♂
♀
J F M A M J J A S O N D

♂ *Drassyllus pusillus* ×4

♀ *Drassyllus praeficus* ×4

♀ *Trachyzelotes pedestris* ×4

♀ *Drassyllus lutetianus* ×4

Urozelotes   🔍 1 British species (illustrated)

NA *Urozelotes rusticus*   🔍   **Extremely rare**

♂6·0–6·5mm ♀7·0–8·5mm   [PAGE 326 B]

Observation tips/habitat: Typically found in and around houses. **It has an overall orange appearance distinguishing it from other** *Zelotes*-**type species.** Its very scattered distribution may suggest occasional introductions to Britain which have not established.

Description: CARAPACE Pale brown to orange, occasionally with indistinct, radiating lines. ABDOMEN Dull greyish-brown with a short, pale orange cardiac mark. Thickly covered with dark hairs. LEGS Coloured as carapace.

Similar species: None.

Distribution/Status: Extremely rare, with very scattered records from England and Wales, the most recent from 1994.

♂   NO PHENOLOGY DATA
♀
   J F M A M J J A S O N D

Drassyllus   ♟ 3 British species (3 illustrated)

LC *Drassyllus pusillus*   ♟   **Common, widespread**

♂3–4mm ♀4–5mm   [PAGE 327 TL]

Observation tips/habitat: Favours open, dry habitats such as sandy heaths and chalk downland in similar situations to other spiders in the *Zelotes* group. The smallest and commonest of the *Drassyllus* genus.

Description: CARAPACE Dark brown. ABDOMEN Dark brown to black. Ventrally, the **branchial opercula are brown and not as obvious as in other** *Zelotes*-**type species.** LEGS Metatarsi and tarsi are pale brown; all the other segments are dark brown/black.

Similar species: *Drassyllus lutetianus* (*p. 329*). Habitat preferences may help in species identification.

Distribution/Status: Widespread but scattered distribution in lowland areas of southern Britain and central-eastern Scotland.

♂
♀
   J F M A M J J A S O N D

LC *Drassyllus praeficus*

♂4·5–5·0 mm   ♀5–6 mm   [PAGE 327 TR]

Observation tips/habitat: Most frequently found on chalk grassland under stones but occasionally recorded from dry heathland. Its general appearance is of an entirely black spider.

Description: CARAPACE Black with very faint radial markings. ABDOMEN Black; ventrally the **branchial opercula are yellow-orange.** LEGS Black, apart from **yellow tarsi.**

Similar species: None.

Distribution/Status: Concentrated in central-southern England with a few scattered records elsewhere.

J F M A M J J A S O N D

LC *Drassyllus lutetianus*

♂4–5 mm   ♀5·0–7·5 mm   [PAGE 327 BR]

Observation tips/habitat: Predominantly a coastal spider preferring damp conditions. It occurs in plant litter in marshes, on sand dunes, among stones and in strandline litter on the sea shore. Occasionally recorded from marshes inland.

Description: CARAPACE + ABDOMEN + LEGS Similar to *D. pusillus.*

Similar species: *Drassyllus pusillus* (*p. 328*). Habitat preferences may help in species identification.

Distribution/Status: Scarce. Recorded mainly from coastal sites in England and Wales, predominantly in the south.

J F M A M J J A S O N D

Gnaphosa

🔍 **4 British species (4 illustrated)**

The four species are uncommon and, apart from size differences, they closely resemble each other. They are **quite robust spiders with a dull, greyish-brown and hairy appearance.** They differ from other gnaphosids in the **row of posterior eyes, which is strongly recurved.** All are found under stones and amongst plant litter and debris in low vegetation and are generally nocturnal in their activities, although occasionally they may be observed running around in bright sunny conditions. Sexes are similar but ♀s are generally larger. Microscopic examination of the genitalia (see page 96) is necessary to separate the species.

VU ## *Gnaphosa lugubris*

♂9–12mm ♀10–13mm

Observation tips/habitat: Occurs in dry stony areas usually on hillsides on open heathland and occasionally on coastal chalk grassland.

Description: CARAPACE Dark brown to black. ABDOMEN Dark brown to sooty-black with six faint indentations and covered in dark hairs. Ventrally, the branchial opercula are yellow. LEGS Coloured as carapace. Fairly robust.

Similar species: Other *Gnaphosa* species.

Distribution/Status: Rare. Main concentration in Dorset with a very few records from coastal sites elsewhere.

J F M A M J J A S O N D

♀ *Gnaphosa lugubris* ×4

LC

Gnaphosa leporina

♂ 5·5–7·0 mm ♀ 7–9 mm [BL]

Nationally Scarce

Scarce, regional

Observation tips/habitat: Similar to *G. lugubris* (*p. 330*) but smaller and may be paler in colour. Occurs in damp, heathland. It is more active than other *Gnaphosa* species and often seen running rapidly over bare ground. It is by far the commonest member of the genus in Britain.

Description: CARAPACE Dark brown to black, similar to *G. lugubris*. ABDOMEN Similar to *G. lugubris* although colour may be a paler brown compared to the carapace. LEGS Paler than carapace.

Similar species: Other *Gnaphosa* species.

Distribution/Status: Scarce but widespread in appropriate habitat in central-southern Britain and in parts of northern England, north Wales and Scotland.

J F M A M J J A S O N D

VU

Gnaphosa nigerrima

♂ 6–7 mm ♀ 7·5–9·0 mm [BR]

Nationally Rare

Extremely rare

Observation tips/habitat: Similar to *G. lugubris* (*p. 330*) but smaller and prefers a moister habitat amongst moss in boggy areas.

Description: CARAPACE + ABDOMEN + LEGS Similar to *G. lugubris*.

Similar species: Other *Gnaphosa* species.

Distribution/Status: Very rare. Known from a single site in Cheshire.

NO PHENOLOGY DATA

♀ *Gnaphosa leporina* × **4**

♀ *Gnaphosa nigerrima* × **4** 331

Gnaphosa occidentalis 🔬

♂9–11mm ♀10–12mm

Observation tips/habitat: Closely resembles *G. lugubris* (*p. 330*). Occurs in dry stony areas, usually on hillsides on open heathland, and occasionally on coastal grassland.

Description: CARAPACE + ABDOMEN + LEGS
Very similar to *G. lugubris*.

Similar species: Other *Gnaphosa* species.

Distribution/Status: Very rare. Known from a single site in Cornwall.

♂ NO PHENOLOGY DATA
♀
J F M A M J J A S O N D

♀ *Gnaphosa occidentalis* × **4**

Gnaphosa species – identification pointers			
SPECIES	CARAPACE	ABDOMEN	HABITAT
G. lugubris*	Dark brown to black	Dark brown to sooty black; covered in dark hairs; 6 faint indentatons	Dry stony areas in heathland; also coastal grassland
G. occidentalis*			
G. nigerrima*			Moss in boggy areas
G. leporina*		As above; may be paler	Damp heathland

* Only safely distinguished by microscopic examination of the genitalia (see *page 96*).

Micaria

🔍 **5 British species (4 illustrated)**

These are all **small, ant-mimicking spiders with an iridescent abdomen.** They run around very rapidly in sunny conditions, when the iridescence is most obvious. Although sometimes living in close association with ants they are not known to feed on them; their mimicry appears to be a ploy to deter potential predators. Only one species, *M. pulicaria*, is likely to be encountered; all the others are rare. The sexes are similar in general appearance and the species strongly resemble each other. As well is being very similar, abdominal markings (lines and spots) are also variable both within and between species and even though habitat may be a useful pointer as to the species involved microscopic examination of the genitalia (see page 96) is necessary to confirm identification.

LC *Micaria pulicaria* 🔬

Common, widespread

♂ 3·0–3·5 mm   ♀ 2·7–4·5 mm   [PAGE 335 TL]

♂♀ **Observation tips/habitat:** Occurs in a wide range of habitats, particularly warm, sunny spots and bare, dry areas in open sandy heaths, chalk downlands, dunes and brownfield sites. Also recorded from damper habitats such as saltmarshes and moss in broadleaved woodland.

Description: CARAPACE Black, with lines of white hairs radiating from the fovea. ABDOMEN Black and strongly iridescent with a short, white transverse line on the anterior margin. Centrally a longer, white transverse line stretches to either side. Occasionally a central, longitudinal line of white spots extends the length of the abdomen. LEGS Pale brown, apart from femora I and II which are black. Femora III and IV are dark brown.

♂
♀
J F M A M J J A S O N D

Similar species: Other *Micaria* species.

Distribution/Status: Common and widespread throughout Britain.

Micaria species – identification pointers		
SPECIES	TYPICAL ABDOMINAL MARKINGS NB highly variable within and between species	HABITAT
M. pulicaria*	Black; strongly iridescent; two white transverse lines; a central longitudinal line of spots may be present	Bare, warm areas on sandy heaths, chalk downland, dunes and brownfield sites; also saltmarshes and broadleaved woodland
M. subopaca*		Trunks of pine trees
M. albovittata*	As *M. pulicaria* but spots (if present) less distinct	Short grassland on clifftops
M. silesiaca*		Dry heath and sandy ground
M. alpina*	As *M. pulicaria* transverse lines less distinct or absent	Moss and grass > 750 m altitude

* Only safely distinguished by microscopic examination of the genitalia (see *page 96*).

VU *Micaria albovittata*

♂3·5–4·5mm ♀4·5–5·0mm [PAGE 335 TR]

Nationally Rare

Rare, regional

Observation tips/habitat: The largest member of the genus. It is confined to coastal locations where it occurs under stones on short chalk grassland on cliff tops. It runs about in warm sunny conditions.

Description: CARAPACE Similar to *M. pulicaria* (p. 333). ABDOMEN Similar to *M. pulicaria*, but the white spots may not be so obvious. LEGS Similar to *M. pulicaria*.

Similar species: Other *Micaria* species.

Distribution/Status: Rare. Recorded from just a few sites on the south coast of England.

J F M A M J J A S O N D

NT *Micaria silesiaca*

♂3·5–4·0mm ♀4–5mm [PAGE 335 M]

Nationally Rare

Rare, regional

Observation tips/habitat: Usually occurs on dry heath and sandy ground under stones and in low vegetation, often in association with ants. May also occasionally be found in wetter areas.

Description: CARAPACE Similar to *M. pulicaria* (p. 333). ABDOMEN Similar to *M. pulicaria*, but the white markings are often less distinct. LEGS Similar to *M. pulicaria*.

Similar species: Other *Micaria* species.

Distribution/Status: Rare and confined to appropriate habitats in southern England.

J F M A M J J A S O N D

♀ *Micaria pulicaria* × **10**

♀ *Micaria albovittata* × **10**

♂ *Micaria silesiaca* × **10**

♀ *Micaria subopaca* × **4**

LC *Micaria subopaca*

♂2·5–3·3mm ♀2·5–3·3mm [PAGE 335 B]

♂♀ **Observation tips/habitat:** Occurs mainly on the trunks
of pine trees and can be observed running about in bright
sunny conditions, often accompanied by ants.

Description: CARAPACE + ABDOMEN + LEGS
Similar to *M. pulicaria* (*p. 333*).

Similar species: Other *Micaria* species.

Distribution/Status: Very local and mainly confined to
southern England. Records from Liverpool and Glasgow
are probably the result of chance importations.

♂
♀
J F M A M J J A S O N D

VU *Micaria alpina*

♂2·7–4·0mm ♀2·7–4·0mm [NOT ILLUSTRATED]

♂♀ **Observation tips/habitat:** Occurs amongst moss and grass
and under stones at high altitudes, usually above 750m.

Description: CARAPACE Similar to *M. pulicaria* (*p. 333*).
ABDOMEN Similar to *M. pulicaria*, but the white transverse
lines may be less obvious or completely absent.
LEGS Similar to *M. pulicaria*.

Similar species: Other *Micaria* species.

Distribution/Status: Rare. Known only from Welsh
mountains and northern Scotland.

NO PHENOLOGY DATA

ZORIDAE   Ghost spiders   **1 British genus**

In Britain this eight-eyed family contains just a single genus. They are all similar in appearance and the yellow body contrasts markedly with the brown markings.

Zora   🔍 **4 British species (4 illustrated)**

Four species occur in Britain. **The carapace is pale yellow with a pair of brown longitudinal bands. The eyes are all roughly the same size with the posterior row being strongly recurved.** Markings on the femora may help in suggesting species but microscopic examination of the genitalia (see *page 96*) is necessary to confirm identification.

LC   # *Zora spinimana*   🔬   **Common, widespread**

♂ 4·5–5·0 mm   ♀ 5·0–6·5 mm   [PAGE 338 B]

♂ ♀

Observation tips/habitat: Typically a grassland spider found low down amongst grass roots and litter, but has also been recorded from a wide range of habitats including hedgerows and open woodland. The ♀ is often found under debris, guarding her loosely woven egg-sac. *Z. spinimana* is by far the commonest member of the genus.

Description: CARAPACE Pale brown with wide dark brown median band within which is a paler central band with a covering of white hairs, the whole appearing as alternating dark and light longitudinal bands. ABDOMEN Pale brown with scattering of dark markings at sides enclosing a paler central area which itself contains a whitish cardiac mark with a broken dark edging. LEGS Dark grey apart from pale brown femora which have darker streaks on legs I and II.

♂
♀
J F M A M J J A S O N D

Similar species: Other *Zora* species.

Distribution/Status: Common and widespread in southern half of Britain, more scattered in northern England and Scotland.

Zora species – identification pointers

SPECIES	CARAPACE	ABDOMEN	LEGS: FEMORA I AND II
*Z. nemoralis**	**dark bands usually wider than light bands**	usually darker than other *Zora* spp.	darker streaks
*Z. spinimana**			
*Z. armillata**	light bands usually wider than dark bands	pale brown with dark markings	fewer dark markings
*Z. sylvestris**			clear dark spots

* Only safely distinguished by microscopic examination of the genitalia (see *page 96*).

VU *Zora nemoralis*

♂3–4 mm ♀3·5–5·5 mm

Observation tips/habitat: Typically found amongst moss and heather in woodland habitats.

Description: CARAPACE Similar to *Z. spinimana* (*p. 337*). Dark bands usually wider than pale ones.
ABDOMEN Similar to *Z. spinimana* but usually darker.
LEGS Similar to *Z. spinimana*.

Similar species: Other *Zora* species.

Distribution/Status: Very local and scattered distribution in Wales, northern England and Scotland.

♂
♀
J F M A M J J A S O N D

Generally darker and with wider dark carapace bands than other *Zora* spp. of the region.

♀ *Zora nemoralis* × **4**

Dark streaks on femora I and II

♀ *Zora spinimana* × **4**

Zora armillata

CR

♂3·5–4 mm   ♀4·0–6·5 mm

Observation tips/habitat: Occurs in Britain in two different habitats: wet heathland and fenland.

Description: CARAPACE + ABDOMEN As *Z. spinimana* (*p. 337*). LEGS Similar to *Z. spinimana* but with fewer dark markings.

Similar species: Other *Zora* species.

Distribution/Status: Rare. Known from a very few sites in East Anglia and southern England and last recorded in 1980.

♀ *Zora armillata* ×4

Fewer dark markings on femora I and II than *Z. spinimana*

♂
♀
J F M A M J J A S O N D

Zora silvestris

CR

♂3–4 mm   ♀3·5–4·0 mm

Observation tips/habitat: Occurs on dry heathland mainly in stands of mature heather. Similar to, but more greyish-brown than, *Z. spinimana*.

Description: CARAPACE + ABDOMEN As *Z. spinimana* (*p. 337*). LEGS Similar to *Z. spinimana*. Femora have clear dark spots.

Similar species: Other *Zora* species.

Distribution/Status: Rare. Known from just a few localities in southern and central England.

♂   NO PHENOLOGY DATA
♀
J F M A M J J A S O N D

♀ *Zora silvestris* ×4

Clear dark spots on femora I and II

ZOROPSIDAE   False wolf spiders   **1 British genus**

This eight-eyed family resembles the Lycosidae (*p. 206*) and is sometimes referred to as the 'false wolf spiders'. However, the eye arrangement is distinctly different.

Zoropsis   👁 **1 British species (illustrated)**

A single species is known in Britain. **Only found within buildings, it resembles a wolf spider but is larger, moves more slowly and has smaller eyes of equal size in two rows.**

NA   *Zoropsis spinimana*   👁   **Rare, regional**

♂10–13mm   ♀10-19mm

Observation tips/habitat: A large, distinctive synanthropic spider recently (2011) recorded as well-established in the London area.

♂♀ **Description:** CARAPACE Pale brown with darker, dentate lateral bands enclosing a paler median band with irregular black, butterfly-shaped outline posteriorly and a white area anteriorly. ABDOMEN Mottled greyish-brown with darker cardiac mark edged with black dashes. In ♂ cardiac mark can be black. LEGS Greyish-brown with darker speckling and greyish spots. Legs I and II may be darker than III and IV. Tibia I has 6–7 pairs of spines ventrally.

Similar species: None.

Distribution/Status: Limited to the south-east of England but likely to extend its range.

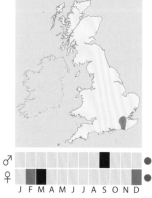

♂
♀
J F M A M J J A S O N D

♀ *Zoropsis spinimana* ×**4**

SPARASSIDAE Huntsman spiders   **1 British genus**

Contains one genus in Britain with a single distinctive eight-eyed species.

Micrommata   **1 British species (illustrated)**

The single species in this genus is unmistakable. Its size and bright colouring should allow easy recognition, and the avoidance of confusion with any other species. However, it can be difficult to find as it tends to remain motionless, sitting amongst foliage waiting to ambush passing insects.

LC *Micrommata virescens* Green Huntsman Spider

♂7–10mm ♀10–15mm

Nationally Scarce

Scarce, regional

Observation tips/habitat: Typically found in damp, sheltered woodland, often on the lower branches of young oak, on tall grass or sedge tussocks. The ♀ constructs a large retreat for herself and the egg-sac by binding together a number of small leaves with silk. The retreat is usually positioned less than half a metre above the ground. The eggs are green.

Description: CARAPACE Bright emerald green (♂ slightly duller). The eyes are ringed with white hairs. ABDOMEN ♀ and immatures of both sexes yellowish-green with darker green cardiac mark outlined in yellow. ♂ yellow with deep red median and lateral bands. LEGS Green.

Similar species: None.

Distribution/Status: Widespread; very scattered in the southern half of Britain with very few records in the north.

♂
♀
J F M A M J J A S O N D

♂   *Micrommata virescens* × **4**   ♀

PHILODROMIDAE　Running crab spiders　　3 British genera

Contains 17 eight-eyed species, in three genera. They have a rather flattened appearance with an almost circular carapace and oval abdomen which is sometimes elongated (particularly in *Tibellus*). The legs are relatively long, ɪ and ɪɪ being longer than ɪɪɪ and ɪᴠ.

Philodromus　Running crab spiders　　👁️ 13 British species (13 illustrated)

The common name of running crab spiders derives from their general crab-like body shape, fairly long, laterally inclined legs and rapid, erratic movement (sometimes sideways). They are normally fairly sedentary, only displaying their speed and living up to their common name when hunting and catching prey amongst the lower branches of trees and shrubs.

The ♂s and ♀s of some species are quite different, but in other species can be similar with the ♂ just having a slimmer abdomen and more distinct markings.

The egg-sacs vary in appearance; in some cases they are covered with plant debris or sand grains, and in others simply hidden beneath a covering of silk.

Although a few *Philodromus* spiders have distinctive markings and may be recognisable in the field with the use of a hand lens, there is great variation in the appearance of many species because of cryptic coloration and camouflage. This is particularly true in the *P. aureolus* group of seven species (*Philodromus dispar, P. aureolus, P. praedatus, P. cespitum, P. longipalpis, P. collinus* and *P. buxi*) where past misidentifications affect the reliability of our present understanding of their distributions. Microscopic examination of the genitalia (see page 96) is necessary to confirm identification of all species in the genus.

Philodromus species – habitat preferences; see individual species accounts for more details									
SPECIES	WOODLAND				OPEN HABITATS			HEATHLAND		DUNE
	Broad leaved	Pine	Wood edge	Wood pasture	Scrub	Hedges	Park/ Garden	Wet	Dry	
P. dispar	●				●	●	●			
P. aureolus	●				●	●	●			
P. cespitum					●	●		●	●	
P. praedatus			●	●	●					
P. longipalpis				●			●			
P. collinus	●	●				●	●		●	
P. buxi							●			
P. emarginatus		●							●	
P. albidus	●		●	●						
P. rufus				●	●					
P. margaritatus	●	●								
P. fallax										●
P. histrio									●	

● Preferred habitats
● Additional habitats where sometimes found

Philodromus dispar 🔍[♂] | ⚲ [♀]

LC

Common, regional

♂4mm ♀4–5mm   [PAGE 344 T]

Observation tips/habitat: Found on the lower branches of trees and shrubs in a wide range of wooded habitats including mature woodland, scrub and hedgerows. It is also found in gardens and occasionally within houses. There is great disparity between the two sexes giving the species its specific name. The ♂ is identifiable in the field.

Description: CARAPACE ♀ brown with thin, white, marginal line and pale brown, wide median band which includes a white wedge-shaped marking behind the eyes. ♂ **iridescent bluish-black, with thin white marginal line.** ABDOMEN ♀ brown with pale brown central area containing vague pattern of darker spots and chevrons posteriorly, and sometimes a darker cardiac mark. ♂ as carapace, sometimes appearing jet black in the field. LEGS Pale pinkish-brown with a few dark spots.

♂
♀
J F M A M J J A S O N D

Similar species: Other members of the *P. aureolus* group – see under Genus description (*p. 342*).

Distribution/Status: Common in southern Britain, much less frequent farther north and almost completely absent from Scotland.

Philodromus aureolus ⚲

LC

Common, widespread

♂4mm ♀5–6mm   [PAGE 344 CL]

Observation tips/habitat: Occurs in a similar range of habitats to *P. dispar*. Probably the commonest member of the genus.

Description: CARAPACE ♀ similar to *P. dispar* (*above*) but white marking behind eyes may be absent. ♂ similar to ♀ but can be much darker and iridescent. ABDOMEN ♀ similar to *P. dispar* but when guarding an egg-sac may be uniformly pale yellow with darker sides. ♂ as carapace. LEGS Yellowish-brown, sometimes reddish, with very few, if any, darker markings.

Similar species: Other members of the *P. aureolus* group – see under Genus description (*p. 342*).

Distribution/Status: Common and widespead throughout much of Britain, more scattered in the west and north.

♂
♀
J F M A M J J A S O N D

343

♂ *Philodromus dispar* × **4** ♀

♀ *Philodromus aureolus* × **4**

♀ *Philodromus cespitum* × **4**

♂ *Philodromus praedatus* × **4** ♀

♂ *Philodromus longipalpis* × **4**

♀ *Philodromus collinus* × **4**

♀ *Philodromus buxi* × **4**

♀ *Philodromus emarginatus* × **4**

♀ *Philodromus albidus* × **4**

♂ *Philodromus rufus* × **4**

♀ *Philodromus margaritatus* × **4**

♂ *Philodromus fallax* × **4**

LC *Philodromus cespitum*

Common, widespread

♂4mm ♀5–6mm [PAGE 344 CR]

♂♀ **Observation tips/habitat:** Occurs on heather-dominated, wet and dry heathland and also recorded from wooded habitats such as scrub and hedgerows. Seems to favour low herbage and scrub more than other species in the *P. aureolus* group.

Description: CARAPACE + ABDOMEN + LEGS
Similar to *P. aureolus* (*p. 343*)

Similar species: Other members of the *P. aureolus* group
– see under genus description (*p. 342*).

Distribution/Status: Common and widespread in southern Britain in lowland areas, much less frequent in northern England and Scotland.

J F M A M J J A S O N D

LC *Philodromus praedatus*

Common, regional

♂3·5–4·0mm ♀5–6mm [PAGE 344 B]

♂♀ **Observation tips/habitat:** Typically occurs on mature oak trees in open habitats such as wood pasture, the margins of woodland rides or old hedgerows. Occasionally recorded from other trees in similar situations.

Description: CARAPACE + ABDOMEN Similar to *P. aureolus* (*p. 343*) and *P. cespitum* (*above*). LEGS Pale yellow with dark annulations, particularly in ♀.

Similar species: Other members of the *P. aureolus* group
– see under genus description (*p. 342*).

Distribution/Status: Widespread in southern and eastern England.

J F M A M J J A S O N D

Philodromus longipalpis

♂3·5–4·0 mm ♀5–6 mm [PAGE 345 TL]

Observation tips/habitat: Adults restricted to the lower branches and trunks of old oak trees in open situations such as parkland. Has a similar body length to others in the *P. aureolus* group but the longer legs make it look significantly larger. Immatures, which have a characteristic reddish appearance, have been collected from heather underneath old trees.

Description: CARAPACE + ABDOMEN + LEGS Similar to *P. aureolus* (*p.343*) and *P. cespitum* (*p.346*).

Similar species: Other members of the *P. aureolus* group – see under genus description (*p.342*).

Distribution/Status: Scarce. Recorded from widely scattered sites in south-east England.

♂
♀
J F M A M J J A S O N D

Philodromus collinus

♂3–4 mm ♀4–6 mm [PAGE 345 TR]

Observation tips/habitat: Typically found on the branches of evergreen trees, particularly pine and Yew on heathland. Occasionally recorded from broadleaved trees in mixed woodland and from evergreen trees and bushes in urban parks and churchyards.

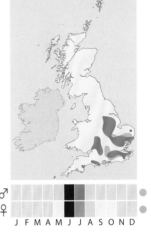

Description: CARAPACE Similar to *P. aureolus* (*p.343*) and *P. cespitum* (*p.346*). ABDOMEN Reddish-brown with median band of white hairs tapering towards the spinnerets. LEGS Greyish-brown.

Similar species: Other members of the *P. aureolus* group – see under genus description (*p.342*).

Distribution/Status: Uncommon and restricted to southern and eastern England.

♂
♀
J F M A M J J A S O N D

NE *Philodromus buxi* ⚲

Extremely rare

♂4mm ♀5–7mm   [PAGE 345 HML]

Observation tips/habitat: Thought to be extinct in Britain until it was rediscovered in 2014 in London on a vegetated green roof. Occurs on bushes and trees in Europe.

Description: CARAPACE + ABDOMEN Similar to *P. aureolus* (*p. 343*) and *P. cespitum* (*p. 346*). LEGS Pale brown with darker annulations/spots.

Similar species: Other members of the *P. aureolus group* – see under Genus description (*p. 342*).

Distribution/Status: Very rare.

♂
♀
J F M A M J J A S O N D

VU *Philodromus emarginatus* ⚲

Nationally Rare

Rare, local

♂4–5mm ♀5–6mm   [PAGE 345 HMR]

Observation tips/habitat: Generally occurs on pine trees, and occasionally on heather under pine in heathland areas. It lacks any distinct markings and has a pinkish-brown overall appearance.

Description: CARAPACE Similar to *P. aureolus* (*p. 343*) and *P. cespitum* (*p. 346*) but contrasting median and lateral banding is less distinct. ABDOMEN Similar to *P. aureolus* and *P. cespitum* but pattern less clear. LEGS Greyish-brown with darker markings.

Similar species: Members of the *P. aureolus* group – see under Genus description (*p. 342*).

Distribution/Status: Rare and very local. Very widely scattered throughout Britain as far north as central Scotland.

♂
♀
J F M A M J J A S O N D

Philodromus albidus

♂3·0–3·5mm ♀3·4–5·0mm [PAGE 345 LML]

Observation tips/habitat: One of the smallest species in the genus, *P. albidus* is typically found on the lower branches of broadleaved trees, particularly oak, on the margins of clearings and rides in woodland. The overall appearance is similar to ♀ *P. dispar* (p. 343) but the pattern is generally rather vague.

Description: CARAPACE Greyish-brown with broad, paler median band. Both sexes similar to ♀ *P. dispar* but paler. ABDOMEN Pale yellowish-brown with vague pattern of darker chevrons posteriorly. LEGS Greyish-brown.

Similar species: *P. rufus* (*below*) and members of the *P. aureolus* group – see under Genus description (p. 342).

Distribution/Status: Common and widespread in southern England. Appears to be extending its range.

Common, regional

♂
♀
J F M A M J J A S O N D

P. albidus and *P. rufus* can only be safely identified by microscopic examination and dissection of the genitalia (see *page 96*).

Philodromus rufus

♂3·3–4·0mm ♀4–6mm [PAGE 345 LMR]

Observation tips/habitat: Indistinguishable from *P. albidus* (*above*) in appearance and habitat. Until recently (2000) both species were identified as *P. rufus*. The majority are now confirmed as *P. albidus*. The few confirmed records of *P. rufus* suggest it has a more reddish appearance than *P. albidus* and is found in more open scrub habitats.

Description: CARAPACE + ABDOMEN As *P. albidus*. LEGS Pale pinkish-brown.

Similar species: *P. albidus* (*above*) and members of the *P. aureolus* group – see under Genus description (p. 342).

Distribution/Status: Rare. Recorded from a very few sites in south-east England.

Rare, regional

♂
♀
J F M A M J J A S O N D

Egg-sac: *p.89*

NT *Philodromus margaritatus* 🔍

♂4–5mm ♀5–6mm   [PAGE 345 BL]

Observation tips/habitat: The spider has a rather broad and flattened body, and typically occurs on lichen-covered trunks of both evergreen and broadleaved trees. Both sexes show colour and markings that are variable, and which generally reflect the substrate on which the individual spiders are found, providing them with excellent camouflage. However **the overall greenish-grey colouring together with its general shape make this species quite distinctive.**

Description: CARAPACE White to greenish-grey with darker lateral bands containing white markings. The whole having a rather mottled appearance. ABDOMEN Two pattern forms are recognized. One is greenish-grey with mottling and indistinct paler chevrons posteriorly. The other form has the whole dorsal area white to pale greenish-grey with dark 'shoulders' and a conspicuous transverse row of black spots centrally. LEGS Grey with dark annulations.

Similar species: None.

Distribution/Status: Rare. Known from scattered localities in southern England and central Scotland.

♂
♀
J F M A M J J A S O N D

VU *Philodromus fallax* Sand Running Spider 👁

♂4–5mm ♀4·5–6·0mm   [PAGE 345 BR]

Observation tips/habitat: A coastal species occurring on sand dunes and Marram Grass. **Distinctive both because of its habitat and being the only *Philodromus* species found at ground level.** Its superb camouflage renders it almost invisible in its sandy habitat. Both sexes are similar.

Description: CARAPACE Pale, sandy colour with brown markings. ABDOMEN Sandy-brown with darker cardiac mark and posteriorly darker lateral bands containing white spots. LEGS Sandy-brown with dark spots.

Similar species: None.

Distribution/Status: Rare around the coasts of England and Wales.

♂
♀
J F M A M J J A S O N D

Philodromus histrio

LC

♂5–6mm ♀6–7mm

Observation tips/habitat: This distinctive, handsome spider typically occurs on heathland amongst heather where its cryptic markings provide excellent camouflage. It can be confused with *Oxyopes heterophthalmus* but the latter has very conspicuous leg spines not present on *P. histrio*.

Description: CARAPACE Dark brown with pale brown median band and white marginal line. ABDOMEN Distinct, dark brown cardiac mark with white edging within pale brown median band tapering towards the spinnerets. Dark brown sides with oblique white marks. LEGS Greyish-brown with paler annulations.

Similar species: *Oxyopes heterophthalmus* (p. 243).

Distribution/Status: Scarce and local. Widely scattered throughout Britain with two areas of concentrated records in southern England.

Nationally Scarce

Scarce, local

♂
♀
J F M A M J J A S O N D

♀ *Philodromus histrio* ×4

Tibellus

 **2 British species (1 illustrated)**

These species have a **very distinctive appearanc**e and differ markedly from other philodromids. They are **straw coloured with a narrow, elongated abdomen and long legs which are typically extended along the blades and stems of tall ground vegetation**. They remain motionless in this position awaiting prey and as such are extremely well camouflaged, particularly in dry conditions. The genus is recognisable in the field; the only possible confusion is with the *Tetragnatha* (*pp. 165–170*), but *Tibellus* does not have enlarged chelicerae and never has a metallic, silvery appearance. The sexes are similar, as are the species themselves. Microscopic examination of the genitalia (see *page 96*) is necessary to confirm identification of the species in the genus.

♀ *Tibellus oblongus* ×**6**

LC *Tibellus oblongus* 🔬

♂7–8 mm ♀8–10 mm [PAGE 352]

Observation tips/habitat: Occurs on coarse grasses, rushes and heather in a range of habitats including bogs, sandhills and rough ground, similar to *T. maritimus*. *T. oblongus* is the commoner of the two species, and more frequent inland and in damper habitats.

Description: CARAPACE Pale sandy-brown with darker median band. ABDOMEN Similar colouring and pattern as carapace such that a dark median stripe appears to run entire length of body. Two pairs of faint spots may be present posteriorly on either side of the median line. ♂ abdomen is thinner than that of ♀. LEGS Pale sandy-brown, sometimes with dark spots at the base of femora.

♂
♀
J F M A M J J A S O N D

Similar species: *Tibellus maritimus* (below).

Distribution/Status: Widespread and common in southern Britain. More local and scattered in the north.

LC *Tibellus maritimus* 🔬

♂7–8 mm ♀8–10 mm [NOT ILLUSTRATED]

Observation tips/habitat: Similar to *T. oblongus*, occuring on coarse grasses, rushes and heather in a range of habitats including bogs, sandhills and rough ground. Although *T. maritimus* is found inland it appears to favour coastal locations where, particularly in sand dunes, it is usually the more frequent *Tibellus* species.

Description: CARAPACE Similar to *T. oblongus* but often also has dark brown spots on margins of carapace. ABDOMEN Similar to *T. oblongus* but, in addition to the spots posteriorly, also usually has a line of clear dark spots on either side of the median line. ♂ abdomen is thinner than that of ♀. LEGS Similar to *T. oblongus*.

♂
♀
J F M A M J J A S O N D

Similar species: *Tibellus oblongus* (above).

Distribution/Status: Uncommon but widely scattered throughout Britain.

Thanatus

👁 **3 British species (3 illustrated)**

These species have a similar appearance to *Philodromus* (pp. 342–351) but differ **in leg IV being longer than the others.** The oval abdomen has a conspicuous cardiac mark. Unlike *Philodromus* they are generally found at ground level amongst grass and undergrowth.

LC *Thanatus striatus* ◆ 🔍

♂ 3–4 mm ♀ 4–5 mm

Nationally Scarce

Uncommon, regional

♂♀ **Observation tips/habitat:** Typically occurs at ground level in a variety of usually sandy habitats including grassland, wet heathland, fens, dunes and saltmarsh. The whole spider is covered with coarse black hairs. Sexes are similar.

Description: CARAPACE Wide, yellowish-brown median band with dark central stripe in posterior half, the whole flanked by darker lateral bands. ABDOMEN Pale brown with distinct dark cardiac mark tapering to a point about half-way to the spinnerets. In posterior half, two dark lines converge towards the spinnerets forming a 'V'-shape. LEGS Yellowish-brown with dark brown spots and thick covering of hairs.

Similar species: None.

Distribution/Status: Uncommon and fairly local. Widespread in East Anglia and southern England, very scattered and much less frequent in the rest of England and Wales. Absent from Scotland.

♂
♀

J F M A M J J A S O N D

♀ *Thanatus striatus* ×**6**

NA *Thanatus vulgaris* 🔍

♂4–6mm ♀6–9mm

Observation tips/habitat: Not native to Britain. Regularly found in consignments of imported live crickets but rarely recorded.

Description: CARAPACE Dark brown with white marginal line and pale greyish-brown median band containing, anteriorly, a dark brown wedge-shaped tapering towards the rear. ABDOMEN Mottled greyish-brown with distinct dark brown cardiac mark edged in white. LEGS Grey and relatively long.

Similar species: *T. formicinus* (p. 356).

Distribution/Status: Not thought to be established in Britain although of rare but regular occurrence.

♂ ●
♀ ●
J F M A M J J A S O N D

♀ *Thanatus vulgaris* ×**4**

PE *Thanatus formicinus* 🔍

♂5–7mm ♀7–12mm

Observation tips/habitat: Typically occurs in boggy areas on wet heathland at the base of vegetation. Occasionally recorded from drier, sandy areas. Similar in general appearance to *T. vulgaris* but larger.

Description: CARAPACE + ABDOMEN + LEGS Similar to *T. vulgaris*.

Similar species: *T. vulgaris* (p. 355).

Distribution/Status: Formerly recorded in the Ashdown Forest and New Forest in southern England; last seen in 1969.

NO PHENOLOGY DATA

♀ *Thanatus formicinus* ×**6**

THOMISIDAE Crab spiders   **7 British genera**

These are broad-bodied, eight-eyed spiders with legs I and II longer and more robust than legs III and IV. Until recently they were included in a single family with the Philodromidae (*p.342*), but their squat, dumpy appearance and shorter legs give them much more of a crab-like appearance. They are fairly sedentary, lying in wait for prey and grabbing hold of it with the first two pairs of legs, which usually have a number of strong spines to aid prey capture and retention. They are able to move sideways but this is usually fairly slow and ungainly. Five thomisid genera contain just a single species, all of which have a distinctive and individual appearance. However, the other two genera, *Xysticus* (*p.362*) and *Ozyptila* (*p.371*), contain spiders which are fairly similar in general appearance.

Thomisus   👁️ **1 British species (illustrated)**

The British *Thomisus* species is one of our most striking spiders. Its appearance, body shape and colouring allow for fairly easy recognition.

LC *Thomisus onustus*   👁️   Nationally Scarce

Scarce, regional

♂2·5–3·5mm ♀6–7mm   [PAGE 358 T]

Observation tips/habitat: Occurs on heathland where it is typically found on the flowers of Bell Heather and Cross-leaved Heath where it awaits prey. Occasionally may be found on other plants, where its ability to change colour according to its surroundings gives it excellent camouflage. The ♂ and ♀ are quite different.

Description: CARAPACE ♀ broad, whitish-yellow central band flanked by brown lateral bands. ♂ dark brown with narrow, paler median band. In both sexes lateral eyes are on conspicuous tubercles at the anterior corners of the head area. ABDOMEN ♀ very variable in colour – can be pink, yellow, white or a combination of the three. When viewed from above, the abdomen has a distinctly triangular shape which is truncated anteriorly. There is a distinct conical tubercle on each of the two posterior points of the triangle, with a flattened triangular area to the rear between these points. ♂ are similar in shape but much smaller than ♀ and usually a darker, brownish-orange. LEGS ♀ colour variable, matching that of the abdomen, sometimes with paler markings on legs I and II. Tibia and metatarsus I with short spines. ♂ legs I and II relatively long.

Similar species: *Pistius truncatus* (*p.361*).

Distribution/Status: Restricted to southern-central England where it is very local.

♂
♀
J F M A M J J A S O N D

A ♂ sitting on the rear of the abdomen of the much larger ♀.

Yellow and pink variations

Thomisus onustus × **6**

♀ *Misumena vatia* × **6**

Misumena

1 British species (illustrated)

The ♀ of the single British species is unmistakable and field recognition should present no problem. It can change colour (varying from white to yellow and occasionally green) to match that of the flower head where it sits waiting to ambush visiting insects. The ♂ also has a distinctive appearance – very different from the ♀ and much smaller. In both sexes legs I and II are much longer than legs III and IV.

LC

Misumena vatia

Common, regional

♂3–4mm ♀9–11mm   [BELOW AND PAGE 358 B]

Observation tips/habitat: The ♀ is typically found on flower heads among grass and scrub along woodland margins, and occasionally in more open locations, including gardens. The ♂ tends to be found lower down in the vegetation.

Description: CARAPACE ♀ broad white median band with olive-green lateral bands. ♂ dark brown with whitish-green median band. ABDOMEN ♀ variable in colour from white to bright yellow, sometimes with two pink, oblique, lateral lines in the anterior half. ♂ white with two, dark brown, longitudinal bands in the posterior half, and dark brown sides. LEGS ♀ coloured as carapace with many conspicuous spines on tibia I and metatarsus I. ♂ noticeably long (particularly I and II) but lacking spines. Femora and patellae I and II dark brown with remaining segments annulated. Legs III and IV pale-yellow.

♂
♀
J F M A M J J A S O N D

Similar species: None.

Distribution/Status: Fairly common and widespread in southern England and parts of Wales, absent in the north and Scotland.

♂ *Misumena vatia* ×**6**

359

Diaea

👁 **1 British species (illustrated)**

The single species in this genus has a **distinctive appearance** and should be readily recognized in the field.

LC *Diaea dorsata*   Green Crab Spider   👁

Common, regional

♂ 3–4 mm   ♀ 5–6 mm

Observation tips/habitat: This spider strongly favours woodland habitat where it typically occurs amongst the foliage of evergreens such as Box, Yew and other conifers. Also recorded from oak.

Description: CARAPACE ♀ bright, emerald green with eyes encircled in white and slightly elevated. ♂ greenish-yellow (sometimes brown), with darker blotches or spots bearing long bristles. Immatures of both sexes, ♂s particularly, are typically distinctly green. ABDOMEN ♀ dark brown folium with irregular margin covering most of dorsal surface. Sides are a pale yellowish-green. ♂ similar to ♀ but usually darker. LEGS ♀ as carapace with tarsi and metatarsi usually tinged with pale brown. Tibia I and metatarsus I with conspicuous spines ventrally. ♂ similar to ♀ but with dark brown annulations and spots on legs I and II.

♂
♀
J F M A M J J A S O N D

Similar species: None.

Distribution/Status: Local and widespread in southern England as far north as Yorkshire. Absent from much of Wales, northern England and Scotland.

♂   *Diaea dorsata* ×**6**   ♀

Pistius

 1 British species (illustrated)

The single British species in this genus has a **similar abdominal shape to *Thomisus onustus* but any confusion is avoided by the overall brown appearance of *Pistius truncatus*** and recognition in the field should be straightforward. The sexes are similar; the ♂ being slightly darker.

CR *Pistius truncatus*

♂4–5mm ♀7–9mm

Observation tips/habitat: Thought to be extinct in Britain but was re-discovered in 1985 (and since then recorded a few times) at a single location where it occurs in woodland on the lower branches of coppiced oak. Appears to overwinter under loose bark or dead wood.

Description: CARAPACE Brown, mottled and with pale spots. ABDOMEN Similar shape to *T. onustus* but browner in colour and with less pronounced tubercles. Sometimes paler chevrons are present posteriorly. LEGS I and II dark brown sometimes with paler annulations, contrasting strongly with the pale, yellowish-brown legs III and IV.

Similar species: *Thomisus onustus* (*p. 357*).

Distribution/Status: Very rare, currently known from a single location in south-east England.

♂ NO PHENOLOGY DATA
♀ [phenology chart]
J F M A M J J A S O N D

♀ *Pistius truncatus* ×**6**

Xysticus

🔍 **12 British species (12 illustrated)**

Like *Ozyptila* (*p. 371*), these spiders are very crab-like. **They have a squat, rounded appearance but are larger and have more definite body patterns than** *Ozyptila*. The carapace usually has dark lateral bands flanking a paler median band that normally contains a slightly darker triangular area anteriorly. Also, the whole spider usually has a sparse covering of long spines. Most species are generally found at ground level or amongst low vegetation, where they lie in wait to ambush prey in a similar fashion to other members of the family. ♂s are smaller than ♀s but often have much stronger markings. There is considerable variation in the depth of colour in many of the species and, although the genus itself is readily recognized in the field, microscopic examination of the genitalia (see *page 96*) is necessary to confirm identification of all species in the genus.

LC # *Xysticus cristatus*

Abundant, widespread

♂3–5mm ♀6–8mm   [PAGE 364 T]

Observation tips/habitat: By far the commonest *Xysticus*. Occurs in low vegetation in almost every habitat type but is intolerant of shade and therefore rarely found in woodland.

Description: CARAPACE ♀ mottled, pale brown lateral bands flank a whitish median band which contains a slightly darker wedge shape. This extends ⅔ the carapace length ending in a distinctive dark brown point. Lateral bands have a darker tip posteriorly. ♂ similar to ♀ but darker. ABDOMEN ♀ pale creamy-brown with similar coloured central band made up of three or four overlapping triangles on a darker brown folium. Depth of colour can vary. ♂ similar to ♀ but darker. LEGS ♀ pale brown with some darker streaks and spots. Tibia I usually has four conspicuous pairs of spines ventrally. ♂ similar to ♀ but darker.

Similar species: All other *Xysticus* species.

Distribution/Status: Abundant and widespread throughout Britain.

♂
♀
J F M A M J J A S O N D

LC # *Xysticus kochi*

Common, regional

♂4–5mm ♀6–8mm   [PAGE 364 BR]

Observation tips/habitat: Appears to favour more open, sparsely vegetated conditions than *X. cristatus* (*above*). Occurs in a variety of habitats, including waste ground, sand dunes and south facing chalk scarps.

Description: CARAPACE + ABDOMEN + LEGS Similar to *X. cristatus*.

Similar species: All other *Xysticus* species.

Distribution/Status: Widespread but scattered distribution in southern England and on the Welsh coast. Much less frequent elsewhere and almost completely absent from Scotland.

♂
♀
J F M A M J J A S O N D

LC *Xysticus audax* ♀

♂3–5mm ♀6–8mm   [PAGE 364 M]

Observation tips/habitat: Typically occurs on gorse and
heather on heathland, and occasionally in grassland. Similar
in general appearance to *X. cristatus* (*p. 362*) but usually darker
with more pronounced pattern and occuring at a higher level in
the vegetation.

Description: CARAPACE ♀ similar pattern to *X. cristatus* but the
wedge shape within median band does not extend quite as far,
and is often darker. Lateral bands black. ♂ darker. ABDOMEN
♀ similar pattern to *X. cristatus* but usually darker and more
distinct. ♂ darker. LEGS Brown with more extensive areas of
black markings than *X. cristatus*, particularly in ♂.

Similar species: All other *Xysticus* species.

Distribution/Status: Very scattered throughout England
and Wales, much less frequent elsewhere.

Uncommon, regional

♂
♀
J F M A M J J A S O N D

LC *Xysticus ulmi* ♀

♂3–4mm ♀5–8mm   [PAGE 364 BL]

Observation tips/habitat: Typically found in low vegetation
in damp, marshy habitats. **It differs from other *Xysticus* in
having a slightly more elongated abdomen which makes
indicative field identification easier.** The body pattern resembles
that of *X. cristatus* (*p. 362*) but the two species have quite
different habitat requirements.

Description: CARAPACE ♀ similar to *X. cristatus* but the wedge
shape in the median band extends nearly the whole length of
the carapace and has a white edging in darker specimens.
The lateral bands are thinner with pale spotting. ♂ similar
but darker. ABDOMEN ♀ and ♂ anterior edge overhangs the
carapace. Usually has white sides with brown folium
sometimes edged with a thin black line. Within the folium is a
pale median band in the anterior half with pale transverse lines
posteriorly. LEGS ♀ pale brown with numerous small spots.
♂ legs I and II have black femora and patellae; remaining segments
and other legs pale brown with small spots.

Similar species: All other *Xysticus* species.

Distribution/Status: Widespread and local in south-east England apart from the extreme
south-east. Scattered elsewhere.

Common, widespread

♂
♀
J F M A M J J A S O N D

♂ *Xysticus cristatus* × **4** ♀

♂ *Xysticus audax* × **4** ♀

♀ *Xysticus ulmi* × **4**

♀ *Xysticus kochi* × **4**

♀ *Xysticus sabulosus* × **4**

colour variation

♂

Xysticus luctator × **4**

♀

♀ *Xysticus bifasciatus* × **4**

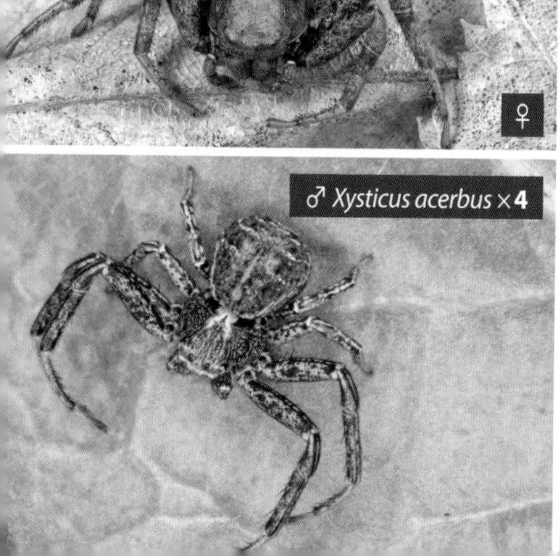

♂ *Xysticus acerbus* × **4**

♀ *Xysticus luctuosus* × **4**

365

LC *Xysticus bifasciatus* ◆

♂6–7mm ♀7–10mm   [PAGE 365 MR]

Observation tips/habitat: Its large size and robust appearance make *X. bifasciatus* quite distinctive in the field. It is found in low vegetation and under stones on chalk grassland and grassy heathland, usually in warm situations. In ♂ carapace almost equal in size to abdomen.

Description: CARAPACE Both sexes have a similar appearance to *X. cristatus* (*p. 362*) but the markings are usually less distinct. ♂ usually much darker than ♀ and has a swollen appearance. ABDOMEN ♀ similar to *X. cristatus* but pattern can be vague and sometimes completely absent. ♂ has white sides with dark brown folium sometimes containing white spots and transverse lines. LEGS ♀ noticeably robust; pale brown with darker lines and spots particularly on femora and tibiae. ♂ pale-yellow apart from dark brown femora and patellae I and II.

Similar species: All other *Xysticus* species.

Distribution/Status: Scarce but widely scattered throughout Britain; most frequent in central-southern England.

♂
♀
J F M A M J J A S O N D

EN *Xysticus luctuosus*

♂4–5mm ♀7–8mm   [PAGE 365 BR]

Observation tips/habitat: A woodland species, occurring on low plants and vegetation. The ♀ is similar to *X. cristatus* (*p. 362*) in general appearance but pattern is usually less well defined. ♂ is generally a uniform dark brown.

Description: CARAPACE ♀ similar to *X. cristatus*. ♂ dark brown to black with very few markings, if any. ABDOMEN ♀ similar to *X. cristatus* but less distinct pattern. ♂ very dark with no obvious pattern. LEGS ♀ pale brown but heavily mottled with black, and furnished with stout spines. ♂ legs I and II have dark brown femora and paler patellae and tibiae; legs III and IV yellow-brown with darker markings.

Similar species: All other *Xysticus* species.

Distribution/Status: Rare; very scattered distribution throughout Britain.

♂   NO PHENOLOGY DATA
♀
J F M A M J J A S O N D

EN *Xysticus luctator* ♀

♂6–7mm ♀7–10mm [PAGE 365 ML]

Nationally Rare

Extremely rare

Observation tips/habitat: Similar to *X. bifasciatus* (*p. 366*) in size and general appearance but much rarer. Locations where it has occurred have been mature dry heathland and Beech woodland where it has been found at ground level amongst heather and Beech litter, and under dead wood.

Description: CARAPACE ♀ brown with broad pale brown median band and two dark crescent-shaped spots on posterior margin. ♂ dark brown to black with rather indistinct paler median band (sometimes including darker wedge shape anteriorly) and two dark brown crescent-shaped spots (sometimes two additional brighter ones) on posterior margin. ABDOMEN ♀ light brown, without clear pattern. ♂ dark brown, with thin cream margin. LEGS ♀ yellowish-brown with dark mottling on femora, patellae and tibiae. Metatarsi I with numerous spines. ♂ coxae, femora and patellae dark brown to glossy black with white junctions, remaining segments pale yellow.

♂
♀ NO PHENOLOGY DATA

Similar species: All other *Xysticus* species.

Distribution/Status: Very rare; known from just four locations in southern England.

LC *Xysticus acerbus* ♀

♂4–5mm ♀7–8mm [PAGE 365 BL]

Nationally Rare

Rare, regional

Observation tips/habitat: Similar to *X. luctuosus* (*p. 566*) in terms of size, the vagueness of markings and the variability of appearance (usually dark). Typically occurs in a variety of grassland habitats, sand dunes and heathland.

Description: CARAPACE ♀ greyish-brown sometimes with a vague 'V'-shaped marking. ♂ similar but usually darker. ABDOMEN ♀ greyish-brown, lacking any distinct pattern. ♂ brownish-grey to black, some with faint, white transverse lines. LEGS Brown with darker marks and, in paler specimens, some white mottling.

Similar species: All other *Xysticus* species.

Distribution/Status: Rare and very local; scattered records in southern England.

♂
♀
J F M A M J J A S O N D

367

LC *Xysticus erraticus* ♂♀

Common, widespread

♂4–5mm ♀6–8mm   [PAGE 370 T]

Observation tips/habitat: Typically occurs at ground level amongst grass tussocks or under stones and dead plant litter in grassland and heathland, particularly where the sward is short. **Dark colouring of ♂** gives it a distinctive appearance in the field.

Description: CARAPACE ♀ broad, pale, median band flanked by well-defined thin, dark bands outside of which are pale brown bands and then dark edges. Wedge shape in median band very indistinct but margin is outlined in white. ♂ similar but with edges a deep, rich brown, and white wedge margin very clear. ABDOMEN ♀ creamy-white sides with brown folium containing creamy-white median band extending almost the whole length of the abdomen. ♂ similar but folium a rich dark brown and with a clear, dark brown cardiac mark. LEGS ♀ yellowish-brown. ♂ similar but coxae, femora and patellae I and II very dark brown. In both sexes strong spines present ventrally on tibia I.

♂
♀
J F M A M J J A S O N D

Similar species: All other *Xysticus* species.

Distribution/Status: Common. Widespread but fairly scattered throughout Britain.

LC *Xysticus lanio* ♂♀

Uncommon, regional

♂4–5mm ♀6–7mm   [PAGE 370 M]

Observation tips/habitat: Occurs on bushes and young trees, particularly oak, in woodland, usually at a higher level than other *Xysticus*. The depth of abdominal pattern, particularly in the ♂, is very variable and the pattern may be completely absent. **The spider has a distinctive reddish appearance** which helps field identification.

Description: CARAPACE ♀ yellowish-brown median band with slightly darker wedge shape in anterior half. Lateral bands reddish-brown. ♂ pale, central median band has darker, ill-defined, wedge shape anteriorly; lateral bands much darker than ♀, sometimes almost black. ABDOMEN ♀ broad and rounded posteriorly with reddish sides and rather indistinct brown folium. ♂ dark reddish-black folium containing white transverse and lateral lines. LEGS ♀ reddish with faint darker annulations; tibia I with strong spines ventrally. ♂ femora I deep reddish-brown with conspicuous spines dorsally, remaining segments and other legs pale yellow.

♂
♀
J F M A M J J A S O N D

Similar species: All other *Xysticus* species.

Distribution/Status: Widespread but scarce in southern and eastern England with very scattered records elsewhere.

EN *Xysticus robustus* ♀

♂ 5–6 mm ♀ 7–10 mm [PAGE 370 B]

Nationally Rare

Extremely rare

Observation tips/habitat: Clearly characterized by its very dark appearance and broad, squat form and should be readily recognized in the field. Occurs on dry heathland and coastal chalk grassland, usually in open stony areas at ground level; occasionally amongst grass and heather.

Description: CARAPACE ♀ laterally, dark greyish-brown with the central area only slightly paler. The whole usually appears as a uniform colour; head area spiny. ♂ almost uniformly a rich, deep black. ABDOMEN ♀ greyish-brown, sometimes with pinkish tinge, lacking any distinct pattern. ♂ dark brown to black. LEGS Dark brown to black.

Similar species: All other *Xysticus* species.

NO PHENOLOGY DATA

Distribution/Status: Extremely rare. Confined to the south coast of England but last recorded in 1998.

LC *Xysticus sabulosus* ◆ ♀

♂ 5–6 mm ♀ 7–9 mm [PAGE 365 T]

Nationally Scarce

Scarce, local

Observation tips/habitat: Typically occurs on sandy heathland on low vegetation or at ground level where its pattern and colouring provide excellent camouflage. Colour and pattern are very variable and mature specimens can be almost completely black.

Description: CARAPACE ♀ dark brown lateral bands (almost black posteriorly) flank a broad white median band which contains a greyish-brown wedge shape in the anterior two-thirds; the whole is thickly covered with short spines. ♂ similar but darker with fewer spines. ABDOMEN Grey with brown folium containing greyish median band with lateral extensions posteriorly. LEGS ♀ femora whitish with dark brown to black spots; remaining segments brown with some white spotting on patellae and tibiae. ♂ legs I and II can be almost completely black, the remainder similar to ♀.

J F M A M J J A S O N D

Similar species: All other *Xysticus* species.

Distribution/Status: Scarce and very local; very patchy and scattered distribution throughout Britain.

369

♂ *Xysticus erraticus* × **4** ♀

♂ *Xysticus lanio* × **4** ♀

♂ *Xysticus robustus* × **4** ♀

Ozyptila

🔍 **10 British species (10 illustrated)**

These are all small spiders generally occurring at ground level. **They resemble *Xysticus* (*p.362*) species but are smaller, have a more squat appearance and the carapace is clothed with clavate hairs which are apparent with the use of a hand lens.** The abdomen usually has a flattened anterior edge and its pattern, if present, lacks the folium of *Xysticus* and is much less structured. *Ozyptila blackwalli*, *O. scabricula*, *O. nigrita* and *O. pullata* are all rather similar to each other and are rare. They are dark, have numerous clavate hairs and are often covered with soil particles. The other species in the genus have fewer clavate hairs, and are generally more variable in their appearance. Microscopic examination of the genitalia (see *page 96*) is necessary to confirm identification of all species in the genus.

Clavate hairs on the carapace separate *Ozyptila* spp. from *Xysticus* spp.

LC *Ozyptila praticola* ⚲

Common, regional

♂ 2·5–3·0 mm ♀ 3–4 mm   [BELOW AND PAGE 377 TR]

Observation tips/habitat: Usually found amongst plant litter and debris in a wide variety of habitats including woodland, grassland, gardens and even disturbed areas. Occasionally recorded from the lower branches of trees and under bark.

Description: CARAPACE ♀ dark brown to black laterally with reddish median band. ♂ can be slightly darker but depth of colour is variable in both sexes. ABDOMEN Both sexes greyish-brown mottled with black. LEGS Brown with darker annulations on femora, tibiae and patellae.

Similar species: All other *Ozyptila* species except *O. scabricula*, *O. nigrita* (both *p.378*), *O. pullata* and *O. blackwalli* (both *p.378*). ♂

Distribution/Status: Widespread in much of England and Wales, less frequent in the west and absent in Scotland. ♀

J F M A M J J A S O N D

×4

♀ *O. praticola*, like all *Ozyptila* ♀s, is much smaller than any *Xysticus* ♀s, though it is close in size to ♂s of the smaller *Xysticus* spp.

LC *Ozyptila trux*

Common, widespread

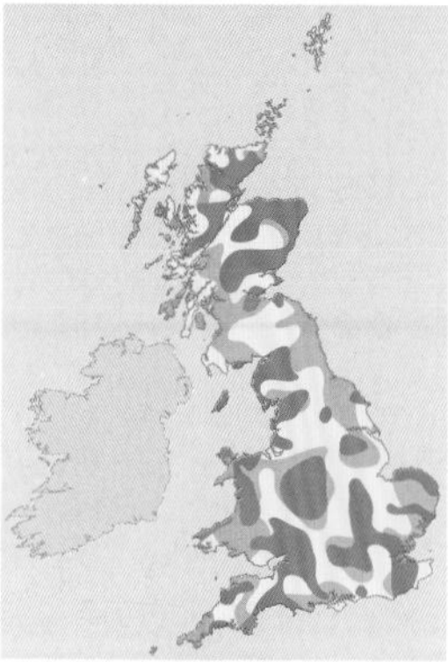

♂
♀
J F M A M J J A S O N D

♂3–4 mm ♀4–5 mm [PAGE 373 TL]

Observation tips/habitat: The commonest *Ozyptila* species and probably the most likely to be encountered. It occurs in all types of wet and dry grassland, heath and woodland.

Description: CARAPACE ♀ yellowish-brown with two, thin, dark brown longitudinal stripes. Some clavate hairs present, particularly in the central band. ♂ similar to ♀ but the longitudinal bands are darker and broader and the whole carapace may have a thin, dark margin. ABDOMEN Both sexes pale brown with black and white mottling. LEGS ♀ pale yellowish-brown. ♂ similar to ♀ apart from dark brown femora I and II.

Similar species: *Ozyptila simplex* (*p. 373*), *O. atomaria* (*below*).

Distribution/Status: Widespread and scattered throughout Britain, commoner in the north and west.

LC *Ozyptila atomaria*

Common, widespread

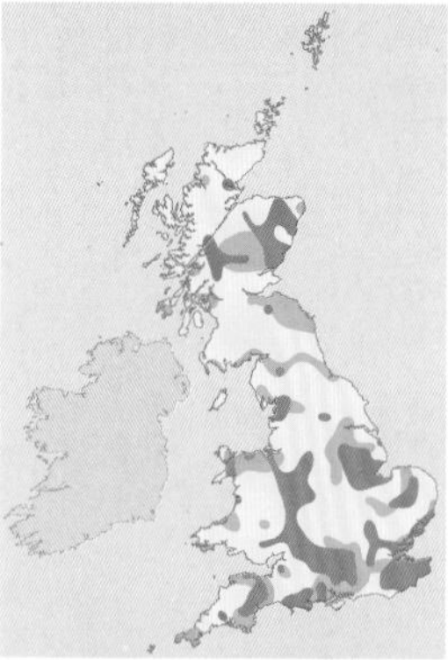

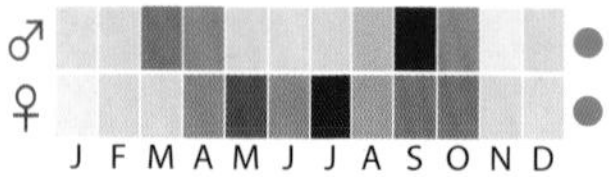
♂
♀
J F M A M J J A S O N D

♂3–4 mm ♀4–6 mm [PAGE 373 TR]

Observation tips/habitat: After *O. trux* the next commonest species in the genus. It typically occurs on limestone grassland and mature heathland where it is found at ground level amongst plant debris and occasionally under stones. The two sexes have a similar appearance but depth of colour can vary considerably.

Description: CARAPACE ♀ similar to ♀ *O. trux* but longitudinal lines may be less definite and lateral areas may be suffused with black. ♂ similar to ♀ but often darker with lateral areas almost entirely dark and central band orange-brown posteriorly. ABDOMEN Distinctly squared anterior edge. ♀ brownish-grey with darker markings posteriorly and lines of black spots on anterior sides. ♂ similar to ♀ but often darker. LEGS Pale brown. ♂ femora I and II slightly darker than other segments.

Similar species: *Ozyptila trux* (*above*), *Ozyptila simplex* (*p. 373*).

Distribution/Status: Common with widespread but scattered distribution throughout Britain.

♀ *Ozyptila trux* × **6**

♀ *Ozyptila atomaria* × **6**

♂   *Ozyptila simplex* × **6**   ♀

LC *Ozyptila simplex*

[ABOVE]

♂3–4mm ♀4–5mm

Observation tips/habitat: Typically associated with sandy habitats, particularly in coastal areas, where it occurs at the base of plants and in plant litter. In both sexes the depth of colour and strength of markings is variable.

Description: CARAPACE ♀ similar to ♀ *O. trux* but slightly paler. ♂ dark brown to black sides and head area, with the remaining central posterior median region pale brown. ABDOMEN ♀ pale greyish-brown sometimes with a few darker spots. ♂ similar to ♀ but often darker posteriorly. LEGS ♀ pale yellowish-brown. ♂ similar to ♀ apart from dark brown femora I and II.

Similar species: *Ozyptila trux, O. atomaria* (both *p. 372*).

Distribution/Status: Local; scattered and patchy distribution in southern Britain with most records from the south-east.

Uncommon, regional

♂
♀
J F M A M J J A S O N D

LC *Ozyptila brevipes*

♂2–3mm ♀3–4mm [PAGE 375 TL]

Observation tips/habitat: Occurs in a variety of wet and dry situations but appears to favour wet marsh and fenland habitats, with fewer records from drier grassland and heathland areas.

Description: CARAPACE ♀ dark brown sides, variegated with paler lines and patches, enclosing a paler, central band, fading to white posteriorly. ♂ similar to, but darker than, ♀. ABDOMEN ♀ greyish-white mottled with brown patches, particularly towards the posterior. ♂ similar to ♀ but darker and the posterior mottling is almost black. In both sexes four brownish dots forming a square are sometimes discernible in the anterior half. LEGS Pale yellowish-brown with dark brown annulations. In ♂ femora I are dark brown.

Similar species: All other *Ozyptila* species except *O. scabricula*, *O. nigrita* (both *p. 378*), *O. pullata* and *O. blackwalli* (both *p. 378*)

♂
♀
J F M A M J J A S O N D

Distribution/Status: Uncommon. Widespread and scattered throughout England. Less frequent in the north and absent from Scotland.

LC *Ozyptila sanctuaria*

♂2–3mm ♀3–4mm [PAGE 375 TR]

Observation tips/habitat: Occurs in a variety of open habitats including chalk and acid grassland, roadside verges, old sand and chalk pits and occasionally heathland. It is usually found at ground level under stones or among low vegetation.

Description: CARAPACE ♀ dark brown lateral bands with paler median region, particularly in the posterior half, and a thin, white, marginal line to the whole. ♂ similar to ♀ but darker and the posterior median region is yellowish-orange and usually smaller. ABDOMEN ♀ greyish-brown, usually with vague, black, flattened chevrons posteriorly. ♂ black. LEGS ♀ yellowish-brown with clavate hairs dorsally. ♂ femora I and II almost black, remaining segments lighter brown with tarsi and metatarsi paler. Some clavate hairs present.

♂
♀
J F M A M J J A S O N D

Similar species: All other *Ozyptila* species except *O. scabricula*, *O. nigrita* (both *p. 378*), *O. pullata* and *O. blackwalli* (both *p. 378*).

Distribution/Status: Uncommon and local; widespread in the southern half of Britain. Absent from the north and Scotland.

♀ *Ozyptila brevipes* ×**6**

♀ *Ozyptila sanctuaria* ×**6**

♀ *Ozyptila* species – identification pointers and habitat preferences
NB ♂'s generally similar but darker – see individual species accounts for fuller information

SPECIES	CARAPACE	ABDOMEN	LEGS	HABITAT
O. praticola*	Dark brown to black; reddish central band	Greyish-brown mottled with black	Brown with darker annulations on femora, tibiae and patellae	Woodland, grassland, gardens, disturbed areas
O. sanctuaria*	Dark brown; paler median region	Greyish-brown with vague black chevrons at rear	Yellowish brown	Open habitats such as grassland, roadside verges, sand and chalk pits, heathland
O. brevipes*	Dark brown ± variegated; paler median band	Greyish-white mottled with brown	Pale yellowish-brown with dark brown annulations	A variety, including dry grassland and heath, but favours wet marsh and fenland
O. trux*	Yellowish-brown with two dark brown stripes	Pale brown with black and white mottling	Pale yellowish-brown	Wet and dry grassland, heath, woodland
O. simplex*	As O. trux but slightly paler	Pale greyish-brown, sometimes a few darker spots		Sandy habitats
O. atomaria*	As O. trux but lines may be less defined and lateral areas suffused with black	Brownish-grey with dark markings at rear; black spots on sides at front	Pale brown	Limestone grassland and mature heathland
O. pullata*	Dark brown with broad, slighter paler median band	Pale greyish-brown with black mottling and short white streaks on back edge and sides	LEGS I + II mid brown; others paler brown	Disused chalk quarry (1 record)
O. blackwalli*	Deep brown with paler median band NB O. nigrita median band can be reddish	Greyish-brown with dark spots and bars	Brown with darker spots; 3 clavate hairs and conspicuous spines ventrally on femora I	Cliff tops and undercliffs
O. scabricula*			Brown with darker markings on femora	Dry, sandy heathland and coastal sand dunes
O. nigrita*				Chalk and limestone grassland

* Only safely distinguished by microscopic examination of the genitalia (see *page 96*).

LC *Ozyptila scabricula* ♀

♂2–3mm ♀3–4mm [PAGE 377 TL]

♂♀ **Observation tips/habitat:** Occurs on sparsely vegetated, dry, sandy heathland and coastal sand dunes where it is found under stones and amongst low vegetation. Both sexes can be particularly dark, the ♂ especially so.

Description: CARAPACE Similar to *O. blackwalli*. ♂'s can be very dark, almost black. ABDOMEN Similar to *O. blackwalli*. ♂'s can be very dark, almost black. LEGS ♀ brown with darker markings on the femora. ♂ similar but the femora very dark, almost black.

Similar species: *Ozyptila nigrita* (*below*), *O. pullata* and *O. blackwalli* (both *p. 378*).

Distribution/Status: Scarce. A mainly southern and eastern distribution with a few scattered records from the Welsh and Cornish coasts.

♂
♀
J F M A M J J A S O N D

LC *Ozyptila nigrita* ♀

♂2–3mm ♀3–4mm [PAGE 377 M]

♂♀ **Observation tips/habitat:** Occurs on short chalk and limestone grassland, often amongst stones.

Description: CARAPACE Similar to *O. blackwalli*. ♀ central band can be reddish. ♂'s can be very dark, almost black. ABDOMEN Similar to *O. blackwalli*. ♂'s can be very dark, almost black. LEGS ♀ brown with darker markings on femora. ♂ similar but femora very dark, almost black.

Similar species: *Ozyptila scabricula* (*above*), *O. pullata* and *O. blackwalli* (both *p. 378*).

Distribution/Status: Scarce. Confined to southern-central and south-east England.

♂
♀
J F M A M J J A S O N D

♀ *Ozyptila scabricula* ×**6**

♀ *Ozyptila praticola* ×**6**

♂   *Ozyptila nigrita* ×**6**   ♀

♀ *Ozyptila blackwalli* ×**6**

♀ *Ozyptila pullata* ×**6**

EN *Ozyptila blackwalli* 🔬

Nationally Rare

Extremely rare

⚦ ⚦ ♂2–3mm ♀3–4mm [PAGE 377 BL]

♂♀ **Observation tips/habitat:** Typically occurs near the coast under stones and in short grass, for example on cliff tops and undercliffs. The whole spider is covered with numerous clavate hairs.

Description: CARAPACE Deep-brown laterally with a paler central band. ABDOMEN Greyish-brown with a peppering of dark spots and bars. LEGS Brown with darker spots. Three small clavate hairs on femora I and conspicuous spines ventrally on femora and metatarsi I.

Similar species: *Ozyptila pullata* (*below*), *O. nigrita* and *O. scabricula* (both *p. 376*).

Distribution/Status: Very rare; restricted to coastal locations in southern England.

♂
♀

J F M A M J J A S O N D

VU *Ozyptila pullata* 🔬

Nationally Rare

Extremely rare

⚦ ⚦ ♂3.1–3.3mm ♀3.3–3.6mm [PAGE 377 BR]

♂♀ **Observation tips/habitat:** The single British site for *O. pullata* is from a disused chalk quarry.

Description: CARAPACE Both sexes have dark brown lateral bands with a slightly paler, broad (less so in ♂), median band tapering towards the posterior. The whole carapace is densely covered with clavate hairs. ABDOMEN ♀ pale greyish-brown with black mottling and short, white streaks on the anterior and lateral edges. ♂ similar to ♀ but darker. Densely covered with clavate hairs in both sexes. LEGS ♀ legs I and II mid-brown, III and IV slightly paler brown. ♂ legs I and II mid-brown with femora I and II dark brown; legs III and IV paler brown with white streaks, with femora III and IV mid-brown.

Similar species: *Ozyptila blackwalli* (*above*), *O. nigrita* and *O. scabricula* (both *p. 376*).

Distribution/Status: Very rare. Known from just one location in south-east England.

♂
♀

J F M A M J J A S O N D

Synema

 1 British species (illustrated)

The British representative of this genus has an **unmistakable appearance**. It sits in flower heads pouncing on nectar- and pollen-feeding insects as they approach. However, it is unclear at present whether *Synema globosum* is an established British species or whether the few British records to date (2016) represent introductions by way of garden centres and imported garden shrubs.

Synema globosum

Extremely rare

♂3–4mm ♀6.0–8.5mm

Observation tips/habitat: In Europe occurs in grassland and occasionally in the foliage of shrubs.

Description: CARAPACE Black and shiny with a thin covering of hairs. Lateral eyes are on small tubercles. ABDOMEN ♀ yellow background (but on the continent it can also be white or orange/red) with a broad, deeply dentate, dark brown to black folium. ♂ similar but the abdomen is smaller and the pattern may be less distinct. LEGS Mostly dark with pale annulations. Femora I and II may be completely dark , particularly in ♂.

Similar species: None.

Distribution/Status: Very rare. Known from four widely scattered locations in England.

♂ NO PHENOLOGY DATA ●
♀ ●
J F M A M J J A S O N D

♀ *Synema globosum* ×**6**

SALTICIDAE Jumping spiders   17 British genera

This family is easily recognized in the field by the square front edge of the cephalothorax carrying a row of four large, forward-facing eyes with the central pair much larger than those on either side (see *page 398*). These characters are usually obvious without the need for a hand lens. The other four eyes are smaller and are located on top of the cephalothorax in two widely spaced rows. Salticids have a compact body and short, robust legs. They are commonly known as jumping spiders because of their method of catching prey by leaping onto it, occasionally from some distance away. The large forward-facing eyes are well developed and are able to judge accurately the required jumping distance to catch prey. The spider awaits the arrival of a potential meal, picking up any nearby movement with the eyes on the top of the cephalothorax. It then shifts its position to face its prey, judging the required distance with its large eyes, before leaping forwards onto its victim. They are often attractively marked – the males particularly can have brightly coloured or contrasting front legs, pedipalps and eye fringes which are used during courtship displays directed at the female.

LC *Salticus scenicus*   Common Zebra Spider

Abundant, widespread

♂5–6mm ♀5–7mm

Observation tips/habitat: Often seen on sunny walls and fences around houses and in gardens, where it sits on the vertical surface hunting for prey.

Description: CARAPACE Black with patches of white iridescent hairs, appearing sometimes as an X-shaped marking in ♀. There is a wide band of white hairs on the lateral margins. ♂ has very long chelicerae. ABDOMEN Black with white patches, often appearing as black and white stripes across the abdomen. A wide band of white hairs curves around the anterior margin and two or three pairs of white bars taper from each side towards the centre, sometimes obliquely. ♂s often have a less obvious pattern than ♀s. LEGS ♀ legs mottled yellow-brown with darker annulations at the joints and with numerous white hairs. ♂'s legs are darker.

Similar species: Other *Salticus* species.

Distribution/Status: Abundant and widespread throughout England and Wales, less so in Scotland.

J F M A M J J A S O N D

♂   *Salticus scenicus* × 6   ♀

380

Salticus

◉ 3 British species (3 illustrated)

All three species have a **black and white striped appearance**. ♂'s have **enlarged and projecting chelicerae**. Variability in the pattern and strength of colour in all three species means that microscopic examination of the genitalia (see *page 96*) is necessary to confirm identification.

LC

Salticus zebraneus

♂ 3–4 mm ♀ 3–4 mm

Observation tips/habitat: Recorded from the trunks of old trees, particularly pine, oak and willow. The spider is well camouflaged and will hide in the cracks and fissures of bark, only appearing at the surface in warm, sunny conditions.

Description: CARAPACE Similar to *S. scenicus* (*p. 380*). ABDOMEN Similar to *S. scenicus* but much smaller and with less obvious white striping. LEGS Similar to *S. scenicus*.

Similar species: Other *Salticus* species.

Distribution/Status: Generally scarce and mostly confined to south-east England.

Nationally Scarce

Scarce, regional

♂
♀
J F M A M J J A S O N D

Salticus zebraneus × **6**

♀ *Salticus cingulatus* × **6**

LC *Salticus cingulatus* ♀♂

♂ 5–6 mm ♀ 5–7 mm [PAGE 381 B]

Observation tips/habitat: Recorded from old tree trunks, and fenceposts in woodlands, wetlands and heathlands, away from habitation.

Description: CARAPACE Similar to *S. scenicus* (*p. 380*). ABDOMEN Similar to *S. scenicus* but the white bands are usually more oblique and larger, giving the general impression of black markings on a white background, rather than vice versa as in *S. scenicus*. LEGS Paler than *S. scenicus* but with more distinct, darker annulations.

Similar species: Other *Salticus* species.

Distribution/Status: Widespread throughout much of England but much less common than *S. scenicus*.

♂
♀
J F M A M J J A S O N D

Neon 🔍 4 British species (2 illustrated)

These are **small spiders with large posterior eyes.** The **head area (containing the eye arrangement) of the carapace is often distinctly longer than the thoracic area.** Just one of the species has a widespread distribution. Habitat preferences can be useful pointers for identification but the small size and variability in appearance of all four *Neon* species means that microscopic examination of the genitalia (see *page 96*) is necessary for safe identification.

LC *Neon reticulatus* ♀♂

♂ 2·0–2·5 mm ♀ 2–3 mm [PAGE 383 L]

Observation tips/habitat: Occurs in two distinct habitats – in woodland leaf-litter which may be quite dry and amongst moss in bogs and marshes.

Description: CARAPACE ♀ brown with black around eyes. ♂ darker with the head area having a metallic sheen. ABDOMEN Pale brown with darker spots and bars. Darker chevrons in a herringbone pattern are sometimes present towards the posterior end. ♂ is generally darker with a stronger pattern than ♀. LEGS I dark brown, the remainder are paler.

Similar species: Other *Neon* species.

Distribution/Status: Widespread and fairly common throughout much of Britain.

♂
♀
J F M A M J J A S O N D

NT *Neon pictus*

♂2·7 mm ♀3 mm   [BELOW R]

Observation tips/habitat: General appearance is yellowish-brown. It occurs on bare and thinly vegetated shingle near the shoreline and on shingle ridges up to three kilometres inland.

Description: CARAPACE + ABDOMEN Similar to *N. reticulatus* (*p. 382*). LEGS Pale yellow with dark annulations and dark bands on femora I, II and III. The femur, patella, tibia and metatarsus of legs I are dark brown.

Similar species: Other *Neon* species.

Distribution/Status: Rare. Known from four locations on the coast of southern England.

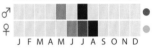

♂
♀

J F M A M J J A S O N D

♀ *Neon reticulatus* ×**10**

♀ *Neon pictus* ×**10**

Neon species – identification pointers				
SPECIES	CARAPACE	ABDOMEN	LEGS	HABITAT
*N. robustus**	♂ Brown; metallic sheen to head area

♀ Pale brown; black around eyes | Pale brown with darker spots and bars; ♂ darker than ♀ | LEG I dark brown; others paler | South facing rocky slopes and cliffs; bare shingle |
*N. reticulatus**				**Woodland leaf litter; mossy areas in bogs and marshes**
*N. pictus**			LEG I dark brown, tarsus pale yellow; others with distinct pattern	Bare and thinly vegetated shingle
*N. valentulus**	As above but usually darker		LEG I often entirely black apart from pale brown to white tarsus tip; others brown with distinct, darker annulations	Grass and moss in sedge fens

* Only safely distinguished by microscopic examination of the genitalia (see *page 96*).

LC *Neon robustus*

♂2·5–2·8mm ♀2·5–3·2mm [NOT ILLUSTRATED]

Nationally Scarce

Scarce, local

Observation tips/habitat: Very closely resembles
N. reticulatus (*p. 382*) but is slightly larger. It has been recorded
from south-facing areas of scree on rocky slopes and cliff faces
with little or no vegetation, and also from bare shingle at coastal
sites. In the past it has been misidentified as *N. reticulatus* but
that species favours an entirely different habitat.

Description: CARAPACE + ABDOMEN + LEGS
Similar to *N. reticulatus*.

Similar species: Other *Neon* species.

Distribution/Status: Locally abundant within its specific
habitats.

J F M A M J J A S O N D

CR *Neon valentulus*

♂2·0–2·5mm ♀2–3mm [NOT ILLUSTRATED]

Nationally Rare

Extremely rare

Observation tips/habitat: Occurs in grass and moss in
sedge fens.

Description: CARAPACE + ABDOMEN Both similar to *N. reticulatus*
(*p. 382*) but usually much darker. LEGS I often entirely black apart
from tarsi tips which range from pale brown to white; other legs
are brown with distinct, darker annulations

Similar species: Other *Neon* species.

Distribution/Status: Rare. Recorded from a few fenland
sites in East Anglia.

♂ NO PHENOLOGY DATA

♀

J F M A M J J A S O N D

Marpissa

 3 British species (3 illustrated)

This genus includes our largest jumping spiders. **All have an elongated abdomen and front legs that are darker and more robust than the rest.**

LC *Marpissa nivoyi* ◆

Nationally Scarce

Scarce, regional

♂4–5mm ♀4–6mm

Observation tips/habitat: A coastal species occurring almost exclusively on sand dunes amongst Marram Grass. **A distinctive spider with its elongated body and large dark forelegs.**

Description: CARAPACE Noticeably elongated. Brown with two lines of white hairs located on either side of the central section. ABDOMEN Elongated. Pale brown with whitish markings. Three rows of black spots running longitudinally are often present. LEGS I enlarged and dark brown to black. The other legs are pale.

Similar species: None.

Distribution/Status: Scarce, with scattered, mainly coastal distribution in England and Wales. Absent from Scotland.

♂
♀

J F M A M J J A S O N D

♀ *Marpissa nivoyi* × **6**

LC *Marpissa muscosa* Fencepost Jumping Spider

♂6–8mm ♀8–10mm

Observation tips/habitat: Generally found in wooden fences and under the bark of old trees and fallen branches, where it spins a silk cell. It is frequently recorded from dry stone walls on the south coast.

Description: CARAPACE Head area dark brown to black in both sexes. ♀ thoracic area reddish brown. Whole head area coated in white hairs. ABDOMEN Greyish-brown with a paler median band, which has an irregular edging of black linear patches. There are thin white lines at an angle to the central band on either side. LEGS I are large, robust and almost black in colour. The remainder are paler with darker annulations and long silky hairs.

Similar species: None.

Distribution/Status: Widespread but scarce in south-east England with a few records from the rest of Britain.

♂
♀

J F M A M J J A S O N D

♀ *Marpissa muscosa* ×**6**

VU *Marpissa radiata* 🔍

♂ 6–7 mm ♀ 8–10 mm

Observation tips/habitat: Occurs in the heads of common reed where females spin their egg-sacs. The two sexes have a similar general appearance, but the depth of colour of both abdomen and carapace varies from pale to dark.

Description: CARAPACE Brown with the head area darker and a paler median band. Clothed in white hairs. ABDOMEN Pale brown with a yellow-brown median band with dark edging. Covered in pale hairs. ♂'s abdomen is sometimes completely black. LEGS Pale brown with long hairs.

Similar species: None.

Distribution/Status: Largely confined to the fenland areas of East Anglia, where it can be widespread. It is also recorded from Somerset and West Glamorgan.

♂
♀
J F M A M J J A S O N D

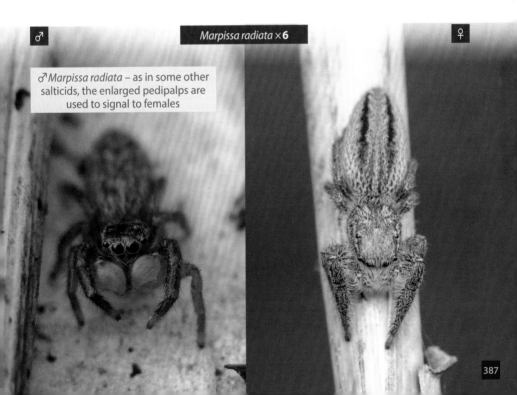

♂ *Marpissa radiata* × 6 ♀

♂ *Marpissa radiata* – as in some other salticids, the enlarged pedipalps are used to signal to females

Pellenes

🔍 **1 British species (illustrated)**

A single species of this genus is known in Britain. There is a **conspicuous abdominal pattern** in both sexes. **Found on shingle beaches.**

VU ## *Pellenes tripunctatus* 🔍

♂4–5mm ♀6·0–6·5mm   [PAGE 389 T]

♂♀ **Observation tips/habitat:** A coastal spider occurring on thinly vegetated shingle beaches, occasionally inside empty whelk shells. Field identification is assisted by the **conspicuous abdominal pattern in both sexes**.

Description: CARAPACE Rich blackish-brown with a covering of white hairs. The eyes have a fringe of orange hairs, particularly in the ♂.
ABDOMEN Brown with a white median band widening into diamond shapes throughout. LEGS Coxae and trochanters pale brown; remaining segments brownish black. Legs I more robust than others. All covered in long fine hairs.

Similar species: None.

Distribution/Status: Rare. Known from coastal sites in east Kent and Dorset.

Nationally Rare

Rare, regional

♂
♀
J F M A M J J A S O N D

Sibianor

🔍 **1 British species (illustrated)**

A single species in this genus is known in Britain. **Carapace and abdomen dark to almost black with a metallic sheen in both sexes. Legs I dark and swollen**

LC ## *Sibianor aurocinctus* 🔍

♂3·0–3·5mm ♀3–4mm   [PAGE 389 BL]

♂♀ **Observation tips/habitat:** This rare spider has a **coppery appearance**. It seems to favour dry, sparsely vegetated conditions such as post-industrial sites and other brownfield habitats.

Description: CARAPACE Dark to almost black with a metallic sheen in both sexes. In ♀ with a covering of white hairs. The head area of ♂ is pitted. ABDOMEN Similar colouring and sheen to the carapace. LEGS I dark and greatly swollen (slightly less so in ♀). The remaining legs are paler with some darker markings.

Similar species: None.

Distribution/Status: Scarce. Presence in Britain concentrated in the Thames corridor with very few records elsewhere.

Nationally Scarce

Scarce, regional

♂
♀
J F M A M J J A S O N D

Pellenes tripunctatus × **6**

♂ | ♀

♀ *Sibianor aurocinctus* × **6**

♀ *Ballus chalybeius* × **6**

Ballus

🔍 **1 British species (illustrated)**

The single species in this genus is one of the few salticids **found in the foliage of trees and bushes. The coloration of legs I contrasts with that of the others.**

LC *Ballus chalybeius*

🔍

♂3–4 mm ♀4·5–5·0 mm

[ABOVE R]

♂♀ **Observation tips/habitat: Distinctive appearance**; almost exclusively recorded from broadleaved trees and bushes, particularly oak.

Description: CARAPACE Dark brown to black, clothed with pale brown hairs. ABDOMEN ♀ greyish-brown with a darker median band with pale margins in the anterior half, and two pairs of pale chevron bands across the posterior half. In ♂, dark red to black with no defined pattern. LEGS Conspicuous in the field. Forelegs are large and robust with femur and tibia darkened in ♂; less so in ♀. Remainder are pale with dark annulations at joints and dark streaks on femur and tibia.

Similar species: None.

Distribution/Status: Widespread but scattered distribution in south-east England with some scattered records in the south-west and Midlands.

Nationally Scarce

Scarce, regional

♂
♀
J F M A M J J A S O N D

Heliophanus Sun jumping spiders | 4 British species (4 illustrated)

Four species occur in Britain. ♀s are recognisable in the field, having a black body and pale, yellowish-green legs. ♂s tend to have darker legs and a metallic sheen to the body. Both sexes have a **thin band of white hairs on the anterior edge of the abdomen.**

LC ## *Heliophanus cupreus*

Common, regional

♂3–4mm ♀5–6mm [PAGE 391 TL]

Observation tips/habitat: Found in a variety of habitats, usually low down amongst vegetation in dull weather but becoming very active around the tops of plants in warm sunny conditions.

Description: CARAPACE Black with a metallic sheen. ABDOMEN Black with thin, white band around the anterior margin. Occasionally with one or two pairs of faint white spots in the posterior half. LEGS ♀ greenish-yellow occasionally with black streaking on femora. ♂ similar to ♀ but usually darker and with white hairs.

Similar species: Other *Heliophanus* species.

Distribution/Status: Common with a widespread but patchy distribution throughout Britain apart from northern Scotland.

♂
♀
J F M A M J J A S O N D

LC ## *Heliophanus flavipes*

Common, regional

♂3–4mm ♀5–6mm [PAGE 391 TR]

Observation tips/habitat: Occurs in similar habitats to *H. cupreus* (*above*).

Description: CARAPACE + ABDOMEN Similar to *H. cupreus*. LEGS Similar to *H. cupreus* but much paler.

Similar species: Other *Heliophanus* species.

Distribution/Status: Widespread in southern England and central Scotland but scattered distribution elsewhere.

♂
♀
J F M A M J J A S O N D

♂ *Heliophanus cupreus* × **6**

♀ *Heliophanus flavipes* × **6**

♀ *Heliophanus auratus* × **6**

♀ *Heliophanus dampfi* × **6**

Heliophanus species – identification pointers				
SPECIES	CARAPACE	ABDOMEN	LEGS	HABITAT
H. flavipes*	Black with metallic sheen	Black with thin white band around the anterior margin	As *H. cupreus* but much paler	WIDE RANGE
H. cupreus*			Greenish-yellow, ♂ darker than ♀	
H. auratus*				Thinly vegetated coastal shingle
H. dampfi*				Raised bogs

* Only safely distinguished by microscopic examination of the genitalia (see **page 96**).

VU *Heliophanus auratus*

Nationally Rare

Rare, regional

♂3–4mm ♀4–5mm   [PAGE 391 BL]

♂♀ **Observation tips/habitat:** Found in areas of thin vegetation on shingle beaches near the tide line.

Description: CARAPACE + ABDOMEN + LEGS Similar to *H. cupreus* (*p. 390*).

Similar species: Other *Heliophanus* species.

Distribution/Status: Rare. Recorded from coastal sites in south-east and southern England.

J F M A M J J A S O N D

VU *Heliophanus dampfi*

Nationally Rare

Rare, regional

♂3–4mm ♀3–5mm   [PAGE 391 BR]

♂♀ **Observation tips/habitat:** Occurs on raised bogs.

Description: CARAPACE + ABDOMEN + LEGS Similar to *H. cupreus* (*p. 390*).

Similar species: Other *Heliophanus* species.

Distribution/Status: Rare. Only recorded from only one site in Wales and two in central Scotland.

J F M A M J J A S O N D

Macaroeris **1 British species (illustrated)**

First recorded in 2002, the single species in this genus is a recent addition to the British spider fauna. **It has a distinctive carapace and abdominal patterns in both sexes.**

NA *Macaroeris nidicolens*

Rare, regional

♂ 6 mm ♀ 7·5 mm

Observation tips/habitat: A medium-sized spider restricted to brownfield sites, where it is found on pines and low scrub in sunny conditions. The species is widespread in southern Europe and its presence and potential spread in the UK may be due to rising mean temperatures as a result of climate change.

Description: CARAPACE ♀ brown to black head area with a thin median line of white hairs widening to a central triangular patch at the posterior margin. The sides and thoracic area are covered in white hairs. ♂ head area is black with two patches of white hairs at the front edge above the anterior line of eyes. The central thoracic area is dark brown flanked by distinctive patches of white hairs on either side running the length of the carapace. ABDOMEN ♀ pale brown with pattern of white markings (chevrons towards the posterior). The anterior edge of the abdomen has a white band extending around sides. ♂ is similar to ♀ but darker and with more distinct white markings. LEGS ♀ pale yellow-brown with darker annulations on legs IV; legs I are darker and stouter. ♂ is darker than ♀ with legs I longer, more robust and darker than the rest.

♂
♀
J F M A M J J A S O N D

Similar species: None.

Distribution/Status: Rare and restricted to the Thames corridor.

♀ *Macaroeris nidicolens* × **6**

The following three genera *Euophrys*, *Pseudeuophrys* and *Talavera* were formerly all included under one genus, *Euophrys*. Small differences observed in the mature ♂ pedipalps have resulted in the split into separate genera. ♂'s often have distinctly darker front legs and brightly coloured hairs fringing the anterior eyes. The spiders themselves all have a similar appearance, however this can vary – causing some difficulty in field identification and therefore microscopic examination of the genitalia (see *page 96*) is necessary to confirm the species, particularly ♀ s.

Euophrys

🔍 **2 British species (2 illustrated)**

The two species are both small spiders with a clear, dark patterned abdomen. ♂'s frequently have an iridescent body with darkened legs I which are used in courtship displays.

LC | # *Euophrys frontalis*

♂ 2–3 mm ♀ 3–5 mm

♂♀

Observation tips/habitat: Occurs in a wide variety of habitats, particularly grassland and heath. The dark abdominal spotting in both sexes is conspicuous in the field.

Description: CARAPACE ♀ brown with a darker head area and black edging to the carapace. ♂ has a black head area with bright orange hairs fringing the anterior eyes. ♂ pedipalps have conspicuous tufts of white hairs. ABDOMEN ♀ pale brownish-yellow with longitudinal rows of black spots which, in the centre line, are triangular. ♂ is similar to ♀ but darker and with a more definite central line of triangular spots. LEGS ♀ pale brown with no markings. Legs I of ♂ have a metallic appearance and are black with white tarsi. The other legs are pale brown with darker streaking, particularly legs II.

Similar species: *Euophrys herbigrada* (p. 395).

Distribution/Status: Widespread throughout England and Wales with records from coastal areas farther north.

Common, regional

♂
♀

J F M A M J J A S O N D

Euophrys frontalis × **10**

♂ ♀

Euophrys herbigrada

♂ 2·5 mm ♀ 3–4 mm

Observation tips/habitat:
Occurs amongst grass and
heather and under stones on dry,
sunny slopes or cliff-tops within
a few hundred metres of the sea.
It is possibly restricted to frost-
free sites.

Description: CARAPACE
As *E. frontalis* but darker. In the
♂ the pedipalp lacks the white hairs
of *E. frontalis* and the eyes have no fringing orange hairs.
ABDOMEN As *E. frontalis* but darker. LEGS As *E. frontalis*.

Similar species: *Euophrys frontalis* (p. 394).

Distribution/Status: Rare. Known from scattered sites on
the coast of southern England.

♂ Euophrys herbigrada × **10**

♂
♀
J F M A M J J A S O N D

♂ *Euophrys, Pseudeuophrys* and *Talavera* species – identification pointers

SPECIES	PEDIPALPS	CARAPACE		ABDOMEN	LEGS	
E. frontalis	Conspicuous tufts of white hairs	Brown with darker head area	**Bright orange hairs around eyes**	Brownish-yellow with longitudinal black spots, triangular in centre	LEG I metallic black with white tarsi; others pale brown with dark streaks	
E. herbigrada	No white hairs		No orange hairs			
P. erratica	Brown; femur and patella yellow	Black; with orange and brown hairs		**Dark on pale** inverted 'Y' + chevron pattern	LEG I dark brown; others pale yellow with dark streaks	
P. lanigera				**Pale on dark** inverted 'Y' + chevron pattern	LEG I brown; others yellowish-brown with dark streaks	
P. obsoleta	Brown to black; white hairs at joints	Black; with orange and white hairs giving a dark purplish-brown appearance		Brown with clear white markings	Purple-brown with darker annulations	
T. petrensis	Conspicuous tufts of white hairs	Dark brown to black; with white hairs; **orange hairs around eyes**		As carapace but paler; no real pattern	LEGS I + II black; LEGS III + IV brown	
T. thorelli	Yellowish	Dark brown to black; with yellowish-white hairs		As carapace but paler; no real pattern	LEGS pale yellow	FEMORA I black
T. aequipes						FEMORA I pale yellow

Pseudeuophrys

🔍 **3 British Species (3 illustrated)**

All three species are **similar in appearance to** *Euophrys* **but slightly smaller and darker.** ♂'s **typically have an iridescent body with darkened legs** I which are used in courtship displays.

LC *Pseudeuophrys erratica* 🔬

┇ ┇ ♂3–4 mm ♀3–4 mm [PAGE 397 BL]
♂♀

Nationally Scarce

Scarce, regional

Observation tips/habitat: Found on walls and amongst piles of stones and rubble. Occasionally recorded from under the bark of ancient trees, amongst dead wood fragments and leaf-litter.

Description: CARAPACE Black with margins of light hairs. The head area has white hairs centrally with the remainder covered with orange and brown hairs. In ♀ the pedipalps are pale yellow whereas on ♂ pedipalps only the femur and patella are pale yellow; the other segments are brown. ABDOMEN Brownish with an anterior band of white hairs. ♀ has a darker inverted 'Y'-shaped marking in the anterior half with darker chevrons behind. ♂ has a less distinct pattern. LEGS ♀ pale yellow with dark annulations, more distinct on legs III and IV. In ♂ legs I are dark brown, the remainder as for ♀ but with less distinct annulations and more dark streaks.

♂
♀
J F M A M J J A S O N D

Similar species: *Pseudeuophrys lanigera* (p. 397).

Distribution/Status: Scattered distribution in northern and western Britain. Almost completely absent from eastern and southern England.

LC *Pseudeuophrys obsoleta* 🔬

┇ ┇ ♂2·5–3·0 mm ♀3·0–3·5 mm [PAGE 397 T]
♂♀

Biodiversity List (En) Nationally Scarce

Scarce, regional

Observation tips/habitat: Occurs on shingle beaches where it is found in tide litter and inside empty whelk shells.

Description: CARAPACE ♀ black but covered with orange and white hairs giving an overall purplish-brown appearance. ♂ is similar but darker. Pedipalps vary from brown to black, with white hairs at the joints. ABDOMEN ♀ general appearance and colouring similar to that of the carapace with faint pattern of pale chevrons posteriorly. ♂ is similar but usually has clearer white markings. LEGS Purple-brown with darker annulations.

Similar species: *Sitticus caricis* (p. 404), but this species occupies a very different habitat..

Distribution/Status: Scarce. Recorded from a few sites on the south-east coast.

♂
♀
J F M A M J J A S O N D

Pseudeuophrys lanigera

♂♀

♂3·5–4·0 mm   ♀4–5 mm

[BR]

Uncommon, widespread

Observation tips/habitat: First recorded in Britain in 1930, it has since spread throughout most of England and will probably extend its distribution into Scotland and Wales. It is strongly associated with human habitation and is often recorded from the roofs and walls of buildings.

Description: CARAPACE Similar to *P. erratica* (*p. 396*). ABDOMEN Similar to *P. erratica* but light and dark markings in the abdominal pattern are reversed in ♀, *i.e.*. the inverted 'Y'-shaped marking is paler than the background and the chevrons at the posterior end of the abdomen are light. LEGS In both sexes, legs I have some dark brown colouring; in ♀ only the femora, in ♂ the whole leg. The remaining legs are yellowish-brown with dark streaks and annulations, particularly in ♀.

♂
♀
J F M A M J J A S O N D

Similar species: *Pseudeuophrys erratica* (*p. 396*).

Distribution/Status: Widespread but local in much of England, with a few records in Wales and Scotland.

♀ *Pseudeuophrys obsoleta* × **10**

♂ *Pseudeuophrys erratica* × **6**

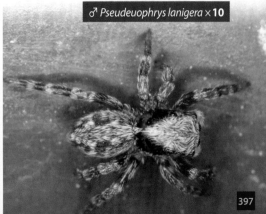
♂ *Pseudeuophrys lanigera* × **10**

Talavera

🔍 **3 British species (2 illustrated)**

All three species generally have a much lighter thoracic area of the carapace compared with the head area containing the eye field. ♂'s frequently have an iridescent body with darkened legs I which are used in courtship displays.

NT *Talavera petrensis* 🔍

I I
♂♀

♂3mm ♀3mm

Observation tips/habitat: The ♂ has a very distinctive appearance in the field with orange hairs around the eyes and at the front of the head area. This species occurs in bare stony areas on dry heathland sites, particularly in southern England. Farther north it is generally found under stones.

Description: CARAPACE Both sexes dark brown to black with a thick scattering of white hairs. ♂ has bright orange hairs fringing the anterior eyes and over the front edge of the carapace. ♂ **pedipalps have conspicuous tufts of white hairs**, whereas ♀ pedipalps are pale yellow. ABDOMEN Similar to the carapace but paler. In ♀ there is a faint pattern of chevrons towards the rear. LEGS ♀ **femora black, remaining segments orange-brown with annulations**. In ♂ legs I and II are black and legs III and IV brown with darker annulations.

Similar species: None.

Distribution/Status: Occurs mainly in southern England where it can be common in suitable habitat. Few records from northern England and Scotland.

♂
♀
J F M A M J J A S O N D

Talavera petrensis × **10**

♂

♀

Close up and seen from the front ♂ *Talavera petrensis* is an amazing looking creature

LC *Talavera aequipes*

Uncommon, regional

I I ♂ 2·0–2·5 mm ♀ 2–3 mm
♂ ♀

Observation tips/habitat: The spider has a dull yellow appearance. It favours sunny, open, stony sites where it hunts on the ground.

Description: CARAPACE Dark brown to black with a covering of yellowish-white hairs. Both sexes have yellowish pedipalps. ABDOMEN Similar to carapace, but paler. LEGS ♀ pale yellow with black annulations. ♂ is similar but leg I has a **black femur.**

Similar species: *Talavera thorelli* (*below*).

Distribution/Status: Scattered distribution throughout England, more frequently found in the south.

♂
♀

J F M A M J J A S O N D

 ♂ *Talavera aequipes* × **10**

VU *Talavera thorelli*

Nationally Rare

Extremely rare

I I ♂ 1·9–2·3 mm ♀ 2·3–2·5 mm [NOT ILLUSTRATED]
♂ ♀

Observation tips/habitat: Occurs on steep, south-facing chalk grassland.

Description: CARAPACE + ABDOMEN Similar to *T. aequipes.* LEGS ♀ pale yellow with black annulations (similar to *T. aequipes*). ♂ differs from *T. aequipes* in **not having a blackened femur** on leg I.

Similar species: *Talavera aequipes* (*above*).

Distribution/Status: Very rare. Known from one site in south-east England.

NO PHENOLOGY DATA

Sitticus 🔍 **6 British species (6 illustrated)**

These are **rather plump spiders with a fairly drab appearance**. They are superficially greyish-brown but closer examination reveals patterning on the abdomen, sometimes including white markings and light hairs. All species except *S. pubescens* are rare. Habitat requirements are quite specific and this can be helpful in identification.

LC ## *Sitticus pubescens* 🔬

Uncommon, regional

⚲ ♂4mm ♀4–5mm [PAGE 402 TL]

♂♀ **Observation tips/habitat:** A covering of light hairs gives a distinctly greyish appearance. The spider is strongly associated with human habitation – on walls, window frames (sometimes indoors) and fencing. It is occasionally found on tree trunks and fence posts away from buildings.

Description: CARAPACE ♀ dark brown to black with numerous light hairs. Two small, linear patches of white hairs occur in the median line. ♂ is darker. ABDOMEN ♀ similar to carapace with two pairs of white spots centrally positioned, the larger pair to the rear. The sides have some small white patches. ♂ is similar but with clearer white markings. LEGS Brown with darker annulations.

Similar species: *Sitticus saltator, S. floricola* (both *p. 401*), *S. inexpectus* (*p. 404*).

♂
♀
J F M A M J J A S O N D

Distribution/Status: Distributed widely throughout much of England but scarce in the south-west, Wales and the north, and very rare in Scotland.

CR ## *Sitticus distinguendus* Distinguished Jumping Spider 🔍

Biodiversity List (En)
Nationally Rare

Extremely rare

♂3·5mm ♀5·5–6·0mm [PAGE 402 M]

⚲ **Observation tips/habitat:** Larger than other *Sitticus*
♂♀ **species in Britain and generally much paler and lacking a distinct pattern**. The whole spider appears a uniform grey in the field. It favours dry, sparsely vegetated ground that has developed on brownfield sites.

Description: CARAPACE Dark brown to black but a thick covering of white hairs gives a pale grey appearance. ABDOMEN Similar to carapace. LEGS Pale brown with darker markings, particularly in ♂.

Similar species: None.

Distribution/Status: A very rare spider recorded from just two brownfield sites in the Thames corridor.

♂
♀
J F M A M J J A S O N D

S. pubescens, S. saltator, S. floricola and *S. inexpectus* are similar in general appearance and microscopic examination of the genitalia (see *page 96*) is necessary for safe identification.

LC *Sitticus saltator* ◆

Nationally Scarce

Scarce, regional

♂3mm ♀3–4mm   [PAGE 402 TR]

Observation tips/habitat: Similar pattern to, but noticeably smaller than, other *Sitticus* species. It is largely restricted to coastal sites where it is found on sand dunes in sunny conditions and also in open sandy areas on heathland. It can jump considerable distances.

Description: CARAPACE ♀ black head area with a slightly paler thoracic area and a broken median line of white hairs. ♂ is like ♀ but with fewer hairs. ABDOMEN ♀ brown with vague pattern of white hairs and long black hairs. ♂ is similar but with more white hairs. LEGS Yellowish-brown with faint darker annulations, covered with white hairs and carrying stout spines. Legs IV much longer than the others.

Similar species: *Sitticus pubescens* (p. 400), *S. floricola* (*below*), *S. inexpectus* (p. 404).

Distribution/Status: Very local and infrequent around the coast of England and Wales with few inland records. Absent from Scotland.

J F M A M J J A S O N D

NT *Sitticus floricola*

Nationally Rare

Rare, regional

♂4mm ♀5mm   [PAGE 402 B]

Observation tips/habitat: Occurs in wet and swampy areas of fen meadow and *Sphagnum* bog where it spins an egg-sac in the flower and seed heads of tall plants.

Description: CARAPACE ♀ black head area. Thoracic area dark brown with scattered white hairs covering the whole carapace. There is often a patch of white hairs in the fovea. ♂ is similar but with more definite patches of white hairs and the anterior eyes are fringed with white and orange hairs. ABDOMEN ♀ similar to *S. pubescens* but the larger pair of white markings are elongated laterally. ♂ is similar to ♀ but smaller. LEGS ♀ orange-brown with darker annulations. ♂ has less obvious annulations but the femora are brownish.

Similar species: *Sitticus pubescens* (p. 400), *S. saltator* (*above*), *S. inexpectus* (p. 404).

Distribution/Status: Rare. Known from just a few sites in Cheshire and one in Scotland.

J F M A M J J A S O N D

♀ *Sitticus pubescens* × **10**

♀ *Sitticus saltator* × **10**

♂ *Sitticus distinguendus* × **10** ♀

♂ *Sitticus floricola* × **10** ♀

♀ *Sitticus inexpectus* × **10**

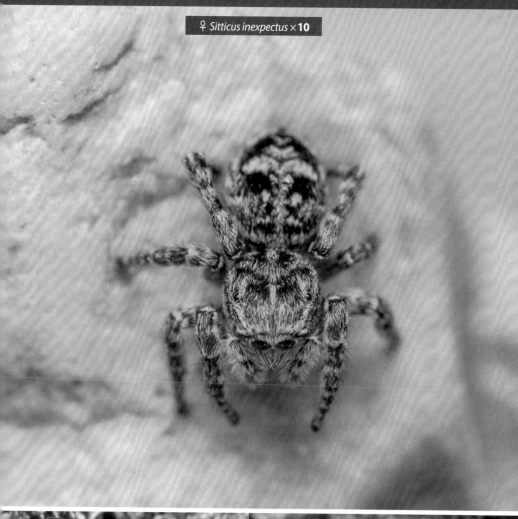

♂ *Sitticus caricis* × **10** ♀

LC *Sitticus inexpectus*

♂4–5mm ♀6–7mm   [PAGE 403 T]

Observation tips/habitat: The whole spider is slightly darker in colour than *S. floricola*. It occurs on shingle beaches and amongst tidal litter.

Description: CARAPACE Similar to *S. floricola*. ABDOMEN Similar to *S. floricola* but the paired white markings are smaller and more rounded. LEGS Similar to *S. floricola*.

Similar species: *Sitticus pubescens* (*p. 400*), *Sitticus saltator*, *S. floricola* (both *p. 401*).

Distribution/Status: Restricted to coastal locations in the south-east and around the Bristol Channel.

Nationally Scarce

Scarce, regional

♂
♀
J F M A M J J A S O N D

LC *Sitticus caricis*

♂3–4mm ♀3–4mm   [PAGE 403 B]

Observation tips/habitat: Favours bog, marsh and fen habitats where it is found amongst low vegetation and areas of *Sphagnum* moss.

Description: CARAPACE ♀ black but covered with orange and white hairs giving an overall purplish-brown appearance. ♂ is similar but darker. ABDOMEN ♀ general appearance and colouring similar to that of the carapace with faint pattern of pale chevrons posteriorly. ♂ is similar but usually has clearer white markings. LEGS Purple-brown with darker annulations.

Similar species: *Pseudoeuophrys obsoleta* (*p. 396*), but this species occupies a very different habitat.

Distribution/Status: Rare, with a scattering of records in south-central England, East Anglia, Anglesey and Cumbria.

Biodiversity List (En, Wa)

Nationally Rare

Rare, regional

♂
♀
J F M A M J J A S O N D

Aelurillus

🔍 **1 British species (illustrated)**

The single species known in Britain has excellent jumping capabilities. **The two sexes have very different, but distinctive, appearances.**

LC ## *Aelurillus v-insignitus* 🔍

♂4–5mm ♀6–7mm

Observation tips/habitat: The almost equal size of the abdomen and the cephalothorax of this species (particularly in the ♂) give it a squat appearance and should aid recognition in the field. It favours open heathland and short, stony grassland habitats in sunny situations, often near the coast.

Description: CARAPACE ♀ black, thickly covered with black and white hairs giving a greyish overall appearance. In ♂, black with a metallic sheen. The head area has white hairs in two inverted 'U'-shapes, one inside the other. ABDOMEN ♀ similar to carapace with an ill-defined pale median line. In ♂, black with a median band of white hairs forming a clear contrast with the rest of the abdomen. LEGS ♀ yellowish-brown with darker annulations and markings. ♂ is similar to, but slightly darker than, ♀. In both sexes the legs have a thick covering of hairs.

Similar species: None.

Distribution/Status: Distribution is concentrated in south-central England with scattered records around the south-west and Welsh coasts and the Firth of Forth.

Nationally Scarce

Scarce, regional

♂
♀
J F M A M J J A S O N D

The distinctive pattern of the ♂ head area

♂   *Aelurillus v-insignitus* ×**6**   ♀

Evarcha

👁 **2 British species (2 illustrated)**

These are handsome, medium-sized spiders with **distinctive features recognisable in the field.** Legs I and II are slightly longer and more robust than legs III and IV. In both species there is a distinct difference between the appearance of males and females.

LC *Evarcha arcuata* 🔍

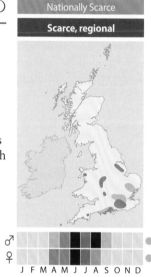

Nationally Scarce

Scarce, regional

♂5–6mm ♀6–8mm

Observation tips/habitat: A distinctive spider, the ♂ in particularly is quite robust. It favours damp, often boggy areas on otherwise dry, mature heathland.

Description: CARAPACE ♀ **brown with a darker metallic sheen in the head area.** ♂ is totally dark brown to black with a metallic sheen. Both sexes have conspicuous lines of white hairs below the anterior eyes (see *front cover*). ABDOMEN ♀ brown with a short, dark cardiac stripe. Pairs of dark, oblique stripes occur in the rear half. In ♂, **similar to the carapace, giving whole spider a metallic-black appearance.** LEGS ♀ yellowish-brown. Leg I of ♂ has the femur, patella and tibia enlarged. All the legs are dark brown to black apart from paler metatarsi and tarsi.

Similar species: None.

Distribution/Status: Concentrated distribution in south-central England with scattered records in the rest of England and Wales.

♂
♀
J F M A M J J A S O N D

Evarcha arcuata × **4**

♂   ♀

LC *Evarcha falcata*

♂5mm ♀6–8mm

Observation tips/habitat: A distinctive spider with features (particularly in ♂) recognisable in the field. It is a woodland species found in the lower branches of trees and on gorse and heather in woodland clearings.

Description: CARAPACE ♀ **black head area with a metallic sheen and the thoracic area covered with brown hairs.** ♂ similar to ♀ but with a conspicuous, broad band of pale brown to white hairs on either side. ABDOMEN ♀ greyish-brown with paler sides and occasionally some vague black markings. ♂ has a distinctive pattern of a greyish-brown median band, containing reddish spots, which is edged with black longitudinal bands. **The whole abdomen is circled by a conspicuous band of white hairs.** LEGS ♀ yellow to dark brown. Legs I darker than others. In ♂, legs I have very large, black femora, the tarsi are yellow and the remaining segments dark brown. Other legs have darkened femora with the remaining segments yellowish-brown.

Similar species: None.

Distribution/Status: Widespread throughout much of England and Wales becoming less common in the north and Scotland.

♂
♀
J F M A M J J A S O N D

Evarcha falcata × **4**

Myrmarachne

🔍 **1 British species (illustrated)**

This spider is an **ant mimic**. Its body shape and ant-like movement sometimes makes it difficult to distinguish from the ants with which it is often associated. Both *Myrmarachne* and *Synageles* (*p.409*) differ markedly in appearance from other jumping spiders, but both species still have the row of large forward-facing eyes typical of the salticid family. **It differs from *Synageles* in that there is no transverse white band across the abdomen.**

LC ## *Myrmarachne formicaria*   🔍

♂5·5–6·5mm   ♀5–6mm

Observation tips/habitat: Grassland and low vegetation, often on undercliffs near the sea. **The large chelicerae of the ♂ are conspicuous features and readily observed in the field**.

Description: CARAPACE ♀ head area dark brown to black with metallic sheen, clearly elevated from the thoracic area, which is reddish-brown. ♂ is very similar to ♀ but with elongated, flattened chelicerae projecting forwards, almost as long as the head area. ABDOMEN ♀ anterior half dark orange to brown separated from a darker posterior half by curved white bands. Sexes similar. LEGS Both sexes pale yellow with black streaking, particularly on legs I.

Similar species: None.

Distribution/Status: Largely confined to the south coast of England.

Nationally Scarce

Scarce, regional

♂
♀
J F M A M J J A S O N D

♂ *Myrmarachne formicaria* × **10**

Synageles

As with *Myrmarachne* (*p. 408*) the single spider in this genus is distinctly ant-like and is usually found associated with them. **It differs from *Myrmarachne* in that there is a transverse white band across the abdomen.**

LC *Synageles venator* 🔍

I I ♂3 mm ♀3·5–4·0 mm
♂♀

Nationally Scarce

Scarce, regional

Observation tips/habitat: Largely confined to coastal sand dune habitats with a few records from inland fenland sites. **Ant–like appearance makes identification in the field straightforward if the spider can be distinguished from the ants!**

Description: CARAPACE ♀ and ♂ very similar. Length at least 2× width. The head area is iridescent black, the thorax lighter. A transverse band of white hairs crosses the carapace about halfway along, behind the posterior eyes. ABDOMEN ♀ and ♂ similar. The pedicel is clearly visible. Dark brown to black with a contrasting, transverse white line of hairs roughly halfway down. LEGS ♀ brown with black longitudinal markings. ♂ is similar but legs I more robust and darker.

Similar species: None.

Distribution/Status: Locally distributed but can be common where it occurs.

♂
♀
J F M A M J J A S O N D

♂ *Syngales venator* × **10**

Phlegra
🔍 **1 British species (illustrated)**

The ♀ and ♂ of the single British species differ markedly but **their appearance is characteristic.**

NT *Phlegra fasciata* 🔍

Nationally Rare

Rare, regional

♂5–6mm ♀6–7mm

Observation tips/habitat: Favours dry coastal habitats, occurring on dunes, shingle and steep sea cliffs. **Both ♀ and ♂ have a distinctive appearance and field recognition should be possible, particularly of the ♀.**

Description: CARAPACE ♀ black with pale brown edging and two light-brown bands running longitudinally from the posterior eyes. ♂ has a black head area and a reddish-brown thorax, with very vague suggestion of lighter brown bands as in ♀. Both sexes have a covering of white hairs and, in ♂ particularly, long black hairs. ABDOMEN ♀ whitish-brown, with two conspicuous dark bands running the whole length. ♂ has a dark, glossy appearance with a faint pattern, as in ♀. LEGS ♀ mid-brown with darker annulations and markings. In ♂, dark reddish-brown with black hairs.

♂
♀
J F M A M J J A S O N D

Similar species: None.

Distribution/Status: Rare. Restricted to a few sites on the south coasts of England and Wales.

Phlegra fasciata × **6**

LINYPHIIDAE Money spiders

123 British genera

This is the largest family of spiders in Britain, containing around 280 species. All have eight eyes. The majority are extremely small and impossible to identify without the use of a high magnification microscope. Shown here are a few of the more common larger species which are likely to be encountered in the field. The typical linyphiid web is a densely woven, horizontal sheet supported above and below by a looser framework of threads attached to surrounding vegetation. The spider itself hangs upside-down on the underside of the sheet waiting for prey to blunder into the upper framework of threads and fall onto the surface of the sheet.

Stemonyphantes

🔍 **1 British species (illustrated)**

A single species is found in Britain. **Its carapace and abdominal patterns are characteristic.**

LC ## *Stemonyphantes lineatus* 🔍

Common, widespread

♂ 4·0–5·4 mm   ♀ 4·0–6·8 mm

Observation tips/habitat: Typically occurs at ground level amongst low vegetation, stones and debris where it spins a flimsy sheet web usually with only a few threads noticeable.

Description: CARAPACE Yellowish-brown with usually rather thin black median and marginal bands. ABDOMEN Greyish-white but can be tinged with green, pink or yellow. Three dark longitudinal lines are often broken into spots or can be completely absent. LEGS Yellowish-brown with dark annulations and carrying numerous spines. ♂ metatarsus I swollen ventrally.

Similar species: None.

Distribution/Status: Widespread throughout England. More scattered in Wales and Scotland.

♂
♀
J F M A M J J A S O N D

♀ *Stemonyphantes lineatus* ×**6**

Drapetisca

 1 British species (illustrated)

The distinctive, single British species of this genus spins a very fine web on the bark of trees. Its mottled appearance provides excellent camouflage in this setting, particularly where the bark is covered with lichen. Both sexes have a similar appearance.

LC *Drapetisca socialis*

Common, widespread

♂ 3·2–4·0 mm ♀ 3·2–4·0 mm

♂♀ **Observation tips/habitat:** Commonly occurs in woodland on tree trunks, particularly pine and Beech, and amongst leaf-litter.

Description: CARAPACE Yellowish-brown with black median band forked anteriorly, a black margin and short black streaks opposite each leg. ABDOMEN Variable in depth of colour, but usually has white anterior and sides with, posteriorly, an ill-defined dark folium containing whitish chevrons. Sometimes has a pinkish tinge. LEGS Yellowish-brown with dark annulations.

Similar species: None.

Distribution/Status: Fairly common and widespread throughout much of Britain.

♂
♀

J F M A M J J A S O N D

♀ *Drapetisca socialis* ×**6**

Floronia

 1 British species (illustrated)

The single British species has a **distinctive appearance and should be identifiable with a hand lens**. It has a slight resemblance to *Linyphia triangularis (p.415)* but the abdomen, particularly in the ♀, has a more globular, teardrop appearance. The spider spins a sheet web in bushes and low vegetation and, if disturbed, will drop to the ground and remain stationary, its white abdominal markings contracting almost entirely, rendering it virtually invisible in the undergrowth.

Floronia bucculenta

Uncommon, regional

♂4–5mm ♀4–5mm

Observation tips/habitat: Occurs in damp places amongst low vegetation in a variety of habitats, including marshy areas, unmanaged scrubby grassland, and open woodland.

Description: CARAPACE Pale brown with conspicuous, darker marginal bands. ♂ head area is elevated and has many forward-directed spines. ABDOMEN Reddish-brown with many white spots. Darker on anterior edge and at sides. Pattern sometimes vague. LEGS Long and thin with numerous long spines. Yellow-brown with faint annulations at segment apices.

Similar species: None.

Distribution/Status: Widespread but uncommon in much of England; less frequent in Wales and the south-west and becoming much scarcer northwards into Scotland.

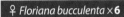

♂
♀
J F M A M J J A S O N D

♀ *Floriana bucculenta* ×**6**

Pityohyphantes

🔍 **1 British species (illustrated)**

The single species of the genus *Pityohyphantes* is a fairly recent addition to the British spider fauna, recorded for the first time in the 1970s. **It has a distinctive abdominal pattern.**

LC *Pityohyphantes phrygianus* 🔍

♂4–5mm ♀4–6mm

Nationally Scarce

Scarce, regional

Observation tips/habitat: The spider spins its sheet web in the lower branches of conifers particularly in plantations of Norway spruce and Sitka spruce. Its distinctive abdominal pattern makes field recognition with a hand lens relatively easy.

Description: CARAPACE Pale brown with a thin dark marginal line, and dark brown median band with a thin, pale central line anteriorly. ABDOMEN Grey with dark brown, laterally indented median stripe appearing as a series of roughly triangular patches running the length of the abdomen. The pattern has some resemblance to that of *Neriene peltata* but the sides lack any dark markings and the median band indentations are much deeper. LEGS Pale brown with faint annulations and clear black spots on femora.

Similar species: *Neriene peltata* (p. 420).

Distribution/Status: Confined largely to Scotland and northern England.

♂
♀
J F M A M J J A S O N D

Pityophantes phrygianus × 6

♂ ♀

Linyphia   Sheetweb spiders

🔍 **2 British species (2 illustrated)**

These two species both spin a horizontal sheet web in low vegetation and hedgerows. *Linyphia triangularis* is extremely common and its webs are often seen festooning hedgerows on misty autumn mornings, each individual thread highlighted by tiny water droplets. The similar spiders of the *Microlinyphia* (*p. 417*) and *Neriene* (*p. 418*) genera were formerly included in *Linyphia* – the genera are separated by microscopic differences in their genitalia. As such it is difficult to identify obvious differences that separate them. All three genera are referred to here as the '*Linyphia* group'.

LC ## *Linyphia triangularis*   Common Sheetweb Spider 🔍

Abundant, widespread

♂ 4·6–6·0 mm   ♀ 5·0–6·6 mm   [PAGE 416 T]

Observation tips/habitat: Occurs on bushes and low vegetation with stiff foliage in a wide variety of habitats. Sheet web spun up to six metres above the ground.

Description: CARAPACE Pale brown with darker marginal bands. The dark median band splits into two in the anterior half; the whole having a tuning-fork shape. ♂ has long, divergent chelicerae and less obvious dark markings. ABDOMEN ♀ white with speckled brown median band, deeply dentated and with darker edges. Sides have dark streaks. ♂ slimmer than ♀ and with no clear pattern; generally a purplish-brown. LEGS Yellowish-brown with numerous spines.

Similar species: None.

Distribution/Status: Very common and widespread throughout much of Britain.

♂
♀
J F M A M J J A S O N D

LC ## *Linyphia hortensis*   🔬

Common, widespread

♂ 3–5 mm   ♀ 4–5 mm   [PAGE 416 BL]

Observation tips/habitat: Typically found in woodland on low vegetation such as Dog's Mercury. Also recorded from hedgerows.

Description: CARAPACE Dark brown with the head area sometimes very dark, particularly in ♂. ABDOMEN ♀ dark brown folium with rounded lobes and white margins. A dark band edges whole dorsal area. ♂ usually darker with vague folium outline and a pair of white patches anteriorly, which can cause confusion with ♂ *Microlinyphia pusilla*. LEGS Pale yellow.

Similar species: *Microlinyphia pusilla* [♂] *Microlinyphia impigra* [♂] (both *p. 417*).

Distribution/Status: Widespread and fairly common in England and Wales. Much less frequent in Scotland.

♂
♀

J F M A M J J A S O N D

♀ *Linyphia triangularis* × **6**

♀ *Linyphia hortensis* × **6**

♀ *Microlinyphia pusilla* × **6**

Microlinyphia   **2 British species (1 illustrated)**

These species both spin the typical linyphiid sheet web, **often in marshy areas.** The ♂s are very different from the ♀s, having a dark tubular abdomen which usually has a pair of white markings anteriorly.

LC *Microlinyphia pusilla*   ♀

Abundant, widespread

♂3–4mm ♀3–5mm   [PAGE 416 BR]

♂♀ **Observation tips/habitat:** Typically occurs in grassland but also known from a wide range of damp habitats. By far the commoner of the two *Microlinyphia* species.

Description: CARAPACE Dark brown to black. ABDOMEN ♀ white with dark cardiac mark of varying width, usually including overlapping triangular patches posteriorly. Sometimes this is a thinner band with faint oblique lines. The whole dorsal area surrounded by dark band. ♂ dark brown with pair of white patches anteriorly. LEGS Pale brown.

Similar species: *Linyphia hortensis* [♂] (*p. 415*), *Microlinyphia impigra* [♂] (*below*).

Distribution/Status: Abundant. Widespread throughout much of Britain.

♂
♀
J F M A M J J A S O N D

LC *Microlinyphia impigra*   ♀

Uncommon, regional

♂3·5–4·0mm ♀3·6–5·4mm   [NOT ILLUSTRATED]

♂♀ **Observation tips/habitat:** Found in low vegetation in marshy areas.

Description: CARAPACE ♀ yellowish-brown with darker median band and margins. ♂ dark brown. ABDOMEN ♀ white with dark, sometimes dentated cardiac mark, followed by pairs of dark triangular marks in posterior half. ♂ similar to *M. pusilla*, sometimes lacking white patches. LEGS ♀ pale brown sometimes with faint annulations. ♂ reddish-brown with no annulations.

Similar species: *Microlinyphia pusilla* [♂] (*above*), *Linyphia hortensis* [♂] (*p. 415*).

Distribution/Status: Uncommon. Widespread but scattered in southern Britain. Much less frequent in the north and Scotland.

♂
♀
J F M A M J J A S O N D

Neriene 6 British species (3 described and illustrated)

Only the three commonest *Neriene* species are described here. They are similar in general appearance to the other spiders in the *Linyphia* group (*Linyphia* (p. 415) and *Microlinyphia* (p. 417) genera). **The width of the abdominal folium can be a helpful diagnostic feature.**

LC ## *Neriene clathrata*

Abundant, widespread

♂3·4–4·8mm ♀3·7–5·0mm

Observation tips/habitat: Occurs in a wide range of habitats including grassland, heathland, marshes, scrub, woodland and gardens where it occurs on or near the ground in leaf-litter, vegetation and in low undergrowth.

Description: CARAPACE Brown to very dark brown. Elongated in ♂. ABDOMEN ♀ has white shoulder areas with broad, brown folium covering remainder of dorsal area. Folium has darker lobed edges and W-shaped markings within. ♂ similar to ♀ but narrower and usually much darker. LEGS Pale brown.

Similar species: *Neriene montana* (p. 420).

Distribution/Status: Abundant and widespread throughout much of Britain. Less frequent in north-west Scotland.

J F M A M J J A S O N D

♀ *Neriene clathrata* ×**6**

♀ *Neriene peltata* ×**6**

♀ *Neriene montana* ×**6**

LC *Neriene peltata* 🔬

♂ 2·2–3·5 mm ♀ 2·8–3·7 mm [PAGE 419 T]

♂♀

Observation tips/habitat: The smallest of the *Linyphia* group. Occurs in low vegetation and bushes but generally at a higher level than other *Neriene* species and favours conifers in open parkland habitats.

Description: CARAPACE Reddish-brown with darker median band, broad in the head area and tapering posteriorly. ABDOMEN ♀ dorsal area white with dark bands laterally and dentated brown median band contrasting sharply with white flanks. ♂ similar to ♀ but median band often broader and less dentated. LEGS Pale brown.

Similar species: *Pityohyphantes phrygianus* (p. 414).

Distribution/Status: Abundant and widespread throughout Britain.

♂
♀
J F M A M J J A S O N D

LC *Neriene montana* 🔬

♂ 4–7 mm ♀ 4·4–7·4 mm [PAGE 419 B]

♂♀

Observation tips/habitat: The largest of the *Linyphia* group of species, *Neriene montana* favours shady habitats, typically in woodland, where it spins a strong sheet web low down in bushes and under logs. The web is rather similar to that of *Tegenaria* but lacks the tubular retreat. It is the only *Neriene* species with annulated legs.

Description: CARAPACE Dark brown with darker margins and thin median line. ABDOMEN ♀ has broad brown folium with indented edges. Sides are white with black line anteriorly. ♂ similar to ♀ but narrower and with darker folium. LEGS Yellowish-brown with narrow dark brown annulations.

Similar species: *Neriene clathrata* (p. 418).

Distribution/Status: Common and widespread in much of central and southern England. Less frequent and scattered in the south-west, Wales and the north.

♂
♀
J F M A M J J A S O N D

Working in the field

The scope of this field guide has been restricted to the identification of live spiders in the field, without removing or killing them. Many fewer regulations are involved, and permissions required, to examine and then release live spiders at the site of capture than in collecting them for later identification (described in the British Arachnological Society's *Arachnologists' Handbook* (see *Further reading – page 464*)). However, some basic principles for the conduct of fieldwork should still be observed and there is also one legal matter to be aware of.

Two British spider species, the Ladybird Spider *Eresus sandaliatus* and the Fen Raft Spider *Dolomedes plantarius*, have specific legal protection. Both are very rare although they are now the subject of successful programmes to reduce their vulnerability by establishing new populations through translocation. Their protection under Schedule 5 of the Wildlife and Countryside Act 1981 (as amended) means that neither they nor their habitat can be disturbed in any way (although there are provisions for conservation, research and education to be carried out under licence). Fieldwork on sites where either species is known to be present should be avoided without specific consent.

When searching for spiders for identification, whether on nature reserves with public access, or on private land that you have permission to access, the land manager's permission should be sought to catch and examine specimens. Seeking permission, particularly on protected sites, also means that you have an opportunity to enquire about, or to be informed of, areas where rare species – whether plants, nesting birds or invertebrates – are present and disturbance should be avoided. Your search should in any case minimize environmental damage. For example, excessive trampling should be avoided, and beating for arachnids in trees and shrubs should not damage the twigs. Leaf-litter, moss, stones, rocks and bark that are moved in search of spiders should be

carefully returned to their original positions; only small areas of bark on dead wood should be lifted in order to search underneath. In the bird breeding season, care should be taken to stay well away from nests. If nests are detected during your work you should immediately leave the vicinity.

More information on working in the field, including advice on your own safety, can be found in the British Arachnological Society's *Arachnologists' Handbook* (see *Further reading – page 464*) and other sources. Amongst all the common sense advice available, the increasing incidence of Lyme disease in Britain, and the consequent need to be 'tick aware' during and after working in the field, should be highlighted. More information on all aspects of the disease can be found at www.lymediseaseaction.org.uk.

Recording spiders

The British Arachnological Society's Spider Recording Scheme (SRS) was established in 1987 to map the distributions of British spiders and, since 2002, has also gathered information on many aspects of their biology. Building on an earlier scheme set up in 1964, it now holds in excess of a million records of spiders covering the great majority of the 10-km Ordnance Survey (OS) grid squares in Britain, including the Isle of Man and the Channel Isles. The SRS website provides accounts of the habitat, status, and adult seasons of all British species together with distribution maps that are updated on a daily basis. The many additional facilities on the website include a forum for discussion of identification queries and guidance on the identification of some of the most difficult species.

A basic spider record for submission to the SRS consists of the following information: species recorded; recorder's name; record date; and where found (with four- or six-figure OS grid reference) – see srs.britishspiders.org.uk/portal.php/p/Recording+spiders). This information is used to record and map the changing distributions of spider species (*e.g.* Wasp Spider *Argiope brunennichi* (shown below)) and to assess the impacts on them of habitat and climate change. These records underpin the conservation of our rare and declining species (see *page 424*). It is not just first records for a particular grid square or site

that are important; all records of spiders matter. Whilst it is important to know that a species was present at a specific site in a given year, it is even more valuable to know whether specimens were male or female, adult or juvenile, the range of dates on which they were present and the habitats in which they occurred (habitat classification codes are provided by the SRS – see srs.britishspiders.org.uk/portal. php/p/Recording%20Methodology). This additional information makes a major contribution to our understanding of the ecology and phenology of British spider species.

The Spider Recording Scheme distribution maps for the Wasp Spider *Argiope brunennichi* in 1996 and 2016, showing its major range expansion.

The SRS is run by a National Organiser supported by Area Organisers, each responsible for one or more **vice-counties**. In areas covered by an Area Organiser, records are submitted to them, preferably in Mapmate (a popular biological recording and mapping software package: www.mapmate.co.uk) format, although they can also be accepted as suitably formatted Microsoft Excel files.

Because of the difficulty of identifying many species of spiders, careful checking of records is needed. This is first done by the Area Organiser who may ask to see preserved specimens. The records are then forwarded to the National Organiser for a decision on whether further expert verification is required. For any area not covered by the network of Area Organisers, records are sent directly to the National Organiser (see the SRS website srs.britishspiders.org.uk for contact details and for a wealth of additional guidance on recording spiders).

For a small but growing number of our most easily recognized species, records can be submitted directly via the SRS website. For these species, the SRS website provides identification guidance and a facility to enter key information about the record and to upload a photograph of the specimen. If it is difficult to obtain a good quality image, dorsal images of live spiders can be obtained by using a spi-pot (see *page 48*).

In addition to the website, the SRS produces a triannual *SRS News*, included as part of the British Arachnological Society's newsletter, which contains articles and notes submitted by recorders on all aspects of the recording of spiders and harvestmen, as well as updates on the recording scheme. Training in spider identification is offered across Britain through courses led by British Arachnological Society experts. These are advertised on the Society's website – www.britishspiders.org.uk – and through the social media – on Twitter @BritishSpiders and www.facebook.com/BritishSpiders.

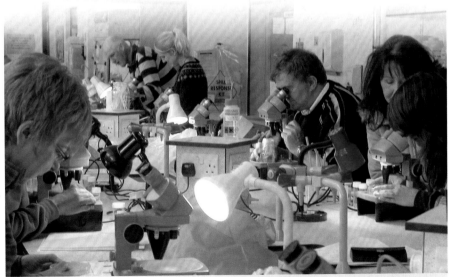

Training courses and workshops are an excellent way to improve your spider knowledge and identification skills.

Legislation and conservation

The conservation of spiders, like that of many invertebrate taxa, was neglected for many years, but spiders are just as vulnerable to habitat degradation and loss, and to the impacts of agrochemicals and climate change, as other groups of animals. Many of Britain's spider species give cause for conservation concern and this is now reflected in a variety of designations aimed to help protect the most vulnerable of them. These include listings under the UK's domestic wildlife legislation and national biodiversity policies, together with Red Lists of species under threat of extinction, based on internationally agreed criteria and categories. An Amber List has recently been introduced to highlight major declines in relatively common species. Rarity Status, although not an assessment of threat, is allocated to species on the basis of restricted distributions. This section summarizes these listings and highlights the high proportion of Britain's spiders that are of concern. The listings relevant to each species are given in the *Species accounts* and in the *List of British spiders* (*page 427*).

Legislation

Wildlife and Countryside Act 1981 (as amended) Just two species of spider – Ladybird Spider *Eresus sandaliatus* and Fen Raft Spider *Dolomedes plantarius* – are listed under this act. They receive full legal protection, which includes disturbance or destruction of the spiders or their habitats, possession, sale and intentional killing or injuring. A licence is required for any activity that breaks these conditions. These species are annotated in the *Species accounts* as: LEGALLY PROTECTED.

The Natural Environment and Rural Communities (NERC) Act 2006 Sections 41 and 42 of the NERC Act require the publication of lists of habitats and species of principal importance for the conservation of biodiversity in England and Wales. These lists are used to guide public authorities in implementing their duty under the Act *"to have regard to the conservation of biodiversity in England and Wales, when carrying out their normal functions"*. They took into account, and effectively supersede, the priority lists in the UK Biodiversity Action Plan (UK BAP: jncc.defra.gov.uk/default.aspx?page=5155).

NERC Act S41 (England) The 31 species of spiders listed under this section of the NERC Act are: *Agroeca cuprea, Alopecosa fabrilis, Altella lucida, Arctosa fulvolineata, Centromerus serratus, Clubiona rosserae, Dictyna pusilla, Dipoena inornata, Dolomedes plantarius* (Fen Raft Spider), *Eresus sandaliatus* (Ladybird Spider), *Erigone welchi, Glyphesis cottonae, Haplodrassus dalmatensis, Mecopisthes peusi, Meioneta mollis, Midia midas* (Midas Tree Weaver Spider), *Monocephalus castaneipes, Nothophantes horridus* (Horrid Ground Weaver Spider), *Notioscopus sarcinatus, Ozyptila nigrita, Philodromus fallax, Philodromus margaritatus, Praestigia duffeyi, Pseudeuophrys obsoleta, Saaristoa firma, Semljicola caliginosus* (Cloud Living Spider), *Silometopus incurvatus, Sitticus caricis, Sitticus distinguendus, Tapinocyba mitis* and *Walckenaeria corniculans*. These are coded in the *Species accounts* as: Biodiversity List (En) and in the *List of British spiders* as S41 (Eng).

NERC Act S42 (Wales) The 11 species of spiders listed under this section of the NERC act are: *Dipoena inornata, Dolomedes plantarius* (Fen Raft Spider), *Erigone welchi, Haplodrassus dalmatensis, Mecopisthes peusi, Meioneta mollis, Monocephalus castaneipes, Notioscopus sarcinatus, Philodromus fallax, Saaristoa firma* and *Sitticus caricis*. These are coded in the *Species accounts* as: Biodiversity List (Wa) and in the *List of British spiders* as S42 (Wal).

Nature Conservation Act (Scotland) 2004 In Scotland, the Nature Conservation Act (Scotland) 2004 provides similar measures requiring public bodies and office-holders to have *"a duty to further the conservation of biodiversity"* and to publish lists of species and habitats considered to be of principal importance for the conservation of biodiversity (The Scottish Biodiversity List). Spiders included on the Scottish Biodiversity List are: *Centromerus levitarsis, Clubiona subsultans, Dictyna major, Dipoena torva, Haplodrassus soerenseni, Mecynargus paetulus, Palliduphantes antroniensis* and *Robertus scoticus*. These are coded in the *Species accounts* as: Biodiversity List (Sc) and in the *List of British spiders* as BDL (Sco).

Red Lists

Red Lists provide an assessment of the threat of extinction of species based on internationally agreed criteria developed by the International Union for Conservation of Nature (IUCN 2012). These criteria include rates of decline, geographic range and population size. The IUCN maintains and regularly updates global inventories of threatened species. In Britain, the same IUCN Red List guidelines are now used to produce national Red Lists for different groups of animals and plants (see http://jncc.defra.gov.uk/page-1773). Both internationally and within Britain, Red Lists provide an indicator of the health of our biodiversity, and a tool to inform and catalyse conservation action. Species assessed as being threatened with extinction (Red Listed) are categorized as **Critically Endangered** CR , **Endangered** EN and **Vulnerable** VU . In addition, species may be recognized as **Extinct** EX , **Extinct in the Wild** EW , or as **Near Threatened** NT or of **Least Concern** LC . Where the IUCN criteria are used to produce national Red Lists, species believed to be extinct are categorized as **Regionally Extinct** RE . Species for which the data are considered inadequate to make an assessment, may be categorized as **Data Deficient** DD . A few species are deemed ineligible for assessment because they are recent imports or colonists. They are placed in the category of **Not Applicable** NA . A final category of **Not Evaluated** NE covers species recently discovered in Britain which have not yet been evaluated against the IUCN criteria.

International Red List Two British spider species are listed on the IUCN Red List (IUCN 2016); *Dolomedes plantarius* (Fen Raft Spider) (*page 240*) is categorized as **Vulnerable** on the basis of its rarity and threats to its wetland habitat across its European range, and the linyphiid *Nothophantes horridus* (Horrid Ground Weaver Spider) is considered **Critically Endangered** because it is a threatened **endemic** with a highly restricted range.

British Red List A recent revision of the UK Red List identified 16% of British spider species as being at threat of extinction (Harvey *et al.*, in press). When **Near Threatened** species are included this figure rises to 20% – a fifth of our spider species.

13 species are categorized as **Critically Endangered** with five of these (*Altella lucida, Centromerus albidus, Orchestina* sp., *Palliduphantes antroniensis* and *Thanatus formicinus*) additionally tagged as **Possibly Extinct** PE . 30 species are categorized as **Endangered**, 54 species are categorized as **Vulnerable** and a further 29 species are assigned **Near Threatened** status. 13 very rare species (11 listed in this book) are regarded as **Data Deficient**. 25 recent additions to the British spider fauna for which the IUCN criteria are not applicable are listed as: **NA**. The remainder of the species are categorized as being of **Least Concern**.

NB In the *Species accounts* threat assessment icons for the British Red List have an icon with a black border (as above); the icons for those on the International Red List lack the black border.

British Rarity Status

Spiders have also been assigned to categories specific to Britain, based on restricted distribution rather than on extinction risk (Harvey *et al.*, in press). The term **Nationally Scarce** is applied to species expected to occur in 16–100 10-km grid squares. **Nationally Rare** species are those thought to be confined to 15 or fewer 10-km squares. **Nationally Scarce** replaces the term **Nationally Notable** (sometimes further split into Notable A and Notable B) used in earlier assessments of invertebrate groups (including spiders: see Merrett 1990), while the Nationally Rare category replaces the former Red Data Book Categories 1–3.

In the recent review (Harvey *et al.*, in press), 152 species are categorized as Nationally Rare and a further 171 as Nationally Scarce. These are annotated in the *Species accounts*, respectively as:

Nationally Rare

Nationally Scarce

The Amber List

The recent review of the status of Britain's spiders (Harvey *et al.*, in press) introduces, for the first time, an **Amber List f**or spider species that are still widespread but have undergone substantial decline. They have the potential to qualify for IUCN Near Threatened status in the future if their decline is not ameliorated. The new list serves to highlight both the species at risk of qualifying for threatened status if current trends continue, and the need for targeted research and surveys. Amber-listed species are annotated in the *Species accounts* as ◆.

References

HARVEY, P. , DAVIDSON, M. , DAWSON, I. , FOWLES, A. , HITCHCOCK, G. , LEE, P. , MERRETT, P. , RUSSELL-SMITH, T. & SMITH, H. (in press). *A review of the scarce and threatened spiders (Araneae) of Great Britain: Species Status No.22*. NRW Evidence Report No. 11, 184pp. Cardiff: Natural Resources Wales.

IUCN 2012. *IUCN Red List Categories and Criteria: Version 3.1*. Second Edition. Gland, Switzerland and Cambridge, UK: IUCN. iv + 32pp.

IUCN 2016. *The IUCN Red List of Threatened Species*. Version 2015-4. www.iucnredlist.org

MERRETT, P. 1990. *A review of the Nationally Notable spiders of Great Britain*. Peterborough: Nature Conservancy Council.

List of British spiders

The great majority of spider species recorded in Britain (excluding the Channel Isles) up to September 2016 are included in the following table. This includes some that are still exclusively associated with human habitation (**synanthropic** species) and excludes most of those not thought to have established populations.

The British spider fauna is changing rapidly as a result of climate change, global trade and habitat loss; to check on updates visit the Spider Recording Scheme website at srs.britishspiders. org.uk. The nomenclature follows Merrett, Russell-Smith & Harvey (2014) (see *Further reading – page 464*) and shows the families and genera, both listed alphabetically, as well as the species within them. Recent taxonomic revisions and **synonyms** that are still in common use are listed but most of those resulting from recent, more controversial taxonomic revisions are not.

For each species an indication of the magnification required for identification is provided. Three categories are used:

 identification possible with the naked eye

 identifiable with a hand lens

 requires study under a microscope

An indication of how widespread each species was between 1993 and 2016 is given by the percentage of the total 10-km Ordnance Survey (OS) Grid Squares in Britain in which it was recorded (but excluding those squares where no spider species have ever been recorded). These are summarized in five categories: <1%, 1–5%, 6–25%, 26–50% and >50%. Species recorded in Britain before, but not since, 1993 are all assigned to the <1% category. It is noteworthy that only two species fall into the >50% category and 234 species into the <1% category. These figures take account only of the frequency with which a species has been recorded at a 10-km square level – species with restricted distributions may be abundant at a local scale. The maps and notes on distribution provided in the *Species accounts* should be used as a further guide to the likelihood of encountering a particular species.

Key to **IUCN Status designation** columns: British Red List assessment (see *page 425*)

PE	Critically Endangered (Presumed Extinct)
CR	Critically Endangered
EN	Endangered
VU	Vulnerable
NT	Near Threatened
LC	Least Concern
DD	Data Deficient
NA	Not Applicable
NE	Not Evaluated

British Rarity status (see *page 426*)

NR	Nationally Rare
NS	Nationally Scarce
◆	British Amber List

Key to **Relevant Legislation** columns

WCA 81	Schedule 5 of Wildlife and Countryside Act 1981
S41 (Eng)	Section 41 of NERC Act
S41 (Wal)	Section 42 of NERC Act
SBL (Sco)	Scottish Biodiversity List

Common name	SPECIES	Authorities	Synonyms	ID	% 10km squares	IUCN	Nat.	Amber	Relevant legislation	Page
Funnelweb spiders	**AGELENIDAE**									**244**
	Agelena									244
Labyrinth Spider	A. labyrinthica	(Clerck, 1757)			6–25%	LC				244
House spiders	Tegenaria									246
	T. agrestis	(Walckenaer, 1802)	[Eratigena agrestis (Walckenaer, 1802)]		1–5%	LC				249
Large house spider	T. atrica	C. L. Koch, 1843	[Eratigena atrica (C. L. Koch 1843)]		<1%	LC				248
Common House Spider	T. domestica	(Clerck, 1757)			6–25%	LC				252
	T. ferruginea	(Panzer, 1804)			<1%	NA				250
Large house spider	T. gigantea	Chamberlin & Ivie, 1935	[T. duellica (Simon 1875), Eratagena atrica (C. L. Koch 1843)]		6–25%	LC				247
Cardinal Spider	T. parietina	(Fourcroy, 1785)			<1%	LC				249
	T. picta	Simon, 1870	[Eratigena picta (Simon, 1870)]		<1%	VU	NR			252
Large house spider	T. saeva	Blackwall, 1844	[Eratigena atrica (C. L. Koch 1843)]		6–25%	LC				248
	T. silvestris	L. Koch, 1872			6–25%	LC				251
	Textrix									245
	T. denticulata	(Olivier, 1789)			6–25%	LC				245
Laceweb spiders	**AMAUROBIIDAE**									**272**
	Amaurobius									274
	A. fenestralis	(Stroem, 1768)			26–50%	LC				276
	A. ferox	(Walckenaer, 1830)			6–25%	LC				276
	A. similis	(Blackwall, 1861)			6–25%	LC				274
	Coelotes									272
	C. atropos	(Walckenaer, 1830)			6–25%	LC				272
	C. terrestris	(Wider, 1834)			1–5%	LC	NS			272
Buzzing spiders	**ANYPHAENIDAE**									**287**
	Anyphaena									287
Buzzing Spider	A. accentuata	(Walckenaer, 1802)			6–25%	LC				287
	A. sabina	L. Koch, 1866			<1%	NA				288

Common name	SPECIES	Synonyms	Authorities	ID	% 10km squares	Status designations IUCN	Nat.	Amber	Relevant legislation	Page
Orbweb spiders	**ARANEIDAE**									**177**
	Agalenatea			👁						188
	A. redii		(Scopoli, 1763)	👁	6–25%	LC				188
	Araneus			👁						177
Strawberry Spider	A. alsine		(Walckenaer, 1802)	👁	1–5%	LC	NS			181
Angular Orbweb Spider	A. angulatus		Clerck, 1757	👁	1–5%	LC	NS			178
Garden Spider	A. diadematus		Clerck, 1757	👁	>50%	LC				178
	A. marmoreus		Clerck, 1757	👁	1–5%	LC				182
Four-spotted Orbweb Spider	A. quadratus		Clerck, 1757	👁	6–25%	LC				177
	A. sturmi		(Hahn, 1831)	🔍	1–5%	LC				180
	A. triguttatus		(Fabricius, 1775)	🔍	1–5%	LC				180
Cucumber spiders	**Araniella**			👁						**190**
Cucumber spider	A. alpica		(L. Koch, 1869)	🔍	<1%	EN	NR			191
Common Cucumber Spider	A. cucurbitina		(Clerck, 1757)	🔍	6–25%	LC				190
Cucumber spider	A. displicata		(Hentz, 1847)	🔍	<1%	NT	NR			192
Cucumber spider	A. inconspicua		(Simon, 1874)	🔍	1–5%	LC	NS			192
Cucumber spider	A. opisthographa		(Kulczyński, 1905)	🔍	6–25%	LC				190
	Argiope			👁						204
Wasp Spider	A. bruennichi		(Scopoli, 1772)	👁	6–25%	LC				204
	Cercidia			🔍						198
	C. prominens		(Westring, 1851)	🔍	1–5%	LC	NS			198
	Cyclosa			👁						203
	C. conica		(Pallas, 1772)	👁	6–25%	LC				203
	Gibbaranea			🔍						186
Humped Orbweb Spider	G. gibbosa		(Walckenaer, 1802)	🔍	6–25%	LC				186
	Hypsosinga			🔍						194
	H. albovittata		(Westring, 1851)	🔍	1–5%	LC	NS			194
	H. heri		(Hahn, 1831)	🔍	<1%	VU	NR			196

Common name	SPECIES	Authorities	Synonyms	ID	% 10km squares	Status designations			Relevant legislation	Page
						IUCN	Nat.	Amber		
	H. pygmaea	(Sundevall, 1831)		🔍	6–25%	LC				194
	H. sanguinea	(C. L. Koch, 1844)		🔍	1–5%	LC	NS			196
	Larinioides			🔍						**183**
	L. cornutus	(Clerck, 1757)		🔍	26–50%	LC				183
	L. patagiatus	(Clerck, 1757)		🔍	1–5%	LC	NS	◆		185
Bridge Orbweb Spider	*L. sclopetarius*	(Clerck, 1757)		🔍	6–25%	LC				184
	Mangora			🔍						**202**
	M. acalypha	(Walckenaer, 1802)		🔍	6–25%	LC				202
	Neoscona									**189**
	N. adianta	(Walckenaer, 1802)			6–25%	LC				189
	Nuctenea									**187**
Walnut Orbweb Spider	*N. umbratica*	(Clerck, 1757)			26–50%	LC				187
	Singa			🔍						**197**
	S. hamata	(Clerck, 1757)		🔍	<1%	LC	NS			197
	Stroemiellus			🔍						**201**
	S. stroemi	(Thorell, 1870)	[*Zygiella stroemi* (Thorell, 1870)]	🔍	<1%	NT	NR			201
	Zilla			🔍						**193**
	Z. diodia	(Walckenaer, 1802)		🔍	6–25%	LC				193
Missing-sector orbweb spiders	**Zygiella**			🔍						**199**
Missing-sector orbweb spider	*Z. atrica*	(C. L. Koch, 1845)		🔍	6–25%	LC				200
Missing-sector orbweb spider	*Z. x-notata*	(Clerck, 1757)		🔍	26–50%	LC				199
Purseweb spiders	**ATYPIDAE**									**98**
	Atypus									**98**
Purseweb Spider	*A. affinis*	Eichwald, 1830		🔍	1–5%	LC	NS	◆		98
Sac spiders	**CLUBIONIDAE**									**290**
	Cheiracanthium			🔍						**305**
	C. erraticum	(Walckenaer, 1802)		🔍	6–25%	LC				306
	C. pennyi	O. Pickard-Cambridge, 1873		🔍	<1%	EN	NR			307
	C. virescens	(Sundevall, 1833)		🔍	1–5%	LC	NS			305

Common name	SPECIES	Synonyms	Authorities	ID	% 10km squares	Status designations			Relevant legislation	Page
						IUCN	Nat.	Amber		
	Clubiona			🔍						**290**
	C. brevipes		Blackwall, 1841	⚲	6–25%	LC				294
	C. caerulescens		L. Koch, 1867	⚲	<1%	VU	NR			302
	C. comta		C. L. Koch, 1839	🔍	6–25%	LC				291
	C. corticalis		(Walckenaer, 1802)	🔍	6–25%	LC				291
	C. diversa		O. Pickard-Cambridge, 1862	⚲	6–25%	LC				300
	C. frisia		Wunderlich & Schütt, 1995	⚲	<1%	NT	NR			304
	C. genevensis		L. Koch, 1866	⚲	<1%	NT	NR			304
	C. juvenis		Simon, 1878	⚲	<1%	NT	NR			295
	C. lutescens		Westring, 1851	⚲	6–25%	LC				293
	C. neglecta		O. Pickard-Cambridge, 1862	⚲	6–25%	LC				292
	C. norvegica		Strand, 1900	⚲	<1%	LC	NS	◆		299
	C. pallidula		(Clerck, 1757)	⚲	6–25%	LC				302
	C. phragmitis		C. L. Koch, 1843	⚲	6–25%	LC				303
	C. pseudoneglecta		Wunderlich, 1994	⚲	<1%	VU	NR			293
	C. reclusa		O. Pickard-Cambridge, 1863	⚲	26–50%	LC				294
Rosser's Sac Spider	C. rosserae		Locket, 1953	⚲	<1%	VU	NR		S41 (Eng)	300
	C. stagnatilis		Kulczyński, 1897	⚲	6–25%	LC				298
	C. subsultans		Thorell, 1875	⚲	<1%	NT	NR		BDL (Sco)	298
	C. subtilis		L. Koch, 1867	⚲	1–5%	LC				299
	C. terrestris		Westring, 1851	⚲	6–25%	LC				292
	C. trivialis		C. L. Koch, 1843	⚲	6–25%	LC				295
Ant-like sac spiders	**CORINNIDAE**									**288**
	Phrurolithus			🔍						**288**
	P. festivus		(C. L. Koch, 1835)	⚲	6–25%	LC				289
	P. minimus		C. L. Koch, 1839	⚲	<1%	LC	NS			289

Common name	SPECIES	Authorities	Synonyms	ID	% 10km squares	IUCN	Nat.	Amber	Relevant legislation	Page
						Status designations				
Soft spiders	**CYBAEIDAE**									**270**
	Argyroneta									270
Water Spider	*A. aquatica*	(Clerck, 1757)			6–25%	LC				271
Meshweb spiders	**DICTYNIDAE**									**257**
	Altella									265
	A. lucida	(Simon, 1874)			<1%	PE	NR		S41 (Eng)	265
	Argenna									266
	A. patula	(Simon, 1874)			<1%	LC	NS			266
	A. subnigra	(O. Pickard-Cambridge, 1861)			1–5%	LC	NS			266
	Cicurina									261
	C. cicur	(Fabricius, 1793)			1–5%	LC	NS	◆		261
	Cryphoeca									264
	C. silvicola	(C. L. Koch, 1834)			6–25%	LC				264
	Dictyna									257
	D. arundinacea	(Linnaeus, 1758)			26–50%	LC				258
	D. latens	(Fabricius, 1775)			6–25%	LC				257
	D. major	Menge, 1869			<1%	CR	NR		BDL (Sco)	260
	D. pusilla	Thorell, 1856			<1%	LC	NS		S41 (Eng)	260
	D. uncinata	Thorell, 1856			6–25%	LC				258
	Lathys									267
	L. humilis	(Blackwall, 1855)			6–25%	LC				267
	L. nielseni	(Schenkel, 1932)			<1%	VU	NR			268
	L. stigmatisata	(Menge, 1869)			<1%	VU	NR			268
	Mastigusa									269
	M. macrophthalma	(Kulczyński, 1897)			<1%	VU	NR			269
	Nigma									262
	N. puella	(Simon, 1870)			1–5%	LC	NS			262
	N. walckenaeri	(Roewer, 1951)			1–5%	LC				262

Common name	SPECIES	Authorities	Synonyms	ID	% 10km squares	Status designations			Relevant legislation	Page
						IUCN	Nat.	Amber		
	Tuberta									264
	T. maerens	(O. Pickard-Cambridge, 1863)			<1%	EN	NR			264
Woodlouse spiders	**DYSDERIDAE**									**106**
Woodlouse spiders	*Dysdera*									106
Woodlouse Spider	*D. crocata*	C. L. Koch, 1838			6–25%	LC				106
	D. erythrina	(Walckenaer, 1802)			1–5%	LC				106
	Harpactea									108
	H. hombergi	(Scopoli, 1763)			6–25%	LC				108
	H. rubicunda	(C. L. Koch, 1838)			<1%	VU	NR			108
Velvet spiders	**ERESIDAE**									**114**
	Eresus									114
Ladybird Spider	*E. sandaliatus*	(Martini & Goeze, 1778)			<1%	VU	NR		WCA 81; S41 (Eng)	114
Ground spiders	**GNAPHOSIDAE**									**311**
	Callilepis									321
	C. nocturna	(Linnaeus, 1758)			<1%	VU	NR			321
	Drassodes									311
	D. cupreus	(Blackwall, 1834)			6–25%	LC				311
	D. lapidosus	(Walckenaer, 1802)			6–25%	LC				312
	D. pubescens	(Thorell, 1856)			1–5%	LC	NS			312
	Drassyllus									328
	D. lutetianus	(L. Koch, 1866)			<1%	LC	NS			329
	D. praeficus	(L. Koch, 1866)			<1%	LC	NS			329
	D. pusillus	(C. L. Koch, 1833)			6–25%	LC				328
	Gnaphosa									330
	G. leporina	(L. Koch, 1866)			<1%	LC	NS			331
	G. lugubris	(C. L. Koch, 1839)			<1%	VU	NR			330
	G. nigerrima	L. Koch, 1877			<1%	VU	NR			331
	G. occidentalis	Simon, 1878			<1%	NT	NR			332

Common name	SPECIES	Synonyms	Authorities	ID	% 10km squares	IUCN	Nat.	Amber	Relevant legislation	Page
	Haplodrassus									**314**
	H. dalmatensis		(L. Koch, 1866)		<1%	LC	NS	◆	S41 (Eng); S42 (Wal)	314
	H. minor		(O. Pickard-Cambridge, 1879)		<1%	LC	NS			317
	H. signifer		(C. L. Koch, 1839)		6–25%	LC				314
	H. silvestris		(Blackwall, 1833)		<1%	LC	NS			317
	H. soerenseni		(Strand, 1900)		<1%	EN	NR		BDL (Sco)	315
	H. umbratilis		(L. Koch, 1866)		<1%	DD	NR			315
	Micaria									**333**
	M. albovittata	[*Micaria romana* L. Koch, 1866]	(Lucas, 1846)		<1%	VU	NR			334
	M. alpina		L. Koch, 1872		<1%	VU	NR			336
	M. pulicaria		(Sundevall, 1831)		6–25%	LC				333
	M. silesiaca		L. Koch, 1875		<1%	NT	NR			334
	M. subopaca		Westring, 1861		<1%	LC	NS			336
	Phaeocedus									**320**
	P. braccatus		(L. Koch, 1866)		<1%	VU	NR			320
Mouse spiders	*Scotophaeus*									**318**
Mouse Spider	S. blackwalli		(Thorell, 1871)		6–25%	LC				318
	S. scutulatus		(L. Koch, 1866)		<1%	NA				318
	Trachyzelotes									**327**
	T. pedestris		(C. L. Koch, 1837)		1–5%	LC				327
	Urozelotes									**328**
	U. rusticus		(L. Koch, 1872)		<1%	NA				328
	Zelotes									**322**
	Z. apricorum		(L. Koch, 1876)		1–5%	LC				323
	Z. electus		(C. L. Koch, 1839)		1–5%	LC	NS			325
	Z. latreillei		(Simon, 1878)		6–25%	LC				323
	Z. longipes		(L. Koch, 1866)		<1%	VU	NR			325

Common name	SPECIES	Authorities	Synonyms	ID	% 10km squares	IUCN	Nat.	Amber	Relevant legislation	Page
Lesser cobweb spiders	Z. petrensis	(C. L. Koch, 1839)		🔍	<1%	LC	NR			324
	Z. subterraneus	(C. L. Koch, 1833)		🔍	<1%	LC	NS			324
	HAHNIIDAE									**253**
	Antistea			🔍						
	A. elegans	(Blackwall, 1841)		🔍	6–25%	LC				253
	Hahnia			🔍						**254**
	H. candida	Simon, 1875		🔍	<1%	VU	NR			256
	H. helveola	Simon, 1875		🔍	1–5%	LC				255
	H. microphthalma	Snazell & Duffey, 1980		🔍	<1%	DD	NR			255
	H. montana	(Blackwall, 1841)		🔍	6–25%	LC				254
	H. nava	(Blackwall, 1841)		🔍	6–25%	LC				254
	H. pusilla	C. L. Koch, 1841		🔍	<1%	LC	NS			256
Money spiders	**LINYPHIIDAE**									**411**
	Acartauchenius			🔍						—
	A. scurrilis	(O. Pickard-Cambridge, 1872)		🔍	<1%	NT	NR			—
	Agnyphantes			🔍						—
	A. expunctus	(O. Pickard-Cambridge, 1875)	[Lepthyphantes expunctus (O. Pickard-Cambridge, 1875)]	🔍	1–5%	LC	NS			—
	Agyneta			🔍						—
	A. cauta	(O. Pickard-Cambridge, 1902)		🔍	1–5%	LC	NS	◆		—
	A. conigera	(O. Pickard-Cambridge, 1863)		🔍	6–25%	LC				—
	A. decora	(O. Pickard-Cambridge, 1871)		🔍	6–25%	LC	NS			—
	A. olivacea	(Emerton, 1882)		🔍	1–5%	LC				—
	A. ramosa	Jackson, 1912		🔍	1–5%	LC				—
	A. subtilis	(O. Pickard-Cambridge, 1863)		🔍	1–5%	LC		◆		—
	Allomengea			🔍						—
	A. scopigera	(Grube, 1859)		🔍	1–5%	LC		◆		—
	A. vidua	(L. Koch, 1879)		🔍	1–5%	LC	NS			—

Common name	SPECIES	Synonyms	Authorities	ID	% 10km squares	Status designations			Relevant legislation	Page
						IUCN	Nat.	Amber		
Aphileta										—
	A. misera		(O. Pickard-Cambridge, 1882)	⌁	1–5%	LC				—
Araeoncus										—
	A. crassiceps		(Westring, 1861)	⌁	1–5%	LC	NS			—
	A. humilis		(Blackwall, 1841)	⌁	1–5%	LC		◆		—
Asthenargus										—
	A. paganus		(Simon, 1884)	⌁	1–5%	LC	NS			—
Baryphyma										—
	B. gowerense		(Locket, 1965)	⌁	<1%	VU	NR			—
	B. maritimum		(Crocker & Parker, 1970)	⌁	<1%	NT	NR			—
	B. pratense		(Blackwall, 1861)	⌁	1–5%	LC				—
	B. trifrons		(O. Pickard-Cambridge, 1863)	⌁	6–25%	LC				—
Bathyphantes										—
	B. approximatus		(O. Pickard-Cambridge, 1871)	⌁	6–25%	LC				—
	B. gracilis		(Blackwall, 1841)	⌁	26–50%	LC				—
	B. nigrinus		(Westring, 1851)	⌁	6–25%	LC				—
	B. parvulus		(Westring, 1851)	⌁	6–25%	LC				—
	B. setiger		F. O. Pickard-Cambridge, 1894	⌁	1–5%	LC	NS	◆		—
Bolyphantes										—
	B. alticeps		(Sundevall, 1833)	⌁	1–5%	LC				—
	B. luteolus		(Blackwall, 1833)	⌁	6–25%	LC				—
Carorita										—
	C. limnaea		(Crosby & Bishop, 1927)	⌁	<1%	VU	NR			—
Caviphantes										—
	C. saxetorum		(Hull, 1916)	⌁	<1%	NT	NR			—
Centromerita										—
	C. bicolor		(Blackwall, 1833)	⌁	6–25%	LC				—
	C. concinna		(Thorell, 1875)	⌁	6–25%	LC				—

Common name	SPECIES	Authorities	Synonyms	ID	% 10km squares	Status designations			Relevant legislation	Page
						IUCN	Nat.	Amber		
	Centromerus									—
	C. albidus	Simon, 1929			<1%	PE	NR			—
	C. arcanus	(O. Pickard-Cambridge, 1873)			1–5%	LC				—
	C. brevivulvatus	Dahl, 1912			<1%	EN	NR			—
	C. capucinus	(Simon, 1884)			<1%	NT	NR			—
	C. cavernarum	(L. Koch, 1872)			<1%	NT	NR			—
	C. dilutus	(O. Pickard-Cambridge, 1875)			6–25%	LC				—
	C. incilium	(L. Koch, 1881)			<1%	LC				—
	C. levitarsis	(Simon, 1884)			<1%	EN	NS		BDL (Sco)	—
	C. minutissimus	Merrett & Powell, 1993			<1%	DD	NR			—
	C. persimilis	(O. Pickard-Cambridge, 1912)			<1%	DD	NR			—
	C. prudens	(O. Pickard-Cambridge, 1873)			1–5%	LC				—
	C. semiater	(L. Koch, 1879)			<1%	EN	NR			—
	C. serratus	(O. Pickard-Cambridge, 1875)			<1%	EN	NR		S41 (Eng)	—
	C. sylvaticus	(Blackwall, 1841)			6–25%	LC				—
	Ceratinella									—
	C. brevipes	(Westring, 1851)			6–25%	LC				—
	C. brevis	(Wider, 1834)			6–25%	LC				—
	C. scabrosa	(O. Pickard-Cambridge, 1871)			1–5%	LC				—
	Ceratinopsis									—
	C. romana	(O. Pickard-Cambridge, 1872)			<1%	LC	NR			—
	C. stativa	(Simon, 1881)			1–5%	LC	NS			—
	Cnephalocotes									—
	C. obscurus	(Blackwall, 1834)			6–25%	LC				—
	Dicymbium									—
	D. brevisetosum	Locket, 1962			1–5%	LC				—
	D. nigrum	(Blackwall, 1834)			6–25%	LC				—
	D. tibiale	(Blackwall, 1836)			6–25%	LC				—

Common name	SPECIES	Authorities	Synonyms	ID	% 10km squares	Status designations IUCN	Nat.	Amber	Relevant legislation	Page
	Diplocentria									—
	D. bidentata	(Emerton, 1882)			1–5%	LC	NS	◆		—
	Diplocephalus									—
	D. connatus	Bertkau, 1889			<1%	CR	NR			—
	D. cristatus	(Blackwall, 1833)			6–25%	LC				—
	D. graecus	(O. Pickard-Cambridge, 1872)			<1%	NA				—
	D. latifrons	(O. Pickard-Cambridge, 1863)			6–25%	LC				—
	D. permixtus	(O. Pickard-Cambridge, 1871)			6–25%	LC				—
	D. picinus	(Blackwall, 1841)			6–25%	LC				—
	D. protuberans	(O. Pickard-Cambridge, 1875)			<1%	VU	NR			—
	Diplostyla									—
	D. concolor	(Wider, 1834)			6–25%	LC				—
	Dismodicus									—
	D. bifrons	(Blackwall, 1841)			6–25%	LC				—
	D. elevatus	(C. L. Koch, 1838)			<1%	VU	NR			—
	Donacochara									—
	D. speciosa	(Thorell, 1875)			<1%	LC	NS			—
	Drapetisca									412
	D. socialis	(Sundevall, 1833)			6–25%	LC				412
	Drepanotylus									—
	D. uncatus	(O. Pickard-Cambridge, 1873)			1–5%	LC		◆		—
	Entelecara									—
	E. acuminata	(Wider, 1834)			6–25%	LC				—
	E. congenera	(O. Pickard-Cambridge, 1879)			1–5%	LC	NS			—
	E. errata	O. Pickard-Cambridge, 1913			1–5%	LC	NS			—
	E. erythropus	(Westring, 1851)			1–5%	LC				—
	E. flavipes	(Blackwall, 1834)			1–5%	LC	NS			—
	E. omissa	O. Pickard-Cambridge, 1902			<1%	LC	NS			—

Common name	SPECIES	Synonyms	Authorities	ID	% 10km squares	Status designations			Relevant legislation	Page
						IUCN	Nat.	Amber		
	Erigone									—
	E. aletris		Crosby & Bishop, 1928	🕷	1–5%	LC				—
	E. arctica		(White, 1852)	🕷	1–5%	LC				—
	E. atra		Blackwall, 1833	🕷	26–50%	LC				—
	E. capra		Simon, 1884	🕷	<1%	LC	NR			—
	E. dentipalpis		(Wider, 1834)	🕷	26–50%	LC				—
	E. longipalpis		(Sundevall, 1830)	🕷	1–5%	LC				—
	E. promiscua		(O. Pickard-Cambridge, 1872)	🕷	6–25%	LC				—
	E. psychrophila		Thorell, 1871	🕷	<1%	NT	NR			—
	E. tirolensis		L. Koch, 1872	🕷	1–5%	LC	NS			—
	E. welchi		Jackson, 1911	🕷	<1%	EN	NR		S41 (Eng); S42 (Wal)	—
	Erigonella									—
	E. hiemalis		(Blackwall, 1841)	🕷	6–25%	LC				—
	E. ignobilis		(O. Pickard-Cambridge, 1871)	🕷	1–5%	LC	NS			—
	Evansia									—
	E. merens		O. Pickard-Cambridge, 1900	🕷	1–5%	LC	NS			413
	Floronia			🔍						
	F. bucculenta		(Clerck, 1757)	🔍	1–5%	LC				413
	Glyphesis			🕷						—
	G. cottonae		(La Touche, 1945)	🕷	<1%	VU	NR		S41 (Eng)	—
	G. servulus		(Simon, 1881)	🕷	<1%	NT	NR			—
	Gnathonarium			🕷						—
	G. dentatum		(Wider, 1834)	🕷	6–25%	LC				—
	Gonatium			🕷						—
	G. paradoxum		(L. Koch, 1869)	🕷	<1%	EN	NR			—
	G. rubellum		(Blackwall, 1841)	🕷	6–25%	LC				—
	G. rubens		(Blackwall, 1833)	🕷	6–25%	LC				—

Common name	SPECIES	Authorities	Synonyms	ID	% 10km squares	IUCN	Nat.	Amber	Relevant legislation	Page
	Gongylidiellum									
	G. latebricola	(O. Pickard-Cambridge, 1871)		🕷	1–5%	LC	NS	◆		—
	G. murcidum	Simon, 1884		🕷	<1%	VU	NS			—
	G. vivum	(O. Pickard-Cambridge, 1875)		🕷	6–25%	LC				—
	Gongylidium									
	G. rufipes	(Linnaeus, 1758)		🕷	6–25%	LC				—
	Halorates									
	H. distinctus	(Simon, 1884)		🕷	<1%	LC	NS			—
	H. holmgreni	(Thorell, 1871)		🕷	<1%	LC	NS			—
	H. reprobus	(O. Pickard-Cambridge, 1879)		🕷	1–5%	LC	NS			—
	Helophora									
	H. insignis	(Blackwall, 1841)		🕷	6–25%	LC				—
	Hilaira									
	H. excisa	(O. Pickard-Cambridge, 1871)		🕷	6–25%	LC				—
	H. frigida	(Thorell, 1872)		🕷	1–5%	LC				—
	H. nubigena	Hull, 1911		🕷	<1%	VU	NR			—
	H. pervicax	Hull, 1908		🕷	1–5%	LC	NS			—
	Hybocoptus									
	H. decollatus	(Simon, 1881)		🕷	<1%	LC	NS			—
	Hylyphantes									
	H. graminicola	(Sundevall, 1830)		🕷	6–25%	LC				—
	Hypomma									
	H. bituberculatum	(Wider, 1834)		🕷	26–50%	LC				—
	H. cornutum	(Blackwall, 1833)		🕷	6–25%	LC				—
	H. fulvum	(Bösenberg, 1902)		🕷	1–5%	LC	NS			—
	Hypselistes									
	H. jacksoni	(O. Pickard-Cambridge, 1902)		🕷	1–5%	LC	NS	◆		—

Common name	SPECIES	Authorities	Synonyms	ID	% 10km squares	Status designations IUCN	Nat.	Amber	Relevant legislation	Page
	Improphantes									—
	I. complicatus	(Emerton, 1882)	[*Lepthyphantes complicatus* (Emerton, 1882)]	ID	<1%	NT	NR			—
	Jacksonella									—
	J. falconeri	(Jackson, 1908)		ID	<1%	LC	NS	◆		—
	Kaestneria									—
	K. dorsalis	(Wider, 1834)		ID	6–25%	LC				—
	K. pullata	(O. Pickard-Cambridge, 1863)		ID	6–25%	LC				—
	Karita									—
	K. paludosa	(Duffey, 1971)	[*Carorita paludosa* Duffey, 1971]	ID	<1%	VU	NR			—
	Labulla									—
	L. thoracica	(Wider, 1834)		ID	6–25%	LC				—
	Latithorax									—
	L. faustus	(O. Pickard-Cambridge, 1900)		ID	1–5%	LC	NS	◆		—
	Lepthyphantes									—
	L. leprosus	(Ohlert, 1865)		ID	6–25%	LC				—
	L. minutus	(Blackwall, 1833)		ID	6–25%	LC				—
	Leptorhoptrum									—
	L. robustum	(Westring, 1851)		ID	6–25%	LC				—
	Leptothrix									—
	L. hardyi	(Blackwall, 1850)		ID	<1%	LC	NS	◆		—
	Lessertia									—
	L. dentichelis	(Simon, 1884)		ID	1–5%	LC	NS			—
Sheetweb spiders	*Linyphia*									**415**
	L. hortensis	Sundevall, 1830		ID	6–25%	LC				415
Common Sheetweb Spider	L. triangularis	(Clerck, 1757)		ID	26–50%	LC				415
	Lophomma									—
	L. punctatum	(Blackwall, 1841)		ID	6–25%	LC				—

Common name	SPECIES	Authorities	Synonyms	ID	% 10km squares	IUCN	Nat.	Amber	Relevant legislation	Page
	Macrargus									—
	M. carpenteri	(O. Pickard-Cambridge, 1894)		⚥	<1%	LC	NS			—
	M. rufus	(Wider, 1834)		⚥	6–25%	LC				—
	Maro			⚥						—
	M. lepidus	Casemir, 1961		⚥	<1%	EN	NR			—
	M. minutus	O. Pickard-Cambridge, 1906		⚥	<1%	LC	NS			—
	M. sublestus	Falconer, 1915		⚥	<1%	EN	NR			—
	Maso			⚥						
	M. gallicus	Simon, 1894		⚥	<1%	LC	NS			—
	M. sundevalli	(Westring, 1851)		⚥	6–25%	LC				—
	Mecopisthes			⚥						—
	M. peusi	Wunderlich, 1972		⚥	<1%	LC	NS		S41 (Eng); S42 (Wal)	—
	Mecynargus									—
	M. morulus	(O. Pickard-Cambridge, 1873)		⚥	1–5%	LC	NS	◆		—
	M. paetulus	(O. Pickard-Cambridge, 1875)		⚥	<1%	VU	NR		BDL (Sco)	—
	Megalepthyphantes									—
	M. nebulosus	(Sundevall, 1830)		⚥	<1%	LC				—
	Megalepthyphantes. sp.			⚥	<1%	NA				—
	Meioneta									—
	M. beata	(O. Pickard-Cambridge, 1906)		⚥	1–5%	LC				—
	M. fuscipalpa	(C. L. Koch, 1836)		⚥	<1%	VU	NR			—
	M. gulosa	(L. Koch, 1869)		⚥	1–5%	LC	NS			—
	M. innotabilis	(O. Pickard-Cambridge, 1863)		⚥	1–5%	LC				—
	M. mollis	(O. Pickard-Cambridge, 1871)		⚥	<1%	NT	NR		S41 (Eng); S42 (Wal)	—
	M. mossica	Schikora, 1993		⚥	1–5%	LC	NS			—
	M. nigripes	(Simon, 1884)		⚥	1–5%	LC	NS			—
	M. rurestris	(C. L. Koch, 1836)		⚥	6–25%	LC				—

Common name	SPECIES	Authorities	Synonyms	ID	% 10km squares	Status designations			Relevant legislation	Page
						IUCN	Nat.	Amber		
	M. saxatilis	(Blackwall, 1844)		🔍	6–25%	LC				–
	M. simplicitarsis	(Simon, 1884)		🔍	1–5%	LC	NS			–
	Mermessus			🔍						–
	M. trilobatus	(Emerton, 1882)		🔍	<1%	NA				–
	Metopobactrus									–
	M. prominulus	(O. Pickard-Cambridge, 1872)		🔍	1–5%	LC				–
	Micrargus									–
	M. apertus	(O. Pickard-Cambridge, 1871)		🔍	6–25%	LC				–
	M. herbigradus	(Blackwall, 1854)		🔍	6–25%	LC				–
	M. laudatus	(O. Pickard-Cambridge, 1881)		🔍	<1%	LC	NS			–
	M. subaequalis	(Westring, 1851)		🔍	6–25%	LC				–
	Microctenonyx									–
	M. subitaneus	(O. Pickard-Cambridge, 1875)		🔍	1–5%	LC	NS			–
	Microlinyphia			🔍						417
	M. impigra	(O. Pickard-Cambridge, 1871)		🔍	1–5%	LC				417
	M. pusilla	(Sundevall, 1830)		🔍	26–50%	LC				417
	Microneta			🔍						–
	M. viaria	(Blackwall, 1841)		🔍	6–25%	LC				–
	Midia									–
Midas Tree Weaver Spider	M. midas	(Simon, 1884)		🔍	<1%	EN	NR		S41 (Eng)	–
	Milleriana			🔍						–
	M. inerrans	(O. Pickard-Cambridge, 1885)		🔍	6–25%	LC				–
	Minicia			🔍						–
	M. marginella	(Wider, 1834)		🔍	<1%	DD	NR			–
	Minyriolus			🔍						–
	M. pusillus	(Wider, 1834)		🔍	6–25%	LC				–
	Mioxena									–
	M. blanda	(Simon, 1884)		🔍	<1%	DD	NR			–

Common name	SPECIES	Synonyms	Authorities	ID	% 10km squares	IUCN	Nat.	Amber	Relevant legislation	Page
	Moebelia			ﭢ						—
	M. penicillata		(Westring, 1851)	ﭢ	1–5%	LC	NS	◆		—
	Monocephalus									—
	M. castaneipes		(Simon, 1884)	ﭢ	1–5%	LC	NS		S41 (Eng); S42 (Wal)	—
	M. fuscipes		(Blackwall, 1836)	ﭢ	6–25%	LC				—
	Mughiphantes			ﭢ						—
	M. whymperi	[Lepthyphantes whymperi F. O. Pickard-Cambridge, 1894]	(F. O. Pickard-Cambridge, 1894)	ﭢ	1–5%	LC	NS			—
	Neriene			🔍						418
	N. clathrata		(Sundevall, 1830)	ﭢ	26–50%	LC				418
	N. emphana		(Walckenaer, 1841)	ﭢ	<1%	NA				—
	N. furtiva		(O. Pickard-Cambridge, 1871)	ﭢ	<1%	LC	NS			—
	N. montana		(Clerck, 1757)	ﭢ	6–25%	LC				420
	N. peltata		(Wider, 1834)	ﭢ	26–50%	LC				420
	N. radiata		(Walckenaer, 1841)	ﭢ	<1%	NT	NR			—
	Nothophantes			ﭢ						—
Horrid Ground Weaver Spider	N. horridus *		Merrett & Stevens, 1995	ﭢ	<1%	CR	NR		S41 (Eng)	—
	Notioscopus			ﭢ						—
	N. sarcinatus		(O. Pickard-Cambridge, 1872)	ﭢ	<1%	LC	NS		S41 (Eng); S42 (Wal)	—
	Obscuriphantes			ﭢ						—
	O. obscurus	[Lepthyphantes obscurus (Blackwall, 1841)]	(Blackwall, 1841)	ﭢ	6–25%	LC				—
	Oedothorax			ﭢ						—
	O. agrestis		(Blackwall, 1853)	ﭢ	6–25%	LC				—
	O. apicatus		(Blackwall, 1850)	ﭢ	6–25%	LC				—
	O. fuscus		(Blackwall, 1834)	ﭢ	26–50%	LC				—
	O. gibbosus		(Blackwall, 1841)	ﭢ	6–25%	LC				—
	O. retusus		(Westring, 1851)	ﭢ	6–25%	LC				—

Status designations

* Also designated as CR on IUCN International Red List.

Common name	SPECIES	Authorities	Synonyms	ID	% 10km squares	IUCN	Nat.	Amber	Relevant legislation	Page
	Oreonetides									—
	O. vaginatus	(Thorell, 1872)		🔍	1–5%	LC	NS			—
	Oryphantes									—
	O. angulatus	(O. Pickard-Cambridge, 1881)	[*Lepthyphantes angulatus* (O. Pickard-Cambridge, 1881)]	🔍	1–5%	LC	NS			—
	Ostearius									—
	O. melanopygius	(O. Pickard-Cambridge, 1879)		🔍	6–25%	LC				—
	Palliduphantes									—
	P. antroniensis	(Schenkel, 1933)	[*Lepthyphantes antroniensis* Schenkel, 1933]	🔍	<1%	PE	NR		BDL (Sco)	—
	P. ericaeus	(Blackwall, 1853)	[*Lepthyphantes ericaeus* (Blackwall, 1853)]	🔍	26–50%	LC				—
	P. insignis	(O. Pickard-Cambridge, 1913)	[*Lepthyphantes insignis* O. Pickard-Cambridge, 1913]	🔍	1–5%	LC	NS			—
	P. pallidus	(O. Pickard-Cambridge, 1871)	[*Lepthyphantes pallidus* (O. Pickard-Cambridge, 1871)]	🔍	6–25%	LC				—
	Panamomops									—
	P. sulcifrons	(Wider, 1834)		🔍	1–5%	LC	NS			—
	Pelecopsis									—
	P. elongata	(Wider, 1834)		🔍	<1%	NT	NR			—
	P. mengei	(Simon, 1884)		🔍	1–5%	LC				—
	P. nemoralioides	(O. Pickard-Cambridge, 1884)		🔍	1–5%	LC	NS	◆		—
	P. nemoralis	(Blackwall, 1841)		🔍	1–5%	LC				—
	P. parallela	(Wider, 1834)		🔍	6–25%	LC				—
	P. radicicola	(L. Koch, 1872)		🔍	<1%	EN	NR			—
	Peponocranium									—
	P. ludicrum	(O. Pickard-Cambridge, 1861)		🔍	6–25%	LC				—
	Piniphantes									—
	P. pinicola	(Simon, 1884)	[*Lepthyphantes pinicola* Simon, 1884]	🔍	<1%	LC	NR			—
	Pityohyphantes									**414**
	P. phrygianus	(C. L. Koch, 1836)		🔍	1–5%	LC	NS			414

Common name	SPECIES	Authorities	Synonyms	ID	% 10km squares	Status designations			Relevant legislation	Page
						IUCN	Nat.	Amber		
	Pocadicnemis									–
	P. juncea	Locket & Millidge, 1953		⚘	6–25%	LC				–
	P. pumila	(Blackwall, 1841)		⚘	6–25%	LC				–
	Poeciloneta			⚘						–
	P. variegata	(Blackwall, 1841)		⚘	6–25%	LC				–
	Porrhomma			⚘						–
	P. cambridgei	Merrett, 1994		⚘	<1%	DD	NR			–
	P. campbelli	F. O. Pickard-Cambridge, 1894		⚘	1–5%	LC	NS			–
	P. convexum	(Westring, 1851)		⚘	1–5%	LC	NS	◆		–
	P. egeria	Simon, 1884		⚘	<1%	LC	NS			–
	P. errans	(Blackwall, 1841)		⚘	<1%	LC	NS			–
	P. microphthalmum	(O. Pickard-Cambridge, 1871)		⚘	6–25%	LC				–
	P. montanum	Jackson, 1913		⚘	1–5%	LC	NS			–
	P. oblitum	(O. Pickard-Cambridge, 1871)		⚘	1–5%	LC	NS			–
	P. pallidum	Jackson, 1913		⚘	1–5%	LC				–
	P. pygmaeum	(Blackwall, 1834)		⚘	6–25%	LC				–
	P. rosenhaueri	(L. Koch, 1872)		⚘	<1%	NT	NR			–
	Praestigia			⚘						–
	P. duffeyi	Millidge, 1954	[*Baryphyma duffeyi* (Millidge, 1954)]	⚘	<1%	EN	NR		S41 (Eng)	–
	Prinerigone			⚘						–
	P. vagans	(Audouin, 1826)		⚘	1–5%	LC				–
	Pseudomaro			⚘						–
	P. aenigmaticus	Denis, 1966		⚘	<1%	DD	NR			–
	Saaristoa			⚘						–
	S. abnormis	(Blackwall, 1841)		⚘	6–25%	LC				–
	S. firma	(O. Pickard-Cambridge, 1905)		⚘	1–5%	LC	NS		S41 (Eng); S42 (Wal)	–

Common name	SPECIES	Authorities	Synonyms	ID	% 10km squares	IUCN	Nat.	Amber	Relevant legislation	Page
	Saloca									—
	S. diceros	(O. Pickard-Cambridge, 1871)		✿	<1%	LC	NS			—
	Satilatlas									—
	S. britteni	(Jackson, 1913)		✿	<1%	LC	NS			—
	Savignia									—
	S. frontata	Blackwall, 1833		✿	6–25%	LC				—
	Scotinotylus									—
	S. evansi	(O. Pickard-Cambridge, 1894)		✿	1–5%	LC	NS			—
	Semljicola									—
Cloud Living Spider	*S. caliginosus*	(Falconer, 1910)		✿	<1%	EN	NR		S41 (Eng)	—
	Silometopus									—
	S. ambiguus	(O. Pickard-Cambridge, 1905)		✿	1–5%	LC	NS			—
	S. elegans	(O. Pickard-Cambridge, 1872)		✿	6–25%	LC				—
	S. incurvatus	(O. Pickard-Cambridge, 1873)		✿	<1%	VU	NR		S41 (Eng)	—
	S. reussi	(Thorell, 1871)		✿	1–5%	LC				—
	Sintula									—
	S. corniger	(Blackwall, 1856)		✿	1–5%	LC	NS	◆		—
	Stemonyphantes									411
	S. lineatus	(Linnaeus, 1758)		🔍	6–25%	LC				411
	Syedra									—
	S. gracilis	(Menge, 1869)		✿	<1%	LC	NS			—
	S. myrmicarum	(Kulczynski, 1882)		✿	<1%	NE				—
	Tallusia									—
	T. experta	(O. Pickard-Cambridge, 1871)		✿	6–25%	LC				—
	Tapinocyba									—
	T. insecta	(L. Koch, 1869)		✿	1–5%	LC	NS	◆		—
	T. mitis	(O. Pickard-Cambridge, 1882)		✿	<1%	EN	NR		S41 (Eng)	—
	T. pallens	(O. Pickard-Cambridge, 1872)		✿	1–5%	LC				—
	T. praecox	(O. Pickard-Cambridge, 1873)		✿	1–5%	LC				—

Common name	SPECIES	Authorities	Synonyms	ID	% 10km squares	Status designations			Relevant legislation	Page
						IUCN	Nat.	Amber		
	Tapinocyboides									—
	T. pygmaeus	(Menge, 1869)			<1%	DD	NR			—
	Tapinopa									—
	T. longidens	(Wider, 1834)			6–25%	LC				—
	Taranucnus									—
	T. setosus	(O. Pickard-Cambridge, 1863)			1–5%	LC	NS	◆		—
	Tenuiphantes									—
	T. alacris	(Blackwall, 1853)	[*Lepthyphantes alacris* (Blackwall, 1853)]		6–25%	LC				—
	T. cristatus	(Menge, 1866)	[*Lepthyphantes cristatus* (Menge, 1866)]		6–25%	LC				—
	T. flavipes	(Blackwall, 1854)	[*Lepthyphantes flavipes* (Blackwall, 1854)]		6–25%	LC				—
	T. mengei	(Kulczyński, 1887)	[*Lepthyphantes mengei* Kulczyński, 1887]		6–25%	LC				—
	T. tenebricola	(Wider, 1834)	[*Lepthyphantes tenebricola* (Wider, 1834)]		6–25%	LC				—
	T. tenuis	(Blackwall, 1852)	[*Lepthyphantes tenuis* (Blackwall, 1852)]		>50%	LC				—
	T. zimmermanni	(Bertkau, 1890)	[*Lepthyphantes zimmermanni* Bertkau, 1890]		26–50%	LC				—
	Thyreosthenius									—
	T. biovatus	(O. Pickard-Cambridge, 1875)			1–5%	LC	NS			—
	T. parasiticus	(Westring, 1851)			1–5%	LC				—
	Tiso									—
	T. aestivus	(L. Koch, 1872)			1–5%	LC	NS			—
	T. vagans	(Blackwall, 1834)			6–25%	LC				—
	Tmeticus									—
	T. affinis	(Blackwall, 1855)			1–5%	LC	NS			—
	Trematocephalus									—
	T. cristatus	(Wider, 1834)			1–5%	LC	NS			—
	Trichoncus									—
	T. affinis	Kulczyński, 1894			<1%	LC	NR			—
	T. hackmani	Millidge, 1955			<1%	VU	NR			—
	T. saxicola	(O. Pickard-Cambridge, 1861)			<1%	VU	NR			—

Common name	SPECIES	Authorities	Synonyms	ID	% 10km squares	IUCN	Nat.	Amber	Relevant legislation	Page
	Trichopterna									—
	T. cito	(O. Pickard-Cambridge, 1872)			<1%	EN	NR			—
	Trichopternoides									—
	T. thorelli	(Westring, 1861)	[*Trichopterna thorelli* (Westring, 1861)]		1–5%	LC		◆		—
	Troxochrus									—
	T. scabriculus	(Westring, 1851)			6–25%	LC				—
	Typhochrestus									—
	T. digitatus	(O. Pickard-Cambridge, 1872)			1–5%	LC	NS	◆		—
	T. simoni	Lessert, 1907			<1%	CR	NR			—
	Wabasso									—
	W. replicatus	(Holm, 1950)	[*Wabasso quaestio replicatus* (Holm, 1950)]		<1%	VU	NR			—
	Walckenaeria									—
	W. acuminata	Blackwall, 1833			6–25%	LC				—
	W. alticeps	(Denis, 1952)			1–5%	LC	NS			—
	W. antica	(Wider, 1834)			6–25%	LC				—
	W. atrotibialis	(O. Pickard-Cambridge, 1878)			6–25%	LC				—
	W. capito	(Westring, 1861)			1–5%	LC	NS			—
	W. clavicornis	(Emerton, 1882)			1–5%	LC	NS	◆		—
	W. corniculans	(O. Pickard-Cambridge, 1875)			<1%	CR	NR		S41 (Eng)	—
	W. cucullata	(C. L. Koch, 1836)			1–5%	LC				—
	W. cuspidata	Blackwall, 1833			6–25%	LC				—
	W. dysderoides	(Wider, 1834)			1–5%	LC	NS	◆		—
	W. furcillata	(Menge, 1869)			1–5%	LC	NS	◆		—
	W. incisa	(O. Pickard-Cambridge, 1871)			<1%	LC	NS	◆		—
	W. kochi	(O. Pickard-Cambridge, 1872)			1–5%	LC	NS	◆		—
	W. mitrata	(Menge, 1868)			<1%	VU	NR			—

Common name	SPECIES	Authorities	Synonyms	ID	% 10km squares	IUCN	Nat.	Amber	Relevant legislation	Page
	W. monoceros	(Wider, 1834)			1–5%	LC	NS	♦		—
	W. nodosa	O. Pickard-Cambridge, 1873			1–5%	LC	NS	♦		—
	W. nudipalpis	(Westring, 1851)			6–25%	LC				—
	W. obtusa	Blackwall, 1836			1–5%	LC	NS			—
	W. stylifrons	(O. Pickard-Cambridge, 1875)			<1%	VU	NR			—
	W. unicornis	O. Pickard-Cambridge, 1861			6–25%	LC				—
	W. vigilax	(Blackwall, 1853)			6–25%	LC				—
	Wiehlea									—
	W. calcarifera	(Simon, 1884)			<1%	EN	NR			—
Running foliage spiders	**LIOCRANIDAE**									**277**
	Agraecina									282
	A. striata	(Kulczyński, 1882)			1–5%	LC	NS			282
	Agroeca									277
	A. brunnea	(Blackwall, 1833)			1–5%	LC				278
	A. cuprea	Menge, 1873			<1%	NT	NR		S41 (Eng)	280
	A. dentigera	Kulczyński, 1913			<1%	DD	NR			280
	A. inopina	O. Pickard-Cambridge, 1886			1–5%	LC				279
	A. lusatica	(L. Koch, 1875)			<1%	EN	NR			279
	A. proxima	(O. Pickard-Cambridge, 1871)			6–25%	LC				278
	Apostenus									283
	A. fuscus	Westring, 1851			<1%	VU	NR			283
	Liocranum									286
	L. rupicola	(Walckenaer, 1830)			<1%	LC	NS			286
	Scotina									284
	S. celans	(Blackwall, 1841)			1–5%	LC	NS			284
	S. gracilipes	(Blackwall, 1859)			1–5%	LC	NS			284
	S. palliardii	(L. Koch, 1881)			<1%	EN	NR			285

Common name	SPECIES	Synonyms	Authorities	ID	% 10km squares	Status designations IUCN	Nat.	Amber	Relevant legislation	Page
Wolf spiders	**LYCOSIDAE**									**206**
	Alopecosa			🔍						221
	A. barbipes		(Sundevall, 1833)		1–5%	LC		◆		222
	A. cuneata		(Clerck, 1757)		1–5%	LC	NS			221
	A. fabrilis		(Clerck, 1757)	🔍	<1%	CR	NR		S41 (Eng)	222
	A. pulverulenta		(Clerck, 1757)		26–50%	LC				221
	Arctosa			🔍						**228**
	A. alpigena		(Doleschall, 1852)	🔍	<1%	VU	NR			232
	A. cinerea		(Fabricius, 1777)		1–5%	LC	NS			229
	A. fulvolineata		(Lucas, 1846)		<1%	NT	NR		S41 (Eng)	230
	A. leopardus		(Sundevall, 1833)		1–5%	LC				230
	A. perita		(Latreille, 1799)	🔍	6–25%	LC				228
	Aulonia			🔍						**227**
	A. albimana		(Walckenaer, 1805)	🔍	<1%	CR	NR			227
	Hygrolycosa									**218**
	H. rubrofasciata		(Ohlert, 1865)	🔍	<1%	EN	NR			218
	Pardosa			🔍						**207**
	P. agrestis		(Westring, 1861)		1–5%	LC	NS			210
	P. agricola		(Thorell, 1856)		1–5%	LC				215
	P. amentata		(Clerck, 1757)		26–50%	LC				212
	P. hortensis		(Thorell, 1872)		1–5%	LC				213
	P. lugubris		(Walckenaer, 1802)		<1%	LC	NS			216
	P. monticola		(Clerck, 1757)		6–25%	LC				207
	P. nigriceps		(Thorell, 1856)		26–50%	LC				211
	P. paludicola		(Clerck, 1757)		<1%	EN	NR			217
	P. palustris		(Linnaeus, 1758)		6–25%	LC				207
	P. prativaga		(L. Koch, 1870)		6–25%	LC				212
	P. proxima		(C. L. Koch, 1847)		1–5%	LC	NS			215

Common name	SPECIES	Synonyms	Authorities	ID	% 10km squares	IUCN	Nat.	Amber	Relevant legislation	Page
	P. pullata		(Clerck, 1757)		26–50%	LC				211
	P. purbeckensis		F.O.Pickard-Cambridge, 1895		1–5%	LC				210
	P. saltans		Töpfer-Hofmann, 2000		6–25%	LC				216
	P. trailli		(O. Pickard-Cambridge, 1873)		<1%	VU	NR			213
Otter spiders	*Pirata*									**233**
	P. hygrophilus		Thorell, 1872		6–25%	LC				235
	P. latitans		(Blackwall, 1841)		6–25%	LC				233
	P. piraticus		(Clerck, 1757)		26–50%	LC				235
	P. piscatorius		(Clerck, 1757)		1–5%	LC	NS	♦		234
	P. tenuitarsis		Simon, 1876		1–5%	LC	NS			237
	P. uliginosus		(Thorell, 1856)		1–5%	LC				237
	Trochosa									**224**
	T. robusta		(Simon, 1876)		<1%	VU	NR			224
	T. ruricola		(De Geer, 1778)		6–25%	LC				224
	T. spinipalpis		(F. O. Pickard-Cambridge, 1895)		1–5%	LC	NS	♦		226
	T. terricola		Thorell, 1856		26–50%	LC				226
	Xerolycosa									**219**
	X. miniata		(C. L. Koch, 1834)		1–5%	LC	NS			220
	X. nemoralis		(Westring, 1861)		1–5%	LC	NS			219
Pirate spiders	**MIMETIDAE**									**110**
Pirate spiders	*Ero*									**110**
	E. aphana		(Walckenaer, 1802)		1–5%	LC	NS			112
	E. cambridgei		Kulczyński, 1911		6–25%	LC				110
	E. furcata		(Villers, 1789)		6–25%	LC				110
	E. tuberculata		(De Geer, 1778)		<1%	LC	NS			112
Dwarf cobweb spiders	**MYSMENIDAE**									**164**
	Trogloneta									**164**
	T. granulum		Simon, 1922		<1%	NE	NR			164

Common name	SPECIES	Synonyms	Authorities	ID	% 10km squares	IUCN	Nat.	Amber	Relevant legislation	Page
Comb-footed cellar spiders	**NESTICIDAE**									**119**
	Nesticus									119
	N. cellulanus		(Clerck, 1757)		6–25%	LC				119
Discweb spiders	**OECOBIIDAE**									**115**
	Oecobius									115
	O. navus		Blackwall, 1859		<1%	NE				115
Goblin spiders	**OONOPIDAE**									**109**
	Oonops									109
	O. domesticus		Dalmas, 1916		1–5%	LC				109
	O. pulcher		Templeton, 1835 , 1916		6–25%	LC				109
	Orchestina									—
	Orchestina. sp.				<1%	PE	NR			—
Lynx spiders	**OXYOPIDAE**									**243**
Lynx spiders	*Oxyopes*									243
Lynx Spider	*O. heterophthalmus*		Latreille, 1804		<1%	VU	NR			243
Running crab spiders	**PHILODROMIDAE**									**342**
Running crab spiders	*Philodromus*									342
	P. albidus		Kulczyński, 1911		6–25%	LC				349
	P. aureolus		(Clerck, 1757)		6–25%	LC				343
	P. buxi		Simon, 1884		<1%	NE				348
	P. cespitum		(Walckenaer, 1802)		6–25%	LC				346
	P. collinus		C. L. Koch, 1835		1–5%	LC				347
	P. dispar		Walckenaer, 1826		6–25%	LC				343
	P. emarginatus		(Schrank, 1803)		<1%	VU	NR			348
Sand Running Spider	*P. fallax*		Sundevall, 1833		<1%	VU	NR		S41 (Eng); S42 (Wal)	350
	P. histrio		(Latreille, 1819)		1–5%	LC	NS			351
	P. longipalpis		Simon, 1870		<1%	LC	NS			347
	P. margaritatus		(Clerck, 1757)		<1%	NT	NR		S41 (Eng)	350

Common name	SPECIES	Authorities	Synonyms	ID	% 10km squares	Status designations			Relevant legislation	Page
						IUCN	Nat.	Amber		
	P. praedatus	O. Pickard-Cambridge, 1871			6-25%	LC				346
	P. rufus	Walckenaer, 1826			<1%	NE				349
	Thanatus									**354**
	T. formicinus	(Clerck, 1757)			<1%	PE	NR			356
	T. striatus	C. L. Koch, 1845			1-5%	LC	NS	♦		354
	T. vulgaris	Simon, 1870			<1%	NA				355
	Tibellus									**352**
	T. maritimus	(Menge, 1875)			1-5%	LC				353
	T. oblongus	(Walckenaer, 1802)			6-25%	LC				353
Cellar spiders	**PHOLCIDAE**									**101**
	Holocnemus									103
	H. pluchei	(Scopoli, 1763)			<1%	NA				103
	Pholcus									101
Daddy Long-legs Spider	P. phalangioides	(Fuesslin, 1775)			6-25%	LC				101
	Psilochorus									102
	P. simoni	(Berland, 1911)			<1%	LC				102
Nurseryweb spiders	**PISAURIDAE**									**238**
	Dolomedes									240
Raft Spider	D. fimbriatus	(Clerck, 1757)			1-5%	LC	NS			242
Fen Raft Spider	D. plantarius *	(Clerck, 1757)			<1%	VU	NR		WCA 81; S41 (Eng); S42 (Wal)	240
	Pisaura									238
Nurseryweb Spider	P. mirabilis	(Clerck, 1757)			26-50%	LC				238
Jumping spiders	**SALTICIDAE**									**380**
	Aelurillus									405
	A. v-insignitus	(Clerck, 1757)			1-5%	LC	NS			405
	Ballus									389
	B. chalybeius	(Walckenaer, 1802)			1-5%	LC	NS			389

* Also designated as VU on IUCN International Red List.

Common name	SPECIES	Authorities	Synonyms	ID	% 10km squares	Status designations IUCN	Nat.	Amber	Relevant legislation	Page
	Euophrys									**394**
	E. frontalis	(Walckenaer, 1802)			6–25%	LC				394
	E. herbigrada	(Simon, 1871)			<1%	VU	NR			395
	Evarcha									**406**
	E. arcuata	(Clerck, 1757)			1–5%	LC	NS			406
	E. falcata	(Clerck, 1757)			6–25%	LC				407
Sun jumping spiders	*Heliophanus*									**390**
	H. auratus	C. L. Koch, 1835			<1%	VU	NR			392
	H. cupreus	(Walckenaer, 1802)			6–25%	LC				390
	H. dampfi	Schenkel, 1923			<1%	VU	NR			392
	H. flavipes	(Hahn, 1832)			6–25%	LC				390
	Macaroeris									**393**
	M. nidicolens	(Walckenaer, 1802)			<1%	NA				393
	Marpissa									**385**
Fencepost Jumping Spider	*M. muscosa*	(Clerck, 1757)			1–5%	LC	NS			386
	M. nivoyi	(Lucas, 1846)			<1%	LC	NS	◆		385
	M. radiata	(Grube, 1859)			<1%	VU	NR			387
	Myrmarachne									**408**
	M. formicaria	(De Geer, 1778)			<1%	LC	NS			408
	Neon									**382**
	N. pictus	Kulczyński, 1891			<1%	NT	NR			383
	N. reticulatus	(Blackwall, 1853)			6–25%	LC				382
	N. robustus	Lohmander, 1945			1–5%	LC	NS			384
	N. valentulus	Falconer, 1912			<1%	CR	NR			384
	Pellenes									**388**
	P. tripunctatus	(Walckenaer, 1802)			<1%	VU	NR			388
	Phlegra									**410**
	P. fasciata	(Hahn, 1826)			<1%	NT	NR			410

Common name	SPECIES	Authorities	Synonyms	ID	% 10km squares	IUCN	Nat.	Amber	Relevant legislation	Page
	Pseudeuophrys									**396**
	P. erratica	(Walckenaer, 1826)			1–5%	LC	NS			396
	P. lanigera	(Simon, 1871)			1–5%	LC				397
	P. obsoleta	(Simon, 1868)			<1%	LC	NS		S41 (Eng)	396
	Salticus									**380**
	S. cingulatus	(Panzer, 1797)			6–25%	LC				382
Common Zebra Spider	S. scenicus	(Clerck, 1757)			6–25%	LC				380
	S. zebraneus	(C. L. Koch, 1837)			6–25%	LC	NS			381
	Sibianor									**388**
	S. aurocinctus	(Ohlert, 1865)	[Bianor aurocinctus (Ohlert, 1865)]		1–5%	LC	NS			388
	Sitticus									**400**
	S. caricis	(Westring, 1861)			<1%	LC	NR		S41 (Eng); S42 (Wal)	404
Distinguished Jumping Spider	S. distinguendus	(Simon, 1968)			<1%	CR	NR		S41 (Eng)	400
	S. floricola	(C. L. Koch, 1837)			<1%	NT	NR			401
	S. inexpectus	Logunov & Kronestedt, 1997			1–5%	LC	NS			404
	S. pubescens	(Fabricius, 1775)			1–5%	LC				400
	S. saltator	(O. Pickard-Cambridge, 1868)			<1%	LC	NS	♦		401
	Synageles									**409**
	S. venator	(Lucas, 1836)			<1%	LC	NS			409
	Talavera									**398**
	T. aequipes	(O. Pickard-Cambridge, 1871)			1–5%	LC				399
	T. petrensis	(C. L. Koch, 1837)			<1%	NT	NR			398
	T. thorelli	(Kulczyński, 1891)			<1%	VU	NR			399
Spitting spiders	**SCYTODIDAE**									**100**
	Scytodes									**100**
Spitting Spider	S. thoracica	(Latreille, 1802)			1–5%	LC				100

Common name	SPECIES	Authorities	Synonyms	ID	% 10km squares	Status designations IUCN	Nat.	Amber	Relevant legislation	Page
Tubeweb spiders	**SEGESTRIIDAE**									**104**
	Segestria									104
	S. bavarica	C. L. Koch, 1843			<1%	LC	NR			105
	S. florentina	(Rossi, 1790)			1–5%	LC				104
	S. senoculata	(Linnaeus, 1758)			6–25%	LC				104
Huntsman spiders	**SPARASSIDAE**									**341**
	Micrommata									341
Green Huntsman Spider	*M. virescens*	(Clerck, 1757)			1–5%	LC	NS			341
Long-jawed orbweb spiders	**TETRAGNATHIDAE**									**165**
Cave spiders	*Meta*									175
	M. bourneti	Simon, 1922			1–5%	LC	NS			175
	M. menardi	(Latreille, 1804)			1–5%	LC				175
	Metellina									172
	M. mengei	(Blackwall, 1869)			26–50%	LC				173
	M. merianae	(Scopoli, 1763)			26–50%	LC				174
	M. segmentata	(Clerck, 1757)			26–50%	LC				172
	Pachygnatha									170
	P. clercki	Sundevall, 1823			26–50%	LC				170
	P. degeeri	Sundevall, 1830			26–50%	LC				172
	P. listeri	Sundevall, 1830			1–5%	LC				171
Stretch spiders	*Tetragnatha*									165
Common Stretch Spider	*T. extensa*	(Linnaeus, 1758)			26–50%	LC				165
	T. montana	Simon, 1874			26–50%	LC				167
	T. nigrita	Lendl, 1886			1–5%	LC				168
	T. obtusa	C. L. Koch, 1837			6–25%	LC				168
	T. pinicola	L. Koch, 1870			1–5%	LC				167
	T. striata	L. Koch, 1862			1–5%	LC				170

Common name	SPECIES	Synonyms	Authorities	ID	% 10km squares	IUCN	Nat.	Amber	Relevant legislation	Page
Comb-footed spiders	**THERIDIIDAE**									**120**
	Achaearanea									136
	A. lunata		(Clerck, 1757)		6–25%	LC				138
	A. riparia		(Blackwall, 1834)		<1%	LC	NS			138
	A. simulans		(Thorell, 1875)		6–25%	LC				136
	A. tepidariorum		(C. L. Koch, 1841)		1–5%	LC				136
	Anelosimus									134
	A. vittatus		(C. L. Koch, 1836)		6–25%	LC				134
	Coleosoma									159
	C. floridanum		Banks, 1900		<1%	NA				159
	Crustulina									128
	C. guttata		(Wider, 1834)		1–5%	LC				128
	C. sticta		(O. L. Pickard-Cambridge, 1861)		<1%	LC	NS			128
	Cryptachaea									139
	C. blattea		(Urquhart, 1886)		<1%	NA				139
	C. veruculata	[*Achaearanea veruculata* (Urquhart, 1885)]	(Urquhart, 1885)		<1%	NA				139
	Dipoena									124
	D. erythropus		(Simon, 1881)		<1%	VU	NR			126
	D. inornata		(O. Pickard-Cambridge, 1861)		<1%	LC	NS		S41 (Eng); S42 (Wal)	126
	D. melanogaster		(C. L. Koch, 1837)		<1%	EN	NR			124
	D. prona		(Menge, 1868)		<1%	EN	NR			127
	D. torva		(Thorell, 1875)		<1%	NT	NR		BDL (Sco)	125
	D. tristis		(Hahn, 1833)		<1%	LC	NS			125
	Enoplognatha									154
Scarce Candy-striped Spider	*E. latimana*		Hippa & Oksala, 1982		6–25%	LC				154
	E. mordax		(Thorell, 1875)		<1%	LC	NS			156
	E. oelandica		(Thorell, 1875)		<1%	CR	NR			157
Common Candy-striped Spider	*E. ovata*		(Clerck, 1757)		26–50%	LC				154

Common name	SPECIES	Authorities	Synonyms	ID	% 10km squares	IUCN	Nat.	Amber	Relevant legislation	Page
	E. tecta	(Keyserling, 1884)			<1%	VU	NR			156
	E. thoracica	(Hahn, 1833)			6–25%	LC				157
	Episinus									**120**
	E. angulatus	(Blackwall, 1836)			6–25%	LC				120
	E. maculipes	Cavanna, 1876			<1%	LC	NS			122
	E. truncatus	Latreille, 1809			1–5%	LC	NS			122
	Euryopis									**123**
	E. flavomaculata	(C. L. Koch, 1836)			1–5%	LC	NS	♦		123
	Kochiura									**135**
	K. aulica	(C. L. Koch, 1838)	[Anelosimus aulicus (C. L. Koch, 1838)]		1–5%	LC	NS			135
	Neottiura									**150**
	N. bimaculata	(Linnaeus, 1767)			26–50%	LC				150
	Paidiscura									**151**
	P. pallens	(Blackwall, 1834)			26–50%	LC				151
	Pholcomma									**158**
	P. gibbum	(Westring, 1851)			6–25%	LC				158
	Phylloneta									**140**
	P. impressa	(L. Koch, 1881)	[Theridion impressum L. Koch, 1881]		6–25%	LC				141
	P. sisyphia	(L. Koch, 1881)	[Theridion sisyphium (Clerck, 1757)]		26–50%	LC				140
	Platnickina									**148**
	P. tincta	(Walckenaer, 1802)	[Theridion tinctum (Walckenaer, 1802)]		6–25%	LC				148
	Robertus									**160**
	R. arundineti	(O. Pickard-Cambridge, 1871)			1–5%	LC				160
	R. insignis	O. Pickard-Cambridge, 1907			<1%	DD	NR			162
	R. lividus	(Blackwall, 1836)			26–50%	LC				160
	R. neglectus	(O. Pickard-Cambridge, 1871)			1–5%	LC	NS	♦		162
	R. scoticus	Jackson, 1914			<1%	CR	NR		BDL (Sco)	161

Common name	SPECIES	Synonyms	Authorities	ID	% 10km squares	IUCN	Nat.	Amber	Relevant legislation	Page
	Rugathodes									152
	R. bellicosus		(Simon, 1873)		<1%	LC	NR			153
	R. instabilis		(O. Pickard-Cambridge, 1871)		1–5%	LC	NS			152
	R. sexpunctatus		(Emerton, 1882)		<1%	NA				152
	Simitidion									149
	S. simile		(C. L. Koch, 1836)		1–5%	LC				149
False widow spiders	*Steatoda*									129
	S. albomaculata		(De Geer, 1778)		<1%	LC	NR			133
	S. bipunctata		(Linnaeus, 1758)		6–25%	LC				129
	S. grossa		(C. L. Koch, 1838)		6–25%	LC				130
Noble False Widow Spider	S. nobilis		(Thorell, 1875)		6–25%	LC				130
	S. phalerata		(Panzer, 1801)		1–5%	LC				131
	S. triangulosa		(Walckenaer, 1802)		<1%	NA				131
	Theonoe									158
	T. minutissima		(O. Pickard-Cambridge, 1879)		1–5%	LC				158
	Theridion									142
	T. blackwalli		O. Pickard-Cambridge, 1871		1–5%	LC	NS			144
	T. familiare		O. Pickard-Cambridge, 1871		<1%	LC	NS			147
	T. hannoniae		Denis, 1944		<1%	NA				145
	T. hemerobium		Simon, 1914		1–5%	NA	NS			144
	T. melanurum		Hahn, 1831		6–25%	LC				146
	T. mystaceum		L. Koch, 1870		6–25%	LC				146
	T. pictum		(Walckenaer, 1802)		1–5%	LC				142
	T. pinastri		L. Koch, 1872		<1%	LC	NS			145
	T. varians		Hahn, 1833		6–25%	LC				142
Ray's spiders	**THERIDIOSOMATIDAE**									163
	Theridiosoma									163
Ray's Spider	T. gemmosum		(L. Koch, 1877)		1–5%	LC	NS			163

Common name	SPECIES	Authorities	Synonyms	ID	% 10km squares	Status designations			Relevant legislation	Page
						IUCN	Nat.	Amber		
Crab spiders	**THOMISIDAE**									**357**
	Diaea									357
Green Crab Spider	*D. dorsata*	(Fabricius, 1777)			6–25%	LC				360
	Misumena									359
	M. vatia	(Clerck, 1757)			6–25%	LC				359
	Ozyptila									371
	O. atomaria	(Panzer, 1801)			6–25%	LC				372
	O. blackwalli	Simon, 1875			<1%	EN	NR			378
	O. brevipes	(Hahn, 1826)			1–5%	LC				374
	O. nigrita	(Thorell, 1875)			<1%	LC	NS		S41 (Eng)	376
	O. praticola	(C. L. Koch, 1837)			6–25%	LC				371
	O. pullata	(Thorell, 1875)			<1%	VU	NR			378
	O. sanctuaria	(O. Pickard-Cambridge, 1871)			1–5%	LC				374
	O. scabricula	(Westring, 1851)			<1%	LC	NS			376
	O. simplex	(O. Pickard-Cambridge, 1862)			1–5%	LC				373
	O. trux	(Blackwall, 1846)			6–25%	LC				372
	Pistius									361
	P. truncatus	(Pallas, 1772)			<1%	CR	NR			361
	Synema									379
	S. globosum	(Fabricius, 1775)			<1%	NA				379
	Thomisus									357
	T. onustus	Walckenaer, 1806			<1%	LC	NS			357
	Xysticus									362
	X. acerbus	Thorell, 1872			<1%	LC	NR			367
	X. audax	(Schrank, 1803)			1–5%	LC				363
	X. bifasciatus	C. L. Koch, 1837			1–5%	LC	NS	◆		366
	X. cristatus	(Clerck, 1757)			26–50%	LC				362
	X. erraticus	(Blackwall, 1834)			6–25%	LC				368
	X. kochi	Thorell, 1872			6–25%	LC				362

Common name	SPECIES	Synonyms	Authorities	ID	% 10km squares	IUCN	Nat.	Amber	Relevant legislation	Page
	X. lanio		C. L. Koch, 1835		1–5%	LC				368
	X. luctator		L. Koch, 1870		<1%	EN	NR			367
	X. luctuosus		(Blackwall, 1836)		<1%	EN	NR			366
	X. robustus		(Hahn, 1832)		<1%	EN	NR			369
	X. sabulosus		(Hahn, 1832)		<1%	LC	NS	◆		369
	X. ulmi		(Hahn, 1831)		6–25%	LC				363
Cribellate orbweb spiders — ULOBORIDAE										**116**
	Hyptiotes									**118**
Triangle Spider	H. paradoxus		(C. L. Koch, 1834)		<1%	LC	NS			118
	Uloborus									**116**
	U. plumipes		Lucas, 1846		6–25%	NA				117
	U. walckenaerius		Latreille, 1806		<1%	NT	NR			116
Ant-hunting spiders — ZODARIIDAE										**308**
Ant spiders	Zodarion									**308**
	Z. fuscum		(Simon, 1870)		<1%	VU	NR			310
	Z. italicum		(Canestrini, 1868)		1–5%	LC	NS			308
	Z. rubidum		Simon, 1914		<1%	NA	NR			309
	Z. vicinum		Denis, 1935		<1%	VU	NR			310
Ghost spiders — ZORIDAE										**337**
	Zora									**337**
	Z. armillata		Simon, 1878		<1%	CR	NR			339
	Z. nemoralis		(Blackwall, 1861)		<1%	VU	NR			338
	Z. silvestris		Kulczynski, 1897		<1%	CR	NR			339
	Z. spinimana		(Sundevall, 1833)		6–25%	LC				337
False wolf spiders — ZOROPSIDAE										**340**
	Zoropsis									**340**
	Z. spinimana		(Dufour, 1820)		<1%	NA				340

Further reading and useful websites

IDENTIFICATION

BEE, L. & LEWINGTON, R. 2002. *A guide to house and garden spiders*. Fold-out chart. Shrewsbury: Field Studies Council.
A pictorial introduction to 40 species of spiders common in and around the home.

JONES-WALTERS, L. M. 1989. *Keys to the families of British spiders*. AIDGAP. Shrewsbury: Field Studies Council.
A useful addition to the guides in this book when first starting out with spiders, helping with placing a spider in the correct family from general appearance – an essential first step in naming the species. However, some of the characters used require microscopic examination.

LOCKET, G. H. & MILLIDGE, A. F. 1951/1953. *British spiders. Vols. 1, 2* and LOCKET, G. H., MILLIDGE, A. F. & MERRETT, P. 1974. *Vol. 3*. London: Ray Society.
Although out of print, a CD version or download comprising all three volumes is published by Pisces Conservation (www.piscesconservation.com/cube). These volumes were the standard identification work for those wishing to pursue a serious interest in the identification of British spiders before the publication of Roberts (see below). Although the illustrations of diagnostic features are not as detailed as in Roberts, and there have been a number of additions to the British fauna since publication, there is an enormous amount of useful information in the text.

ROBERTS, M. J. 1993. T*he spiders of Great Britain and Ireland*. 2-part Compact edition. Colchester: Harley Books - now published by Brill, Leiden.
Softback. Part 1 text, Part 2 colour plates. The standard current identification works for those aspiring to identify all of Britain's spiders to species level, providing the drawings of the male pedipalps and female epigynes needed for working with a microscope. The colour illustrations are useful with preserved specimens, although less so with living spiders.

ROBERTS, M. J. 1995. *Collins field guide: spiders of Britain and northern Europe*. London: HarperCollins.
This single-volume guide goes well beyond the identification that is possible in the field. It includes exquisite colour plates, together with drawings of all the pedipalps and epigynes. The species coverage differs from the two-volume Roberts in that a small number of additional species from adjacent continental Europe are also featured, but only around 40 money spiders (Linyphiidae) are included.

BIOLOGY

FOELIX, R. 2011. *Biology of spiders*. 3rd edition. New York: Oxford University Press.
The only detailed and comprehensive account of all aspects of spider biology, from anatomy to behaviour. Essential reading for a more advanced understanding of the group.

HERBERSTEIN, M. H. (Ed.). 2011. *Spider behaviour: flexibility and versatility*. Cambridge: Cambridge University Press.
An up-to-date and readable compendium covering academic research on the amazing variety and flexibility of spider behaviours.

NENTWIG, W. 2013. *Spider ecophysiology*. Heidelberg: Springer.
A compendium of the latest research combining functional and evolutionary aspects of morphology, physiology, biochemistry and molecular biology with ecology.

WISE, D. H. 1993. *Spiders in ecological webs*. Cambridge: Cambridge University Press.
Comprehensive coverage of all aspects of spider ecology but although useful as a source of information, the somewhat academic approach does not make for easy reading.

GENERAL

BECCALONI, J. 2009. *Arachnids*. London: Natural History Museum.
An excellent coverage of all arachnid families, with stunning photographs.

BRISTOWE, W. S. 1958. *The world of spiders* (New Naturalist no. 38), London: Collins.
This remains probably the best introduction to spiders for the beginner and conveys brilliantly the sheer fascination of this diverse group of organisms. Essential reading which is well worth tracking down through your local library or purchasing through a print-on-demand service from HarperCollins (www. newnaturalists. com/category/Print+on+Demand). Many of the species' scientific names are, however, now out-of-date.

BRUNETTA, L. & CRAIG, C. L. 2010. *Spider silk*. Yale: Yale University Press.
The subtitle of this popular science text 'evolution and 400 million years of spinning, waiting, snagging, and mating' covers its contents – all about spider silk.

KELLY, K. 2009. *Spiders: learning to love them*. Crows Nest, NSW: Jacana Books – Allen & Unwin.
A general introduction to spiders from an Australian science writer through her journey from arachnophobia to arachnophilia. A good read, particularly for anyone wanting to make the same journey.

MERRETT, P., RUSSELL-SMITH, A. & HARVEY, P. 2014. A revised checklist of British spiders. *Arachnology* 16: 134–144.
Precis available from britishspiders.org.uk/wiki2015/images/e/eb/Spider_Checklist_2014.pdf

RUSSELL-SMITH, A., SMITH, H. & OXFORD, G. (Eds) 2015. *Arachnologists' handbook*. Second edition (revised). York: British Arachnological Society.
The British Arachnological Society's own, wide-ranging compendium of arachnological information; everything an aspiring arachnologist needs to know!

USEFUL WEBSITES

IDENTIFICATION GUIDANCE
www.araneae.unibe.ch
Keys to families and to Linyphiidae, species accounts, maps, images and drawings of critical identification features for European spider species, many of which occur in Britain.

www.ednieuw.home.xs4all.nl/Spiders/spidhome.htm
Information, images and line drawings of critical features of north-west European spiders.

www.jorgenlissner.dk
Species accounts, distributions and images of European spiders, including macro photographs of critical features.

www.pavouci-cz.eu
In situ images of many European spider species.

http://wiki.spinnen-forum.de/index.php?title=Hauptseite
Images, species accounts and reference lists for all European arachnid groups.

www.eurospiders.com
Good basic information on spiders, plus images and video footage of spider behaviours.

srs.britishspiders.org.uk/portal.php/p/Difficult+species
Illustrated accounts based on microscopic examination, to separate difficult British species.

HELP WITH IDENTIFICATION OF SUBMITTED PHOTOGRAPHS
Although many species of British spider cannot be definitively identified from photographs (see page 9), high quality images can be submitted to the following websites for an expert opinion.

www.facebook.com/groups/BritishSpiderIdentification
A forum for discussion and identification, particularly of commoner species.

srs.britishspiders.org.uk/portal.php (the British Arachnological Society's Spider Recording Scheme)
High quality images with full record details can be submitted via the 'Contact Us' page.

The British Arachnological Society

The British Arachnological Society (BAS) is Britain's only charity dedicated exclusively to spiders and their relatives – the arachnids. It uses science and education to advance the wider understanding and appreciation of arachnids and to promote their conservation. Its main focus is Britain's spiders, together with its 27 harvestman and 27 false scorpion (pseudoscorpion) species.

ADVANCING ARACHNOLOGY

The BAS has a strong commitment to providing accurate information to the public on these very important, fascinating, but often misrepresented animals. It encourages active participation in arachnology through the provision of information, training and mentoring to anyone wanting to become more involved in identification, recording or studying the biology of this group. As well as joining a growing community of arachnologists, BAS members are kept in touch through its triannual Newsletter and international scientific journal *Arachnology*, an online discussion forum and benefit from a very extensive library of arachnological books and scientific papers.

The BAS runs the national recording schemes for spiders (see *page 422*) and harvestmen (srs.britishspiders.org.uk/portal.php/p/Harvestmen), and supports the scheme for false scorpions (www.chelifer.com/?page_id=81), providing up-to-date information on the distributions of these species and contributing to our knowledge of their biology and habitat requirements. These recording schemes, together with targeted surveys and research, help to underpin arachnid conservation in Britain, providing impartial scientific information and expert advice to statutory and non-governmental conservation organisations as well as to conservation practitioners and the public.

The BAS owes its origins to a small band of enthusiasts who formed the Flatford Mill Spider Group (in Suffolk) in 1958. By 1963 the expanding group registered as a charity and became the British Arachnological Society. Although it has a growing membership, and with this increasing demands for information, advice and training, the Society remains an entirely voluntary organisation dependent upon the generosity of members and active volunteers, supported by donors and grant-givers. More information can be found on spiders and all aspects of the Society on its website www.britishspiders.org.uk and social media @BritishSpiders and www.facebook.com/BritishSpiders.

Acknowledgements and photographic credits

This book is a successor to the ground-breaking (but long out of print) photographic guide to British spiders by Dick Jones and seeks to complement the excellent identification works currently available by Mike Roberts (*page 463*). We are grateful to many friends and colleagues in the British Arachnological Society for their support, and particularly to Tony Russell-Smith and Peter Merrett, together with Peter Harvey, Chris Holland, Paul Lee, Mike Davidson, Richard Gallon and Peter Smithers, for their invaluable comments on the manuscript. We also thank Rob Still and Andy Swash of **WILD***Guides* for their enthusiasm, expertise and support throughout the production process. Chris and Judith Gibson, Gill Swash, Rachel and Anya Still and Brian Clews provided invaluable help with various stages of the manuscript. The authors would like to give special thanks for the understanding shown by their long-suffering families during the production of this book.

Peter Harvey, the Spider Recording Scheme National Organiser, kindly supplied the data used to produce the distribution maps and adult phenology charts.

The production of this book would not have been possible without the generous contribution of the many photographers who kindly supplied their images. Many more photographs were offered for the project than it was possible to include and we would like to thank all those who took the time and trouble to submit their images, and to recognize the skill, time and patience behind each one of them. In total, 720 images are featured, representing the work of 88 photographers: Ingrid Altmann; Martin Askins; Chris Bentley; Trine Bilde; John Bingham; Andrew Bloomfield; Richard Burkmar; Chris Cathrine; Jonathan Coddington; Martin Cooper; Chris Court; Steve Covey; Ian Cross; Mike Davidson; Pascal Dubois; Steven Falk; Bryan Formstone; Anastasia Fox-Cavendish; Marion Friedrich; Richard Gallon; Philippe Garcelon; Gemma Gates; Will George; Arno Grabolle; Hilary Grant; Mark Gurney; Clive Hambler; Peter Harvey; Horst Helwig; Greg Hitchcock; Mark Horton; Mandy Howe; Harald Hoyer; Ian Hughes; Nik Hunt; Alex Hyde; Evan Jones; Anna Jordan; Joanne Joyce; Steve Kerr; Roger Key; Tone Killick; Jens Kirkeby; Holger Krisp; Jim Lindsay; Jorgen Lissner; Nick Loven; Graeme Lyons; Ed Marshall; John Maxwell; Derek Mayes; Sean McCann; Kevin McGee; John Murphy; Steve Murray; Allan Neilson; Peter Nicholson; Ed Nieuwenhuys; Vincent Oates; Pierre Oger; Geoff Oxford; Mauro Paschetta; Trevor & Dilys Pendleton; Didier Petot; Walter Pflieger; Josh Phangurha; Neil Phillips; Shaun Poland; Cliff Raby; Arthur Rivett; Wolfgang Rutkies; Dragiša Savić; Michael Schäfer; Jurgen Scharfy; Helen Smith; Peter Smithers; Stefan Sollfors; Chris Spilling; Aloysius Staudt; Rose Stephens; Dominik Stodulski; Alan Thornhill; Fritz Vollrath and John Walters.

Special mention must go to John Bingham, Steven Falk, Richard Gallon, Arno Grabolle, Peter Harvey, Nik Hunt, Evan Jones, Jorgen Lissner, Trevor & Dilys Pendleton and Michael Schäfer, each of whom has 20 or more of their images included in this book. Evan Jones supplied, at relatively short notice, the majority of images for the *Guide to spider families*.

Every photograph published in the book is listed in this section, together with the photographer's name. Two images have been reproduced under the terms of the Creative Commons Attribution-ShareAlike 3.0 Unported license; these are indicated by "/CC" after the photographer's name.

Where appropriate, the following codes are used to indicate the position of the image concerned: (T) = top; (M) = middle; (B) = bottom; (R) = right; (H) = higher; (L) = lower; (R) = right; (C) = centre; (L) = left.

Cover: ♀ **Jumping spider** *Evarcha arcuata* [Evan Jones].

Title page: Orb web [Alex Hyde].

INTRODUCTION

p4: ATYPIDAE [Evan Jones]; **SCYTODIDAE** [Martin Cooper]; **PHOLCIDAE** [Evan Jones]; **SEGESTRIIDAE** [Evan Jones]; **DYSDERIDAE** [Evan Jones]; **OONOPIDAE** [Evan Jones]; **MIMETIDAE** [Evan Jones]; **ERESIDAE** [Ian Hughes]; **OECOBIIDAE** [John Maxwell]; **ULOBORIDAE** [Chris Court]; **NESTICIDAE** [Evan Jones]; **THERIDIIDAE** [Evan Jones]; **THERIDIOSOMATIDAE** [Evan Jones]; **MYSMENIDAE** [Richard Gallon]; **TETRAGNATHIDAE** [Evan Jones]; **ARANEIDAE** [Evan Jones]; **LYCOSIDAE** [Evan Jones]. **p5: PISAURIDAE** [Evan Jones]; **OXYOPIDAE** [Evan Jones]; **AGELENIDAE** [Evan Jones]; **HAHNIIDAE** [Evan Jones]; **DICTYNIDAE** [Evan Jones]; **CYBAEIDAE** [Evan Jones]; **AMAUROBIIDAE** [Evan Jones]; **LIOCRANIDAE** [Evan Jones]; **ANYPHAENIDAE** [Evan Jones]; **CORINNIDAE** [Stefan Sollfors]; **CLUBIONIDAE** [Evan Jones]; **ZODARIIDAE** [Evan Jones]; **GNAPHOSIDAE** [Evan Jones]; **ZORIDAE** [Evan Jones]; **ZOROPSIDAE** [Geoff Oxford]; **SPARASSIDAE** [Evan Jones]; **PHILODROMIDAE** [Evan Jones]; **THOMISIDAE** [Evan Jones]; **SALTICIDAE** [Evan Jones]; **LINYPHIIDAE** [Evan Jones]. **p6:** *Argiope bruennichi* [Vincent Oates]. **p8: webs** [Geoff Oxford]. **p10:** *Tegenaria saeva* [Geoff Oxford]. **p12:** *Ixodes ricinus* [Holger Krisp]; *Trombidium holosericeum* [Dominik Stodulski]. **p13: Knotty Shining Claw** [Peter Nicholson]; **spider** [John Bingham]; **harvestman** [Geoff Oxford]; **cranefly** [Geoff Oxford]. **pp14–15:** *Tegenaria gigantea* (ALL) [Geoff Oxford]. **p16: book lung** [Evan Jones]. **p17:** (INSET TR) showing **scutum** [Peter Harvey]; (ALL OTHERS) [Evan Jones]. **p20: recurved eye row** [Geoff Oxford]. **p21: spiracles** [Geoff Oxford]. **p22:** *Araneus diadematus* (BOTH) [Geoff Oxford]. **p23: cribellum** and **calamistrum** (BOTH) [Geoff Oxford]; *Araneus diadematus* [Sean McCann]. **p24: orb web** [Geoff Oxford]; **glue droplets** (INSET) [Fritz Vollrath]. **p25:** *Araneus diadematus* [Geoff Oxford]. **p27:** *Argyroneta aquatica* [Neil Phillips]. **p28:** *Larinioides cornutus* [Geoff Oxford]. **p29:** *Dolomedes plantarius* [Anna Jordan]. **p30:** *Aelurillus v-insignitus* [Horst Helwig]; *Metellina segmentata* [Geoff Oxford]. **p31:** *Evarca arcuata* [Evan Jones]; *Pisaura mirabilis* [Trine Bilde]. **p32:** *Tetragnatha montana* [Ed Nieuwenhuys]; *Enoplognatha ovata* [Geoff Oxford]. **p33: egg-sac** [Geoff Oxford]. **p34:** *Phylloneta sisyphia* [John Murphy]. **p35:** *Neoscona adienta* [Tone Killick]; *Tegenaria saeva* [Geoff Oxford]. **p36: spider prior to ballooning** (TL) [Rose Stephens]; **spider raising legs** (TR) [Alex Hyde]. **p37: gossamer** [Joanne Joyce]. **p39:** *Enoplognatha ovata* **with mites** (TL) [Lightwriter1949 / Alamy Stock Photo]; *Neriene peltata* (TR) [Geoff Oxford]; **spider infected with** *Cordyceps* **fungus** (ML) [Peter Smithers]; *Zygiella x-notata* **eggs** (MR) [Geoff Oxford]; **spider-hunting wasp** (B) [Wolfgang Rutkies]. **p40:** *Ero aphana* (TL) [Tone Killick]; *Theridion melanurum* (TR) [Hilary Grant]; *Misumena vatia* (ML) [Alex Hyde]; **excretory products** (MR) [Geoff Oxford]; **caught prey** (B) [Sean McCann]. **p41:** *Argiope bruennichi* [Josh Phangurha]. **p42: food remains:** *Tegenaria saeva* [Geoff Oxford]; *Misumena vatia* [Stu's Images/CC CC BY-SA 3.0 (http://creativecommons.org/licenses/by-sa/3.0), via Wikimedia Commons]. **p43:** *Araneus quadratus* (BL) [Geoff Oxford]; (BC) [Helen Smith]; (BR) [Geoff Oxford]. **p45:** *Tegenaria saeva* [Geoff Oxford]. **p47:** *Textrix denticulata* [Derek Mayes]. **p48: using a hand lens** [Geoff Oxford]; **spi-pot** [Geoff Oxford]. **p49: pooter** (BOTH) [Geoff Oxford]. **p50: sweep net** [Geoff Oxford]. **p51: beating** [Peter Smithers]. **p52: sweep netting** [Roger Key]. **p53: 'fishing' techniques** (BOTH) [Geoff Oxford]; **pitfall trap** [Geoff Oxford].

GUIDE TO SPIDER FAMILIES

p54: OONOPIDAE: (BOTH) [Evan Jones]. **p55: SCYTODIDAE: carapace** (INSET) [Nik Hunt]; **spider** (TR) [Martin Cooper]. **DYSDERIDAE:** (BOTH) [Evan Jones]. **p56: SEGESTRIIDAE: carapace** (INSET) [Richard Gallon]; **spider** (TR) [Evan Jones]. **MYSMENIDAE:** (BOTH) [Richard Gallon]. **p57: OECOBIIDAE: eyes** (INSET) [Geoff Oxford]; **spider** (TR) [John Maxwell]. **ZODARIIDAE:** (BOTH) [Evan Jones]. **p58: PHOLCIDAE: carapace** (INSET) [Arno Grabolle]; **spider** (TR) [Evan Jones]; **ATYPIDAE:** (BOTH) [Steven Falk]. **p59: HAHNIIDAE: carapace** (INSET: TL) [Arno Grabolle]; **spinnerets** (INSET: TC) [Evan Jones]; **spider** (TR) [Evan Jones]. **DICTYNIDAE:** *Nigma puella* (INSET: BL) [Philippe Garcelon]; *Lathys humilis* (BR) [Evan Jones]. **p60: THERIDIIDAE:** (BOTH) [Evan Jones]. **CORINNIDAE:** (BOTH) [Stefan Sollfors]. **p61: THERIDIOSOMATIDAE:** (BOTH) [Evan Jones]. **MIMETIDAE:** *Ero cambridgei*: **carapace** (INSET: MC) [Evan Jones]; **spider** (MR) [Mark Gurney]; *Ero tuberculata* (BL) [Evan Jones]. **p62: THOMISIDAE:** (BOTH) [Evan Jones]. **NESTICIDAE:** (BOTH) [Evan Jones]. **p63: ARANEIDAE:** *Araniella* sp. **carapace** (INSET) [John Bingham]; *Larinioides cornutus* (TR) [Evan Jones]. **ULOBORIDAE:** *Uloborus plumipes* [Trevor & Dilys Pendleton]; (INSET: BL) [Stefan Sollfors]. **p64: LIOCRANIDAE:** (BOTH) [Evan Jones]. **LINYPHIIDAE:** (BOTH) [Evan Jones]. **p65: CLUBIONIDAE:** (BOTH) [Evan Jones]. **PHILODROMIDAE:** (BOTH) [Evan Jones]. **p66: TETRAGNATHIDAE:** *Metellina* sp. **carapace** (INSET) [Arthur Rivett]; *Tetragnatha obtusa* [Evan Jones]. **AMAUROBIIDAE:** (BOTH) [Evan Jones]. **p67: ANYPHAENIDAE:** (BOTH) [Evan Jones]. **GNAPHOSIDAE:** (BOTH) [Evan Jones]. **p68: SPARASSIDAE:** (BOTH) [Evan Jones]. **AGELENIDAE:** (BOTH) [Evan Jones]. **p69: CYBAEIDAE:** (BOTH) [Evan Jones]. **ZORIDAE:** (BOTH) [Evan Jones]. **p70: ZOROPSIDAE:** (BOTH) [Geoff Oxford]. **SALTICIDAE:** (BOTH) [Evan Jones]. **p71: LYCOSIDAE:** (BOTH) [Evan Jones]. **OXYOPIDAE:** (BOTH) [Evan Jones]. **p72: ERESIDAE: male** [Ed Nieuwenhuys]; **female** [Ian Hughes]. **PISAURIDAE:** (BOTH) [Evan Jones].

GUIDE TO WEBS

p73: Tent: (INSET: MR) [Helen Smith]; (B) [Geoff Oxford]. **p74: Radial:** [Mike Davidson]. **Funnel:** [Geoff Oxford]. **p75: Diving bell:** [Neil Phillips]. **Lace:** [Geoff Oxford]. **p76: Tube: AMAUROBIIDAE:** [Richard Gallon]; **AGELENIDAE:** [Geoff Oxford]. **p77: Tube: ERESIDAE:** [Ian Hughes]; **ATYPIDAE:** [Nik Hunt]. **p78: Orb: TETRAGNATHIDAE:** [Chris Cathrine]. **p79: Orb: ARANEIDAE:** [Geoff Oxford]. **p80: Orb: ULOBORIDAE:** [Nik Hunt]; **THERIDIOSOMATIDAE:** [Jonathan Coddington]. **p81: Sheet: LINYPHIIDAE:** [Helen Smith]; **HAHNIIDAE:** [Sean McCann]. **p82: Tangled: PHOLCIDAE:** [Geoff Oxford]; **DICTYNIDAE:** [Geoff Oxford]. **p83: Tangled:** (T) [Peter Smithers]; (B) [Geoff Oxford].

GUIDE TO EGG-SACS

p84: Inside domestic buildings: *Pholcus phalangioides* [Geoff Oxford]; *Scytodes thoracica* [Nik Hunt]. **p85: Inside domestic buildings:** *Zygiella x-notata* (BOTH) [Geoff Oxford]; *Tegenaria* (BOTH) [Geoff Oxford]; *Araneus diadematus* [Geoff Oxford]; *Scotophaeus blackwalli* [Mandy Howe]. **p86: Inside greenhouses** *etc.*: *Achaearanea tepidariorum* [Geoff Oxford]; *Uloborus plumipes* [Geoff Oxford]. **In caves** *etc.*: *Meta menardi* [Geoff Oxford]; *Nesticus cellulanus* [Evan Jones]. **p87: Under wood** *etc.*: *Drassodes* [Martin Askins]; *Coelotes* [Steve Murray]; *Zelotes etc.* [John Bingham]; *Rugathodes bellicosus* [Mike Davidson]. **p88: Under wood** *etc.*: *Tegenaria agrestis* (TL) [Mandy Howe]; (TR) [Geoff Oxford]. **Attached to vegetation (unstalked):** *Argiope bruennichi* [Tempaccount01 at English Wikipedia/CC]; *Tetragnatha* [Geoff Oxford]. **p89: Attached to vegetation (unstalked):** *Episinus* [Tone Killick]; *Philodromus* [Alex Hyde]; *Paidiscura pallens* [Geoff Oxford]. **p90: Attached to vegetation (stalked):** *Theridiosoma gemmosum* [Evan Jones]; *Ero* (L) [Geoff Oxford], (R) [Gemma Gates]; *Agroeca brunnea* [John Bingham], *A. proxima* [Mike Davidson]. **p91: Within rolled/folded leaves:** (ALL) [Geoff Oxford]. **p92: Within webs/retreats in vegetation:** *Phylloneta sisyphia* and *P. impressa* [Jim Lindsay]; (OTHERS) [Geoff Oxford]. **p93: Within webs/retreats in vegetation:** *Cheiracanthium erraticum* [Martin Askins]; *Micrommata virescens* [Mauro Paschetta]; *Agelena labyrinthica* (BOTH) [Geoff Oxford]. **p94: On vegetation or bare ground:** *Neottiura bimaculata* [Ingrid Altmann]; *Pirata* [Helen Smith]; *Rugathodes sexpunctatus* [Mike Davidson]; *R. instabilis* [Jorgen Lissner]; *Pardosa etc.* [Richard Gallon]. **p95: On vegetation or bare ground:** *Pisaura mirabilis* [Mike Davidson]; *Dolomedes* [Helen Smith].

SPECIES ACCOUNTS

ATYPIDAE: p98: *Atypus affinis* [Evan Jones]. **p99:** *Atypus affinis* (L) [Steven Falk]; (B) [Andrew Bloomfield].

SCYTODIDAE: p100: *Scytodes thoracica* [Greg Hitchcock].

PHOLCIDAE: p101: *Pholcus phalangioides* [Richard Gallon]. **p102:** *Psilochorus simoni* [Arno Grabolle]. **p103:** *Holocnemus pluchei* [Peter Harvey].

SEGESTRIIDAE: p105: *Segestria bavarica* [Richard Gallon]; *Segestria senoculata* [Nik Hunt]; *Segestria florentina:* **carapace** (INSET) [Nik Hunt], **spider** [Steven Falk].

DYSDERIDAE: p107: *Dysdera crocata* **spider** [Richard Gallon], **leg** (INSET) [Geoff Oxford]; *Dysdera* **chelicerae** (INSET) [Cliff Raby]; *Harpactea hombergi* [Richard Gallon].

OONOPIDAE: p109: *Oonops domesticus* [John Bingham].

MIMETIDAE: p111: *Ero* **abdomen** (INSET) [Mark Gurney]; *Ero furcata* (BOXED: TR) [Trevor & Dilys Pendleton]; *Ero cambridgei* (BL) [Mark Gurney], (BOXED: BR) [Bryan Formstone]. **p113:** *Ero* **abdomen** (INSET) and *Ero aphana* (BOXED: TR) (BOTH) [Trevor & Dilys Pendleton]; *Ero tuberculata* [John Walters].

ERESIDAE: p114: *Eresus sandaliatus* (BOTH) [Ian Hughes].

OECOBIIDAE: p115: *Oecobius navus* [Evan Jones].

ULOBORIDAE: p116: *Uloborus walckenaerius* [Arno Grabolle]. **p117:** *Uloborus walckenaerius* [Trevor & Dilys Pendleton]. **p118:** *Hyptiotes paradoxus* **male and female** [Evan Jones]; **web illustration** [Robert Still].

NESTICIDAE: p119: *Nesticus cellulanus* [Richard Gallon]; (INSET) [Arno Grabolle].

THERIDIIDAE: p121: *Episinus truncatus* (BOTH) [Mauro Paschetta]; *Episinus angulatus* (BOTH) [John Bingham]; *Episinus maculipes* (BOTH) [Philippe Garcelon]. **p123:** *Euryopis flavomaculata* [Arno Grabolle]. **p124:** *Dipoena melanogaster* **male** [Jorgen Lissner]; **female** [Arno Grabolle]. **p125:** *Dipoena torva* [Walter Pflieger]. **p129:** *Crustulina guttata* [Trevor & Dilys Pendleton]; *Crustulina sticta* (INSET) [Jorgen Lissner]. **p131:** *Steatoda triangulosa* [Philippe Garcelon]. **p132:** *Steatoda grossa* (MAIN IMAGE) [Steven Falk], (INSET) [Anastasia Fox-Cavendish]; *Steatoda nobilis* (MAIN IMAGE) [Steven Falk], (INSET) [Peter Harvey].

p133: *Steatoda bipunctata* [Nik Hunt]; *Steatoda triangulosa* [Peter Harvey]; *Steatoda albomaculata* [Arno Grabolle]; *Steatoda phalerata* [Peter Harvey]. **p134:** *Anelosimus vittatus* (BOTH) [Tone Killick]; *Kochiura aulica* (INSET) [Philippe Garcelon]. **p135:** *Kochiura aulica* (BL) [Philippe Garcelon]; (BR) [Peter Harvey]. **p137:** *Achaearanea lunata* [Trevor & Dilys Pendleton]; *Achaearanea riparia* [Jorgen Lissner]; *Achaearanea simulans* [Nik Hunt]; *Achaearanea tepidariorum* [Steven Falk]. **p139:** *Cryptachaea blattea* **spider** [Steve Kerr], **tubercle** (INSET) [Tone Killick]. **p140:** *Phylloneta sisyphia* [Nik Hunt]; **abdomen illustrations** [Robert Still]. **p141:** *Phylloneta impressa* [Trevor & Dilys Pendleton]. **p143:** *Theridion pictum* [Nick Loven]; *Theridion hemerobium* [Martin Askins]; *Theridion varians* [Trevor & Dilys Pendleton]; *Theridion blackwalli* (BOTH) [Trevor & Dilys Pendleton]; *Theridion hannoniae* [Peter Harvey]; *Theridion pinastri* [Peter Harvey]. **p147:** *Theridion familiare* [Pierre Oger]; *Theridion mystaceum* [Trevor & Dilys Pendleton]; *Theridion melanurum* [Trevor & Dilys Pendleton]. **p148:** *Platnickina tincta* [Trevor & Dilys Pendleton]. **p149:** *Simitidion simile* [Jorgen Lissner]. **p150:** *Neottiura bimaculata* [Trevor & Dilys Pendleton]. **p151:** *Paidiscura pallens* (BOTH) [Trevor & Dilys Pendleton]. **p153:** *Rugathodes sexpunctatus* (BOTH) [Mike Davidson]; *Rugathodes instabilis* [Jorgen Lissner]; *Rugathodes bellicosus* [Richard Gallon]. **p155:** *Enoplognatha ovata* (ALL) [Geoff Oxford]; *Enoplognatha latimana* **yellow** (T) [Jorgen Lissner]; (OTHERS) [Geoff Oxford]. **p155:** *Enoplognatha mordax* [Chris Bentley]. **p157:** *Enoplognatha thoracica* [Arno Grabolle]. **p159:** *Pholcomma gibbum* [Arno Grabolle]; *Theonoe minutissima* [Arno Grabolle]; *Coleosoma floridanum* (BOTH) [Jorgen Lissner]. **p160:** *Robertus* **leg** [Arno Grabolle]; **linyphiid leg** [Evan Jones]. **p161:** *Robertus scoticus* [Jorgen Lissner]; *Robertus arundineti* [Arno Grabolle]; *Robertus lividus* [Trevor & Dilys Pendleton].

THERIDIOSOMATIDAE: **p163:** *Theridiosoma gemmosum* [Philippe Garcelon].

MYSMENIDAE: **p164:** *Trogloneta granulum* (BOTH) [Richard Gallon].

TETRAGNATHIDAE: **p165:** *Tetragnatha* [Trevor & Dilys Pendleton]. **p166:** *Tetragnatha montana* [Trevor & Dilys Pendleton]; *Tetragnatha extensa* [Trevor & Dilys Pendleton]. **p167:** *Tetragnatha pinicola* [Peter Harvey]; **abdomen illustrations** [Robert Still]. **p169:** *Tetragnatha obtusa* [Trevor & Dilys Pendleton]; *Tetragnatha nigrita* [Trevor & Dilys Pendleton]; *Tetragnatha striata* **male** [Mike Davidson], **female** [Andrew Bloomfield]. **p171:** *Pachygnatha listeri* **male** [Peter Harvey], **female** [Jorgen Lissner]; *Pachygnatha clerki* [Trevor & Dilys Pendleton]; *Pachygnatha degeeri* [Trevor & Dilys Pendleton]. **p173:** *Metellina mengei* [Trevor & Dilys Pendleton]; *Metellina* **sp. carapace** (INSET) [Arthur Rivett]; *Metellina segmentata* [Trevor & Dilys Pendleton]. **p174:** *Metellina merianae* (BOTH) [Geoff Oxford]. **p176:** *Meta bourneti* [Steven Falk]; *Meta menardi* [Trevor & Dilys Pendleton].

ARANEIDAE: **p179:** *Araneus quadratus* [Steven Falk]; *Araneus angulatus* [Shaun Poland]; *Araneus diadematus* [Steven Falk]. **p180:** *Araneus sturmi* [Steven Falk]; *Araneus triguttatus* [Peter Harvey]. **p181:** *Araneus alsine* [John Bingham]. **p182:** *Araneus marmoreus* (ALL) [Trevor & Dilys Pendleton]. **p183:** *Larinioides cornutus* (BOTH) [Steven Falk]. **p184:** *Larinioides sclopetarius* [Steven Falk]. **p185:** *Larinioides patagiatus* [Peter Harvey]. **p186:** *Gibbaranea gibbosa* [Trevor & Dilys Pendleton]. **p187:** *Nuctenea umbratica* [Chris Cathrine]. **p188:** *Agalenatea redii* (BL) [Didier Petot]; (BC) [Aloysius Staudt]; (BR) [Aloysius Staudt]. **p189:** *Neoscona adianta* [Geoff Oxford]. **p191:** *Araniella displicata* [Peter Harvey]; *Araniella cucurbitina/ opisthographa* **male** [John Bingham], **female** [Geoff Oxford]. **p193:** *Zilla diodia* [Nik Hunt]. **p195:** *Hypsosinga albovittata* [Trevor & Dilys Pendleton]; *Hypsosinga pygmaea* [Trevor & Dilys Pendleton]; *Hypsosinga sanguinea* [Jorgen Lissner]; *Hypsosinga heri* (BOTH) [Allan Neilson]. **p197:** *Singa hamata* [Peter Harvey]. **p198:** *Cercidia prominens* (BOTH) [Trevor & Dilys Pendleton]. **p199:** *Zygiella x-notata* [Steven Falk]. **p200:** *Zygiella atrica* [Trevor & Dilys Pendleton]. **p201:** *Stroemiellus stroemi* [Jorgen Lissner]. **p202:** *Mangora acalypha* [Martin Askins]. **p203:** *Cyclosa conica* **male** [John Bingham], **female** [Trevor & Dilys Pendleton]. **p204:** *Argiope bruennichi* [Jens Kirkeby]. **p205:** *Argiope bruennichi* [Mark Gurney].

LYCOSIDAE: **p208:** *Pardosa monticola* [Steven Falk]; *Pardosa palustris* [Trevor & Dilys Pendleton]; *Pardosa agrestis* [Jorgen Lissner]; *Pardosa nigriceps* [Trevor & Dilys Pendleton]; *Pardosa purbeckensis* [Andrew Bloomfield]. **p209:** *Pardosa pullata* [Richard Gallon]; *Pardosa prativaga* [Arno Grabolle]; *Pardosa amentata* (BOTH) [Steven Falk]; *Pardosa trailli* (BOTH) [Walter Pflieger]. **p214:** *Pardosa agricola* [Steven Falk]; *Pardosa hortensis* [Arno Grabolle]; *Pardosa saltans* (BOTH) [Richard Gallon]; *Pardosa lugubris* [Jorgen Lissner]; *Pardosa proxima* [Arno Grabolle]. **p217:** *Pardosa paludicola* [Pascal Dubois]. **p218:** *Hygrolycosa rubrofasciata* (BOTH) [Arno Grabolle]. **p219:** *Xerolycosa nemoralis* [Nik Hunt]. **p220:** *Xerolycosa miniata* **male** [Andrew Bloomfield], **female** [Steven Falk]. **p223:** *Alopecosa cuneata* [Will George]; *Alopecosa pulverulenta* [Peter Harvey]; *Alopecosa barbipes* [John Bingham]; *Alopecosa fabrilis* [Arno Grabolle]. **p225:** *Trochosa ruricola* [Steven Falk]; *Trochosa robusta* [Arno Grabolle]. **p227:** *Trochosa terricola* [Trevor & Dilys Pendleton]; *Trochosa spinipalpis* [Bryan Formstone]; *Aulonia albimana* (BOTH) [Jorgen Lissner]. **p228:** *Arctosa perita* [Will George]. **p229:** *Arctosa cinerea* [Richard Burkmar]. **p231:** *Arctosa fulvolineata* [Arno Grabolle]; *Arctosa leopardus* [Greg Hitchcock]. **p232:** *Arctosa alpigena* [Walter Pflieger]. **p233:** *Pirata latitans* [Andrew Bloomfield]. **p234:** *Pirata piscatorius* (L) [Evan Jones]; (INSET) [Jorgen Lissner]. **p236:** *Pirata piraticus* [Arno Grabolle]; *Pirata tenuitarsis* [Jorgen Lissner]; *Pirata uliginosus* [Jorgen Lissner]; *Pirata hygrophilus* [Trevor & Dilys Pendleton].

PISAURIDAE: **p238:** *Pisaura mirabilis* **nursery web** [Geoff Oxford]. **p239:** *Pisaura mirabilis* (T) [Nik Hunt]; (B) [John Bingham]. **p241:** *Dolomedes plantarius* (T) [Helen Smith]; (B) [Neil Phillips]. **p242:** *Dolomedes fimbriatus* [Nik Hunt].

OXYOPIDAE: **p243:** *Oxyopes heterophthalmus* (BOTH) [Arno Grabolle].

AGELENIDAE: **p244:** *Agelena labyrinthica* [John Bingham]. **p245:** *Textrix denticulata* [Trevor & Dilys Pendleton]. **p246:** *Tegenaria saeva* (BOTH) [Geoff Oxford]; *Tegenaria atrica* [Geoff Oxford]. **p247:** *Tegenaria gigantea* [Steven Falk]. **p250:** *Tegenaria agrestis* [Trevor & Dilys Pendleton]; *Tegenaria parietina* [Arno Grabolle]. **p251:** *Tegenaria ferruginea* [Geoff Oxford]; *Tegenaria silvestris* [Arno Grabolle]; *Tegenaria domestica* [Trevor & Dilys Pendleton].

HAHNIIDAE: **p253:** *Antistea elegans* [Jorgen Lissner]. **p255:** *Hahnia montana* [Jorgen Lissner]; *Hahnia nava* [Richard Gallon]. **p256:** *Hahnia candida* [Arno Grabolle]; *Hahnia pusilla* [Arno Grabolle]; *Hahnia helveola* [Arno Grabolle].

DICTYNIDAE: **p257:** *Dictyna latens* (BL) [Ed Marshall], (BR) [Richard Gallon]. **p259:** *Dictyna arundinacea* [Trevor & Dilys Pendleton]; *Dictyna uncinata* [Trevor & Dilys Pendleton]; *Dictyna pusilla* [Arno Grabolle]. **p261:** *Cicurina cicur* [Arno Grabolle]. **p263:** *Nigma walckenaeri* (BOTH) [John Bingham]; *Nigma puella* **male** [Tone Killick], **female** [Philippe Garcelon]. **p265:** *Cryphoeca silvicola* [Arno Grabolle]; *Tuberta maerens* [Clive Hambler]; *Altella lucida* [Arno Grabolle]. **p267:** *Argenna subnigra* [Arno Grabolle]; *Argenna patula* [Jorgen Lissner]. **p268:** *Lathys humilis* [Mark Horton]; *Lathys nielseni* [Jorgen Lissner]; *Lathys stigmatisata* [Arno Grabolle]. **p269:** *Mastigusa arietina* (ALL) [Jorgen Lissner].

CYBAEIDAE: **p270:** *Argyroneta aquatica* [John Walters]. **p271:** *Argyroneta aquatica* [Arno Grabolle].

AMAUROBIIDAE: **p272:** *Coelotes atropos* [Trevor & Dilys Pendleton. **p273:** *Coelotes terrestris* [Peter Harvey]. **p274:** *Amaurobius similis* [Steven Falk]. **p275:** *Amaurobius ferox* [Richard Gallon]; *Amaurobius ferox* **pedipalps** (INSET) [Tone Killick]; *Amaurobius fenestralis* [Steven Falk].

LIOCRANIDAE: **p277:** *Agroeca brunnea* [Jorgen Lissner]. **p280:** *Agroeca cuprea* [Arno Grabolle]. **p281:** *Agroeca proxima* [Trevor & Dilys Pendleton]; *Agroeca inopina* [Peter Harvey]; *Agroeca lusatica* [Arno Grabolle]. **p282:** *Agraecina striata* [Arno Grabolle]. **p283:** *Apostenus fuscus* (ALL) [Arno Grabolle]. **p285:** *Scotina celans* [Arno Grabolle]; *Scotina gracilipes* [Arno Grabolle]; *Scotina palliardii* [Arno Grabolle]. **p286:** *Liocranum rupicola* [Richard Gallon].

ANYPHAENIDAE: **p287:** *Anyphaena accentuata* [Steven Falk].

CORINNIDAE: **p288:** *Phrurolithus festivus* [Trevor & Dilys Pendleton].

CLUBIONIDAE: **p290:** *Clubiona corticalis* **male** [Richard Gallon], **female** [Tone Killick]; *Clubiona comta* [Trevor & Dilys Pendleton]. **p296:** *Clubiona lutescens* **male** [Mike Davidson], **female** [Arno Grabolle]; *Clubiona neglecta* [Arno Grabolle]; *Clubiona pseudoneglecta* [Dragiša Savić]; *Clubiona terrestris* [Trevor & Dilys Pendleton]; *Clubiona reclusa* [Nik Hunt]. **p297:** *Clubiona brevipes* [Bryan Formstone]; *Clubiona trivialis* [Arno Grabolle]; *Clubiona juvenis* [Peter Harvey]; *Clubiona subsultans* [Arno Grabolle]; *Clubiona stagnatilis* [Jorgen Lissner]; *Clubiona norvegica* [Richard Gallon]. **p301:** *Clubiona subtilis* [Richard Gallon]; *Clubiona diversa* [Peter Harvey]; *Clubiona rosserae* (BOTH) [Peter Harvey]; *Clubiona caerulescens* [Arno Grabolle]. **p303:** *Clubiona pallidula* [Trevor & Dilys Pendleton], *Clubiona phragmitis* [Trevor & Dilys Pendleton]. **p304:** *Clubiona genevensis* [Richard Gallon]. **p305:** *Cheiracanthium virescens* [Dragiša Savić]. **p306:** *Cheiracanthium erraticum* [Nik Hunt]. **p307:** *Cheiracanthium pennyi* [Arno Grabolle].

ZODARIIDAE: **p308:** *Zodarion italicum* (BOTH) [Peter Harvey]; **'igloo'** [Peter Harvey]. **p309:** *Zodarion rubidum* [Arno Grabolle].

GNAPHOSIDAE: **p311:** **spinnerets:** *Drassodes* [Arno Grabolle], **clubionid** [Bryan Formstone]; **posterior median eyes:** (BOTH) [Arno Grabolle]. **p312:** *Drassodes pubescens* [Trevor & Dilys Pendleton]. **p313:** *Drassodes lapidosus* [Arno Grabolle]; *Drassodes cupreus* [Mike Davidson]. **p316:** *Haplodrassus signifer* [Arno Grabolle]; *Haplodrassus dalmatensis* [Arno Grabolle]; *Haplodrassus umbratilis* [Arno Grabolle]; *Haplodrassus soerenseni* [Arno Grabolle]. **p317:** *Haplodrassus silvestris* [Arno Grabolle]; *Haplodrassus minor* [Arno Grabolle]. **p319:** *Scotophaeus scutulatus* [Arno Grabolle]; *Scotophaeus blackwalli* [Steven Falk]. **p320:** *Phaeocedus braccatus* [Nik Hunt]. **p321:** *Callilepis nocturna* [Martin Askins]. **p322:** *Zelotes latreillei* [Steven Falk]. **p326:** *Zelotes latreillei* [Steven Falk]; *Zelotes longipes* [Arno Grabolle]; *Zelotes subterraneus* [Arno Grabolle]; *Zelotes apricorum* [Arno Grabolle]; *Zelotes petrensis* [Jorgen Lissner]; *Zelotes electus* [Arno Grabolle]; *Urozelotes rusticus* [Dragiša Savić]. **p327:** *Drasyllus pusillus* [Richard Gallon]; *Drasyllus praeficus* [Arno Grabolle]; *Trachyzelotes pedestris* [Arno Grabolle]; *Drasyllus lutetianus* [Arno Grabolle]. **p330:** *Gnaphosa lugubris* [Arno Grabolle]. **p331:** *Gnaphosa leporina* [Jorgen Lissner]; *Gnaphosa nigerrima* [Jorgen Lissner]. **p332:** *Gnaphosa occidentalis* [John Walters]. **p335:** *Micaria pulicaria* [Trevor & Dilys Pendleton]; *Micaria albovittata* [Jorgen Lissner]; *Micaria silesiaca* [Jorgen Lissner]; *Micaria subopaca* [Peter Harvey].

ZORIDAE: **p338:** *Zora nemoralis* [Arno Grabolle]; *Zora spinimana* (BOTH) [Trevor & Dilys Pendleton].
p339: *Zora armillata* (BOTH) [Jorgen Lissner]; *Zora silvestris* (BOTH) [Trevor & Dilys Pendleton].

ZOROPSIDAE: **p340:** *Zoropsis spinimana* [Tone Killick].

SPARASSIDAE: **p341:** *Micrommata virescens* male [John Bingham], female [Evan Jones].

PHILODROMIDAE: **p344:** *Philodromus dispar* male [Nik Hunt], female [Steven Falk]; *Philodromus aureolus*
[Steven Falk]; *Philodromus cespitum* [Trevor & Dilys Pendleton]; *Philodromus praedatus* (BOTH) [Arno Grabolle].
p345: *Philodromus longipalpis* [Peter Harvey]; *Philodromus collinus* [Arno Grabolle]; *Philodromus buxi*
[Peter Harvey]; *Philodromus emarginatus* [Arno Grabolle]; *Philodromus albidus* [Peter Harvey]; *Philodromus rufus*
[Peter Harvey]; *Philodromus margaritatus* [John Walters]; *Philodromus fallax* [Mark Gurney].
p351: *Philodromus histrio* [Mark Gurney]. **p352:** *Tibellus oblongus* [Arno Grabolle]. **p354:** *Thanatus striatus*
[Mark Gurney]. **p355:** *Thanatus vulgaris* [Nik Hunt]. **p356:** *Thanatus formicinus* [Arno Grabolle].

THOMISIDAE: **p357:** *Thomisus onustus* [Marion Friedrich]. **p358:** *Thomisus onustus* (MAIN IMAGE) [Steve Covey],
yellow (INSET) [Mauro Paschetta] pink (INSET) [Ian Cross]; *Misumena vatia* [Jurgen Scharfy]. **p359:** *Misumena*
vatia [Jurgen Scharfy]. **p360:** *Diaea dorsata* male [Nik Hunt], female [John Bingham]. **p361:** *Pistius truncatus*
[Jorgen Lissner]. **p364:** *Xysticus cristatus* (BOTH) [Steven Falk]; *Xysticus audax* male [Graeme Lyons], female
[Jorgen Lissner]; *Xysticus ulmi* [Steven Falk]; *Xysticus kochi* [Arno Grabolle]. **p365:** *Xysticus sabulosus* (TL) [Michael
Schäfer], (TR) [Graeme Lyons]; *Xysticus luctator* (BOTH) [Arno Grabolle]; *Xysticus bifasciatus* [John Bingham]; *Xysticus*
luctuosus [Peter Harvey]; *Xysticus acerbus* [Arno Grabolle]. **p370:** *Xysticus erraticus* male [Steven Falk], female
[Arno Grabolle]; *Xysticus lanio* male [Will George], female [Steven Falk]; *Xysticus robustus* (BOTH) [Arno Grabolle].
p371: *Ozyptila carapace* (INSET) [Jorgen Lissner]; *Ozyptila praticola* [Arno Grabolle]. **p373:** *Ozyptila trux* [Trevor &
Dilys Pendleton]; *Ozyptila atomaria* [Trevor & Dilys Pendleton]; *Ozyptila simplex* (BOTH) [Arno Grabolle].
p375: *Ozyptila brevipes* [Jorgen Lissner]; *Ozyptila sanctuaria* [Jorgen Lissner]. **p377:** *Ozyptila scabricula* [Arno
Grabolle]; *Ozyptila praticola* [Arno Grabolle]; *Ozyptila nigrita* (BOTH) [Jorgen Lissner]; *Ozyptila blackwalli* [Dragiša
Savić]; *Ozyptila pullata* [Arno Grabolle]. **p379:** *Synema globosum* [Geoff Oxford].

SALTICIDAE: **p380:** *Salticus scenicus* (BOTH) [Michael Schäfer]. **p381:** *Salticus zebraneus* (BOTH) [Michael Schäfer];
Salticus cingulatus [Trevor & Dilys Pendleton]. **p383:** *Neon reticulatus* [Evan Jones]; *Neon pictus* [Evan Jones].
p385: *Marpissa nivoyi* [Michael Schäfer]. **p386:** *Marpissa muscosa* [Kevin McGee]. **p387:** *Marpissa radiata*
male [Alan Thornhill], female [Mark Gurney]. **p389:** *Pellenes tripunctatus* male [Mark Gurney], female [Michael
Schäfer]; *Sibianor aurocinctus* [Mark Gurney]; *Ballus chalybeius* [Mark Gurney]. **p391:** *Heliophanus cupreus* [Steven
Falk]; *Heliophanus flavipes* [Steven Falk]; *Heliophanus auratus* [Michael Schäfer]; *Heliophanus dampfi* [Jorgen
Lissner]. **p393:** *Macaroeris nidicolens* [Michael Schäfer]. **p394:** *Euophrys frontalis* (BOTH) [Mark Gurney].
p395: *Euophrys herbigrada* [Michael Schäfer]. **p397:** *Pseudeuophrys obsoleta* [Michael Schäfer];
Pseudeuophrys erratica [Richard Gallon]; *Pseudeuophrys lanigera* [Harald Hoyer]. **p398:** *Talavera petrensis*
(ALL) [Michael Schäfer]. **p399:** *Talavera aequipes* [Will George]. **p402:** *Sitticus pubescens* [Trevor & Dilys
Pendleton]; *Sitticus saltator* [Michael Schäfer]; *Sitticus distinguendus* male [Peter Harvey], female [Steven Falk];
Sitticus floricola (BOTH) [Michael Schäfer]. **p403:** *Sitticus inexpectus* [Mark Gurney]; *Sitticus caricis* (BOTH) [Richard
Gallon]. **p405:** *Aelurillus v-insignitus* male, female (BOTH) [Mark Gurney]; (INSET) [Chris Spilling].
p406: *Evarcha arcuata* male [Steven Falk], female [Mark Gurney]. **p407:** *Evarcha falcata* male [Steven Falk],
female [Evan Jones]. **p408:** *Myrmarachne formicaria* [Michael Schäfer]. **p409:** *Synageles venator* [Michael Schäfer].
p410: *Phlegra fasciata* (BOTH) [Michael Schäfer].

LINYPHIIDAE: **p411:** *Stemonyphantes lineatus* [John Bingham]. **p412:** *Drapetisca socialis* [Nik Hunt].
p413: *Floronia bucculenta* [Peter Harvey]. **p414:** *Pityohyphantes phrygianus* (BOTH) [Jorgen Lissner].
p416: *Linyphia triangularis* [Philippe Garcelon]; *Linyphia hortensis* [Trevor & Dilys Pendleton];
Microlinyphia pusilla [Trevor & Dilys Pendleton]. **p418:** *Neriene clathrata* [Trevor & Dilys Pendleton].
p419: *Neriene montana* [Trevor & Dilys Pendleton]; *Neriene peltata* [Trevor & Dilys Pendleton].

BACK SECTION
p421: sweep netting [Peter Smithers]. **p421:** training course [Geoff Oxford].

Index

This index includes the English and *scientific* (in *italics*) names of all the spiders in this book.
Family names are shown in upper case – English names in small capitals, scientific names in capitals.

Bold black figures highlight the main species accounts or introductions to families or genera.
Italicized figures indicate page(s) on which other photographs appear.
Red figures relate to the *Guide to spider families*.
Green figures refer to the *Guide to webs*.
Brown figures relate to the *Guide to egg-sacs*.
Blue figures relate to the entry in the *List of British spiders* table.
Regular text is used to indicate pages where other information may be found.

Alphabetical list of genera with species accounts

About the authors

All three authors are active Council members of the British Arachnological Society.

Lawrence Bee is an ecological consultant and educator, and is the author of the Field Studies Council's *Guide to House and Garden Spiders*.

Geoff Oxford is an Honorary Fellow in Biology at the University of York and an authority on both colour variation and speciation in spiders.

Helen Smith is a conservation biologist and leads the conservation programme for the endangered Fen Raft Spider.